Titles in Counseling and Professional Identity Series

CACREP Standards	Sangganjanavanich, Introduction to Professional Counseling	Watson, Counseling Assessment and Evaluation	Conyne, Group Work Leadership	Parsons, Becoming A Skilled Counselor	Parsons, Counseling Theory	Wong, Counseling Individuals Through the Lifespan	Duan, Becoming a Multiculturally Competent Counselor	Wright, Research Methods for Counseling	Scott, Counselor as Consultant
1. PROFESSIONAL ORIENTATION AND ETHCIAL PRACTICE	1a 1b 1d 1e 1f 1g 1h 1i 1j	1j	1b 1j	1b 1d 1e 1j	1j	1j	1j	1j	1b 1j
2. SOCIAL AND CULTURAL DIVERSITY	2c 2f 2g	2g	2d 2e 2g	2b 2c 2g	2c 2e 2g	2a 2b 2c 2d 2e 2g	2c 2e 2f 2g	2g	2d 2g
3. HUMAN GROWTH AND DEVELOPMENT			3f		3b	3a 3b 3c 3d 3e 3f 3g	3d 3e		
4. CAREER DEVELOPMENT		4f							4c
5. HELPING RELATIONSHIPS	5a 5b 5c 5f 5g 5h		5b 5c 5d 5e	5a 5b 5c 5d	5b 5c 5d 5e 5g	5b	5b 5e		5b 5c 5f 5g 5h
6. GROUP WORK			6a 6b 6c 6d 6e						
7. ASSESSMENT		7a 7b 7c 7d 7e 7f 7g	7b	7b		7f		7c 7d 7e	
8. RESEARCH AND PROGRAM EVALUATION								8a 8b 8c 8d 8e	

Counseling and Professional Identity

Series Editors: Richard D. Parsons, PhD, and Naijian Zhang, PhD

Becoming a Skilled Counselor—Richard D. Parsons and Naijian Zhang

Research Methods for Counseling: An Introduction—Robert J. Wright

Group Work Leadership: An Introduction for Helpers—Robert K. Conyne

Introduction to Professional Counseling—Varunee Faii Sangganjanavanich and Cynthia Reynolds

Counseling Theory: Guiding Reflective Practice—Richard D. Parsons and Naijian Zhang

Counselor as Consultant—David A. Scott, Chadwick W. Royal, and Daniel B. Kissinger

Counseling Assessment and Evaluation: Fundamentals of Applied Practice—Joshua C. Watson and Brandé Flamez

Counseling Individuals Through the Lifespan—Daniel W. Wong, Kimberly R. Hall, Cheryl A. Justice, and Lucy Wong Hernandez

Becoming a Multiculturally Competent Counselor—Changming Duan and Chris Brown

Ethical Decision Making for the 21st Century Counselor—Donna S. Sheperis, Michael Kocet, and Stacy Henning

Career Development and Counseling: Theory and Practice in a Multicultural World—Mei Tang and Jane Goodman

Field Experience: Transitioning From Student to Professional—Naijian Zhang and Richard D. Parsons

Counseling Individuals
Through the Lifespan

Counseling Individuals Through the Lifespan

Daniel W. Wong
Mississippi State University

Kimberly R. Hall
Mississippi State University

Cheryl A. Justice
Mississippi State University

Lucy Wong Hernandez
Mississippi State University

Los Angeles | London | New Delhi
Singapore | Washington DC | Boston

Los Angeles | London | New Delhi
Singapore | Washington DC | Boston

FOR INFORMATION:

SAGE Publications, Inc.
2455 Teller Road
Thousand Oaks, California 91320
E-mail: order@sagepub.com

SAGE Publications Ltd.
1 Oliver's Yard
55 City Road
London EC1Y 1SP
United Kingdom

SAGE Publications India Pvt. Ltd.
B 1/I 1 Mohan Cooperative Industrial Area
Mathura Road, New Delhi 110 044
India

SAGE Publications Asia-Pacific Pte. Ltd.
3 Church Street
#10-04 Samsung Hub
Singapore 049483

Printed in the United States of America.

A catalog record of this book is available from the Library of Congress.

ISBN 978-1-4522-1794-9

This book is printed on acid-free paper.

Acquisitions Editor: Kassie Graves
Editorial Assistant: Carrie Montoya
Production Editor: Bennie Clark Allen
Copy Editor: Michelle Ponce
Typesetter: C&M Digitals (P) Ltd.
Proofreader: Ellen Brink
Indexer: Julie Grayson
Cover Designer: Candice Harmon
Marketing Manager: Shari Countryman

16 17 18 10 9 8 7 6 5 4 3 2

Detailed Contents

PART IV   **259**

Editors Preface: Introduction to the Series

Erik Erikson (1902–1994) noted: "There is in every child at every stage a new miracle of vigorous unfolding." Think about that phrase, "a new miracle of vigorous unfolding." What a glorious way to depict our human development.

As counselors, however, we know that this developmental unfolding is fragile and can be altered, stifled, or even halted as a result of biological, sociocultural, and psychological influences. If we are to assist those who seek our counsel as they attempt to navigate through life's many challenges, then we must understand both that which is normative and that which is not and the resources presented as well as the limitations existing at each point in this "vigorous unfolding" of the human condition.

Counseling Individuals Through the Lifespan is a text written by true experts in the field of human development. It is a text that is essential to a counselor's understanding of the human condition and his or her positioning to facilitate growth and wellness. *Counseling Individuals Through the Lifespan* is unique among texts on human development in that it not only provides the reader with the latest research and theory explaining human development but also guides the reader through to the application of this research, these theories, in the authors' practice as professional counselors. The extensive use of case illustrations and guided exercises not only makes each chapter come alive but also helps the reader translate knowledge to practice. *Counseling Individuals Through the Lifespan* is a more than an academic text—it is core to one's professional development. Not only will the text facilitate your developing knowledge and skills, but it will stimulate further development of your professional identity.

As is obvious, one text, one learning experience, will not be sufficient for mastery of group work or for the successful formation of your professional identity and practice. The formation of both your professional identity and practice will be a lifelong process—a process that we hope to facilitate through the presentation of this text and the creation of our series: *Counseling and Professional Identity in the 21st Century*.

Counseling and Professional Identity in the 21st Century is a new, fresh, pedagogically sound series of texts targeting counselors in training. This series is *not* simply a compilation of isolated books matching that which is already in the market. Rather each book, with its targeted knowledge and skills, will be presented as a part of a larger whole. The focus and content of each text serves as a single lens through which a counselor can view his or her clients, engage in his or her practice, and articulate his or her own professional identity.

Counseling and Professional Identity in the 21st Century is unique not just in the fact that it packages a series of traditional texts but that it provides an *integrated* curriculum targeting the formation of the readers' professional identities and efficient, ethical practice. Each book within the series is structured to facilitate the ongoing professional formation of the reader. The materials found within each text are organized in order to move the reader to higher levels of cognitive, affective, and psychomotor functioning, resulting in his or her assimilation of the materials presented into both his or her professional identity and approach to professional practice. While each text targets a specific set of core competencies (cognates and skills) identified by the Council for Accreditation of Counseling & Related Educational Programs (CACREP) as essential to the practice of counseling (see Table P-1), each book in the series will emphasize each of the following:

a. the assimilation of concepts and constructs provided across the text found within the series, thus fostering the reader's ongoing development as a competent professional;

b. the blending of contemporary theory with current research and empirical support;

c. a focus on the development of procedural knowledge, with each text employing case illustrations and guided practice exercises to facilitate the readers ability to translate the theory and research discussed into professional decision making and application;

d. the emphasis on the need for and means of demonstrating accountability, and;

e. the fostering of the reader's professional identity and with it the assimilation of the ethics and standards of practice guiding the counseling profession.

Table P.1 Books and Corresponding CACREP (Council for the Accreditation of Counseling and Related Educational Programs) Competencies

Counseling and Professional Identity	
Books in the Series	**Typical Courses Served by the Text**
Introduction to Professional Counseling Varunee Faii Sangganjanavanich and Cynthia A. Reynolds	Introductory
Becoming a Skilled Counselor Richard D. Parsons and Naijian Zhang	Basic skills
Becoming a Multiculturally Competent Counselor Changming Duan and Chris Brown	Multicultural and diversity
Counseling Individuals Through the Lifespan Daniel Wai Chung Wong, Kim Hall, Cheryl Justice, and Lucy Wong Hernandez	Human development
Counseling Assessment and Evaluation: Fundamentals of Applied Practice Joshua C. Watson and Brandé Flamez	Assessment
Research Methods for Counseling Robert Wright	Fundamental research
Counseling Theory: Guiding Reflective Practice Richard D. Parsons and Naijian Zhang (Eds.)	Theories
Ethical Decision Making for the 21st Century Counselor Donna S. Sheperis, Michael Koct, and Stacy Henning	Ethics—or sections within each course covering ethical issues
Career Development and Counseling: Theory and Practice in a Multicultural World Mei Tang and Jane Goodman	Career counseling
Counselor as Consultant David Scott, Chadwick Royal, and Daniel Kissinger	Consultation and coordination
Group Work: An Introduction for Helping Professionals Robert Conyne	Group dynamics, group counseling

We are proud to have served as co-editors of this series, feeling sure that all of the texts, just like *Counseling Individuals Through the Lifespan*, will serve as a significant resource to you and your development as a professional counselor.

Richard Parsons, PhD

Naijian Zhang, PhD

Preface

Since the inception of the CACREP standards, human growth and development has been maintained as one of eight established curricular areas in counselor education. The objective of this textbook is to present human development from a counseling perspective, and this unique perspective can be applied in practice across the lifespan of clients. Professional counselors have distinguished themselves among helping professionals through a focus and foundational framework in normal human growth and development over the lifespan. Knowledge of human development incorporated within the counseling practice makes the counselor more sensitive to the complexities of human development and able to translate sound theoretical knowledge into effective counseling practice. Professional counselors are trained and dedicated to the promotion of human growth and development across the lifespan of individuals from diverse backgrounds. They engage in practices that are developmentally appropriate in nature and life stages and act as advocates against any barrier that limits human development.

We hope that this textbook will provide practical, knowledge-based, and educational information to students, professional counselors, and counselor educators in reference to the relationship between human development and counseling. We believe that our mission is accomplished if this textbook is able to facilitate a positive learning experience for the readers.

Acknowledgments

This book could not have been written without the encouragement and support of our family members, colleagues, and our students. We were blessed with their steadfast support during this process. We would like to acknowledge the contributions of Ms. Monyee Lee, Ms. Chelsea Rushing, Ms. Katya Demetriades, and Ms. Laura Hankins for their assistance and research work to complete this book.

The guidance, support, and expertise that the series editors, Drs. Richard D. Parsons and Naijian Zhang, have provided to us was indispensable for the completion of this book. Finally, we are forever indebted to Ms. Kassie Graves, publisher, Human Services, at SAGE Publications for her patience and support during the past 2 years. Finally, our deep appreciation to Ms. Bennie Clark Allen, Ms. Carrie Montoya, and Ms. Michelle Ponce for their excellent editorial work and guidance to accomplish this project.

About the Authors

Daniel W. Wong, PhD

Daniel W. Wong, PhD, is a professor in the Department of Counseling and Educational Psychology, College of Education, at Mississippi State University (MSU). Prior to MSU, Dr. Wong was professor and director of the doctoral program in the Department of Rehabilitation Studies, College of Allied Health Sciences and adjunct professor in the Department of Physical Medicine and Rehabilitation at Brody School of Medicine at East Carolina University. Since 1987, he has taught at the University of North Texas, San Jose State University, Hofstra University, and the University of Hawaii at Manoa. Dr. Wong received the American Counseling Association (ACA) Research Award and the American Rehabilitation Counseling Association Research Award, and he has published more than 80 peer-reviewed articles, book chapters, and numerous disability-rehabilitation policy/position papers nationally and internationally.

Kimberly R. Hall, PhD

Kimberly R. Hall earned a master's of science degree in school counseling in 1997 and the doctorate of philosophy degree in school counseling in 2004 from Mississippi State University. Dr. Hall worked at Virginia Commonwealth University in Richmond, Virginia, exclusively with the school counseling program for several years before returning to Mississippi State. For 6 years, she served as the program coordinator for Graduate Programs in School Counseling, which offered degrees at the master's, educational specialist, and doctoral degree levels. She is now an associate professor at the Meridian campus of Mississippi State University and currently serves as the program coordinator for Graduate Programs in School Counseling and as graduate coordinator for the Division of Education. Dr. Hall specializes in counseling children and adolescents and working with parents.

Cheryl A. Justice, PhD

Cheryl A. Justice earned her undergraduate degree from Indiana University and her master's degree from DePauw University. She later received a PhD in counseling and supervision from the University of Mississippi. Dr. Justice has over 25 years of experience in teaching, counseling, and consultation. She is currently an assistant professor at Mississippi State University. She serves as the clinical and school counseling coordinator for the Department of Counseling and Educational Psychology. In addition, she is the faculty advisor for the Chi Sigma Iota Chapter. Dr. Justice specializes in group work and is an advocate for social justice.

Lucy Wong Hernandez, MS

Lucy Wong Hernandez is an instructor in the Department of Counseling and Educational Psychology at Mississippi State University. She has extensive experience in the fields of rehabilitation and disability studies as they relate to academics, disability rights, social policy, and service provision for persons with disabilities. She teaches in the areas of rehabilitation counseling and disability, gerontology, and human development. She is a frequent speaker, presenter, and trainer at national and international conferences and seminars. She has authored and contributed to numerous articles on disability rights, social policy, and multicultural issues. She has taught at York College-City University of New York, Hofstra University, University of Hawaii at Manoa, and East Carolina University.

PART I

Human Development Through the Lifespan

> You cannot predict the outcome of human development. All you can do is like a farmer create the conditions under which it will begin to flourish.
>
> K. Robinson

The above quote certainly sounds true at an intuitive level, however, one must wonder, especially one who is entering the field of counseling, whether the quote is accurate and, if so, what are the implications to counseling? Counseling is by definition a process that supports and facilitates change. If the outcome of one's development is without prediction, and one can only set conditions that hopefully allow for development to flourish, how will we, as agents of change, engage in our specialized craft? Or, as might be suggested by the quote, are we to be like the farmer and focus our energies, our research, our knowledge, and our skills on creating the conditions that prevent dysfunction and foster the flourishing of the human condition?

The questions posed are not without consequence. Their answers require more than mere opinion or intuitive responses. For the professional counselor, understanding that which nourishes the human condition as well as that which depletes the unfolding of the human potential is essential to our practice. Further, understanding the degree to which this process of development can be influenced is core to any efforts that we may employ to affect beneficial change for our clients. Thus, knowledge of the principles and processes of human development is key to a counselor's effective functioning.

There are central questions addressed by the study of human development, a field of study devoted to understanding constancy and change throughout the lifespan. Great diversity characterizes the interests and concerns of those who study human development. They all share a common goal: to identify those factors that influence consistencies and transformation in people from conception to the end of life.

This chapter provides an overview of those factors influencing consistency and change and highlights the complexity and multidimensional nature of human development as it unfolds through one's lifespan. In addition, the chapter describes the importance and essential contribution that the knowledge and understanding of human development provides to counselors and their effective practice. Specifically, after completing this chapter, readers will be able to

1. describe what is meant by viewing development from a lifespan perspective,

2. explain the multidimensional and multidirectional nature of lifespan development,

3. describe what is meant by viewing development within a contextual framework,

4. discuss the biopsychosocial approach to defining human development and the multiple interactive forces that shape human development, and

5. explain the value of understanding human development across the lifespan for the counseling process.

The Counseling Connection

Counselors, by the very nature of their vocational calling, tend to be doers. As professionals, we review the research and the emerging theories in an attempt to better understand the human condition. However, it is more than for the sake of understanding that we pursue these endeavors. Counselors seek to translate theory-research-knowledge, into practice. And as such, the question to be asked as you proceed through this text is: "What value does understanding human development through the lifespan, or more specifically this theory, have for me, as I attempt to make practice decisions in service of another?"

While the question may be challenging and difficult to answer, it needs to be asked. It is a question that can serve as a guide to extracting meaning throughout the remainder of this text. And it is a question that we feel will not only be answered in the pages that follow but will be answered in a way that makes you a more effective counselor.

Uniqueness of the Counseling Profession Identity

Professional counseling has been defined as "the application of mental health, psychological, or human development principles, through cognitive, affective, behavioral or systemic **intervention** strategies, that address wellness, personal growth, or career development, as well as pathology." (American Counseling Association (ACA), 1997). Further, as noted in the **ACA Code of Ethics** (2005), counselors are dedicated to the promotion of human growth and development across the lifespan, engage in practices that are developmentally appropriate in nature, and act as advocates against any barrier that limits human development. Professional counselors have distinguished themselves among helping professionals through their focus on normal human growth and development over the lifespan. It is in our DNA and is the core of our professional identity.

As contrasted to other helping professionals, counselors dedicate their professional lives to issues of wellness, prevention, and personal growth and development. This is not to suggest that we are not engaged in processes that help those experiencing major disruptions to their lives. Certainly, as counselors we engage in remediation and therapeutic interventions with those who present with problems, dysfunctions, or pathology. However, even when serving in that capacity, counselors as a result of their professional identity, not only seek to assist the client back to the path of stability but do so in a way that prevents their future disruption and promotes or fosters their ongoing wellness and development.

Essential to Counseling Practice

As noted above, counselors engage in practices that foster ongoing wellness and development and act as advocates against barriers that limit human development. Such a professional calling, or mission, is both noble and valuable. However, it is a mission that is clearly impossible to fulfill without (a) professional knowledge of the nature of human development across the lifespan, (b) the understanding of both normative and exceptional challenges that can be and are experienced, and c) the use of research and theory on human development to guide professional practice decisions.

Without a full understanding of that which defines the nature of human development across the lifespan, counselors would be unable to discern that which is normative from that which is a deviation or engage in processes that continue to support healthy development or intervene with that which is less than healthy or optimal. Knowledge of the theory, principles, and research of human development is essential to professional counseling practice. Guided Practice Exercise 1.1 is provided in order to highlight the value of understanding human development when confronted with client concerns. As you review the exercise, ask yourself, would knowledge of human development influence my responses?

Guided Practice Exercise 1.1

Instructions: Below you will find a description of a specific behavior. Your task is simply to reflect on the questions and consider the changing nature of your response as additional data (developmental data) are provided.

Situation 1: Your client presents as noncommunicative, having poor social skills, and appearing as if totally occupied by and within his or her own mental constructs and fantasies.

a. Do you feel this client is in need of counseling?

b. If engaged in counseling, what might be a target or goal for the intervention?

c. What type of approach might you try?

How might your responses change if you knew that

a. The client was 9 months old?

b. The client was 14 years old?

c. The client was 41 years old?

Situation 2: The client presents with behaviors regarding dressing up in female attire. The client is particularly attracted to feminine undergarments and has been reported to have been stimulated while wearing these garments.

a. Do you feel this client is in need of counseling?

b. If engaged in counseling, what might be a target or goal for the intervention?

c. What type of approach might you try?

How might your responses change if you knew that

a. The client was a 13-year-old female?

b. The client was a 27-year-old male?

c. The client was four years old (gender unknown)?

Situation 3: Your client has been described as sullen, moody, withdrawn, and exhibiting a dark side that includes focusing on issues of death and dying.

(Continued)

(Continued)

    a. Do you feel this client is in need of counseling?

    b. If engaged in counseling, what might be a target or goal for the intervention?

    c. What type of approach might you try?

How might your responses change if you knew that

    a. The client was a 14-year-old self-described, gothic male?

    b. The client was a 27-year-old postpartum female?

    c. The client was a 96-year-old cancer patient?

To be effective as a counselor and to truly understand one's client, a counselor must understand the various elements and processes that impact human growth and development. It is important to understand how factors such as an individual's experiences, life maturation processes, and **culture** shape the individual's life at any one stage of human development. Further it is important to know (a) how individuals cope with and make sense of their environment and surroundings; b) how they use their learning experiences to cope with adversity and stress; (c) how they develop resilience and coping skills, and (d) how all of this could be affected by gender, cultural, physical, psychological, and sociological factors.

Integrated in Our Studies

The importance of understanding **human development** is highlighted by the fact that most professional bodies or associations require formal training in developmental theory and research. For example, the **Council on Accreditation of Counseling Related Educational Programs (CACREP)**, the premier accreditation body of counselor education programs, has articulated standards (see Table 1.1 below) and requires its accredited programs to include at least a course in human growth and development in their curricula (Korsmo, Baker-Sennett, & Nicholas, 2009; CACREP, 2009).

Table 1.1   CACREP 2001 Human Growth and Development Standards

Human Growth and Development: Provide an understanding of the nature and needs of individuals at all developmental levels, including all of the following

    a) theories of individual and family development and transitions across the lifespan;

    b) theories of learning and personality development;

    c) human behavior, including understanding of developmental crises, disability, exceptional behavior, additive behavior, **psychopathology,** and situational and environmental factors that affect both normal and abnormal behavior;

    d) strategies for facilitating optimum development over the lifespan; and

    e) ethical and legal considerations.

Even without a specific course in human development, the value of this information is evident by the very fact that numerous courses within the counseling professional training experience find grounding in the theory and research of human development. For example, consider the following brief sampling of course titles typically found in a counselor education program. While unique in their own rights, each offers insight into the nature and dynamic of human development and provides critical information to better understand the nature and needs of individuals at all developmental levels in a diverse cultural and psychosocial context.

1. *Counseling Theory:* Theories of human and personality development, including how genetic, psychosociological, neurobiological, and cognitive factors contribute to behavior and learning development.

2. *Family Counseling:* Theories of family and individuals as related to the transition across the lifespan.

3. *Abnormal Psychology:* Theories of human behavior, both normal and abnormal behavior, to be effected in the development stages of happiness, sadness, loss, crises, health, disability, and situational and environmental factors that may contribute to growth and development stages.

4. *Addiction:* Theories of addictions and addictive behaviors, including strategies for prevention, intervention, and treatment.

5. *Counseling Intervention and Prevention:* Theories for the study of facilitating optimal development, enhancing **quality of life**, and wellness over the lifespan.

6. *Crises Intervention:* Theories of individuals, families, and communities coping with disasters and post-trauma stress and how resilience contributes to the transition of healing and recovery.

7. *Assessment:* Theories of psychosocial, cultural, and economic contributions to the **holistic** assessment of **human growth** and development.

8. *Theories of Counseling and Psychotherapy:* Theories that guide proper diagnoses and appropriate counseling treatment to enhance and optimize the counseling outcome, all placed within the context of the human condition and normative challenges.

The recognition by accrediting bodies of the need and value of knowledge of human development, along with the integration of developmental principles and concepts throughout counselor education curriculum, speaks to the value of this knowledge for professional practice. But, as you continue with your training and reading this chapter, it is our hope that you will come to see that it is more than knowledge that is gained by studying human development across the lifespan. As you begin to understand the complexity of human development, it is our intention that you will also develop an increased appreciation and valuing of uniqueness and commonality, strength and vulnerability, and the simple wonder of the human condition.

The Complexity of Human Development

Human development, while so natural, is very complex and multidimensional. As such, the study of human development is challenging. The study of human development requires an in-depth analysis of the processes that contribute to change while maintaining stability, as uniquely experienced and evidenced throughout one's lifespan. The study of human development attempts to define the elements that contribute to the healthy as well as less-than-healthy unfolding of the human condition. Identifying and defining all of the factors that come together to stimulate growth, development, and change in what is anticipated to be an orderly fashion is quite a task.

The magnitude and complexity implied by the previous statement may be lost to our understanding unless we take time to reflect on our own experience of human development. Consider the apparent seamlessness and

Photo 1.1   The "Crossroad of America—New York's Times Square" represents the numerous factors that impact human development, including socioenvironmental and multigenerational diversity.

fluidity of moving from a two-celled organism to a state of infancy, helpless and dependent in a cradle, to the development of abilities such as walking, talking, remembering, imagining, hypothesizing, empathizing, and even reflecting on one's very being. Certainly, we all celebrate these markers of development, but for most, we also simply take them for granted unless or until something goes wrong. It is at those times of developmental disruption that we seek understanding. And it is that need for understanding and the following direction for intervention that leads to the study of development through the lifespan.

Development: Change and Stability

For the purpose of this chapter and theme, development is defined as the orderly and sequential changes that occur with the passage of time as an organism moves and adapts from the very beginning until the end of life. These changes and development occur through complex interactions between processes that are biologically programmed within the organism and elements presented within the environment. It is an interaction that transforms the organism through the process of orderly, sequential change.

This interactive process is complex; it is multidimensional and not always clear-cut or easily understood. Guided Practice Exercise 1.2 highlights the complexity of this process of development as it gives form to the intricate interplay and interaction between biological and environmental processes.

Guided Practice Exercise 1.2 Human Development:
A Product of Complex Interactions

Instructions: To more fully appreciate the complexity of human development, you are to respond to each of the following questions. After responding, read what is presented. Was this a surprise? Did it change your view? Does it highlight the interactive and complex nature of development?

1. **Identical twins:** Identical twins share the same genetic makeup and thus share physical traits. Many have tried and proved successful in fooling friends and family who may confuse their identities. Can they fool a forensic specialist employing fingerprint analysis?

2. **Sex Role Behaviors:** Much has been written and discussed about the development of sex role behaviors. Some emphasize the cultural influence of boys learning to be boys and girls enculturated to be girls. Others have pointed to the influence of the unique *XX* and *XY* genetics. What is your position—nature (genetics), nurture (cultural influence), or perhaps something else?

3. **Adolescent Brains:** It is likely that you have read about or heard discussions about the storm and stress nature of adolescence: the depiction of adolescents as hormonally driven, emotional, unpredictable, and impulsive. Some have argued that the emotional and social liability and upheaval experienced in adolescence is a function of biological/hormonal changes, whereas other suggest it is merely a function of the frustration of being socially in between childhood and adulthood. What is your position?

Additional data for consideration: Does the following information reshape your initial opinions or expand your view of the complexity of these developmental issues?

1. **Identical Twins:** While identical twins could certainly be said to be genetic carbon copies, their fingerprints need not be. Research shows that the fine details of ridges, valleys, and swirls that define one's fingerprints are influenced by random stresses experienced in the womb. Even a slightly different umbilical cord length can change one's fingerprints.

2. **Sex Role Behaviors:** Research provides evidence regarding the prenatal influences of gonadal steroids on human sexual orientation, as well as sex-typed childhood behaviors that predict subsequent sexual orientation. The evidence supports a role for prenatal testosterone exposure in the development of sex-typed interests in childhood, as well as in sexual orientation in later life, at least for some individuals. It appears, however, that other factors, in addition to hormones, play an important role in determining sexual orientation. These factors have not been well-characterized, but possibilities include direct genetic effects and effects of maternal factors during pregnancy. Although a role for hormones during early development has been established, it also appears that there may be multiple pathways to a given sexual orientation outcome, and some of these pathways may not involve hormones.

3. **Adolescent Brains:** Some of the most exciting new discoveries in neuroscience focus on adolescent brain development. Researchers now know that the adolescent brain is different from an adult's brain and that development continues well into a person's 20s. One particular finding sheds light on the adolescent's characterization as dramatic and overly emotional.

Neuroscience research has shown that adolescents process information differently than do adults. While adults usually rely on the frontal lobes, the center of reasoning and language, to respond to situations, adolescents rely more on the amygdala, which controls a wide range of emotions. As a result, teens are more likely than adults to respond emotionally to a situation.

Perhaps, what is so uniquely human is that we remain in an unending state of development throughout our lifespan. Life is always an unfinished business, and death is its only cessation. And even having stated that change is the essence of the human condition, our understanding of human development highlights the fact that in midst of change, we exhibit stability and that the nature of this change is predictable.

Understanding this orderly, sequential nature of human development not only allows us to understand when development has been thwarted but also provides us with the markers that serve as beacons to guide our decisions as we attempt to facilitate the continuation of healthy growth and development. As a simple illustration, consider the sequence of moving from being an infant to being a toddler. When reflecting on this transition, what changes would you expect to observe? Would you assume increased mobility? Would language and social interaction improve? Would you be concerned if these changes were not evident?

While we can appreciate the realities of individual differences, and that development does not adhere to a rigid time structure, our knowledge of human development helps to establish markers denoting expected orderly sequential change, and when these do not occur, our concerns are alerted.

Development: The Result of Interactive Forces

Human development involves growth, maintenance, and regulation of loss and is constructed through the interaction of biological, cognitive, sociocultural, and individual factors working together, interactively throughout one's lifespan. Human development is both multidimensional and multidirectional. Our development reflects the internal direction of our biological substrate while at the same time is responsive to environmental and contextual demands. Throughout it all, our development demonstrates a unique plasticity that allows each of us to adapt and promote positive change when confronted with challenges (Baltes & Smith, 2003; Baltes, Lindenberger, & Staudinger 2006).

The complexity of developmental interactive forces and the interaction of elements can be seen by simply considering a child's initiation into the world of crawling (see Case Illustration 1.1 below)

CASE ILLUSTRATION 1.1 TRANSITIONING TO CRAWLING

The simple act of initiating crawling highlights the multidimensional and multidirectional nature of development as well as the unique contribution of biological and environmental forces. An infant's engagement in crawling not only signals amazing changes that have occurred but also serves as the source, or the impetus, for additional change to come. Crawling is evidence that the infant is strong enough to sit and to support himself or herself on hands and knees. Crawling indicates the infant's ability (and environmental support) for risk taking, even when the risk is to trust one hand or one knee, being placed one before the other. But once engaged, crawling contributes to the ongoing development of the infant. Crawling contributes to the development of balance, to the practice of bilateral motion, and to the strengthening of muscles that will eventually be used in walking. The increased mobility afforded by crawling provides the infant with increased, and sometimes scary, independence. Being able to move, sit, and hold the body stable and erect changes visual perspective and invites new experiences, which in turn stimulates new cognitive development. Increased mobility results in increased social interaction, whether that is playing with the family pet or with siblings or with parents and caretakers encouraging the crawling while at the same removing obstacles and potential danger.

> Reflect on the following: What appears as such a small thing as moving from sitting up to learning and trusting to rock back and forth to eventually finding the ability to push off one's knees in order to become a crawler is anything but simple or small. The effects of engaging with these new competencies has its impact on physical development, cognitive development, social engagement, and even on development of a worldview with its joys and risks.

Case Illustration 1.1 is certainly simple, but upon reflection, dramatically poignant. The subtle yet impacting interplay between the infant's internal drives, developing muscles, perceptual awareness, environmental supports and encouragers, and the leap of faith exhibited in those first few movements speaks to the multifaceted and multidimensional nature of our development. Further, in reviewing the illustration of the crawling infant it becomes apparent that often these forces are bidirectional, where the biological influences can affect the development of the cognition and vice versa.

This bidirectional quality becomes apparent when one considers what is required and what results from the development of the ability to speak; to reflect on one's own thoughts; to balance and ride a two-wheeled bike; or to feel sympathy, empathy, or loss. Each of these new abilities serves as both the end result of the complicated process called development and at the same time serves as the stimulant, contributor, and even foundation element for what is to follow.

Development: A Lifespan Perspective

There was a time when we viewed children as merely miniature replications of adults. Early pictorial presentations of children, at least those before the 17th century, showed them in adult dress, with eerily adult facial features—truly mini adults. It has been argued that the idea of *childhood* was a social creation appearing during the 1600s (Cunningham, 2006). It is not until the 1600s that we see evidence of children being presented as unique and different from adults. Thus, the study of human development, prior to the 1600s, would have focused simply on the adult experience, generalizing that experience to children as miniature expressions of adults. It could be argued that, somewhat reactively, once childhood was viewed as a unique stage of development, the pendulum swung too far to the emphasis of childhood experience as if development ended with one's passage from adolescence.

We now understand that while these early years and experiences are critical, they are not the entire story. As it will be presented in the upcoming chapters, research has provided us with ample evidence of the continuing nature of our development. Our developmental journey and the changes encountered as we move from childhood to old age are not merely changes of quantity but changes in quality.

Cognitively, for example, an adult not only has more information stored (i.e., quantity) but is also able to employ that information in ways (e.g., hypothetico-deductive reasoning) that are qualitatively different than those that would be used by a child of school age. Similarly, the socioemotional motives that drive people in their 30s are qualitatively different than those that direct life and decisions for people in their 70s. The adjustments we make and the changes we experience, or, more simply, our development, is truly a lifelong process (Charles & Carstensen, 2010; Hoyer & Roodin, 2009).

Lifespan: A Series of Human Developmental Periods

In the upcoming chapters, you will see how the interplay between biological, cognitive, and socioemotional processes impacting development takes on unique characteristics as defined by specific time frames within a person's

Photo 1.2   The journey of human development, from infancy to elderhood, continues to evolve during the lifespan.

Source: Stockphoto.com/Tana26.

life. These time frames, or developmental periods, are marked by the appearance of unique features, tasks, capabilities, and challenges. For purposes of this text's organization, we have identified 10 periods where developmental changes and challenges appear to be somewhat unique. The classification of the human developmental periods can be found in Table 1.2.

Table 1.2   Periods of Human Development

Period	Estimated Age Range	Description
Conception-Prenatal	0	Period involving rapid and extensive growth from single cell to human, with neurological capabilities
Infancy	Birth–24 months	While highly dependent, the development of language, symbolic thought, social skills, and modeling takes place.
Toddler	1–3 (overlap)	Increasing mobility and independence; the terrible 2s.
Early School Age	4–6	Increasing self-sufficiency, peer interest and interaction, and school readiness skills.
Middle Childhood	7–12	Achievement drive becomes evident; the fundamental skills of reading, writing, and arithmetic are mastered.
Early Adolescence	13–18	Rapid physical changes and the development of sexual characteristics. Increased peer interaction and influence. Cognitively moving into formal, abstract reasoning.
Late Adolescence	19–25	The pursuit of independence (socially, psychology, and financially) and desire to identify vocational direction and personal identity.

Period	Estimated Age Range	Description
Early Adulthood	26–35	Focus on establishing personal and economic independence, career development, and, for many, selecting a mate, possibly starting a family, and rearing children.
Middle Adulthood	36–50	While maintaining a satisfying career, interest turns toward social responsibility; in assisting the next generation.
Late Adulthood	51–75	Adjusting to post-work identity and retirement, adjusting to challenges of changing health.
Elderhood (Oldest-Old)	75+	Reflection and life review. Preparing for the end of life.

As you scan these periods of development, begin to consider those challenges, those tasks encountered by an individual at each period, and the role you, as counselor, could play in facilitating his or her development through that period. Your thoughts on these issues will take greater form as you proceed in your reading.

Development as Contextual

While Table 1.1 points out some generalized tasks or challenges confronting individuals at each period of their development, the nature of the challenges as well as the quality of the responses can be influenced by the context in which the development is occurring. Simply consider the situation of two individuals entering a late adult period of their development. Imagine that one has a healthy retirement plan, wonderful physical health, the support of an intimate partner and extended family, and job-related health benefits. Needless to say, addressing the tasks of this period will be different for that individual as opposed to one who is without family support, living on social security and food stamps, and has to employ emergency hospital services as his or her only form of health care. These are contextual variables, and they clearly impact the continuity of development.

Whether it is our local neighborhood or global community, our development occurs and is influenced by the setting and conditions as context. Factors such as culture, ethnicity, social values, histories, and economics come in to play in the unfolding of our personal stories. We are developing, but we as people of the 21st century are developing in a different context than that of our ancestors. As such, when viewing development one must appreciate the influence that context contributes.

According to Baltes & Smith (2003), context exerts three types of influences on human development: (a) normative age-graded influence that presents individuals as similar to those within their age group; (b) normative history-graded influences, such as the widespread impact of major sociopolitical events like world war, the civil rights movements, or even the terrorist attacks of 9/11/2001; and (c) nonnormative or highly individualized life events, such as the death of a loved one, the experience of being abandoned or abused, or even something like winning the lottery.

Life Domains of Human Development

As you proceed in your readings, you will see that the upcoming chapters discuss development by way of reviewing the theories and research targeting specific domains of development within the context of a particular developmental period. These domains refer to specific aspects of growth and change as noted in socioemotional, physical, linguistic, and cognitive development.

Photo 1.3   Healthy lifestyles, including good nutrition, contribute to a healthier longevity.

Source: Digital Vision/Photodisk/Thinkstock.

There are times when it appears that growth in one domain is dominant, even to the point of overriding development in other domains. For example, consider the case of the crawler who almost magically transitioned to taking her first steps. While the physical expression of this child's development may gather attention, the truth is that other domains are changing, perhaps more gradually and less prominently but changing nonetheless. The child's new physical capabilities interact and benefit from improved sensory perception and stimulate increasing cognitive development by way of infusion of new experiences. Change across domains is occurring often but sometimes not in so obvious ways.

Consider the changes accompanying adolescence. While one can see and most certainly experience the physical changes (deepening of the voice, physical development, body hair, etc.) and emotional liability (adolescent moodiness) that accompanies puberty, what may be less apparent are the cognitive changes occurring. Changes that are qualitative in nature and provide the adolescent with an increasing ability to think about his or her own thinking and to operate in the world of the hypothetical.

Development is a multifaceted process consisting of growth, regression, and change in many different domains. Understanding the uniqueness of these changes across domains, as they take form at different chronological periods of development, is essential if counselors are to know what is *normative* and what to do when help is needed.

A Biopsychosocial Approach

For years, the question of the degree to which our development is the product of our biological inheritance or our lived experience has been debated. The question of nature (biological forces) versus nurture (environmental/experiential/learning forces) and the influence of each continues to rear its head, especially when addressing issues of intelligence and behavioral aberrations. Do we simply write off developmental variations and deviations as a function of the luck of genetics, positioning ourselves somewhat impotently on the sidelines allowing nature to run its course? Or do we argue for sociopolitical and environmental changes that will ensure the proper nurturance for all in the human condition? Is it really that simple . . . either nature . . . or nurture? Review of the literature and research outcomes tell us that it is not.

As we noted above, human development is complicated. Development is multifaceted, multidimensional, and contextual. Our development is, at any one point, the result or outcome of the interaction of biological, cultural, and uniquely personal factors (Baltes, Reuter-Lorenz, & Rösler, 2006). As such, development should be viewed and studied from an interactive perspective valuing the influence of biology, psychology, and social context in the same environment.

In the upcoming chapters, information is provided about the unique biological conditions, cognitive capabilities, and psychosocial and emotional dispositions characteristic of a specific period of development. Further, research highlighting the factors both positively and negatively affecting development through that period of one's life will be discussed. But throughout each chapter, the unifying theme is that changes occurring in any one domain do not happen in isolation, rather each affects the other, and the outcome of development is the result of the interplay between these various factors. This integrative model is not new.

George Engel (1980) was one of the pioneers in bringing an integrative model to the field of medicine. Engel (1980) formulated the biopsychosocial model as a dynamic, interactional view of human experience in which there is mutual influence of mind and body, by way of the interactive forces found within the biological, psychological, and sociocultural systems.

Consider the issue of heart disease (Engel, 1977). While it is true that there is a **pathophysiological** component to heart disease (biological system), this biological state is often the end point of a large variety of sociocultural and psychological factors impinging on the **cardiovascular system**. Thus, it is not only important to view the condition from a perspective of the client's genetic vulnerability or biological makeup but also through the perspective social and cultural conditions (e.g., poverty, nutrition, marginalization, etc.) or psychological dispositions (e.g., lifestyle choices, stress encounters, and stress management strategies). It is in employing all systems—biological, psychological, social, and cultural—that one gets a full and accurate understanding of the what is and what needs to done.

Biological System

The biological system, as we know it, consists of a group of organs that work together to perform certain tasks. When applied to the biopsychosocial model, the need is to investigate how the biological or neurological basis affects human growth and development with respect to behavioral issues, how each individual responds to his or her world or has different levels of neurotransmitters in the brain. As such, the biological component of the biopsychosocial model seeks to understand how the functioning of one's body, one's biological system, contributes to the developmental difficulties encountered.

Psychological System

The psychological component of the biopsychosocial model looks for potential contributions from psychological issues that have caused or contributed to developmental difficulty and result in mental and physical health problems, issues such as **irrational thinking**, emotional distress, lack of self-control, and **excessive distress** (Ilham, 2000).

Sociocultural System

The social system aspect of the biopsychosocial model directs one to consider how various social contextual factors, such as social environment, interactive patterns, socioeconomic status (SES), culture, family structure, and religion contribute to healthy or unhealthy development. The social systems aspect of the biopsychosocial model draws attention to the effects of patterns of social roles and norms as well as the timing and sequence of important life events.

Application to Counseling Skills

The perspective gained from such a biopsychosocial model of development is that normative growth and development as was well pathology is influenced by a number of factors. Factors such as age-graded sociocultural factors (race, ethnicity, family, educational setting, friendships, religion, peer pressures, etc.), age-graded biological factors (puberty, **maturation**, menopause, etc.), historical factors (natural disasters, wars, etc.), and nonnormative factors (death of siblings, death of a child, early death of parents, etc.) contribute to formation and development of any one individual at any one of his or her developmental periods.

This integrative approach parallels what we know about the multidimensional and integrative nature of development and, as such, will be integrated throughout the upcoming chapters of the book. While investigating the uniqueness of the human experience as encountered at each of the periods of development, the focus will remain on understanding the interplay of the biological, psychological, and social and cultural processes contributing to that uniqueness and promoting growth and development through that particular period. It is our belief that understanding of lifespan development in the absence of its biological substrate, its psychological components, and its sociocultural context is not possible. This is brought to life in the presentation of Charla's case (Case Illustration 1.2).

CASE ILLUSTRATION 1.2 CHARLA

Instructions: The following case illustration demonstrates and highlights the biopsychosocial model as it depicts the elements contributing to the client's well-being. As you read the case illustration, highlight the biopsychosocial variables that you feel contribute to Charla's depression, anxiety, and other concerns. It is helpful to discuss your observations with a colleague or your instructor.

Charla's Case

Charla is a 28-year-old Caucasian female presenting with symptoms of possible depression and anxiety. Charla reports that her boyfriend, Jack, asked her to marry him 2 months ago, but she has not yet accepted the proposal. Ever since, she has been feeling anxious, overeating, and sleeping 10 to 12 hours at a time. Charla has been withdrawn from her friends because she knows that they do not support her relationship with Jack, as they believe that he is an alcoholic and has abused her. She also lacks interest in her work and has been taking numerous days off and has demonstrated very low performance on the job duties. Charla grew up in a very rigid and religious family. She states that her parents are very supportive of her, but they were always very critical toward her while she was growing up. Her father is very authoritative, and he is also a heavy drinker. While drunk, he often exhibits extreme violent and abusive behavior toward his wife and Charla. Charla's relationship with her mother is strained because she is critical of her father's behavior and often voices her disapproval of her father's actions toward her mother. She reports that her relationship with Jack has been rocky with multiple breakups and a history of heated augments. Jack becomes extremely violent when intoxicated, and it reminds her of her father's behavior and how that affected her family. Charla's religious belief causes her to feel guilt over her father and Jack's drinking problems. She reports having a few good friends whom she sees "from time to time." She expresses that she can "rely on them to vent her frustrations" but has recently "pulled back from them" because they do not approve of her relationship with Jack. Charla and Jack have a history of domestic violence. She reported one incident of domestic violence to the police, in which Jack was arrested and referred to participate in anger management counseling. Although there has not been an incident since then, Charla is worried that when he drinks he might do it again. Charla reports no homicidal ideation, plan, or intent to do so. She also denies any personal alcohol or substance abuse.

In summary, Charla is presenting symptoms of depression and anxiety. The symptoms and findings are prominent and clinically significant: oversleeping, overeating, isolative behavior, and feelings of anxiety. The symptoms are relatively acute. Protective factors include supportive mother and friends, as well as Charla's insight and motivation for treatment. Significant biopsychosocial stressors include absences from work and her relationship with her supervisor and coworkers. Other stressors include her relationship with her boyfriend, Jack, and her traumatic experience while growing up with an abusive alcoholic father, a demanding mother, and also a history of domestic violence with her father and her boyfriend.

Human Development Knowledge Applied to Counseling

The noted developmental psychologist, Lawrence Kohlberg, believes that counseling is important for the development of both the counselor and the client. His explanation for this relationship is established in the Moral Development Theory, originating from his earlier work and writings on moral development and moral education that are applied to the process of schooling, particularly as it relates to teaching and not counseling. After studying Piaget's views on the cognitive development of children's thinking about the physical world, Kohlberg asserts that all the basic processes involved in physical cognition in stimulating development changes are fundamental to social development (Kohlberg, 1969). He further asserts that the counseling process between a counselor and a client is a fundamental social activity, and thus, this process should be considered a developmental process of social interaction. Kohlberg also believed the skill of listening required the empathy and role-taking that are important for both moral and psychological growth between the counselor and the client. Kohlberg offers the view of progressivism, which encourages the nourishment of the individual's natural interaction with a developing society or environment and a cognitive-developmental psychology as compared to other theories offered.

While the case has been made for the value of a counselor's understanding of human development, as he or she differentiates that which is normative from that which is problematic, what might also be obvious is that knowledge of those factors impeding development positions a counselor to serve as an advocate or agent of prevention.

As you read on and begin to identify those biological, cultural, environmental and psychological forces that influence one's development, it will become clear that some individuals, by nature of their conditions of birth or circumstances of life, are more vulnerable to the interferences of healthy development. Whether it is the absence of prenatal medical care and nutritional support or the violence of bullying experienced by a teen, some individuals encounter stressors that exceed their ability to cope and thus impede development. Environmental pollution, infectious diseases, poverty, the absence of early childhood stimulation, or the experience of abuse and abandonment are only a few of the more dramatic forms of assault to human development that many people experience. While these are noted and noteworthy, there are threats that can be much more subtle yet just as insidious. Consider the situation of a student experiencing undue pressure to succeed, or the young adult displaced without social support, or the aging adult confronting physical limitations and medical needs within restricted financial resources. All of these conditions restrict individuals' ability to enjoy their current state of development and grow to the next.

As you begin to more fully understand the natural challenges experienced throughout the various periods of development, you will also come to appreciate those factors and elements that can facilitate and support healthy growth and development. With that knowledge, you will be better positioned to not only intervene as a counselor when called upon but also to proactively engage as an advocate for those who need your support.

The objective of this textbook is to present human growth and development from a counseling perspective and how this unique perspective can be applied through the lifespan of individuals. As discussed in this chapter, to define human development is to define the growth of humans throughout their entire lifespan. The principle of the study of human development is to understand and explain how and why people change throughout the lifespan, and this includes all aspects of human development, including the psychological, physical, emotional, intellectual, social, perceptual, and personality development. These are all variables to be taken into consideration for an effective therapeutic intervention. There is an urgent need to augment research in these areas and place this knowledge in the hands of educators and students.

To understand human development is important to have a clear concept of how factors such as individuals' experiences, life maturation processes, and changes in time, including cultural implications, shape the stages of human development. This process also includes (a) how individuals cope with and make sense of their environment and surroundings; (b) how individuals use their learning experiences to cope with adversity and stress; (c) how individuals develop resilience and coping skills affected by gender, cultural, physical, psychological, and sociological factors; (d) how individuals behave and perceive life expectations; and (e) how life events and changes, transitions, and transformations form from one stage to another to contribute to an individual's identity and integration into one's community and society. This is a complex process with multiple factors that are all equally important, and they need to be emphasized not only during counselor training but also during counseling practice.

Human development awareness is about creating an environment in which people can develop their full potential and have a healthy, active, creative, and productive lifestyle. The advancement of science and technology has contributed greatly to the acceleration of human progress during the past decades. According to many recent studies, modernization and globalization, with the advancement of technology, while generally good for societies, can also create many disadvantages for some sectors of the population. Some individuals are more vulnerable to the wider effects of environmental degradation and social problems because of more significant stressors and fewer coping tools that weaken resilience. Vulnerable individuals must also deal with threats to their immediate environment from pollution, contaminated water, and unimproved sanitation. Forecasts suggest that a continuing failure to reduce grave environmental risks and deepening social inequalities threatens to slow decades of sustained progress by the world's poor majority and can even reverse the global convergence in human development. The is perhaps an urgent warning to develop and strengthen the safety networks of society to make sure that they reach everyone and prevent the physical and mental decline of all people. The counseling profession, with its many roles like working with, assisting, and advocating for its clients, also has a responsibility to act and contribute.

The challenges ahead for counselor education are many; however, the significant ones are to conduct more evidence-based research to study this very complex topic of the relationship between counseling and human development through the lifespan; to conduct research with cultural responsibility in reference to the increased cultural and ethnic diversity among populations in the United States; to explore and study the interaction among learning, physical ability, cultural influence, socioeconomic status, environmental and ecological factors, genetic composition, and biopsychosocial implications with respect to human development through the lifespan.

The world has become a global community, and the proliferation of cultural and knowledge exchange among peoples and nations has provided great incentives for researchers and scholars to study human development from a multidimensional and multilevel perspective, with respect to cultural, psychological, and sociological factors. It is very important for helping professionals, such as counselors, to continue to apply and promote the study of human development through the lifespan today and in the future. It is essential not only to understand human development to be able to understand the individual but also to acquire the knowledge of individual differences, abilities, disabilities, and other diverse characteristics that can enhance and optimize the outcome of counseling services.

SUMMARY

- Human development is an interdisciplinary field dedicated to understanding human constancy and change throughout the lifespan.
- The study of human development requires a comprehensive and systematic approach.
- The study of human development involves the explanation of both change and continuity.
- The field of human development has four major goals: (a) to describe the changes that occur across the human lifespan, (b) to explain these changes, (c) to predict developmental changes, and (d) to intervene in the course of events in order to control them.

➤ It is important to discuss human development through the lifespan perspective, consisting of the multidimensional, multidirectional, multidisciplinary, plastic, and contextual development of humans.

➤ The domain of human development refers to specific aspects of growth and change, and the major domains of development include psychosocial, emotional, physical, language, and cognition.

➤ Understanding human development is important to the counselor's competence because this knowledge will enhance the counselor's ability to apply best practices during the particular life stage of the client and to serve as an advocate for those in need advocacy.

ADDITIONAL RESOURCES

This chapter contains a list of resources including readings and websites that may be useful to readers in their search for more information and in-depth knowledge. However, readers should be aware that the information contained on websites may not always be reliable and should be verified before the source is used as a reference. The following are some websites to obtain further information on human development and lifespan:

The United Nations: www.un.org

The United Nations (UN) is an international organization whose stated aims are facilitating cooperation in international law, international security, economic development, social progress, human rights, and achievement of world peace. The UN was founded in 1945 after World War II to replace the League of Nations, to stop wars between countries, and to provide a platform for dialogue. It contains multiple subsidiary organizations to carry out its missions. The UN currently has a total of 193 member states.

The World Bank: www.worldbank.org

The World Bank is an international financial institution that provides loans to developing countries for capital programs. The World Bank's official goal is the reduction of poverty around the world. The World Bank differs from the World Bank Group, in that the World Bank comprises only two institutions: the International Bank for Reconstruction and Development (IBRD) and the International Development Association (IDA), whereas the latter incorporates these two in addition to three more: the International Finance Corporation (IFC), the Multilateral Investment Guarantee Agency (MIGA), and the International Centre for Settlement of Investment Disputes (ICSID).

The National Association of School Psychologists: www.nasponline.org

The mission of the National Association of School Psychologists (NASP) is to empower school psychologists by advancing effective practices to improve students' learning, behavior, and mental health. The core values of NASP are advocacy, collaborative relationships, continuous improvement, diversity, excellence, integrity, student-centered, and visionary leadership.

The Council on Social Work Education: www.cswe.org

The Council on Social Work Education (CSWE) is a nonprofit national association representing more than 2,500 individual members, as well as graduate and undergraduate programs of professional social work education. Founded in 1952, this partnership of educational and professional institutions, social welfare agencies, and private citizens is recognized by the Council for Higher Education Accreditation as the sole accrediting agency for social work education in the United States.

Centers for Disease Control and Prevention: www.cdc.gov

The Centers for Disease Control and Prevention (CDC) is a United States federal agency under the Department of Health and Human Services. It is headquartered and based in Atlanta, Georgia. The CDC works to protect public health and safety by providing information to enhance health decisions, and it promotes health through partnerships with state health departments and other organizations. The CDC focuses national attention on developing and applying disease prevention and control (especially infectious diseases and foodborne pathogens and other microbial infections), environmental health, occupational safety and health, health promotion, injury prevention, and education activities designed to improve the health of the people of the United States. The CDC is the United States' national public health institute and is a founding member of the International Association of National Public Health Institutes.

Council for Standards in Human Services Education: www.cshse.org

The Council for Standards in Human Service Education (CSHSE) is committed to assuring the quality, consistency, and relevance of human service education through research-based standards and a peer-review accreditation process. The vision of CSHSE is to promote excellence in human service education, provide quality assurance, and support standards of performance and practice through the accreditation process.

Council for Accreditation of Counseling and Related Educational Programs: www.cacrep.org

The Council for Accreditation of Counseling and Related Educational Programs (CACREP) accredits graduate-level counseling programs offered by institutions throughout the United States and some international programs. CACREP accredits many programs, including addiction counseling, clinical mental health counseling, family counseling, and school counseling. The vision of CACREP is to provide leadership and to promote excellence in professional preparation through the accreditation of counseling and related educational programs. As an accrediting body, CACREP is committed to the development of standards and procedures that reflect the needs of a dynamic, diverse, and complex society.

The National Institute on Aging's Featured Health Topic: Healthy Aging/Longevity: www.nia.nih.gov/health/featured/healthy-aging-longevity

The National Institute on Aging (NIA), one of the 27 Institutes and Centers of the National Institutes of Health (NIH), leads a broad scientific effort to understand the nature of aging and to extend the healthy, active years of life. In 1974, Congress granted authority to form NIA to provide leadership in aging research, training, health information dissemination, and other programs relevant to aging and older people.

Annenberg Learner: www.learner.org

Annenberg Learner uses media and telecommunications to advance excellent teaching in American schools. This mandate is carried out chiefly by the funding and broad distribution of educational video programs with coordinated web and print materials for the professional development of K–12 teachers. It is part of the Annenberg Foundation and advances the Foundation's goal of encouraging the development of more effective ways to share ideas and knowledge. Annenberg Learner's multimedia resources help teachers increase their expertise in their fields and assists them in improving their teaching methods. Many programs are also intended for students in the classroom and viewers at home. All Annenberg Learner videos exemplify excellent teaching.

RECOMMENDED SUPPLEMENTARY READINGS

Adams, M. (2006). Towards an existential phenomenological model of lifespan human development. *Existential Analysis, 17*(2), 261–280.

Beckett, C. (2010). *Human growth and development* (2nd ed.). Thousand Oaks, CA: Sage

Chatterjee, S. (2005). Measurement of human development: An alternative approach. *Journal of Human Development, 6*(1), 31–53.

Duck, S. (2007). *Human Relationships* (4th ed.). Thousand Oaks, CA: Sage.

Melchert, T. P. (2011). *Foundations of professional psychology: The end of theoretical orientations and the emergence of the biopsychosocial approach.* Amsterdam: Elsevier.

Robine, J. (2003). Life course, environmental change and lifespan. *Population & Development Review, 29*(1), 229–238.

Salkind, N.J. (2004). *An introduction to theories of human development.* Thousand Oaks, CA: Sage.

REFERENCES

American Counseling Association (1997). Defining the counseling profession: A practitioner's guide to the counseling profession. *Counseling Today,* 6–12. Alexandria, VA: Author.

American Counseling Association. (2005). *ACA code of ethics.* Alexandria, VA: Author.

Baltes, P. B., & Smith, J. (2003). New frontiers in the future of aging: From successful aging of the young old to the dilemmas of the fourth age. *Gerontology, 49,* 123–135.

Baltes, P. B., Lindenberger, U., & Staudinger, U. M. (2006). Lifespan theory in developmental psychology. In R. Lerner & W. Damon (Eds.), *Handbook of child psychology (6th ed.): Vol 1, Theoretical models of human development* (569–664). Hoboken, NJ: John Wiley.

Baltes, P. B., Reuter-Lorenz, P. A., & Rösler, F., (2006). Prologue: Biocultural co-construtivism as a theoretical metascript. In P. B. Baltes, P. Reuter-Lorenz, & F, Rösler (Eds.), *Lifespan development and the brain: The perspective of biocultural co-constructivism* (3–39). New York, NY: Cambridge University Press.

Charles, S. T., & Carstensen, L. L. (2010). Emotion regulation and aging. In J. J. Gross (Ed.), *Handbook of emotion regulation* (2nd ed.). New York, NY: Guilford Press.

Council for Accreditation of Counseling and Related Educational Programs (CACREP). (2009). *The 2013 standards. What is accreditation?* Retrieved from http://www.cacrep.org/template/index.cfm.

Cunningham, H. (2006). *The invention of childhood.* New York, NY: Random House.

Engel, G. (1980). The clinical application of the biopsychosocial model. *American Journal of Psychiatry, 137,* 113–136.

Engel, G. E (1977). The need for a new medical model. *Science, 196,* 129–36.

Hoyer, W. J., & Roodin, P. A. (2009). *Adult development and aging.* New York, NY: McGraw Hill.

Ilham, D. (2000). *Psychology and human behavior: Is there a limit to psychological explanation?* New York, NY: Cambridge University Press.

Kohlberg, L. (1969). Stages and sequences—The cognitive-developmental approach to socialization. In D. Goslin (Ed.), *Handbook of socialization theory and research* (pp. 347–480). Chicago, IL: Rand McNally.

Korsmo, J., Baker-Sennett, J., & Nicholas, T. (2009). Learning through like books: Teaching human growth and development in an emotionally rich community context. *International Journal of Teaching and Learning in Higher Education, 21*(3), 382–389.

Theories of Human Development

We know what we are, but know not what we may be.

W. Shakespeare

Consider the above quote by Shakespeare, from the perspective of a person who is unfamiliar with human development and the multiple changes of transformation that take place from the moment of birth and long into the future lifespan. Imagine looking at newborn babies bundled in blankets, resting peacefully in their bassinets. You may know what is seen but you are unable to know what may be.

Through observation it is clear that there is difference in size, shape, color tone, level of activity, and even the degree to which hair is present. Some may be quiet with eyes closed, sleeping, while others clearly in stress are red faced and screaming. Again, the observer would know these observations but certainly would be hard pressed to describe what may be.

While the process of developing from the joining of two cells to what now appears in a flesh-and-blood bundle in a nursery is in itself quite an amazing, complex, and intricate affair, the complexity or intricacy does not cease at birth. Ask yourself, which of the bundled babies will become a president, a CEO, or a notorious criminal? Which one among those sleeping or crying may fail to thrive or may develop with major physical, intellectual, social, or emotional challenges? Which of this birth class will be tall or short, slim or obese, athletic, academic, artistic, or skilled with his or her hands? Which of those present at that moment will navigate life feeling good about themselves, accomplishing that which they desire and reflecting at the end on a life fulfilled? These are the questions that the observer may ponder, along with one more. What are the factors, the elements, and the processes that give shape or contribute to that which will become?

These above questions were offered as a way to ponder these very same questions that we may have while expanding our knowledge. If we knew what was to be, and what factors gave shape to that future scenario, then we would be better positioned to intervene when danger and blocks were clearly present and supportive to those conditions that facilitated optimal development. And, while we now know so much more about those very factors, there is much to research, investigate, and discover.

As noted in Chapter 1, human development is complex. It is multidimensional, multidirectional, contextual, and in many ways, quite idiosyncratic to each individual. These characteristics make it difficult to study and challenging to know factually. This chapter introduces the theories and research methodologies that are leading us to a more complete and accurate understanding of the nature and conditions of human development. Specifically, after studying this chapter, the student will be able to

1. describe the general focus of seven main theories of human development: Maturationist Theory, Psychoanalytic Theory, E. Erikson's Psychosocial Theory, Behaviorism Theory, Biopsychosocial Theory, Cognitive Development Theory, and Ecological System Theory;

2. identify the J. Piagetian Stages of Cognitive Development as they appear at different periods of development;

3. describe the psychosocial task experienced at each period of development as described by E. Erickson;

4. explain the methods of research employed in the pursuit of knowledge and validation of developmental theories; and

5. describe the fundamental ethical concerns and principles that guide research on human development.

Theories and Theoretical Models of Human Development

The complexity of human development invites the creation of multiple perspectives and theories, some global and grand in nature addressing principles that apply to every domain of development, where others are more domain specific (e.g., focusing on cognitive development).

Theories provide a framework for the study of human development that furthers scientific vision and stimulates the application of science for public policy and social programs. Most importantly, theories help organize a large body of information and provide ways of examining facts. They also help focus our search for new understandings, explain how findings may be interpreted, and identify major disagreements among scholars (Dacey, Travers, & Fiore, 2009).

This chapter will briefly describe the seven major theoretical perspectives or theories on human development: Maturationist Theory, Psychoanalytic Theory, Erikson's Psychosocial Theory, Behaviorism Theory, Biopsychosocial Theory, Cognitive Development Theory, and Ecological System Theory. Like most theories used in counseling, each can serve as a lens through which to view human development and to guide practice decisions. It is useful, as you review each theory, to consider the implication that theory presents for a counselor's intervention and prevention programming.

Photo 2.1   Life adversity, and how an individual copes with it, has an impact on the person's developmental stages and ultimately on quality of life.

Maturationist Theory

Granville Stanley Hall (1844–1924) was a pioneering American psychologist and educator. His interests focused on childhood development, evolutionary theory, and their applications to education. Hall was a strong believer in the scientific method and its application to the study of human nature. He supported empirical research in the then emerging area of child development, developing both theories of psychological development and its application to children's education. Although Hall's understanding was incomplete, and his theories not fully accepted, his work was significant in laying the foundation for the field (Parry, 2006; Ross, 1972). His maturationist theory emphasized the importance of genetics and evolution and was based on the premise that growing children would recapitulate evolutionary stages of species development as they grew up. He concluded that it would be counterproductive to push a child ahead of any one developmental stage since each stage laid the foundation for what was to follow. In very simple terms, the position was that everyone would need to crawl before learning to walk.

Psychoanalytic Theories

While much attention has been given to the psychoanalytic position on issues such as determinism, instinctual drives, and the unconscious, the early works of psychoanalytic theorists, especially the founder, Sigmund Freud (1856–1939) highlighted the essential role played by early childhood experiences. Freud's position was that a person's psychological responses and behaviors were reflections of biological instinctual drives. Freud postulated that

Table 2.1   Freud's Psychosexual Stages of Development

Stage	Age	Characteristics
Oral Stage	Birth to 1	An infant's primary interaction with the world is through the mouth. The mouth is vital for eating, and the infant derives pleasure from oral stimulation through gratifying activities such as tasting and sucking. If this need is not met, the child may develop an oral fixation later in life, examples of which include thumb-sucking, smoking, fingernail biting, and overeating.
Anal Stage	1 to 3	With the development of new cells and the control provided by those cells (sphincters), the focus shifts from oral stimulation to controlling bladder and bowel movements. Toilet training is a primary issue with children and parents. Too much pressure can result in an excessive need for order or cleanliness later in life, while too little pressure from parents can lead to messy or destructive behavior later in life.
Phallic Stage	3 to 6	At this point in development, the focus of the id's instinctual energies shifts to the genitals. It is during this period that children develop an attraction to the opposite-sex parent. It is also at this period that children adopt the values and characteristics of the same-sex parent and form the superego.
Latent Stage	6 to 11	During this stage, children develop social skills, values, and relationships with peers and adults outside of the family.
Genital Stage	11 to 18	During this stage, people develop a strong interest in the opposite sex, and the onset of puberty causes the libido to become active once again. If development has been successful to this point, the individual will continue to develop into a well-balanced person.

objects or means for satisfying our instinctual drive for pleasure shifted throughout our early years of development moving from the mouth and oral stimulation, to the anus and the experience of control, and eventually to the genitals and the inclusion of sex role behaviors and identification (See Table 2.1). Freud posited that it was during our childhood, our first 6 years, that we developed ways to resolve conflicts between the desire for pleasure and the demands, often repressive, encountered in reality. For Freud, it was this dynamic process of conflict resolution that he believed shaped one's development and later lifestyle (Freud, 1962). While many of the tenets originally presented by Freud have been modified by contemporary psychoanalytic theorists, emphasis on the importance of early childhood experiences, especially experience in and with relationships, continues to play a pivotal role in their understanding of adult choices and behavior. Table 2.1 demonstrates Freud's Psychosexual Stages of Development from ages 1 to 18 years old and its implications for human development and growth.

Erik Erikson's Psychosocial Development Theory

Unlike Freud, who focused on early childhood with an emphasis on biological instinctual urges as key to human development, Erik Erikson presented a model emphasizing the challenges and tasks presented across one's lifespan as key to understanding human development. Further, unlike Freud, Erickson emphasized development from within a social context. Erickson's theory is an epigenic theory, which means it focuses on both the biological and genetic origins of behaviors as interacting with the direct influence of environmental forces over time. He posited that this biological unfolding in relation to our sociocultural settings is done in stages of psychosocial development, where progress through each stage is in part determined by our success, or lack of success, in all the previous stages.

Erickson posited that humans pass through 8 stages of development with each presenting the individual with a unique developmental task, or what he termed "crisis" (see Erikson's Stages of Psychosocial Development in Table 2.2). Erickson felt that these psychosocial crises were based on physiological development interacting with the demands put on the individual by parents and society (Erikson, 1982; Stevens, 1983)

Erikson's Stages of Psychosocial Development are presented in Table 2.2. As you review the brief description of each stage, note how the resolution of any one stage may pave the way for subsequent stages. For example, the

Photo 2.2   The early years of schooling are major contributors to children's developmental stages.

Source: Creatas/Creatas/Thinkstock.

child who has difficulty developing a basic trust (trust vs. mistrust, Stage 1) of his or her environment may find it difficult to risk engaging in the types of self-directed behaviors that would allow for a positive resolution to the autonomy versus shame and doubt stage (Stage 2).

Table 2.2   Erikson's Stages of Psychosocial Development

Stages	Life Stage & Age	Meaning & Interpretation
Trust vs. Mistrust	Infant (0–1½)	The infant will develop a healthy balance between trust and mistrust if cared for and responded to consistently. Abuse or neglect will foster mistrust. Positive outcomes consist of the development of hope and drive, while negative outcomes could contribute to withdrawal.
Autonomy vs. Shame & Doubt	Toddler (1–3)	Autonomy means self-reliance or independence of thought and confidence to act for oneself. Toilet training is a significant part of this stage. Positive outcomes consist of willpower and self-control, while negative outcomes could contribute to compulsive behaviors.
Initiative vs. Guilt	Preschool (4–6)	Initiative means aptitude and self-confidence to perform actions, even with the understanding of risks and failure. Guilt results from abandonment or believing an action will draw disapproval. Positive outcomes foster purpose and direction, while negative outcomes encourage inhibition.
Industry vs. Inferiority	School Age (7–12)	Industry means having a meaningful activity and the competence to perform a skill. Inferiority means feeling incapable of experiencing failure or inability to discover one's own strengths. This stage is crucial in the school years. Positive outcomes foster competence, while negative outcomes encourage inertia.
Identity vs. Role Confusion	Adolescent (12–18)	Identity means understanding of self and how one fits into the surrounding world, while role confusion focuses on the inability to understand one's self or personal identity. Positive outcomes foster fidelity and devotion, while negative outcomes encourage repudiation behavior.
Intimacy vs. Isolation	Young Adult (19–40)	Intimacy means developing relationships with friends, family, and partners. Isolation involves feelings of being excluded from relationships or partnership. These encompass sexual maturity, reciprocal love, support, and emotional connection. Positive outcomes foster love and affiliation, while negative outcomes encourage exclusivity.
Generativity vs. Stagnation	Adulthood (41–65)	Generativity means unconditional care for one's offspring or the future generations to come, while stagnation refers to self-absorption/concentration. Positive outcomes foster care and giving, while negative outcomes encourage rejectivity.
Integrity vs. Despair	Mature Adult (65+)	Integrity means understanding of self and satisfaction with life, while despair contributes to feelings of wasted time, opportunity, and chances. Positive outcomes foster wisdom, while negative outcomes encourage despair.

Behaviorism Theory

Whereas, Erikson introduced the importance of social context to development, the Behavioral Theory, at least in its classical form, placed nearly sole emphasis on the impact of environment, experience, and learning about the unfolding development of the human condition.

This orientation can best be illustrated by a quote offered by John B. Watson (1878–1985), deemed the father of American Behaviorism. Watson's emphasis on the role of environment in the shaping of human development is concretized in his statement "Give me a dozen healthy infants, well-formed, and my own specified world to bring them up in and I will guarantee to take any one at random and train him to become any type of specialist I might select . . . doctor, lawyer, artist, merchant-chief . . . and, yes, even beggar-man and thief, regardless of his talents, penchants, tendencies, abilities, vocations, and race of his ancestors" (Watson, 1998, p.82). That is quite a guarantee and clearly highlights the valuing and focuses this behaviorist placed on the role of environment, experience, and learning in the creation of the human condition.

Two main themes or forms of behavioral theory have been presented in explaning how the environment has such a formational impact. One proffered by B. F. Skinner (1904–1990) suggested that behavior was formed, or shaped, as a result of the consequences experienced. His operant conditioning model argued that behavior followed by a rewarding stimulus would be more likely to recur and endure than that followed by a punishing consequence (Cohen, 1987; Skinner, 1974).

Thus, an infant who experiences the comfort of being picked up and cradled following his or her crying is more likely to employ crying behavior in the future. Or, an individual who has experienced ridicule following his or her initiation of a social contact may soon employ withdrawal and isolation as a developmental coping style.

A second behavioral approach to the explanation of the influence of environment on development is that initially presented by Albert Bandura (1997, 2008) as social learning theory. Bandura's model expanded the classic behavioral theory to include cognitive elements. Bandura's work emphasized the importance of observational learning (also called imitation or modeling). For example, consider the situation of a child who was raised in an environment where there was much domestic arguing and physical violence and the employment of alcohol as a stress-reducing strategy. Raised in this setting and observing these social exchanges and coping styles, the child, according to social learning theory, would be very likely to model the observed behavior and engage in similar domestic violence and alcohol use behaviors.

According to Bandura, Barbaranelli, Caprara, and Pastorelli (2001), social learning is connected to perceptions and interpretations of the individual's experience. Self-efficacy, the belief that personal achievement depends on one's actions, teaches people to have high aspirations and to strive for notable accomplishments when they see others solve problems successfully. This premise is contrary to Behavioral Theory, which holds that behavior depends on associations between one stimulus and another and also assumes that all behaviors react from a chain of learned responses. In contrast, social learning maintains that behaviors come from people acting on the stimulation of the environment.

Cognitive Theories

Whereas Behavioral Theory targeted the process of developing behavior and the psychoanalytic models emphasized the role of the unconscious, theorists expressing a Cognitive Theory of development emphasized the unfolding of conscious thought and the developing abilities to process, store, retrieve, and use information. Two major players in the realm of cognitive theory are Jean Piaget, a well-known Swiss psychologist and Lev Vygotsky, an equally well-known psychologist from Russia. Both men contributed significantly to our understanding of the nature of cognitive development.

Piaget's Theory of Cognitive Development

Piaget's theory of cognitive development describes how humans gather and organize information and how this process changes developmentally (Inhelder & Piaget, 1958). He believed that children are born with a very basic mental structure on which all subsequent learning and knowledge is based. For Piaget, the focus was on how mental structures and processes evolved to help individuals make meaning out of their experience and adapt to their changing environments. To understand this process of adaptation, he employed the constructs of schema, assimilation, accommodation, and equilibration.

For Piaget, a schema (or the plural schemata) referred to the cognitive structures by which an individual organizes his or her experience and environment. For example, an infant upon encountering a dog for the first time will experience visual, auditory, and olfactory input. These data, according to Piaget, will be linked in a neural pathway, a schema that will eventually be used as a mental template to represent *dog* each time these stimuli are encountered. However, as we know, not all dogs will be like the first one experienced, and other animals, for example a fox or wolf, while possessing some of the characteristic of our *dog* will be different. It is these subtle differences that will force an individual to develop new schemata to reflect and organize these categories of stimulation. The process by which this is done includes (a) first a new encounter; (b) an experience of disequilibrium, discomfort of not quite understanding or being able to make sense of the new encounter; and then (c) the process of adaptation.

When discussing this process of adaptation, Piaget noted that our first inclination is to attempt to "force" the new experience into an existing template or schema by way of the process of assimilation. Consider the infant who begins to discern the features of a male-daddy from that of a female-mommy. It would not be unexpected that when encountering a new male figure the infant responds with "daddy." But as the infant develops and possesses increased visual clarity and memory, discerning that the new male does not possess all the distinguishing characteristics of "daddy," he or she will be forced to make an adjustment or to create a new schema, perhaps "uncle," as a way of making meaning and organizing this encounter. This condition of making a new schema is call accommodation. For Piaget, humans are continually adjusting knowledge in order to adapt to the environment through a process of equilibration, assimilating when possible and accommodating when necessary (Atherton, 2011).

As Piaget researched cognition and cognitive development, he concluded that a person's cognitive development unfolds through four distinct and qualitatively different stages (see Piaget's Stages of Cognitive Development in Table 2.3). He believed that these stages reflected an invariant sequence of development with all children passing through each in order. Further, he posited that each stage was qualitatively different than the others, such that it was not simply a matter of more knowledge or information but a different way or ability to derive and use that information. Finally, while assuming the necessity of biological readiness as a determining factor in one's progression through the stages, he also acknowledged the potential for the environment to accelerate or even retard that progression.

Although many think Piaget's Cognitive Theory is too narrow to explain lifespan human development, he is credited with discovering that thoughts, not just experience, contribute to human development. The advancement of medical research, particularly brain research, has allowed scientists to study how humans process information and react to various stimulations and will ultimately allow them to understand human cognition development at every age in the near future (Atherton, 2011).

Vygotsky's Sociocultural Perspective

Lev Vygotsky (1896–1934), a pioneer of sociocultural theory, like Piaget, maintained that children actively construct their knowledge. However, he disagreed with Piaget's proposal that progression through the identified cognitive stages was natural and invariant. Vygotsky emphasized the role of culture in promoting certain types of activities (Rogoff & Chavajay, 1995) and emphasized that a child masters tasks that are deemed culturally important.

Vygotsky believed that human development is the result of interactions between people and their social environment. He focused on the connections between people and the sociocultural context in which they act and interact in shared experiences and cultural artifacts such as written languages, number systems, various signs, and symbols (Burns, Bodrova, & Leong, 2012). The purpose of these cultural artifacts is to facilitate the possible adjustment of a growing child into the culture and transform the way the child's mind is formed. Initially, children

Table 2.3   Piaget's Stages of Cognitive Development

Stage	Approximate Age	Description
Sensorimotor	Birth to 18–24 months	Infants adapt and organize experiences by way of sensory and motor actions. Initially, simple reflexes, for example sucking, help them know their world. Later, within this stage, the infant differentiates self from the external world and objects take on their own existence. This is when object permanence occurs with the infant able to symbolize the object and realize that objects exist even if out of sensory experience.
Preoperational	2 to 7 years	While the child at this stage lacks logical operations, he or she is no longer tied to sensorimotor input but is tied to and operates via representational and conceptual frameworks. The child is able to employ symbols to recreate or present experiences. In this stage, the child believes that everyone sees the world the same way that he or she does. This is called egocentrism. Conservation, another achievement of this stage, is the ability to understand that quantity does not change if the shape changes.
Concrete Operational	7 to 11 years	In this stage, the child has the ability to employ logic; however, only to concrete problems and objects.
Formal Operational	Over 11	At this point, children's abstract thinking leads to reasoning with more complex symbols. They can think logically about abstract propositions and test hypotheses systematically. They become concerned with the hypothetical, the future, and ideological problems.

Photo 2.3   Strong intergenerational family bonding is very important throughout the lifespan of family members.

Source: Jack Hollingsworth/Photodisc/Thinkstock.

develop these tools to serve solely as social functions and ways to communicate needs. These cultural tools are an achievement that expands one's mental capacities, allowing individuals to master their own behavior. Children generally learn how to use these cultural tools through interactions with parents, teachers, or more experienced peers (Burns et al., 2012).

Biopsychosocial Theories

The Biopsychosocial theory was discussed in some detail in Chapter 1, and thus will not be expanded upon here. It is sufficient to highlight that the biopsychosocial model focuses on the integration and reciprocal effect that the biological, psychological, and social systems have on our development. The theory helps to highlight the fact that mental and psychological states are influenced by many interacting processes, including internal and external variables and factors such as bodily processes, personality dispositions, and life events.

Ecological Systems Theory

Theories of development classified as ecological theories emphasize environmental factors. One ecological theory that has important implications for understanding life-span development was created by Urie Bronfenbrenner. Bronfenbrenner (1917–2005), a Russian-American, developed the Ecological Systems Theory of human development. According to the theory, a child's development occurs within a complex system of relationships including parent-child interactions (i.e., the microsystem); the extended family, school, and neighborhood (the mesosystem); and the general society and culture (the exosystem). All in all, the theory posited five environmental systems significant for understanding human development: microsystem, mesosystem, exosystem, macrosystem, and chronosystem. Table 2.4 provides descriptions of these systems, whereas Figure 2.1 highlights the dynamic interactive nature of these systems.

Photo 2.4   An environment that is accommodating creates a better society where everyone can function independently.

Source: Toby Burrows/Digital Vision/Thinkstock.

As you review Table 2.4, consider how specific formation of each of the systems can interfere with one's optimal development. Consider, for example, the impact that living in poverty, or in an abusive family, or in a culture/society that is war torn has on development. As you reflect on each of these systems, consider the implications for a counselor's intervention and prevention services.

Table 2.4   Bronfenbrenner's Ecological Systems Theory

System	Description
Microsystem	The *microsystem* refers to the immediate surroundings of the individual and consists of the interactions in his or her immediate surroundings. It is the setting in which a person lives; family, peer groups, neighborhood, and school life are all included in the microsystem. It is in the microsystem that the most direct interactions with social agents take place, with parents, peers, and teachers, for example. The individual is not merely a passive recipient of experiences in these settings but someone who actually helps to construct the social settings.
Mesosystem	The *mesosystem* connects with the structure of the microsystem. The relationship can be seen between school life, the neighborhood, and the family. The child's environment links the child with his or her immediate surroundings. Some common examples are the connections between family experiences and school experiences, school experiences and church experiences, and family experiences and peer experiences. A result of mesosystem interactions could be that children whose parents have rejected them may have difficulty developing positive relations with their friends or peers.
Exosytem	The *exosystem* is the outer shell surrounding both the mesosystem and the microsystem. The inner level of the exosystem is affected by the support of the macrosystem. Bronfenbrenner describes the exosystem as being made up of social settings that do not contain the developing person but nevertheless affect experiences in his or her immediate settings (Berk, 2007). The exosystem includes other people and places that the child may not interact with often but still have a large effect on the child, such as parents' workplaces, extended family members, neighborhoods, and so on. For example, a wife's or child's experience at home may be influenced by the husband's experiences at work. The father might receive a promotion that requires more travel, which might increase conflict with the wife and affect patterns of interaction with the child.
Macrosystem	The *macrosystem* influences the individual directly, but the individual has less influence in determining settings. The macrosystem includes aspects of culture and the relative freedoms permitted by the national government, cultural values, the economy, wars, and so on. Macrosystem also describes the culture in which individuals live, including socioeconomic status, poverty, and ethnicity.
Chronosystem	The *chronosystem* refers to the patterning of environmental events and transitions over the life of an individual as well as sociohistorical circumstance. For example, divorce is one transition. Researchers have found that the negative effects of divorce on children often peak in the first year after the divorce. Two years after the divorce, family interaction is less chaotic and more stable. An example of sociohistorical circumstances would be the increasing opportunities in the last decades for women to pursue a career.

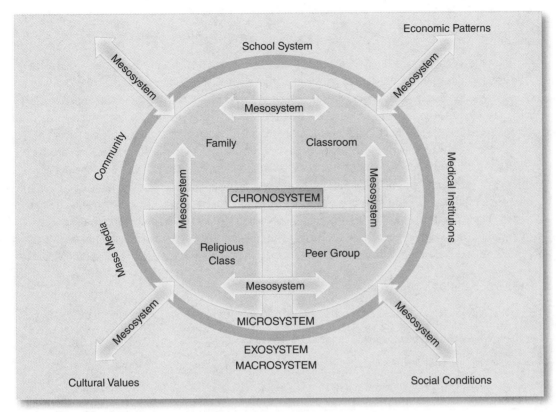

Figure 2.1 Bronfenbrenner's Ecological Systems Theory of Dynamic Interactive Nature

The Ecological Systems Theory developed by Bronfenbrenner has influenced the thinking of developmental psychologists and other psychologists throughout the world. This theory has significantly impacted the field of child and youth care. The umbrella, cube, and ecological onion models, which are widely used by professionals in child and youth care to organize ideas and information and to facilitate planning, are based on Bronfenbrenner's theory (Oswalt, 2008). Guided Practice Exercise 2.1, A Collision of Cultures, is provided to allow you to view a case through the lens of Bronfenbrenner's Ecological Systems theory.

Guided Practice Exercise 2.1 A Collision of Cultures

Instructions: As you read through the case of "Ben," reflect on the information as you filter it through the Ecological Theory of Development. Following your reading, respond to the questions presented. Discuss your responses with a colleague or professor.

The Case of Ben

Ben is an American-Chinese boy growing up in a very traditional American society with very traditional Chinese parents. Ben's parents communicate with each other in Chinese (Mandarin) at home. Ben's

(Continued)

(Continued)

parents are highly educated individuals, and because Ben is their first child, he has been spoiled since he was a toddler. Due to their work responsibilities, the parents live separately, which requires a 2-hour drive to get together, and Ben's mother is the primary caretaker for Ben. The parents have been making an effort to see each other and Ben every weekend. Ben has been attending school, and the majority of his classmates are either White Americans or Black Americans. Since Ben can see his father only on weekends, and was instructed by his father to take care of his mother when his father is not around, Ben has developed a very authoritarian attitude toward his mother. When Ben was 8 his mother gave birth to a sister, and Ben's behavior became more overbearing toward his mother and sister.

Recently, the school informed Ben's mother that Ben has been "acting-up" in school, and he has been frequently disciplined by his teachers. Ben's parents are extremely concerned about Ben's growth and development, especially his mental health and his biopsychosocial development, which can contribute to Ben's growth and development as a dynamic, interactional, and dualistic individual.

Reflection and Discussion Points

a. Can you identify any unique pressures or forces coming from Ben's micro-, meso-, or exosystems?

b. What do you predict will be the impact on Ben's identity?

c. What are your feelings about Ben and his parents' relationship moving forward?

d. How might a counselor intervene?

Cultural Diversity and Human Development

From the cultural diversity perspective, the contributions of Bronfenbrenner and Vygotsky are significant to the study of human development because their theories focus on its socioecological and sociocultural contexts. Bronfenbrenner's theory focuses on the mutual accommodation and interaction between the developing individual and the physical environment; this ecological approach defines the development of the individual who interacts with the environment in a process of mutual accommodation. Vygotsky, in a similar theoretical approach, developed the theory of cognitive development to emphasize that human development is inseparable from social and cultural activities. His theory complements Bronfenbrenner's ecology of human development. According to Vygotsky, by interacting with the environment, society, and people with higher skill levels, children develop higher mental processes and learn to use the tools of culture such as language, mathematics, interpersonal skills, and so on. This interaction process is important because it allows children to become acculturated in the use of their intellectual tools. Most importantly, by interacting with a variety of cultural, ecological, and social contexts, children can understand and learn self-regulation. Guided Practice Exercise 2.2 will further demonstrate Vygotsky's concept of various interactions and their impacts on the child.

Guided Practice Exercise 2.2

Instructions: As you read about "Kate," process the information through your understanding of Vygotsky's and Bronfenbrenner's theories. Your task is to identify the unique contributions and influences, both positive and negative, on Kate's development as she grows up in a culturally diverse family. Discuss your observations with a colleague or instructor.

Kate's Case

Kate grew up in a culturally diverse family on the East Coast. Her father, Paul, comes from a traditional Greek family and migrated to the United States after high school. Kate's father married Linda, Kate's mother, who is of Hispanic descent. Kate's family resided in a middle-upper-class neighborhood since Kate's birth. When Kate started her senior year in high school, she developed an isolative behavior toward her family and her peers in school. Kate also exhibited resentment and anger about her racial identity. Kate has expressed her frustration in reference to comments from her friends and classmates about her multicultural background, the imperfection of her father's English language, her multiracial appearance, and her family's celebration of her parents' special occasions that differ significantly from those of her neighbors. In coping with her unhappiness and frustration, the skill that Kate has developed is to pretend to be tough, not just toward her friends and classmates but also toward her family members. These behaviors have contributed negatively to her school performance and social relationships. She is in transition from high school to college, and without appropriate therapeutic intervention, Kate's behavior can be detrimental to her growth and development, especially her educational attainment and career objectives.

Seeking the Truth: Research Methodologies

According to Miller (2011), a **developmental theory** is a systematic statement of general principles that provides a coherent framework for understanding how and why people change over time with respect to their behaviors, attitudes, thoughts, philosophies, physical, and psychological capabilities. Theories in development are scientific theories and, as such, represent the *systematic* statement and integrated assumptions and hypotheses drawn from the observations and research conducted by developmental theorists. As a scientific theory, theories of development propose explanations of phenomena that can be tested for confirmation or falsification using scientific methodology. Through research, theories are modified to reflect and explain new data. But when the subject is human development, the application of the scientific method is not always easy, and as such, multiple methods of research are employed. The difficulty answering valuable questions regarding the impact and influence of various factors on normative development can be seen in Guided Practice Exercise 2.3. It is suggested that you return to this scenario after reading about the various methods of research employed in studying human development. Consider which of the various methods would be most useful and applicable to studying this situation.

Guided Practice Exercise 2.3

Instructions: Developmental theories have alerted us to the significant influence social and environmental forces have on development. Read the following case of "Monique" and consider the various, multidimensional elements impacting not only Monique's development but also that of her brother. Also, as you read through the various methodologies used to research development, consider which method(s) may reveal the most accurate understanding of this situation.

(Continued)

(Continued)

The Case of Monique

Monique grew up with her brother, who has severe mental retardation. Research studies have indicated that siblings are an integral part of most children's social world during their growing up years. Furthermore, the emotional ties between siblings are next only to those between parents and children.

Reflect on the following questions:

1. How might having a brother with severe mental retardation affect Monique's human growth and development?

2. Would her sense of identity be negatively influenced by the presence of a disabled brother?

3. Would her self-esteem be affected by having a disabled brother?

4. Would she be well-adjusted in her sibling role and accept her brother with a disability as an inseparable part of their lives?

5. Would her peer relationships be altered by the presence of her brother, such as signs of latent shame associated with having a sibling with a disability?

6. What kind of data do we need to collect in order to find out the impact of having a brother with severe mental retardation during developmental years?

7. Further, what other factors may have contributed to Monique's coping mechanisms when she was growing up?

8. How important is the extended family support system, parents as the primary caregivers, independent mobility of the brother, and Monique's awareness regarding the limitations of her brother?

Research Observation

The scientific observation approach in human development research requires the researcher to record human behavior objectively, methodically, and systematically. In employing scientific observations, researchers need to know what they are looking for, what they are observing, when and where they will be observing it, and how the observation will be made. This research approach can be applied to both **qualitative and quantitative research methods**. When a researcher wants to make an observation and attempt to get a comprehensive picture of a specific situation by gathering notes and verbatim or narrative data, this research is considered qualitative. When the researcher uses independent measures such as scales and objective observational recording instruments, the data collected are quantitative (Berger, 2011).

There are two possible settings for making scientific observations: (a) a laboratory, which is a controlled setting in which the researcher can manipulate the environment (removing the real-world experience) to optimize the research result and (b) a real-world setting.

Although conducting behavioral observations in a laboratory setting will provide researchers the ability to control certain factors that may influence behaviors not related to the study, this approach has drawbacks. First, being an artificial setting to that of typical human engagement, the participants in the laboratory research study may perform differently (most work harder and perform better) since they are aware that they are being observed. This phenomenon is called the **Hawthorne Effect**. Second, volunteers who are willing to come to the laboratory to participate may not represent the population the researchers intend to study. Last, due to its complex nature and the amount of variables involved, the study of human development is difficult, if not impossible, to examine in the laboratory.

Human development and lifespan studies often lend themselves to investigation within real-world settings. These naturalistic observations can be conducted in child care centers, classrooms, work settings, shopping malls, sporting arenas, and so on. In conducting observations in natural settings, the researchers can observe people's real behaviors and interactions with one another. As with any other type of research methods and data collection, the major concern of direct scientific observation is its validity and reliability. A well-defined behavior to be measured and a well-trained observer to make the observations will enhance the validity of the data to be collected. A well-trained observer must be aware of his or her own bias, world view, beliefs, and perceptions, which may influence the way he or she observes and interprets the situation. The observer effect, in which people being observed behave differently because they are being observed, may also compromise the research.

Survey Interviews

Often the research question being investigated is best understood by way of direct response from those within the study. For example, in wishing to learn more about peoples' attitudes or beliefs about a particular issue, asking them directly may be the most effective strategy for gaining understanding.

The use of direct interview or the application of a survey or questionnaire can be very effective in gathering this type of self-reported information, especially when seeking it from large groups of people. In a good survey, the questions are clear and unbiased, allowing respondents to answer unambiguously. As is true for all research methodology, survey research has both strengths and weaknesses as a vehicle for gathering insight and understanding (see Strengths and Weaknesses of Survey Research in Table 2.5).

Process of Case Study

In contrast to the large number of people typically included in survey research, a case study is an in-depth look at a single individual. The focus of the case study is to collect complete, detailed information about the individual in a situation or when exhibiting a set of behaviors. A case study is heavy in qualitative data, with extensive detailing of conditions and events and reliance on anecdotal accounts of those involved (Parsons & Brown, 2002).

Typically, the process of a case study starts with a wide view of data collection. Researchers gather as much data as possible that describe the case, while at the same time formulating questions and refining data collection techniques. As the study progresses, attention may shift to gathering information that explains the present situation and the factors contributing to what is observed. Data are collected using a wide variety of methods—observation, questionnaire, interviews, and so on. While the strength of a case study is that it can provide a rich, in-depth look at a single individual, a limitation is that the data collected are not easily generalizable to other individuals.

Research Design: The Experiment

According to Campbell and Stanley (1963), "By experiment, we refer to that portion of research in which variables are manipulated and their effects upon other variables observed" (p. 1.). Thus, the experiment would be one in

Table 2.5   Strengths and Weaknesses of Survey Research

Strengths	Weaknesses
1. Surveys are relatively inexpensive.	1. A methodology relying on standardization forces the researcher to develop questions general enough to be minimally appropriate for all respondents, possibly compromising what is most appropriate to many respondents.
2. Surveys are useful in describing the characteristics of a large population.	
3. Surveys can be administered from remote locations using a website, mail, e-mail, or telephone.	2. The initial study design, including the method and the tool, has to remain unchanged throughout the data collection, and this makes the design inflexible.
4. Collecting large samples is feasible in a survey, making the results statistically significant even when analyzing multiple variables.	3. In order to get a good-sized sample, the researcher must ensure that a large number of the selected samples will respond to the survey.
5. Multiple questions can be asked about a specific topic, giving considerable flexibility to the analysis.	4. In the conclusion of the survey, it may be hard for participants to recall information or to tell the truth about a controversial question.
6. There is flexibility at the creation phase in deciding how the questions will be administered: as face-to-face interviews, by telephone, as a group-administered written or oral survey, or by electronic means.	5. The survey is a widely used research method for gathering data from samples ranging from health concerns and political viewpoints to attitudes and opinions. Surveys tend to be weak on validity (except face validity) and strong on reliability. In addition, survey answers are influenced by the wording and sequence of the questions. The selective memory of the respondents may also contribute to how they answer the questions.
7. Standardized questions make measurement more precise by enforcing uniform definitions upon the participants.	
8. Between-group study can be standardized to ensure that similar data can be collected from groups then interpreted comparatively.	6. The artificiality of the survey format has compromised its validity, and participants are more inclined to respond to questions they perceive to be relevant and meaningful rather than those questions they cannot comprehend. Survey data must have reliability if they are to be useful since survey research presents all subjects with a standardized stimulus and potentially eliminates the unreliability issue in the process of data collection.
9. High reliability is not difficult to obtain by presenting all subjects with a standardized stimulus.	
10. Observer subjectivity is greatly eliminated by this medium of research.	

which the researcher manipulates one or more independent variables, controls any other relevant extraneous variables, and observes the effect of the manipulations on the dependent variable(s).

The independent variable is the variable being manipulated by the researcher, and the dependent variable is the change in behavior measured by the researcher. The independent variable, the variable predicted from, is the presumed cause. The dependent variable, the variable predicted to, is the presumed effect. All other variables that might affect the results, and therefore produce a false set of results, are called confounding variables (also called random variables), and these must in some way be eliminated from influencing the outcome.

Since an experiment is a study of cause and effect, it differs from nonexperimental methods in that it involves the deliberate manipulation of one variable while trying to keep all other variables constant. It is clear that when applied to the study of human development, pure experimentation is difficult at best and impossible when applied to certain research questions. Humans simply don't lend themselves to isolation, laboratory conditions, and manipulation of factors. But it is not impossible, just difficult. For example, if a researcher is interested in understanding how best to affect children's reading abilities, he or she may gather two groups of children matched on variables that could affect reading abilities but that are not the variables under study (for example, intelligence, current reading level, visual acuity, motivation, etc.). Once these variables have been accounted for (i.e., controlled), the method of teaching, which is the focus of the study (i.e., independent variable), will be introduced to one of the groups. The dependent measure might be a reading score or measure of grade-level performance. The hypothesis under investigation would be that the group receiving the test variable (the reading program) would do significantly better than those who did not.

In the above example, we noted a number of other—not tested—factors that could account for differences in the two groups. But this list is not exhaustive. You probably could identify other factors that could influence performance on the group reading test. This is an overly simplified view of an experimental approach to studying a developmental issue but hopefully serves to demonstrate the difficulty one has researching developmental factors. Table 2.6 highlights the strengths and weaknesses of laboratory experimentation when applied to the study of human development.

Table 2.6   Strengths and Weaknesses of Laboratory Research

Strengths	Weaknesses
1. Experiments are the only means by which cause and effect can be established, and a true experimental design is able to deliberately and systematically introduce changes and then observe their consequences.	1. The experiment is not typical of real-life situations, and the unnatural environment may generate the distortion of behaviors because the experimental setting is not ecologically valid (not a real-life setting). The range of behavior to be observed in the laboratory is relatively narrow. By controlling the situation so precisely, the observation and measurement of the behavior may be very limited.
2. Experiments allow the researcher to control the variables; the purpose of control is to enable the researcher to isolate the one key independent variable in order to observe its effect on the dependent variable. To control the variables allows the researcher to conclude that it is the independent variable, and nothing else, that is influencing the dependent variable.	2. A psychological experiment is a social situation in which neither the subjects nor the experimenters are passive; they are active, thinking human beings. The Hawthorne Effect has demonstrated that regardless of the experimental manipulation employed, the workers' production seems to be improved, and the logical conclusion is that the workers are pleased to receive attention from the researchers who expressed an interest in them. Thus, the results do not necessarily reflect how the workers would behave in the same situation if experimenters were not present.

(Continued)

Table 2.6 (Continued)

Strengths	Weaknesses
3. Experiments can be replicated. The experimental method consists of standardized procedures and measures, which allow it to be easily repeated.	3. Often, the experimental method, as it operates in psychology, has a history of using biased or unrepresentative sampling. For instance, the participants in this type of research are often psychology students who are required to partake in research as a course requirement.
4. The data generated by experimental research are normally quantitative data and can be analyzed using inferential statistical tests. The results of the tested data permit statements to be made about how likely the results are to have occurred through chance.	4. The strength of the experimental method is the amount of control that the researcher has over variables. However, it is not possible to completely control all variables. There may be other variables at work of which the experimenter is unaware, and it is extremely difficult to control the mental world of the research participants.
	5. The ethical practice in experimental research is a major concern since experiments nearly always involve deceiving participants to some extent. In fact, the very term *subject* implies that the participant is being treated as something less than a person. It is important for researchers to understand that many areas of human life cannot be studied using the experimental method because it would be too unethical to conduct this type of research in those areas.
	6. Some behavioral researchers consider normative data to have very limited usage because such data tend to describe, rather than explain, phenomena. In addition, grouping people together, many argue, limits researchers' ability to look at individuals' specificities.

The Field Experiment

Sometimes an experiment can be conducted in a more natural setting, that is, in the field. As an example, the television series entitled "Primetime: What Would You Do?" has been a part of the Primetime series, an American news magazine broadcast on ABC (2013) since 2008. The show stages events that people do not experience or expect in everyday life, and these events, as staged, are usually injustices or illegal activity. The producers set up hidden cameras to view the reactions of ordinary people when they encounter these staged injustices or illegal acts as performed by actors. They want to see whether the individuals are compelled to act or mind their own business. In these field experiments, the series looks at how ordinary people react to everyday dilemmas that test their character and values. One of the scenarios involves three teenagers (actors) who beat and taunt a homeless man in front of a passerby on the sidewalk. As with the laboratory experiment, the independent variable of this type of field experiment is still deliberately manipulated by the researcher. Regardless, it still has the advantage of being less artificial than the laboratory experiment.

Natural Experiments

In a natural experiment, behavioral scientists and psychologists can use a natural situation to conduct a research study that they cannot themselves manipulate. For example, a psychologist may use a one-way mirror or a hidden camera or observe from a distance to study aggressive behavior among children. In conducting this type of experiment, the researcher must not allow the children to notice him or her. This is not a true experiment because the psychologist is unable to manipulate or control variables. For this reason, it is sometimes referred to as a quasi-experiment (Kazdin, 1980).

Lifespan Study

Researchers in life-span development often have a special concern with studies that focus on the relation of age to some other variable. Methods that are sometimes employed to study the effect of age involve identifying groups of varying ages and comparing them on some dimension (i.e., cross-sectional research) or at other times following the same individuals across their life span noting changes in the dimensions under investigation (i.e., longitudinal study).

Cross-Sectional Research

A cross-sectional study is a descriptive study in which characteristics under investigation are measured simultane-ously in different age populations. Cross-sectional studies can be thought of as providing a snapshot of contrasting populations at a particular point in time. While the data collected may reveal differences, the actual cause for those differences cannot be isolated nor validly attributed to age alone.

Longitudinal Research

A longitudinal study, like a cross-sectional one, is observational. So, once again, researchers do not interfere with their subjects. However, in a longitudinal study, researchers conduct several observations of the same subjects over a period of time, sometimes lasting many years. The benefit of a longitudinal study is that researchers are able to detect developments or changes in the characteristics of the target population at both the group and individual levels. The key here is that longitudinal studies extend beyond a single moment in time. As a result, they can establish sequences of events.

Rules Governing Human Subject Research

World Opinion

Rules governing research on human subjects has been embedded not just in the parameters of our professional ethic but also within the rules and regulations established by ours and other governments. For example, as a result of the atrocities revealed during the Neuremberg trial following World War II, the Nuremberg Code (1948) was established. This code articulated the basic requirements for conducting research in a way that respects the fun-damental rights of research subjects. The World Medical Association met in Helsinki, Finland, in 1964 to draft the Declaration of Helsinki, a document that would build on the Nuremberg Code of 1948 to outline the standards of ethical research involving human subjects. This declaration was revised in 2000.

Additional rules of study followed upon the experience with Thalidomide (1962). Prior to this time, informed consent prior to taking medication was not required. After significant numbers of pregnant women gave birth to infants with deformities, public outrage over this practice led to an amendment to the Food, Drug, and Cosmetic Act that basically required investigators and researchers to obtain informed consent from potential subjects before giving them investigational medications.

Other events also have had a significant effect on how we regulate research conduct nowadays. These include the Wichita Jury Study (1955), the NIH Ethics Committee (1964), the Ethic of Clinical Research and the New England Journal of Medicine, the Congressional Hearings on the Quality of Health Care and Human Experimentation (1973), the Milgram Studies of Obedience to Authority (1960s), the San Antonio Contraception Study (1970s), the Tearoom Trade Study (1970s), and the Tuskegee Syphilis Study (1932–1972).

Additionally, the National Research Act of 1974 established the National Commission for Protection of Human Subjects of Biomedical and Behavioral Research. The goal of this commission was to clarify the ethical guidelines to apply to research involving human subjects in all research disciplines. The commission conducted a series of meetings at the Belmont Conference Center near Baltimore, Maryland, and generated the report in 1978 to address and explain the fundamental ethical principles that should guide research conduct involving human subjects. This became known as the Belmont Report.

The Three Major Ethical Principles of the Belmont Report are

Principle 1: Respect for persons—Treat individuals as autonomous agents and protect persons with diminished autonomy.

Principle 2: Beneficence—Do unto others as you would have them do unto you.

Principle 3: Justice—Distribute the risks and potential benefits of research equally among those who may benefit from the research.

ACA Guidelines for Ethical Research

According to the American Counseling Association (ACA, 2005): "Counselors who conduct research are encouraged to contribute to the knowledge base of the profession and promote a clearer understanding of the conditions that lead to a healthy and more just society. Counselors support efforts of researchers by participating fully and willingly whenever possible. Counselors minimize bias and respect diversity in designing and implementing research programs" (p. 16).

The Code of Ethics of ACA addresses many areas related to conducting counseling research and provides guidelines:

1. Researchers have responsibilities when using human research participants. They should seek consultation if the research suggests a deviation from standard practices, consult the Institutional Review Board (IRB) procedures, and use precaution to avoid injury to participants. Also, the principal researcher should be mindful of ethical obligations and responsibilities and have minimal interference in the lives of research participants. Finally, the research should consider multicultural and diversity issues.

2. Rights of research participants include informed consent—counselors may not conduct research that involves deception. There are policies on student/supervisee participation, client participation, confidentiality of information, persons not capable of giving informed consent, commitments to participants, explanations after data collection, informing sponsors, and disposal of research documents and records.

3. Nonprofessional relationships with research participants should be avoided. Researchers do not condone or subject research participants to sexual harassment or potentially beneficial interactions.

4. Researchers must report accurate results and are obligated to report unfavorable results and errors while protecting the identity of participants and allowing replications of the study.

5. Publication includes recognizing the contributions of others. Counselors may not plagiarize; they must review republished data or ideas, acknowledge contributors appropriately, and establish agreements in advance of the publication. Students are listed as principal authors if they are the primary contributors and submissions should not be duplicated.

Research Contributing to a Counselor's Identity

Research is not only a data source for ethical and effective practice but is a process in which all professional counselors should seek to contribute. Engaging with the research either as a knowledgeable consumer or contributor is essential not only to effective practice but to the development of one's professional identity.

The field of counseling has been constantly evolving and progressing due to the increasing demands of competent, well-trained professional counselors to work with many emerging modern society issues (substance abuse, family in crisis, posttraumatic stress disorder, etc.) and individuals from diverse cultural and ethnic backgrounds. This also applies to the importance of studying human development through the lifespan because one cannot deny the contribution of life experience to the well-being and quality of life of each individual in society. It is important for counselors to keep up with current research that is being conducted. The more research studies that counselors read, understand, and are able to apply at work, the more they can optimize their abilities to improve counseling services for their clients. New studies can help counselors understand what is important for them to focus on in their work. It can also teach them what is expected of a professional counselor at work. However, over the last two decades, the enthusiasm for research has declined.

According to Reisetter, Korcuska, Yexley, Bonds, Nikels, and McHenry (2004) there is a need to inspire interest in research among counselor education students in training and in practice. Although there has been a lot of research on the development of humans, there is much more to learn. Students in the counseling fields, along with practicing counselors, need to read, understand, and participate in more counseling research activities.

According to Nelson and Southern (2008), there are four areas counselors should consider when determining how scholarly they are on the job and how they can apply this knowledge to optimize their job performance. They believe that the most important area is discovery, where a counselor researches and investigates. The second important area is integration, which occurs when a scholar takes isolated concepts and places them in a larger context that gives new meaning to an emerging perspective. The third area is application, which involves service-related activities geared toward applying knowledge/scholarship to solving individual and community problems. The last, and perhaps least valued, area is teaching with educators in the academic profession. Nelson and Southern (2008) believe that counselors need to acquire a passion for advancing knowledge in ways that satisfy needs for personal growth and innovation in society. We support that notion of counselor as research-practitioner.

SUMMARY

- ➤ Many theories have explained that human development consists of physical, cognitive, and social perspectives and how these are present throughout prenatal, childhood, and adult development
- ➤ Human development is multidimensional, multidirectional, plastic, multidisciplinary, and contextual, and the domains that characterize human development are physical, cognitive, and social.
- ➤ There are 10 major theoretical perspectives on human development: Maturationist Theory, Psychoanalytic Theory, Erikson's Theory, Behaviorism Theory, Social Learning Theory, Evolution Theory, Cultural Theory, Biopsychosocial Theory, Cognitive Development Theory, and Ecological System Theory.
- ➤ Studying the implications of cultural factors is indispensable to the study of human development.
- ➤ The process of scientific inquiry is a very rigorous and systematic journey for the purpose of developing new theories and re-affirming existing ones.
- ➤ Research design requires the in-depth understanding of various methods of collecting data, including different approaches in reference to experimental and nonexperimental designs, cross-sectional research, and longitudinal research.
- ➤ The ACA Code of Ethics contains clear guidelines that provide members with the knowledge of how to conduct ethical research.

ADDITIONAL RESOURCES

SAGE Research Methods (www.srmo.sagepub.com/)

This website was created to help researchers, faculty, and students with their research projects. The platform links over 175,000 pages of SAGE's renowned books and journal and reference content with truly advanced search-and-discovery tools. Researchers can explore method concepts to help them design research projects, understand a particular method or identify a new method, and write up their research. Since this platform focuses on methodology, rather than on disciplines, researchers from the social sciences, health sciences, and more, can use it. SAGE Research Methods contains content from over 640 books, dictionaries, encyclopedias, and handbooks, and the entire *Little Green Book* and *Little Blue Book* series—two major works collating a selection of journal articles and newly commissioned videos.

Examples of Some of the Videos

- Stephen Gorard. (2011). "How do I choose between different research methods?"
- Naomi Jones. (2011). "How do I design policy-focused research?"
- Rachel Thomson & Julie McLeod. (2011). "How do I research social change?"
- Martyn Hammersley. (2011). "Methodology: Who needs it?"
- Bren Neale. (2011). "What is longitudinal research?"

RECOMMENDED SUPPLEMENTAL READINGS

American Psychological Association. (2005). *Policy statement on evidence-based practice in psychology*. Retrieved from http://www.apa.org/practice/ebpreport.pdf.

American Psychological Association. (2009). *Publication manual of the American Psychological Association* (6th ed.). Washington, DC: Author.

Buchwald, D., Delmar, C., & Schantz-Laursen, B. (2011). Ethical dilemmas in conducting research with children. *International Journal for Human Caring, 15*(2), 28–34.

Creswell, J. (2002). *Research design: Qualitative, quantitative and mixed method approaches* (2nd ed.). Thousand Oaks, CA: Sage.

Johnson, B. (2004). *Educational research: Quantitative, qualitative and mixed approaches, research edition* (2nd ed.). Chicago, IL: Allyn & Bacon.

Smith, D. (2003). 10 ways practitioners can avoid frequent ethical pitfalls. *APA Monitor on Psychology, 34*(1), 50. Retrieved from http:// www.ic.ucsc.edu/ ~ vktonay/psyc165/apaethics.html.

REFERENCES

ABC (2013). *What would you do?* Retrieved from http:// www.ABC.org.

American Counseling Associations (ACA) Code of Ethics. (2005). *Section G, research and publication*. Retrieved from: counseling.org.

Atherton, J. S. (2011). Learning and teaching: Piaget's developmental theory. Retrieved from http://www.learningandteaching.info/learning/piaget.htm.

Bandura, A. (1997). *Self-efficacy: The exercise control*. New York, NY: W.H. Freeman.

Bandura, A. (2008). Environment harm. *Psychology Review, 14*(2), 1–5.

Bandura, A., Barbarnelli, C., Caprara, G. V., & Pastorelli, C. (2001). Self-efficacy beliefs as shapers of children's aspirations and career trajectories. *Child Development, 72,* 187–206.

Berger, K. S. (2011). *The developing person through the lifespan* (4th ed.). New York, NY: Worth.

Berk, L. E. (2007). *Development though the life span* (4th ed.). Boston, MA: Pearson.

Burns, S., Bodrova, E., & Leong, D. (2012). *Developmental theory—Vygotskian theory*. Retrieved from http://education.state university.com/pages/1912/Developmental-Theory—VYGOTSKIAN-THEORY.html.

Campbell, D. T., & Stanley, J. C. (1963). *Experimental and quasi-experimental design for research*. Chicago, IL: Rand McNally & Co.

Cohen, D. (1987). Behaviorism. In Richard L. Gregory (Ed.), *The Oxford companion to the mind* (p. 71). New York, NY: Oxford University Press

Dacey, J., Travers, J., & Fiore, L. (2009). *Human development: Across the lifespan*. New York, NY: McGraw-Hill.

Erikson, E. (1982). *The life cycle completed*. New York, NY: Norton.

Freud, S. (1962). *The ego and the id*. New York, NY: W.W. Norton.

Inhelder, B., & Piaget, J. (1958). *The growth of logical thinking from children to adolescence: An essay on the construction of formal operational structures*. New York, NY: Basic Books.

Kazdin, A. (1980). *Research design in clinical psychology*. New York, NY: Harper & Row.

Miller, P. H. (2011). *Theories of developmental psychology* (5th ed.). New York, NY: Worth.

Nelson, K. W., & Southern, S. (2008). Expanding the view of scholarship. *The Family Journal, 16*(3), 197–198.

Oswalt, A. (2008). *Urie Bronfenbrenner and child development*. Retrieved from http://www.mentalhelp.net/poc/view_doc .php?type = doc&id = 7930.

Parry, M. (2006). G. Stanley Hall: Psychologist and early gerontologist. *American Journal of Public Health, 96*(7), 1161.

Parsons, R. D., & Brown, K. S. (2002). *Teacher as reflective practitioner and action researcher*. Belmont, CA: Wadsworth.

Reisetter, M., Korcuska, J. S., Yexley, M., Bonds, D., Nikels, H., & McHenry, W. (2004). Counselor educators and qualitative research: Affirming a research identity. *Counselor Education and Supervision, 44*(1), 2–16.

Rogoff, B., & Chavajay, P. (1995). What's become of the research on the cultural basis of cognitive development? *American Psychologist, 50*, 859–877.

Ross, D. G. (1972). *G. Stanley Hall: The psychologist as prophet*. Chicago, IL: University of Chicago Press.

Skinner, B. F. (1974]. About behaviorism. New York, NY: Vintage Books.

Stevens, R. (1983). *Erik Erikson: An introduction*. New York, NY: St. Martin's.

Watson, J. B. (1998). *Behaviorism*. New Brunswick, NJ: Transaction.

PART II

Conception and Prenatal Development

Giving birth and being born brings us into the essence of creation, where the human spirit
is courageous and bold and the body, a miracle of wisdom.

Harriette Hartigan

The quote by Harriette Hartigan draws our attention to the undeniable wonderment of birth. However, the wonder of human development begins well before that magical moment.

While we celebrate the appearance of the baby bump and the ever increasing maternal girth that signals progression toward the blessed event, those with knowledge of prenatal development will be moved to look deeper behind the bump to find that which is truly unbelievable and deserving of both our celebration and awe. Consider what is taking place. From conception and the joining of cells in fertilization and the resultant creation of a one-celled organism known as a zygote, the wisdom and wonderment of human development unfolds into the creation of a fetus, who while still in utero, can hiccup, react to loud noises, dream, demonstrate primitive learning (habituation), and even exhibit a rudimentary personality (temperament). It is a process that truly deserves our awe, but more so, invites our understanding. It is a process that not only reveals the courage, strength, determination, and resiliency of the human condition but also its vulnerabilities.

This chapter reviews the processes involved in this prenatal stage of human development, as well as those factors that can threaten it. In addition to presenting information about prenatal development, the chapter will review counseling issues that may arise for both the mother and father during pregnancy. After reading the chapter you will be able to

1. describe typical physical, cognitive, and social/emotional development during prenatal development;

2. identify common risks to healthy prenatal development;

3. explain the ways counselors can provide both prevention and intervention services in support of parents experiencing pregnancy and prenatal development; and

4. identify areas of consultation that can be provided with other health care providers.

Healthy Prenatal Development

In discussing **prenatal development**, it is common practice to break this period of development into three phases or trimesters. The **first trimester** includes the first 13 weeks of prenatal development, the **second trimester** includes weeks 14 to 27, and the **third trimester** includes weeks 28 and beyond. Within each of these trimesters, critical developments occur across physical, cognitive, and social-emotional domains

Physical Development

As can be seen in Figure 3.1, the developing **fetus** undergoes dramatic physical changes while in utero. From the union of a microscopic sperm and egg, a fully developed baby forms after only 9 months in the womb. Physically, a fetus undergoes the most dramatic changes in the first 8 weeks of life, but critical growth and development occurs throughout the full 9 months of pregnancy.

First trimester. During the first trimester (weeks 1 to 12), the fetus develops in a cephalocaudal (head to toe) direction, meaning that the structures near the head develop faster than structures near the feet. The embryonic period (weeks 2–8), in particular, is a critical time period in our development. During this time, all the major organs and structures begin to form, such as bones, skin, and internal organs. In fact, all of the major organs are formed by the end of the eighth week. The heart begins to beat, and blood begins to circulate. By the end of the first trimester, the head, face, eyes, ears, arms, fingers, legs, and toes have formed. The lungs have begun to develop, hair has started to grow, and buds for 20 temporary teeth have developed.

Second trimester. During the second trimester (weeks 13–27), the organs continue to develop further and actually begin to function within the body. The fetus can swallow, hear, pass urine, and suck its thumb. Genitals, eyebrows, eyelashes, and fingernails form. The skin is very wrinkled and is covered with **vernix** (a waxy coating) and **lanugo** (fine hair). The fetus moves, kicks, sleeps, and wakes.

Third trimester. During the third trimester (weeks 28 and beyond), the fetus still kicks and stretches; however, this activity may slow down a bit as the fetus grows and space in the uterus declines. The fetus actually gains most of its weight during this period, about one half pound per week until the 37th week. During this time, the lanugo disappears, and the bones harden, but the skull remains soft for delivery.

Guided Practice Exercise 3.1

Review the facts depicted in Figure 3.1. As you do, identify those facts that you find surprising or inspiring.

These are the facts—but we cannot allow the facts to interfere with the wonderment and awe. Guided Practice Exercise 3.1 is provided to help you keep that perspective of wonderment and awe.

Cognitive Development

The brain is the first organ to begin developing (at 18 days of fertilization) in a fetus. Initially, the brain begins as a layer of cells on the neural plate, which folds to form the neural tube. This tube then closes, beginning in its middle and progressing outward. Failure of the plate to properly fold and create a tube by the end of the fourth

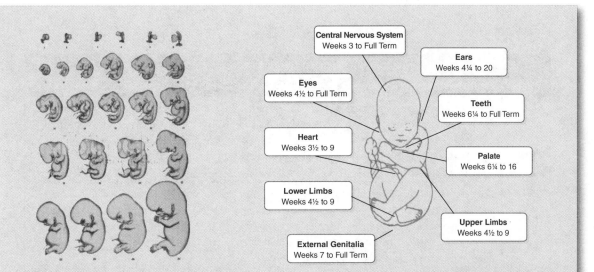

Prenatal Development		
Weeks	Fetal Development & Growth	Size
4	The baby implants into the uterus. The amniotic and yolk sac have started to form. The embryo has three distinct layers of cells. The inner layer (endoderm) that will form the digestive system; the middle layer (mesoderm) that will form heart, sex organs, muscles, bones, and kidneys; and the outer layer (ectoderm) that will form organs, tissues, hair, skin, and nervous system.	Poppy Seed/ one millimeter
8	Small sprouts for arms, legs, and back have appeared. The embryo's upper lip, tip of the nose, and eyelids are forming, creating a more human appearance. The hands and toes are starting to form and appear less webbed. The heart is now beating around 150 beats per a minute.	Blueberry/ ½ inch
12	Hair follicles, toenails, and fingernails have started to form. Bone and cartilage are creating ankles and elbows. Testes or ovaries are developing, and soon the sex of the baby is clear. Many organs are now working, which is why the baby has doubled in size the last few weeks. Hormones are being produced, while bone marrow is helping to form white blood cells to fight infections.	Large Plum/ ½ ounce
16	The baby's head is half the size of the body. The baby is moving and flipping inside the womb. The fetus has a more erect posture, and the baby's neck is becoming much longer. The baby is practicing breathing, sucking, and swallowing. Tiny bones in the ear are forming and enabling the baby to hear voices and sounds.	Palm of Hand/ 3 ½ ounces
20	The baby can now yawn, kick, and punch. Nerves are connecting and forming the complex connections needed for touch, hearing, smell, sight, and taste. The baby can hiccup, and vernix covers the baby to protect his or her sensitive skin. The gender is now easy to see with the ultrasound.	Large Mango/ 6 ounces

(Continued)

Figure 3.1   Prenatal Development

Figure 3.1 (Continued)

Prenatal Development		
Weeks	**Fetal Development & Growth**	**Size**
24	The baby swallows amniotic fluid for nutrition and hydration. Amniotic fluid can taste different on a daily basis due to the mother's diet. Little taste buds are developing so a colorful pallet could encourage future food likes and dislikes. Sense of touch is in high development, while the baby holds the umbilical cord. The baby can also perceive light and dark.	Banana/ 1½ pounds
28	The baby's skin is turning from translucent to pink. Small blood vessels are forming and filling with blood. Lungs are starting to form but will not be fully functioning until birth when oxygen enters the body. The baby can now open and close his or her eyes, and the irises of the eyes are now filled with pigment. Coughing, blinking, and more intense sucking are all developing.	Cucumber/ 2½ pounds
32	Fat is depositing under the baby's skin surface. Buds for future permanent teeth are forming in the gums. Downy hair covers the baby's body, and bone marrow has taken over the production of red blood cells. Information from all five senses is being perceived.	Pineapple/ 3½ pounds
36	Amniotic fluid in the uterus has reached its maximum amount. The baby will start to double his or her weight over the next few weeks to prepare for delivery. The baby opens and closes his or her eyes during sleep and wake cycles. The baby's immune system has developed, which provides critical antibodies to ward off infection.	Coconut/ 4½–5 pounds
40	The baby is inhaling and exhaling, preparing for his or her first breath. Amniotic fluid, bile, and cells move into the intestines, which will turn into the baby's first bowel movement. The lungs are still developing, and surfactant continues to be secreted so that the lungs do not stick together when breathing initiates. Hormones will soon trigger contractions to begin childbirth.	Watermelon/ 6–7½ pounds

Figure 3.1   Prenatal Development

Source: "Periods of Fetal Development. Prenatal Development, Pathogen Profile Dictionary, hosted by the *Journal of Undergraduate Biological Studies*. @2010. http://www.learn.ppdictionary.com/prenatal%20development.htm

week results in neural tube defects, which lead to disorders such as spina bifida or anencephaly. The wall of the tube then thickens and forms the brain and spinal cord. During the fourth week, the neural tube begins to form the hindbrain, the midbrain, and the forebrain.

The **hindbrain** divides into the myelencephalon and metencephalon. The myelencephalon then forms the medulla oblongata, which regulates respiration and heartbeat, while the metencephalon forms the pons and cerebellum. The pons connects the cerebral cortex with the medulla oblongata and serves as a communications center between the two hemispheres of the brain. The cerebellum controls motor movement coordination, balance, equilibrium, and muscle tone.

The **midbrain** forms the inferior and superior colliculi, which control auditory and visual responses; the tegmentum, which controls motor functions, regulates awareness and attention and regulates some autonomic functions; and, finally, the substantia nigra, which controls voluntary movement, produces dopamine, and regulates mood.

The **forebrain** further divides into the diencephalon and telencephalon. The diencephalon forms the thalamus and the hypothalamus, which control and regulate many areas, including body temperature, sleep, emotions, hunger, and thirst, and the pineal body that produces melatonin. The telencephalon develops into the rhinencephalon (the olfactory center) and the neocortex. The neocortex forms most of the mass of the brain. As the bilateral telencephalic vesicles grow, the cerebral hemispheres begin to develop. Initially, these expand outward, but as growth continues, the vesicles develop to the midline of the brain and cover the diencephalon and mesencephalon. The hemispheres initially appear smooth, but as growth continues, the surface folds begin to form sulci (grooves) and gyri (convolutions), which increase the surface area of the brain without increasing the size of the brain cavity. Growth in the brain is particularly noticeable during weeks 28 and 30 of development. Figure 3.2 will help you visualize the anatomy of the brain.

Social and Emotional Development

Prenatal researchers believe that there is a connection between a mother's emotions and how her baby feels in the womb. In fact, emotional involvement and expression can be seen as early as 10 weeks in utero. Around six months, the unborn baby can share the mother's emotions. This is important to note because if mothers experience a significant amount of emotional distress, the child's emotional development can be affected. Mothers who are anxious during pregnancy tend to produce babies who are also anxious (Huizink, de Medina, Mulder, Visser, & Buitelaar, 2002). Additionally, mothers who resented being pregnant and felt no attachment to their unborn children had children who later suffered from emotional problems. On the contrary, mothers who were less anxious and wanted their children generally tended to have emotionally healthy children. Therefore, it is critical that mothers receive counseling services as needed to manage significant emotional distress.

Risks to Healthy Prenatal Development

Throughout the pregnancy, the fetus is vulnerable to many factors. However, during the first trimester, the fetus is especially at risk. Some factors that may impede healthy prenatal development include maternal nutrition, maternal stress, teratogens, and domestic violence.

Maternal Nutrition

A well-balanced diet is critical to the development of a healthy baby. Two conditions that may lead to problems with maternal nutrition are undernutrition and malnutrition. **Undernutrition** occurs when all of the nutrients are available in the mother's diet, but the mother does not ingest a sufficient amount. In addition to eating a healthy diet, expectant mothers must also add certain vitamins, minerals, and other nutrients to their diets for optimal fetal development. Doctors often prescribe specific prenatal vitamins to address the needs of both the mother and unborn child. **Malnutrition** occurs when one or more of the essential nutrients is missing or when nutrients that are needed for healthy development are present but in the wrong proportions. Malnutrition is a worldwide problem that affects millions of unborn babies and can lead to behavioral abnormalities, altered cognitive functioning, and disturbances in learning and memory. Ensuring that pregnant women understand various resources that may be available to them is critical in helping both the mother and the child get the nutrition that is needed in order for them to be healthy.

Maternal Stress

Maternal stress is another factor that directly impacts fetal development. When a mother is emotionally aroused, her body produces hormones that can cross the placental barrier and enter the fetus's bloodstream. If these

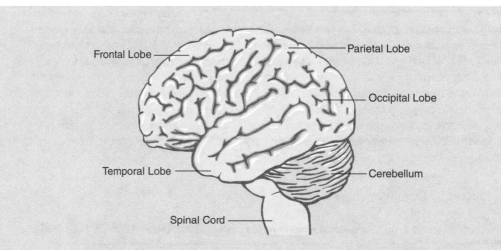

Prenatal Cognitive Development		
Brain Anatomy	Function	Fetal Development
Occipital Lobe	Controls vision and visual recognition	Structural development forms throughout pregnancy, however these pathways develop more with age and exposure to objects.
Parietal Lobe	Controls taste, touch, recognition of objects, and hand-eye coordination	This lobe develops as the baby is exposed to new textures and objects during play
Frontal Lobe	Controls thought, voluntary behavior (walking, speech, problem solving), and some aspects of emotions	Babbling and listening to music directly stimulates the frontal lobe, this lobe matures in spurts as new functions develop.
Temporal Lobe	Controls hearing, some language, smell, portions of memory, emotions, and fear	Hearing is the first sense developed, shortly followed by smell.
Pons	Controls relay signals for sleep, respiration, swallowing, bladder control, hearing, taste, eye movement, and posture	The Pons develops throughout pregnancy and is in high gear after delivery regulating involuntary movements; these will later be refined with environmental exposure and growth.
Medulla	Controls autonomic nervous system functioning and connects the brain and spinal cord; contains reflexes, respiration, and cardiac functions	The medulla forms from a neural tube during pregnancy; this regulates the baby's first nervous system responses and connects senses to brain.
Spinal Cord	Controls nerve tissue and supports cells while connecting the central nervous system; conducts motor information, sensory information, and coordination reflexes	The spinal cord is one of the first visible structures in the developing fetus. At birth it is controlling, stimulating, and developing the neural paths.

Figure 3.2   Anatomy of the Brain and Prenatal Cognitive Development

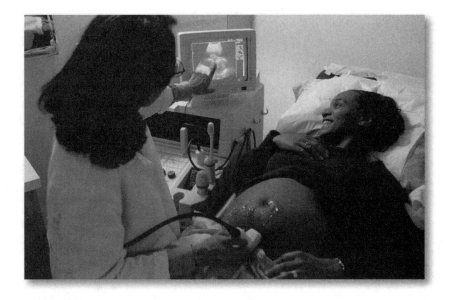

Photo 3.1   Feeling, hearing, and seeing the developmental formation of the fetus contributes to the future mother-baby bonding.

Source: Keith Brofsky/Photodisc/Thinkstock.

hormones cross the placenta often enough, then the fetus gets used to feeling chronically stressed, which prepares its system to overreact to stimuli. Thus, the baby may exhibit more emotional disturbances and gastrointestinal upsets, which may lead the baby to being colicky. While studies indicate that short-term emotional upsets that occur in all pregnancies do not harm the baby, major emotional disturbances and unresolved stresses may lead to emotionally troubled children and can result in spontaneous abortion, preeclampsia, preterm labor, reduced birth weight, and reduced head circumference (Mulder et al., 2002). Therefore, it is important for mothers to seek out support and reduce their stress levels as much as possible during pregnancy. Counselors can work with pregnant mothers to reduce their stress and anxiety and to focus more on positive thinking and solutions. Counselors can also help reduce stress by focusing on topics included in Figure 3.3, which can assist mothers with understanding each step of the pregnancy.

Teratogens

Teratogens include any disease, drug, or other environmental agent that can harm a developing fetus. These include certain medications, chemicals, and infections. The effects of teratogens often depend on when the exposure occurred, how long the exposure lasted, and how much of the teratogen was present in the body. The effects of a teratogen are worst on the fetal development if introduced when the fetal structure is forming and growing most rapidly, which is during the first trimester. Unfortunately, this is also the time when many women do not realize they are pregnant. Counselors, working in consultation with the mother's doctor, can play a critical role in helping pregnant mothers to reduce or eliminate their exposure to teratogens.

Smoking while pregnant is especially dangerous to the developing fetus, as harmful chemicals, such as tar, nicotine, and carbon monoxide, are introduced into the placenta. These chemicals lower the amount of oxygen and nutrition that the fetus receives. Smoking during pregnancy can also lead to an improperly attached placenta, ectopic pregnancy, vaginal bleeding, stillbirth, and low birth weight.

Understand the story of pregnancy	Planed vs. unplanned
	Feelings about pregnancy
	Involved parties
	Complications to date
	Other siblings
Help mother seek out prenatal care	Type of insurance coverage
	Type of care the mother desires
	Type of specialist required, if any
	Fears and concerns around prenatal care
	Financial planning and concerns
	Birthing classes
Provide education regarding bodily changes	Physical changes to body
	Trimester changes for mother and baby
	Emotional changes
	Mental changes
	Breast-feeding
Assist with development of birth plan	Medication vs. natural birth
	Induced labor vs. waiting for water to break
	C-section vs. vaginal birth
	Cutting of umbilical cord
	Viewing arrangements of mother during delivery
	Persons allowed in delivery room

Figure 3.3 Counseling Women During Pregnancy

Alcohol can also be detrimental to the health of a developing fetus. In fact, drinking at any time during the pregnancy can have harmful effects. The same amount of alcohol that the mother consumes transfers to the fetus. While the adult body's liver can break down the alcohol, the fetus's liver is not yet developed enough to do this; therefore, alcohol is much more damaging to the fetus. Alcohol increases the chance of having a miscarriage or preterm baby and is the leading cause of mental retardation.

Using drugs during pregnancy can also cause long-term problems for the developing fetus. There is no safe time during pregnancy to use drugs. During the first trimester, maternal drug use can significantly impact the development of the baby's organs, while during the second and third trimesters, drug use affects fetal brain growth. At the end of the third trimester, maternal drug use can stunt fetal growth and lead to preterm labor.

Prescribed and over-the-counter medications can also negatively impact the developing fetus. Certain medications have been found to cross the placenta and enter the baby's bloodstream. However, some medications are safe. With ongoing research on the risks of medications on developing babies, an expectant mother needs to discuss any and all potential risks with a doctor and pharmacist before taking any prescribed or over-the-counter medication.

It is clear that counselors can contribute to the health of mothers and fetuses by offering proactive preventive education programs as well as offering empirically supported intervention for those struggling with drug and alcohol addictions.

Domestic Violence

According to Ramsay, Richardson, & Carter (2005), **domestic abuse** is one of America's worst health problems. Approximately 42 million women in the United Sates will experience domestic violence during their lifetime (Black et al., 2011). While both men and women experience domestic abuse, the most severe violence is committed by male partners against their female partners. Approximately 1 in 4 women, compared with 1 in 7 men, have been victims of severe physical violence by an intimate partner (Black et al., 2011; Catalano, Smith, Snyder, & Rand, 2009). According to the U.S. Federal Bureau of Investigation, in 2010, 1,095 women were killed by their male partners, as compared with 241 men who were killed by their female partners.

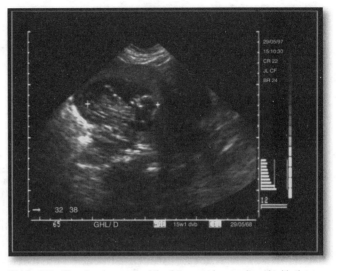

Photo 3.2 The development of the fetus can be monitored with the use of ultrasound images to ensure healthy development and prevent prenatal challenges.

Source: Stockbyte/Stockbyte/Thinkstock.

Domestic abuse is also of concern worldwide. Studies in Australia (Australian Bureau of Statistics 2005–06) and Canada (Ahmad, Hogg-Johnson, Stewart, & Levinson, 2007) both stated that 15% of women reported domestic abuse, while 35% of women in studies conducted in Rwanda (Ntaganira et al., 2008) and India (Silverman, Decker, Saggert, Balaiah, & Raj, 2008) reported domestic abuse. O'Leary, Tintle, Bromet, and Gluzman (2008) found that 20% of women in the Ukraine reported abuse, compared to 32% of women in Spain (Ruiz-Perez, Plazaola-Castano, & Del Rio-Lozano, 2007). Finally, studies in Peru concluded that 45% of women experienced domestic abuse (Perales, Cripe, Lam, Sanchez, & Williams, 2009), while studies in Nicaragua reported 40% to 52% of women reporting abuse (Ellsberg, Peña, Herrera, Liljestrand, & Winkvist, 2009). As you can see, domestic abuse and violence is clearly a worldwide concern.

Researchers disagree about whether the prevalence of domestic abuse and violence decreases, increases, or remains the same during pregnancy. According to the Johnson, Haider, Ellis, & Hay (2003), nearly 1 in 6 pregnant women is abused by her partner, which is almost 20%. Slightly higher rates have been reported in Nicaragua (Salazar, Valladares, Ohman, & Hogberg, 2009), Pakistan (Fikree, Jafarey, Korejo, Afshan, & Durocher, 2006), and Turkey (Deveci, Acik, Gulbayrak, Tokdemir, & Ayar, 2007); while India (Varma, Chandra, Thomas, & Carey, 2007) and Belguim (Roelens, Verstraelen, VanEgmond, & Temmerman, 2008) have reported lower rates of domestic violence experienced by pregnant women. As high as these prevalence rates may be, it is important to note that the actual prevalence of domestic violence experience by pregnant women may be much higher. Many women are reluctant to report abuse, especially during pregnancy.

Many times women believe that becoming pregnant will end domestic violence; however, abuse often begins or worsens during pregnancy, and both the baby and mother are at risk. Dangers include risk of miscarriage, vaginal bleeding, low birth weight, and fetal injury. Working with pregnant mothers to leave an abusive situation can be critical to the health of the mother and infant; however, leaving the relationship may be especially hard since many mothers are worried about financially supporting their children. Counselors can work with pregnant mothers to develop a plan for leaving that includes identifying a safe place to go, making a list of items to take, obtaining a prepaid cellular phone, getting a court order of protection, creating a code word for friends and family when in danger, obtaining an extra set of car keys, keeping evidence of abuse, and identifying financial supports. Of course, mental and emotional needs will also need to be addressed in counseling regardless of whether or not the mother leaves the abusive environment.

Counseling Issues

Now that you have read about healthy prenatal development and risks to healthy development, we turn our attention to other concerns that you may see as a counselor. While this discussion is not all-inclusive, it is our hope that this section will help you to understand the numerous concerns that soon-to-be parents may have.

Having a child can be one of the most joyous events in a person's life, but it can also be one of the most stressful events. Having a child can sometimes strain relationships and trigger confusing emotions. If complications occur, then health issues and financial difficulties may arise. Unplanned pregnancies can create significant strain and unrealistic parenting expectations can lead to struggles. Prior relationship struggles are likely to get worse. However, when both parents desire a child and have a basic agreement concerning parenting and behavior expectations, then a baby can bring a renewed sense of connection between intimate partners. Case Illustration 3.1 further demonstrates the importance of carefully deciding the timing of a pregnancy.

CASE ILLUSTRATION 3.1 DOMESTIC ABUSE

Ayesha has been seeing a counselor at her university for several months. As a newly immigrated student from the Middle East, she has had some difficulties adjusting to the new dominant culture at her school. As sessions progress, Ayesha begins to disclose that her husband is very controlling in their relationship and has been unhappy with her for some time. During this session, she talks about how perhaps having a child would satisfy him and make him happier with her.

There are several issues or concerns that the counselor will need to address with Ayesha. First, it will be important for the counselor to be careful not to impose his or her values on this client. Behavioral expectations for spouses vary across cultures, so it will be important that the counselor respects the client's viewpoint. However, it is also critical that the counselor ensure that abuse is not occurring, and if it is, to provide resources for Ayesha. Through careful questioning, the counselor needs to determine exactly what controlling behavior the husband is exhibiting and how it is affecting Ayesha. The client's thoughts and feelings of the appropriateness of this behavior will need to be clarified. Additionally, what is Ayesha doing that she believes is making her husband unhappy? Or is this simply her perception that he is unhappy with her?

The counselor will also need to address the fact that Ayesha believes that having a child will make her husband happier with her. Because research consistently demonstrates that having a child actually places more strain on a relationship, the counselor needs to make sure that Ayesha is making this decision wisely. The counselor can encourage Ayesha to explore the pros and cons of having a child at this time in her life. Perhaps, the husband would also like to discuss this in counseling to further explore the timing of a pregnancy. Having a child is a life-changing event, and it is important to help Ayesha with this major decision.

Photo 3.3 Maintaining a healthy lifestyle during pregnancy is important for the mother and the baby's development.

Source: Stockbyte/Stockbyte/Thinkstock.

Although all pregnancies have specific similarities, each pregnancy is also very different. Changes in body image, hormones, and attitude toward cultural pressures and expectations all contribute to how a woman feels about her pregnancy. Similar to fetal development, a woman's psychological concerns and issues change throughout each trimester of the pregnancy. For example, during the first trimester, a woman may feel heightened emotionality. While the woman may not physically look any different for several more weeks, her emotions are rapidly changing. Typical emotional highs and lows are magnified, which may lead to confusion and frustration. Additionally if a woman has an increased risk of miscarriage, then this may be a time of heightened anxiety and stress, since the risk of miscarriage approaches 20% in the first trimester. Thankfully, a general sense of well-being typically develops during the second trimester; however, a woman may begin to feel increased dependence on her partner and increased anxiety over her body image. The third trimester is typically filled with anticipation. First-time mothers are usually concerned with labor and delivery; however, this is also quite common with other mothers. Body image concerns may also arise again during this time, especially if her sex drive has diminished.

Fathers also experience psychological changes throughout pregnancy, which also tends to follow the trimester schedule. For many men, the first trimester is filled with a sense of disbelief that the pregnancy is real. Because physical differences in the mother are not typically seen during this time, the father may wonder if the pregnancy is real and may have similar fears to the mother of whether or not the pregnancy will be successful. A man may find it difficult to express his feelings about his partner's pregnancy, and most men experience fear, concern, or even ambivalence toward the pregnancy. Participating in prenatal visits can be helpful to the father, making him feel more involved and connected to the pregnancy. During the second trimester, pregnancy becomes more apparent as physical changes begin to occur in the mother. During this time, if not before, the father may begin reflecting on his own childhood and the way he was fathered. This can bring up many emotions depending on his experiences. During the final trimester, men may get to actually feel the growing child as he or she moves within the womb. This may be the first time that the father really envisions a growing child inside the mother. Additionally, pregnancy can produce profound changes within a relationship. Feelings about the mother's changing body, emotional instability, and shifting sexuality can cause strain on the relationship. Therefore, it is important for both partners to openly communicate during this time. Guided Practice Exercise 3.2 provides an opportunity for you to further explore the various emotions and concerns that both women and men experience during pregnancy.

Guided Practice Exercise 3.2

Interview a new mother and father (with a child 2 years old or younger) or an expecting couple. Considering the general psychological concerns that both women and men experience during each trimester of a pregnancy (discussed earlier in the chapter), interview the couple about their emotions, thoughts, worries, and so on during each trimester. How did each person address these concerns during the pregnancy? Were the concerns similar or were they different from the text?

Family Support

Counselors are in a great position to offer support to families when they are experiencing pregnancy and the birth of a baby. Often times, new parents feel anxious about various concerns, such as the birthing process, caring for an infant, or the upcoming change in lifestyle. Using literature, DVDs, and other materials is a great way to help educate parents about healthy child development and healthy parental development. Counselors may offer workshops designed to address anxieties of parents and include information related to the importance of prenatal care, the prevention of the mother's exposure to teratogens, and strategies for reducing the chance of premature and low birth weight babies. Workshops can also highlight the importance of breast feeding, father involvement, available community resources, and cultural variations in parenting styles. Many of these activities may be held in conjunction with hospital sponsored workshops. Case Illustration 3.2 can help you see how to assist a mother who may be anxious about the upcoming birth of her child.

CASE ILLUSTRATION 3.2 MATERNAL ANXIETY AND SUPPORT

Becky is a 28-year-old, single, expectant mother and has come to counseling once. During the initial session, Becky discloses that she is worried about all of the changes that result in having a child. Becky currently works as a store manager at a grocery store in town. She has limited contact with her baby's father. She lives with her mother, who has attended all prenatal visits with her. This is Becky's first child, and she has become extremely anxious about delivering in 4 months. She does not believe she is ready to balance motherhood and continue her job as a manager, which requires her to be at work at least 60 hours per week. She has not had time to look at day cares and is worried that she may not be able to afford one. Though her mother has been helpful, Becky tells the counselor that her mother has scared her with birthing stories. Becky has not had time to go to birthing classes, and she is worried about the pain during labor. She has chosen to do natural childbirth. Her mother also has told Becky how stressful being a mother can be and has told her that she had postpartum depression after having both Becky and her brother. All of this anxiety is making Becky also worry that she is hurting her baby.

The primary issue that Becky is dealing with is anxiety related to the upcoming birth of her child. The counselor needs to process these feelings with Becky. What, specifically, is making her feel anxious? Is she feeling overwhelmed with everything, or are there one or two specific items that are causing her the most anxiety? She might indicate that she is mostly worried about her job and does not know how to balance her time, or she might say everything. The goal of the counselor is to help her focus on one issue at a time to help minimize the level of anxiety that she is experiencing.

The counselor, in addition to providing emotional support for Becky, may also want to provide some educational materials. High levels of stress do have an impact on the developing fetus, so it is important for the counselor and Becky to find strategies for reducing her stress levels. Working as a team, the counselor may ask Becky to consider times in the past when she felt overwhelmed and anxious. What strategies did she use then to manage her stress and anxiety? Additionally, the counselor can provide literature related to some of the items that Becky is worried about, as well as assign her homework, such as researching local day cares or discussing pain management strategies during birth with her doctor.

Because Becky has indicated that her mother experienced postpartum depression with both of her children, the counselor needs to monitor Becky closely. The counselor may also want to include Becky's mother in a psycho-educational session, during which warning signs of postpartum depression are discussed. Seeing Becky on a continuous basis after the birth of the child is critical to observing her behaviors and ensuring that anxiety levels are kept to a minimum.

Another important area for counselor assistance is in helping parents consider the support that older siblings may need with the arrival of the new baby. Many parents assume that children will not struggle with the addition of a new family member. However, it is critical to help them realize that children may be excited or worried about the upcoming birth. Families undergo tremendous changes during this time, and children can be very susceptible to the stress associated with the changes. Letting a child know that he or she will not be replaced by the new sibling helps establish his or her security within the family. Reading books about siblings, as well as discussing the importance of a being a big brother or sister, can foster a closer relationship to the sibling once born. It is also important for the child to receive special attention once the new baby is born. For example, Dad may want to take the child out for a special day, or Mom may spend an afternoon with the child. With all of the busyness that comes with a new baby, it is important to emphasize that the older child is still an important part of the family.

Grief

Pregnancies do not always go as planned. Many soon-to-be parents are devastated when they experience a miscarriage, stillbirth, or termination of the pregnancy. After any of these losses, many women and their partners experience grief. Unfortunately, this grief is often exacerbated by the lack of recognition of the loss by others, hormonal changes that occur during the postpartum recovery period, and any previous pregnancy-related losses that they may have experienced. It is important for parents, as well as other family members, to work through their grief.

Elisabeth Kübler-Ross (1969) proposed five stages of normal grief that people tend to experience. Typically the first reaction is denial. This stage helps us through the initial shock of the loss. Once this stage wears off, the next stage is typically anger. The anger may be directed toward others, even complete strangers. Families seek out someone to blame—the doctor, God, or so on. Bargaining is another stage that a family may go through. If we had only . . . ; if the doctor had only. . . . Parents may even try to bargain with God (or their higher power). Feelings of depression may begin to emerge. During this time, thoughts are dominated by sadness and regret. Acceptance is the final stage of normal grief; however, not everyone may experience this stage. It is important to note that not everyone experiences each of these stages, and the stages do not flow in a particular order (see more information about Kübler-Ross's five stages of grief in Chapter 13). Coping with loss is a very personal experience and will look differently for each and every family member.

As counselors, we can help our clients to work through the grief process in a healthy manner. Children, in particular, often have a hard time grieving and need special attention through counseling services. Many well-meaning family members try to shield children from grief by distracting them, telling them partial truths, or even lying to them about the death of a loved one. Additionally, the parents may also be so deep in their own grief about the loss of their child that they have a hard time focusing on a living child's needs.

Often times, adults simply do not understand when a child can understand death. During the preschool years (about 2–4 years old), children may not comprehend death, but they do experience a sense of sadness and loss. They often do not have the vocabulary to express their grief, so they act it out. During this age, parents may see a heightened sense of insecurity and clingy behavior, which is normal. It is also important to note that children this age are very literal in their understanding, so adults must be careful about how they explain death. For example, if an adult were to say that the deceased sibling went to sleep for a very long time, then the child may fear going to sleep. During the elementary school years, most children begin to experience the full range of emotions similar to an adult. However, they may not fully understand what it going on simply due to their lack of experience. Children often assume that they are to blame or may worry about who will care for them, particularly if their parents are strongly grieving.

It is important that the child's grief can be expressed to and supported by an attentive adult. It is also important for adults to recognize that grief experienced by a child may look very different than that experienced by adults. For example, children may appear disinterested. This does not mean that they are not grieving; it simply means that they have taken in what they can at the moment. When they are ready, children will reach out for more information. Children need creative outlets, such as art, music, puppets, and so on to help work through their grief. Figure 3.4 further explains typical behavior that may be seen in a grieving child.

Impatience	Child may become easily frustrated or angered during normal daily activities
Inattentive	Child may have trouble focusing on specific tasks (e.g., schoolwork)
Protectiveness	Child may act overly protective of other family members, friends, toys, or pets
Regression	Child may revert to earlier behaviors (e.g., sucking thumb, bedwetting)
Separation Anxiety	Child may begin to have difficulty separating; may become clingy; may fear leaving parents even for a short time
Withdrawal	Child may become unemotional; may separate from family or friends

Figure 3.4   Children's Grief—Common Reactions

In addition to providing counseling services focused on the whole family, counselors can also educate others about the importance of recognizing grief and that each person experiences and demonstrates grief differently. Guided Practice Exercise 3.3 can help you further explore how you can assist parents when a loss of pregnancy occurs.

Guided Practice Exercise 3.3

Unfortunately pregnancies do not always go as planned, and many soon-to-be mothers and fathers are left without a child due to miscarriages, stillbirths, or terminations. Visit or call one of your local OB/GYN clinics and inquire as to their process for helping grieving patients. Do they refer them to counseling? Do they provide educational materials?

Once you understand your local clinic's process, how can you, as a future counselor, develop relationships with medical doctors to provide support services to patients as needed? Write a brief synopsis of your findings and thoughts.

Mental Health Disorders During Pregnancy

While depression and anxiety are the most common mental health issues during pregnancy, with approximately 10% to 15% of pregnant women being diagnosed, some mothers may also experience other mental health issues. Mental health during pregnancy depends on several factors, including past history of mental illness, current treatment of mental illness, recent stressful events, and how the mother feels about the pregnancy. Symptoms of mental illness during pregnancy are similar to those experienced by those not pregnant, although the focus of concerns may be on the pregnancy. For example, anxiety may be specifically related to the health of the unborn child, becoming a mother, or so on. Additionally, if a mother previously suffered from a mental illness, such as an eating disorder, then concerns related to body image may begin to arise again. It is important for the counselor to note that sometimes pregnancy-related issues can be confused with symptoms of a mental health illness. For example, lack of sleep or increased sleep is common in both pregnancy and depression. Anxiety is also normal during pregnancy—most women worry about becoming a mother, being a good parent, difficulties with the pregnancy, and childbirth. However, it is when these fears become overwhelming and interfere with the mother's life that anxiety becomes a diagnosable concern.

Women who previously suffered from a mental illness are at an increased risk of relapsing during pregnancy or after giving birth. Of particular concern are those women who stop using psychotropic medications during pregnancy. According to American College of Obstetricians and Gynecologists and the American Psychiatric Association (2009), approximately 14% to 23% of pregnant women suffer depressive symptoms. Flynn, Blow, and Marcus (2006) followed a group of women with histories of major depression through pregnancy. They found that 26% of the women who maintained antidepressant treatment relapsed compared with 68% who discontinued medication during pregnancy. The authors concluded that women who discontinued medication were 5 times more likely to relapse when compared with women who maintained treatment. High rates of relapse have also been associated with bipolar disorder, with approximately 85.5% of women relapsing who did not comply with their medication treatment during pregnancy, compared with 37% who continued medication treatment. Because many psychotropic medications have either not been determined to be safe during pregnancy or have been determined as unsafe, pregnant women who suffer from mental illness are left in a quandary. Should they take medication to help themselves but possibly cause harm to the fetus? This decision must reflect an understanding of the risks associated with untreated psychiatric illness and the risks associated with fetal exposure. Because mental illness may cause significant struggles for the both the mother and the child, discontinuing or withholding medication during pregnancy may not always be the safest option. It is important for the counselor to work closely with the medical doctor in treating mental illness among pregnant clients.

Depression can affect both mothers and fathers both during pregnancy and after the birth of a child. Numerous studies have indicated high levels of depressive symptoms during pregnancy in the mother (Bunevicius, Kusminskas, Pop, Pedersen, & Bunevicius, 2009; Heron, Haque, Oyebode, Craddock, & Jones, 2009; Lau & Chan,

2009; Skouteris, Wertheim, Rallis, Milgrom, & Paxton, 2009). However, studies have also indicated high levels of depressive symptoms for their partners as well (Condon, Boyce, & Corkindale, 2004; Perren, vonWyl, Burgin, Simoni, & von Klitzing, 2005). Parents may be particularly at risk of depression during the first trimester of pregnancy, as reported symptoms of depression tend to be higher during this time but then decline as the pregnancy progresses (Bunevicius et al., 2009; Teixeira, Figueiredo, Conde, Pacheco, & Costa, 2009). As a counselor, it may be important to work with parents during the first trimester, discussing such topics as what the pregnancy means to them, what changes may need to be made, and how the upcoming birth could impact their current relationships. Helping soon-to-be parents work through these issues at the beginning of pregnancy can help set the stage for a healthier prenatal development of the unborn child and can increase positive parenting after the birth of the child. Additionally, if clients have demonstrated symptoms of depression prior to pregnancy, then there is a greater risk of having a depressive episode during pregnancy and postpartum (Banti et al., 2011; Milgrom et al., 2008). Studies have indicated that individuals who have an anxiety disorder, low socioeconomic status (SES), and multiple children have an increased chance of developing postpartum depression (Banti et al., 2011; Segre, O'Hara, Arndt, & Stuart, 2007). Counselors may want to work with clients to examine their fears about being able to financially take care of their child as well as how to parent multiple children.

Not only have these symptoms been identified during pregnancy but studies have also shown that both mothers and fathers experience these symptoms after the birth of their child (Dorheim, Bondevik, Eberhard-Gran, & Bjorvatn, 2009; Xie, He, Koszycki, Walker, & Wen, 2009). However, the decreasing trend of depressive symptoms tends to persist through the birth of the child with reduced rates of depressive symptoms after the birth (Banti et al., 2011; Heron et al., 2009, Kinsella & Monk, 2009; Lau & Chan, 2009; Skouteris et al., 2009) in both women and men (Figueiredo & Conde, 2011; Perren et al., 2005). However, some studies still indicate a higher rate of postpartum depressive symptoms when compared with symptoms during pregnancy for both women and men (Dietz et al., 2007; Paulson & Bazemore, 2010).

Postpartum depression (PPD) is defined as moderate to severe depression after the birth of a child. Approximately 10% to 15% of women and 10% of men experience PPD (Paulson & Bazemore, 2010). Most parents experience PPD within the first 3 months after birth, but it can take up to 1 year before symptoms arise. Additionally, the risk for PPD peaks in the winter months (Sit, Seltman, & Wisner, 2011). Unfortunately, after the first 42 postnatal days, suicide is the leading maternal cause of death during the first year after birth (Oates, 2003).

Studies indicate that the prevalence of PPD among women in rural settings may be higher than women in urban settings (Villegas, McKay, Dennis, & Ross, 2011). Furthermore, PPD may be even more prevalent among rural women in developing countries as compared to rural women from developed countries. Prevalence rates of PPD among women in rural settings from developing countries is estimated at 31%, compared to rural women in developed countries, which is estimated at 21.5% (Villegas et al., 2011). A review of the literature indicates that rates of PPD among women in rural settings ranges from 23% to 57.8% compared with 10% to 15% in the general population (Villegas et al., 2011). Some common risk factors that have been identified for women in rural settings in general include low socioeconomic status (SEC), being single, history of abuse, low social support, past psychiatric history, depression during pregnancy, and recent stressful events. Women in rural settings in developing countries have additional risk factors that have been identified. These include lack of knowledge of infant care, struggles with in-laws, having an unemployed or uneducated husband, psychopathology of husband, years of marriage, gender of infant, having more than five children, and having two or more children under the age of seven (Ege, Timur, Zincir, Geckil, & Sunar-Reeder, 2008; Gausia, Fisher, Ali, & Oosthuizen, 2009; Kheirabadi et al., 2009; Rahman & Creed, 2007; Savarimuthu et al., 2010).

Living in a rural area may decrease access to mental health services, resulting in fewer diagnoses of depression and lack of appropriate treatment opportunities (Hillemeier, Weisman, Chase, Dyer, & Shaffer, 2008). Women in these settings may also not seek out counseling services (McGarry, Kim, Sheng, Egger, & Baksh, 2009). Jesse, Dolbier, and Blanchard (2008) identify four barriers to seeking assistance, including dissatisfaction with the health care system, lack of trust, fear of stigma, and simply not desiring help. Lack of knowledge about symptoms of PPD may also be a factor (Simmons, Huddleston-Casas, & Berry, 2007). Guided Practice Exercise 3.4 will help you explore how you can help to educate the public about the occurrence of this mental illness.

Guided Practice Exercise 3.4

Unfortunately mental illness still carries a stigma in today's society. Many mothers experience depression during pregnancy and after giving birth, yet are afraid to mention these feelings to their doctors. As a mental health practitioner and advocate, how can you further remove the stigma that depression carries?

Write a few paragraphs about strategies that you could employ within your community to reduce the stigma of depression. Also, include one sample to demonstrate one of the strategies that you identify.

Screening for depression also occurs infrequently in rural communities (Alexander & Fraser, 2008). Counselors may want to develop improved screening tools and referral systems to assist primary health care providers in rural areas with identifying risk factors and detecting PPD earlier. Additionally, group therapy has been found to be an effective intervention for women in rural settings who suffer from PPD (Craig, Judd, & Hodgins, 2005). Case Illustration 3.3 further demonstrates the collaborative role between the client, counselor, and OB/GYN to best help clients suffering from depressive symptoms.

CASE ILLUSTRATION 3.3 DEPRESSION DURING PREGNANCY

Carolyn, a 28-year-old pregnant mother, was referred for counseling by her OB/GYN after disclosing during a prenatal visit that she was beginning to feel depressed. Carolyn was diagnosed with depression during her teenage years but has not been on medication or attended therapy since she was 22. She reports feeling fine and has been doing well since the age of 22 but is now experiencing extreme tiredness, a lack of desire to participate in her hobbies, and negative feelings toward her pregnancy. Her doctor is concerned that she may be relapsing into depression during pregnancy.

Women who have suffered a mental illness prior to getting pregnant are more likely to experience mental illness during pregnancy or after giving birth. While Carolyn may or may not exhibit clinical signs of depression for diagnosis, it is important for both the counselor and the OB/GYN to keep a close eye on her both during her pregnancy and in the months after giving birth. The first step that the counselor will want to begin with is to assess the extent of these emotions that Carolyn is experiencing. Are the symptoms strong enough for a clinical diagnosis, or are the symptoms somewhat typical for a new mother-to-be? Tiredness and moodiness are quite common in pregnancies, but negative feelings toward the pregnancy may be of concern. The counselor will want to explore these negative thoughts. Was the pregnancy planned? What emotional and financial support does Carolyn have? The client may simply need to work through some of these concerns, or the problem may be more severe. If the concerns are of clinical significance and diagnosis is given, treatment options will need to be explored with Carolyn, in consultation with her OB/GYN. Counseling can of course be continued throughout pregnancy and after the birth of the baby, but medication use will need to be carefully considered. What are the side effects of the various medications? What impact does the medication have on the developing fetus? Will the mother breast-feed, and if so, what impact will taking medications have on that process? Ultimately, the counselor, client, and OB/GYN will need to determine what is in the best interest of *both* the mother and the child.

While depression, especially postpartum depression, receives primary attention in the literature, it is important for counselors to understand that women may also experience other emotional issues. Sometimes anxiety and stress during delivery can trigger past traumas (such as abuse) or be traumatic in itself. Symptoms of posttraumatic stress disorder (PTSD) and obsessive-compulsive disorder (OCD) may be seen in some mothers. Again, concerns become diagnosable when they are severe. It is important for health care providers to recognize the warning signs of emotional distress and make appropriate referrals. Our job, as counselors, is to facilitate that understanding and provide resources and treatment when needed. Healthy parents lead to healthy children.

SUMMARY

- Understanding prenatal development is critical to understanding human development.
- Pregnancy is broken down into trimesters, typically lasting for a total of 40 weeks.
- A fetus undergoes the most dramatic changes in the first 8 weeks of gestation, but critical growth and development occur throughout the full 9 months of pregnancy.
- During the first trimester, all the major organs and structures begin to form.
- The brain is the first organ that begins to develop in a fetus.
- The organs begin to function in the body during the second trimester.
- The fetus gains most of its weight during the third trimester.
- Prenatal researchers believe that there is a connection between a mother's emotions and how her baby feels.
- Risks to healthy prenatal development include poor maternal nutrition, maternal stress, presence of teratogens in the mother, and maternal exposure to domestic violence.
- Counselors are in a great position to offer support to families when they are experiencing problems during pregnancy, including specific mental health disorders such as depression, PTSD, and OCD, as well as other general concerns.

ADDITIONAL RESOURCES

Websites

http://www.acog.org/
http://www.marchofdimes.com/pregnancy/prenatal-care.aspx
http://www.mayoclinic.com/health/pregnancy-week-by-week/MY00331
http://www.nlm.nih.gov/medlineplus/prenatalcare.html
http://www.womenshealth.gov/publications/our-publications/fact-sheet/prenatal-care.html
http://www.womenshealth.gov/publications/our-publications/pregnancy-dos-donts.pdf

Videos

Alexander Tsiarias. (2010). "Conception to birth." Retrieved from http://www.ted.com/talks/alexander_tsiaras_conception_to_birth_visualized.html.
BabyCenter. (2012). Pregnancy videos. Retrieved from http://www.babycentre.co.uk/search?q = pregnancy + videos.
National Geographic. (n.d.). "In the womb." Retrieved from http://channel.nationalgeographic.com/channel/in-the-womb/videos/in-the-womb/.
National Geographic. (n.d.). "In vitro fertilization." Retrieved from http://video.nationalgeographic.com/video/science/health-human-body-sci/human-body/ivf-sci/

RECOMMENDED SUPPLEMENTAL READINGS

Books

Bennett, S., & Indman, P. (2011). *Beyond the blues, understanding and treating prenatal and postpartum depression & anxiety*. San Jose, CA: Moodswings Press.

Harms, R. W. (Ed.). (2011). *Mayo Clinic guide to a healthy pregnancy*. Intercourse, PA: Good Books.

International Childbirth Education Association (ICEA). (2007). *The ICEA guide to pregnancy & birth*. Hopkins, MN: Meadowbrook Press.

Sears, W., & Sears, M. (2003). *The baby book*. New York, NY: Little, Brown.

REFERENCES

Ahmad, F., Hogg-Johnson, S., Stewart, D. E., Levinson, W. (2007). Violence involving intimate partners: Prevalence in Canadian family practice. *Canadian Family Physician, 53*(3), 461–468.

Alexander, C., & Fraser, J. (2008). General practitioners' management of patients with mental health conditions: The views of general practitioners working in rural north-western New South Wales. *Australian Journal of Rural Health, 16*(6), 363–369.

American College of Obstetricians and Gynecologists, & American Psychiatric Association. (2009). *Depression during pregnancy: Treatment recommendations*. Retrieved from http://www.acog.org/About_ACOG/News_Room/News_Releases/2009/Depression_During_Pregnancy

Australian Bureau of Statistics. (2005–06). *Personal safety*. Canberra, Australia: Author.

Banti, S., Mauri, M., Oppo, A., Borri, C., Rambelli, C., Ramacciotti, D., & Cassano, G. B. (2011). From the third month of pregnancy to 1 year postpartum: Prevalence, incidence, recurrence, and new onset of depression. Results from the Perinatal Depression Research & Screening Unit study. *Comprehensive Psychiatry, 52*(4), 343–351.

Black, M., Basile, K., Breiding, M., Smith, S., Walters, M., Merrick, M. . . . Stevens, M. (2011). *National intimate partner and sexual violence survey (NISVS): 2010 summary report*. Atlanta, GA: National Center for Injury Prevention and Control, Centers for Disease Control and Prevention. Retrieved from http://www.cdc.gov/ViolencePrevention/pdf/NISVS_Report2010-a.pdf.

Bunevicius, A., Kusminskas, L., Pop, V. J., Pedersen, C. A., & Bunevicius, R. (2009). Screening for antenatal depression with the Edinburgh Depression Scale. *Journal of Psychosomatic Obstetrics & Gynecology, 30*(4), 238–243.

Catalano, S., Smith, E., Snyder, H., & Rand, M. (2009). *Female victims of violence* (NCJ 228356). Washington, DC: U.S. Department of Justice, Bureau of Justice Statistics.

Condon, J. T., Boyce, P., & Corkindale, C. J. (2004). The first-time fathers' study: A prospective study of the mental health and wellbeing of men during the transition to parenthood. *Australian and New Zealand Journal of Psychiatry, 38*, 56–64.

Craig, E., Judd, F., & Hodgins, G. (2005). Therapeutic group programmed for women with postnatal depression in rural Victoria: A pilot study. *Australian Psychiatry, 13*(3), 291–295.

Deveci, S. E., Acik, Y., Gulbayrak, C., Tokdemir, M., & Ayar, A. (2007). Prevalence of domestic violence during pregnancy in a Turkish community. *Southwest Asian Journal of Tropical Medical Public Health, 38*(4), 754–760.

Dietz, P. M., Williams, S. B., Callaghan, W. M., Bachman, D. J., Whitlock, E. P., & Hornbrook, M. C. (2007). Clinically identified maternal depression before, during, and after pregnancies ending in live births. *American Journal of Psychiatry, 164*, 1515–1520.

Dorheim, S. K., Bondevik, G. T., Eberhard-Gran, M., & Bjorvatn, B. (2009). Sleep and depression in postpartum woman: A population based study. *Sleep, 32*(7), 847–855.

Ege, E., Timur, S., Zincir, H., Geckil, E., & Sunar-Reeder, B. (2008). Social support and symptoms of postpartum depression among new mothers in Eastern Turkey. *Journal of Obstetrics and Gynecology Research, 34*(4), 585–593.

Ellsberg, M. S., Peña, R., Herrera, A., Liljestrand, J., & Winkvist, A. (2009). Wife abuse among women of childbearing age in Nicaragua. *American Journal of Public Health, 89*(2), 241–244.

Federal Bureau of Investigation. (2010). *Crime in the United States.* Washington, DC: Author. Retrieved from http://www.fbi.gov/about-us/cjis/ucr/crime-in-theu.s/2010/crime-in-the-u.s.-010/tables/10shrtb110.xls.

Figueiredo, B., & Conde, A. (2011). Anxiety and depression symptoms in women and men from early pregnancy to 3-months postpartum: Parity differences and effects. *Journal of Affective Disorders, 132*(1–2), 146–157. doi: 10.1016/j.jad.2011.02.007

Fikree, F. F., Jafarey, S. N., Korejo, R., Afshan, A., & Durocher, J. M. (2006). Intimate partner violence before and during pregnancy: Experiences of postpartum women in Karachi, Pakistan. *Journal of Pakistan Medical Association, 56*(6), 252–257.

Flynn, H. A., Blow, F. C., & Marcus, S. M. (2006). Rates and predictors of depression treatment among pregnant women in hospital-affiliated obstetrics practices. *General Hospital Psychiatry, 28*(4), 289–295.

Gausia, K., Fisher, C., Ali, M., & Oosthuizen, J. (2009). Magnitude and contributory factors of postnatal depression: A community-based cohort study from a rural sub-district of Bangladesh. *Psychological Medicine, 39*(6), 999–1007.

Heron, J., Haque, S., Oyebode, F., Craddock, N., & Jones, I. (2009). A longitudinal study of hypomania and depression symptoms in pregnancy and the postpartum period. *Bipolar Disorders, 11*(4), 410–417.

Hillemeier, M. M., Weisman, C. S., Chase, G. A., Dyer, A. M., & Shaffer, M. L. (2008). Women's preconceptional health and use of health services: Implications for preconception care. *Health Services Research, 43*(1p1), 54–75.

Huizink, A. C., de Medina, P. G., Mulder, E. J., Visser, G. H., & Buitelaar, J. K. (2002). Psychological measures of prenatal stress as predictors of infant temperament. *Journal of the American Academy of Child and Adolescent Psychiatry, 41,* 1078–1085.

Jesse, D. E., Dolbier, C. L., & Blanchard, A. (2008). Barriers to seeking help and treatment suggestions for prenatal depressive symptoms: Focus groups with rural low-income women. *Issues in Mental Health Nursing, 29*(1), 3–19.

Johnson, J. K., Haider, F., Ellis, D. M., & Hay, S. W. (2003). The prevalence of domestic violence in pregnant women. *BJOG: An International Journal of Obstetrics and Gynecology, 110*(3), 272–275.

Kheirabadi, G. R., Maracy, M. R., Barekatain, M., Salehi, M., Sadri, G. H., Kelishadi, M., & Cassy, P. (2009). Risk factors of postpartum depression in rural areas of Isfahan Province, Iran. *Archives of Iranian Medicine, 12*(5), 461–467.

Kinsella, M. T., & Monk, C. (2009). Impact of maternal stress, depression and anxiety on fetal neurobehavioral development. *Clinical Obstetrics and Gynecology, 52*(3), 425–440.

Kübler-Ross, E. (1969). *On death and dying.* New York, NY: Touchstone.

Lau, Y., & Chan, K. S. (2009). Perinatal depressive symptoms, socio-demographic correlates, and breast-feeding among Chinese women. *Journal of Perinatal & Neonatal Nursing, 23*(4), 335–345.

McGarry, J., Kim, H., Sheng, X., Egger, M., & Baksh, L. (2009). Postpartum depression and help seeking behavior. *Journal of Midwifery & Women's Health, 54*(1), 50–56.

Milgrom, J., Gemmill, A. W., Bilszta, J. L., Hayes, B., Barnett, B., Brooks, J. . . . Buist, A. (2008). Antenatal risk factors for postnatal depression: A large prospective study. *Journal of Affective Disorders, 108,* 147–157.

Mulder, E. J. H, Robles de Medina, P. G., Huizink, A. C., Van den Bergh, B. R. H., Buitelaar, J. K., & Visser, G. H. A. (2002). Prenatal maternal stress: Effects on pregnancy and the (unborn) child. *Early Human Development, 70,* 3–14.

Ntaganira, J., Muula, A. S., Masaisa, F., Dusabeyezu, F., Siziya, S., & Rudatsikira, E. (2008). Intimate partner violence among pregnant women in Rwanda. *BMC Women Health, 8,* 17.

Oates, M. (2003). Suicide: The leading cause of maternal death. *British Journal of Psychiatry, 62,* 279–281.

O'Leary, K. D., Tintle, N., Bromet, E. J., & Gluzman, S. F. (2008). Descriptive epidemiology of intimate partner aggression in Ukraine. *Social Psychiatry Psychiatric Epidemiology, 43*(8), 619–626.

Paulson, J. F., & Bazemore, S. D. (2010). Prenatal and postpartum depression in fathers and its association with maternal depression: A meta-analysis. *Journal of the American Medical Association, 303*(19), 1961–1969.

Perales, M. T., Cripe, S. M., Lam, N., Sanchez, E., & Williams, M. A. (2009). Prevalence, types, and pattern of intimate partner violence among pregnant women in Lima, Peru. *Violence Against Women, 15*(2), 224–250.

Perren, S., von Wyl, A., Burgin, D., Simoni, H., & von Klitzing, K. (2005). Depressive symptoms and psychosocial stress across the transition to parenthood: Associations with parental psychopathology and child difficulty. *Journal of Psychosomatic Obstetrics & Gynecology, 26,* 173–183.

Rahman, A., & Creed, F. (2007). Outcome of prenatal depression and risk factors associated with persistence in the first postnatal year: Prospective study from Rawalpindi, Pakistan. *Journal of Affective Disorders, 100*(1–3), 115–121.

Ramsay, J., Richardson, J., & Carter Y. H. (2005). Should healthcare professionals screen for domestic violence? Special issue in women's health: Intimate partner violence and domestic violence. *American College of Obstetricians and Gynecologists 325*(7359), 314–324.

Roelens, K., Verstraelen, H., VanEgmond, K., & Temmerman, M. (2008). Disclosure and health seeking behavior following intimate partner violence before and during pregnancy in Flanders, Belgium: A survey surveillance study. *European Journal of Obstetrics & Gynecology and Reproductive Biology, 137,* 37–42.

Ruiz-Perez, I., Plazaola-Castano, J., & Del Rio-Lozano, M. (2007). Physical health consequences of intimate partner violence in Spanish women. *European Journal of Public Health, 17*(5), 437–443.

Salazar, M., Valladares, E., Ohman, A., & Hogberg, U. (2009). Ending intimate partner violence after pregnancy: Findings from a community-based longitudinal study in Nicaragua. *BMC Public Health, 9,* 350.

Savarimuthu, R. J., Ezhilarasu, P., Charles, H., Antonisamy, B., Kurian, S., & Jacob, K. S. (2010). Post-partum depression in the community: A qualitative study from rural South India. *International Journal of Social Psychiatry, 56*(1), 94–102.

Segre, L. S., O'Hara, W., Arndt, S., & Stuart, S. (2007). The prevalence of postpartum depression. The relative significance of three social status indices. *Social Psychiatry and Psychiatric Epidemiology, 42,* 316–321.

Silverman, J. G., Decker, M. R., Saggert, N., Balaiah, D., & Raj, A. (2008). Intimate partner violence and HIV infection among married Indian women. *Journal of the American Medical Association, 300*(6), 703–710.

Simmons, L. A., Huddleston-Casas, C., & Berry, A. A. (2007). Low-income rural women and depression: Factors associated with self-reporting. *American Journal of Health Behaviors, 31*(6), 657–666.

Sit, D., Seltman, H., & Wisner, K. L. (2011). Seasonal effects on depression risk and suicidal symptoms in postpartum women. Depression and Anxiety. *ADAA: Journal of Anxiety and Depression of America, 28*(5), 400–405.

Skouteris, H., Wertheim, E. H., Rallis, S., Milgrom, J., & Paxton, S. J. (2009). Depression and anxiety through pregnancy and the early postpartum: An examination of prospective relationships. *Journal of Affective Disorders, 113*(3), 303–308.

Teixeira, C., Figueiredo, B., Conde, A., Pacheco, A., & Costa, R. (2009). Anxiety and depression during pregnancy in women and men. *Journal of Affective Disorders, 119,* 142–148.

Varma, D., Chandra, P. S., Thomas, T., & Carey, M. P. (2007). Intimate partner violence and sexual coercion among pregnant women in India: Relationship with depression and post-traumatic stress disorder. *Journal of Affective Disorders, 102,* 227–235.

Villegas, L., McKay, K., Dennis, C. L., & Ross, L. E. (2011). Postpartum depression among rural women from developed and developing countries: A systematic review. *Journal of Rural Health, 27*(3), 278–288. doi: 10.1111/j.1748–0361.2010.00339.x

Xie, R. H., He, G., Koszycki, D., Walker, M., & Wen, S. W. (2009). Prenatal social support, postnatal social support, and postpartum depression. *Annals of Epidemiology, 19,* 637–643. doi: 0.1016/j.annepidem.2009.03.008

Infancy (Birth to 24 Months Old)

4

The way parents are with children is how children will be with the rest of the world.

Dr. Karl Menninger

This statement by Dr. Karl Menninger is quite an eye-opener. While there is room to disagree with the expanse of this statement, it is hard to deny the power to influence and the awesome responsibility that comes with parenthood. And yet—even with such a powerful and significant role being played—for most, jumping in to or falling into parenthood occurs without any formal training, education, or credentialing.

There are some, as suggested in Menninger's quote, that will simply argue that "it (the way I was parented) was good enough for me, and as such, is good enough for my daughter or son," but is good enough, good enough?

As you read on, you will discover that we now know so much more about human development then we did a generation or two ago. We know so much more about conditions facilitating development as well as those that can threaten and damage development. And as it is our duty, our responsibility is to employ that knowledge to guide our intervention and prevention services.

The current chapter will review typical human development during the infancy stage and explore physical, cognitive, and social/emotional changes that occur during this period of development. After reading and discussing this chapter, you will be able to

1. describe typical physical, cognitive, and social/emotional development during the infant stages of life;

2. apply various theories of development as related to the infant stages of life;

3. evaluate common risks to healthy infant development;

4. distinguish areas of counseling that may be needed for parents, including prevention and intervention strategies; and

5. demonstrate areas of consultation that can be provided with other health care providers.

Healthy Infant Development

Healthy nutrition and a supportive environment are critical to the development of the infant once born. **Breast-feeding is highly recommended, as is delaying solid foods until after 4 to 6 months.** According to the **American Academy of Pediatrics** (AAP, 2012), breast milk should be the only nutrient fed to infants until 4 to 6 months of age. For those mothers who are unable to breast-feed or choose not to breast-feed, a prepared infant formula can be used. However, human breast milk is ideal for infants because it contains lactose, a sugar that provides energy and lipids, which are healthy fats. The AAP recommends breastfeeding for at least 1 year, and the **World Health Organization (WHO)** recommends breastfeeding for at least 2 years. Infants who are breast-fed have less diarrhea, fewer cases of ear and urinary tract infections, fewer infectious diseases, and lower obesity rates (AAP, 2012). The AAP also states that breast-fed babies have lower incidences of sudden infant death syndrome in the first year of life. In addition to the benefits of breast-feeding for infants, mothers also experience decreased postpartum bleeding, more rapid uterine involution, and decreased menstrual blood during monthly cycles.

The AAP recommends that juice not be introduced to infants younger than 6 months of age. In fact, consuming the whole fruit is preferred over giving children juice. An excessive consumption of juice can lead to malnutrition, short stature, and dental cavities in children. If juice is given, both the AAP and the American Academy of Periodontics (1978) recommend that it should be offered in a cup. Children between the ages of one and six should only be allowed 4 to 6 ounces of juice per day.

According to the American Academy of Pediatrics (AAP) and Hassink (2006), solids should not be introduced to an infant until he or she is able to sit alone and can grab for items to put into his or her mouth. This typically occurs between 4 and 6 months of age. Simple basic foods should be introduced one at a time. A popular first food is infant cereal mixed with warm breast milk or formula. The AAP also recommends infant cereals that are enriched with iron because the natural stores of iron become depleted around 6 months of age. New foods should then be introduced one at a time, every 2 to 3 days, so that any food sensitivity or allergy can be easily identified. Within 2 to 3 months of beginning solid foods, the infant's daily diet can consist of breast milk (or formula), cereal, vegetables, fruits, and meats; however, these need to be spread throughout the course of the day rather than offering the infant all of these food groups at one sitting. Around 8 to 9 months old, the infant can begin eating finger foods. The AAP states, however, that raisins, nuts, popcorn, or other small or hard foods should be avoided as infants can easily aspirate on them.

The Advisory Committee on Immunization Practices (Centers for Disease Control and Prevention, 2014a), the AAP (2014), the American Academy of Family Physicians (2014), and the American Congress of Obstetricians and Gynecologists (2014) also recommend that an immunization schedule be followed to deter illnesses and diseases that have been problematic in the past. However, recently immunizations have been a source of suspicion regarding their link to physical and mental disorders.

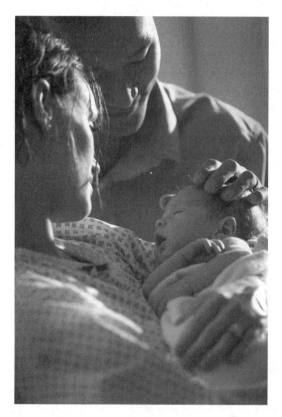

Photo 4.1   The emotional attachment of mother and child begins before the baby is born.

Source: Photodisc/Photodisc/Thinkstock

A study in 1998 (Wakefield et al.) claimed to find a link between the measles, mumps, and rubella (MMR) vaccine and autism, which led to the refusal of many parents to get their children vaccinated. However, the study has since been deemed flawed and has been retracted by the journal that published it. In 2004, the Institute of Medicine released a report that found no scientific evidence of a link. Another scare in the vaccination world was that thimerosal, which was used as a preservative in several vaccines, was linked to autism. However, in a study published in the October 2010 issue of *Pediatrics,* Price et al. reviewed the cases of a total of 1,008 children (256 diagnosed with autism spectrum disorder and 752 without autism) and found that none of the autism outcomes were related to prenatal or early life receipt of thimerosal-containing vaccines.

The Centers for Disease Control and Prevention (CDC, 2014b) does, however, document that the MMR vaccine can cause encephalitis or severe allergic reactions. They caution, though, that we must compare the risk from measles, mumps, and rubella with the risk of the vaccine. For example, the CDC estimates that measles causes 6 out of 100 patients to suffer pneumonia, 1 out of 1,000 to suffer encephalitis, and 2 in 1,000 to die. This is compared to the risk of 1 in 1 million patients receiving the MMR vaccine of developing encephalitis. Similar findings are found when viewing the risks of the diphtheria, tetanus, and pertussis (DTaP) vaccine. Diphteria leads to death for 1 in 20 people, death for 2 in 100 for tetanus, and death for 1 in 1,500 for pertussis (with 1 in 20 developing encephalitis). While there are risks of the vaccine, such as acute encephalopathy, (0–10.5 in 1 million), there have been no associated deaths with the vaccine.

Another concern that has been noted in the literature is the link between the DTaP vaccine and sudden infant death syndrome (SIDS). The root of this concern is that a moderate proportion of children who died of SIDS had recently been vaccinated with DTaP; however, most SIDS deaths occur during the age range when three shots of DTaP are given. Therefore, it may simply be a coincidence. A number of controlled studies conducted during the 1980s indicated that there was no association between SIDS and the DTaP vaccine.

While these links have not been proven, it is important to realize that all vaccines can have side effects. However, for most, these side effects are minor and may only include a low-grade fever or a sore arm. But other, more severe side effects have been noted as previously described. However, the effects of various diseases can also be devastating. It is important for counselors who work with parents of young children to realize the benefits and risks of vaccinations and to be vigilant about staying on top of the current research.

Providing a supportive environment is also vital to the healthy development of the infant. Parents and caregivers should create an environment that is safe and conducive for child exploration. Because infants are natural explorers, safety is a primary concern. All electrical outlet plugs should be covered; breakable items should be put away for the time being, and movable, top-heavy furniture should be made stationary. Parents and caregivers should also provide a nurturing environment, including activities to encourage large motor development, such as small steps and stools, as well as provide a variety of materials and toys for children to develop their fine motor skills, such as items that require grasping and carrying. While there is nothing shocking about any of the above, and in fact, it may appear as simply intuitively logical, the conditions of safety and nurturance are not automatic, and for some living in poverty or experiencing daily threats to their well-being, these provisions may not be possible. It is our responsibility, as counselors, to advocate for those whose life conditions challenge their abilities to provide for such safe and nurturing environments.

Physical Development

Physical growth during infancy is very rapid. Many parents voice that their infant seems to have grown overnight. In fact, infants and toddlers grow in spurts, meaning they grow for several days, often at night, and then rest. The World Health Organization released new international growth charts for six countries (see http://www.who.int/childgrowth/standards/en) that describe optimal growth for children up to the age of five, while the Centers for Disease Control and Prevention provides growth charts for children ages two to 20 living in the United States (see http://www.cdc.gov/growthcharts/clinical_charts.htm).

Sensory and Perceptual Development. During the first few months of life, the sensory system seems to function at a higher level than the motor system. Vision, hearing, taste, smell, and touch are more developed at birth. When first born, a baby is able to see about 8 inches in front of his or her face, which is the approximate distance of a parent's face when holding the baby. Babies also see the world in black and white, but by 3 months of age, they can see blue, green, yellow, and red. Babies also prefer to look at faces. In one study, researchers found that newborns prefer to see faces that are oriented correctly rather than upside down (Leo & Simion, 2009), and by 3 months of age, they can distinguish between genders (Quinn, Yahr, Kuhn, Slater, & Pascalis, 2002) and different races (Sangrigoli & de Schonen, 2004a, 2004b).

Hearing actually begins early during the gestational period. At around 20 weeks, prenatally, fetuses turn toward the source of a sound. In fact, very loud noises can cause an infant to increase his or her movements for approximately 30 minutes after hearing the sound (LeCanuet & Schaal, 2002). Additionally, an infant, at birth, is able to distinguish the difference between the voice of the mother and that of a stranger (Kisilevsky et al., 2003).

Taste and smell are also well formed before birth. At 12 weeks, prenatally, taste buds form. Newborns have shown preferences regarding smells, which indicates that infants' sense of smell is highly developed at birth (Pomares, Schirrer, & Abadie, 2002). Newborns can distinguish between sweet, salty, sour, bitter, and savory flavors (Beauchamp & Mennella, 2009). These researchers found that infants actually prefer sweet, savory, and salty flavors while they reject bitter and sour substances. Schaal, Marlier, and Soussignan (2000) found that the infant's preference is also influenced by the mother's diet during pregnancy and breast-feeding.

Touch is a profoundly powerful sense that is often forgotten. Studies have indicated that premature and high-risk newborns gain more weight when their parents hold them skin-to-skin against their chests (Suman, Udani, & Nanavati, 2008; Worku & Kassie, 2005). Massage is also effective in nurturing healthy development and increasing weight gain (Diego, Field, & Hernandex-Reif, 2005; Hernandez-Reif, Diego, & Field, 2007).

Motor Development. At birth, an infant has poor control of his or her muscles; however, babies are born with certain reflexes, such as the Moro reflex, rooting reflex, and grasp reflex. The **Moro reflex**, also called the startle reflex, occurs in response to a loud noise or when a person nearby makes a sudden movement. The baby throws out his or her arms, lengthens the neck, and then draws his or her arms back into the chest. The **rooting reflex**, or sucking reflex, demonstrates the baby's natural instinct to search for and suckle the breast for nutrition. Shortly after delivery, a baby can suck and swallow milk. Finally, the **grasp reflex** encourages the baby to wrap his or her fingers tightly around anything that touches his or her palm. Over time, each of these behaviors leads to more muscle control and voluntary actions. This transition from involuntary to voluntary action results through a process of repeated discovery, exploration, and practice.

Other motor skills begin to develop as the infant's bones, muscles, and nervous system matures. During the first year of life, babies typically develop in the following order: (1) able to hold chest and head up while lying on stomach, (2) able to roll over, (3) able to sit with support, (4) able to sit alone, (5) able to crawl, (6) able to stand holding on to something or someone, (7) able to walk when led, (8) able to stand alone, and finally (9) able to walk alone. Figure 4.1 further displays motor skill development according to age.

Language Development. As newborns, babies can discriminate speech sounds. At birth, newborns prefer to hear their mothers' voices over a stranger's voice (Kisilevsky et al., 2009), indicating that they have been listening to their mother's voice while in the womb. Infants begin with cooing and then progress to babbling around 5 months of age. **Babbling** increases to include well-formed syllables, which is required for later speech development. Therefore, it is important for parents and caregivers to encourage, imitate, and respond to babbling. By 9 months old, babies may begin to say "da-da" or "ma-ma" intentionally.

While infants are born ready to learn any language, by 12 months old, they have lost the ability to discriminate the sounds in different languages. By 7 to 12 months of age, infants focus on and practice the sounds of the language that they most commonly hear (Kuhl et al., 2006; Rivera-Gaxiloa, Silvia-Pereyra, & Kuhl, 2008). However, Kuhl, Tsao, and Liu (2003) found that after hearing a language and interacting with the speaker for 5 hours at 8

Months	Fine Motor Development
0–4	• Lifts head when back is supported, eventually holding head more stable • Wiggles and kicks with arms and legs • Turns head to familiar voices and sounds • Moves body to continue interaction and can hold body still • Lifts and reaches for toys while grasping objects • Sucks on fingers, hands, and toys • Lifts head off the ground when placed on stomach
4–8	• Reaches with one arm and grasps • Plays with toes • Bounces when held • Opens mouth for food • Turns from back to side and later begins to roll over • Crawls on stomach with hands and knees • Moves objects between hands and holds bottle • Begins to sit with support, and later, alone • Laughs and smiles
8–12	• Pulls up to stand alone • Walks with some help and support • Can sit in chairs supporting own weight • Uses hands to feed and can use spoon and sippy cup • Accomplishes simple goals • Raises arms when he or she wants to be held • Kneels and pulls up • Enjoys looking at objects and mirror

Figure 4.1 Infant Motor Development

months to 10 months old, infants retained their ability to differentiate the sounds of the foreign language, but listening to the language on television or other media did not produce the same results. Therefore, it is important for parents and caregivers to constantly talk to their child because infants learn language best when an adult talks directly to them (Thiessen, Hill, & Saffran, 2005).

Cognitive Development

While the brain grows exponentially during prenatal development, it continues to develop at a rapid pace during the first 3 years of life. It is during this time that a young child's experiences literally shape the neural connections in the brain. **Synapses** are overproduced in the cerebral cortex and then pruned based on the experiences that the infant has. For example, as an event occurs and reoccurs, the synapses storing the information about the event become more active, thicker, and stronger. However, those synapses that are not exercised are deleted from the brain. This pruning enables the brain to become more finely tuned and functional (Thomas & Johnson, 2008). In fact, almost half of the neurons that are created during infant development survive to function in adults (Society for Neuroscience, 2009).

Both physical maturation and experience play a role in positively influencing optimal brain development in infants. Parents and caregivers play a critical role in optimal cognitive development. Halfon, Shulman, and

Hochstein (2001) note that not only is a child's brain immature at birth, and that it changes based on experiences, but that these specific experiences, as well as relationships with caregivers, are critical to the healthy development of a child's social and emotional functioning. Being sensitive to an infant's distress, being emotionally available, and being responsive to a baby's cues are critical parenting skills. Infants learn how to regulate their emotions and behaviors by watching the caregiver's attempts. Responding to infant cues, such as crying and cooing, leads to increased language and cognitive development.

Social and Emotional Development

Identity is a person's self-definition that focuses on enduring traits of the self. Infants learn who they are and how they are perceived by how they are treated. Loving, caring relationships with caregivers are critical to healthy social-emotional development. Early experiences in childhood shape the development of skills to form friendships, communicate emotions, and respond positively to challenges. Supportive relationships help children to develop trust, compassion, and empathy. The following section describes several aspects of identity development that begins in infancy.

Emotional development refers to a child's ability to recognize, express, and regulate his or her emotions. Although all infants express universal emotions, the frequency and use of these emotions is influenced by the child's culture, adult-child interactions, and context. Researchers and practitioners consider social referencing, temperament, self-regulation, and attachment as constructs of emotional development.

Social referencing refers to the ability to observe and understand emotional cues of others and then to use those cues to guide personal behavior. For example, a child may see his or her mother smiling at a toy, so he or she responds by crawling toward it. However, if the mother looks fearful, then the child stops. The baby is using the emotional cue from his or her mother to determine if he or she should crawl toward the object. Most research

Photo 4.2   Healthy parental stimulation contributes to the healthy development of the baby.

Source: Jupiterimages/Creatas/Thinkstock.

indicates that social referencing begins around 7 months of age; however, new studies have indicated that infants, as young as 3 months old, respond to emotional cues (Hoehl, Wiese, & Striano, 2008).

Temperament refers to an individual's personality, disposition, and tendencies. Each child has a unique personality; some are more relaxed, some are more energetic, and some are more irritable. Some infants enjoy being around a lot people, while others want to be around only a few. Originally discussed by Thomas, Chess, Birch, Hertzig, and Korn (1963), temperament includes nine dimensions: activity level, biological rhythms, approach/withdrawal, mood, intensity of reaction, sensitivity, adaptability, distractibility, and persistence. These nine dimensions are then divided into three temperament types, including easy, difficult, and slow to warm. While some babies may have varying levels of intensity on different temperament dimensions, one type usually dominates. Children with easy temperaments are typically more cheerful, recover fairly quickly to changes in routine, have regular biological rhythms, and are moderately active. Conversely, children with **difficult temperaments** tend to be fussy, have intense emotional reactions, and are fearful of new situations. **Slow to warm** children are passive, need time to adjust to new situations, and withdraw or negatively react to new situations.

While temperament describes a child's basic personality, the most important factor in the child's future outcome is the goodness of fit between the caregiver's temperament and the child's temperament. Goodness of fit cannot only be how well the caregiver's temperament matches that of the child but also how well the caregiver understands, accepts, and works with the child's temperament. For example, the way a caregiver views the temperament of the child can impact parenting behaviors and thus the caregiver-child relationship. A child with a difficult temperament who experiences intense emotions may be viewed as overly emotional and demanding or vivacious. The viewpoint of the caregiver directs his or her responses to the child and thus encourages or discourages the parent-child bond.

Self-regulation refers to the ability to regulate and attend to emotions and behaviors. While this development begins as early as the occurrence of the first reciprocal, sensitive interaction between adult and child (Rochat, 2007), self-regulation continues to develop throughout the lifespan. Children who are provided with positive, empathetic support regarding emotions are able to learn how to express their emotions in culturally acceptable ways. However, children who are mistreated, abused, or neglected have a difficult time controlling their emotions and behavior. These children may resort to aggression and other maladaptive behaviors in an effort to control their intense emotions.

The emotional bond between the child and caregivers is referred to as **attachment**. According to Bowlby (1979) and Ainsworth, Blehar, Waters, and Wall (1978), attachment is an affectional bond between two individuals that is persistent and emotionally significant. The attachment produces a desire to maintain closeness as well as to seek security and comfort and results in distress when the two individuals are involuntarily separated (Ainsworth, 1989; Bowlby, 1969/1982). Children are typically described as being securely attached, insecurely attached–anxious-resistant, insecurely attached–avoidant, or insecurely attached–disorganized-disoriented. Children who are **securely attached** seem to feel safe and protected by their caregivers. They seek the parent after separation and go to the parent for comfort. They feel safe to explore their environment and are more socially competent (Braungart-Rieker, Garwood, Powers, & Want, 2001; McElwain, Cox, Burchinal, & Macfie, 2003). In contrast, children who are identified as **anxious-resistant** are fearful to explore the environment and often stay close to their caregiver because of the adult's inconsistent responses to the child's distress. This leads to a limited exploration of the environment, which may then lead to feelings of incompetence, especially if parents are intrusive and negatively controlling (McElwain et al., 2003). Children who are **avoidant-attached** see their caregivers as being unavailable, so they learn to suppress their negative emotions of distress. Therefore, they avoid the adult (e.g., look away, arch their backs). These children often struggle socially because they seem to prefer playing with objects rather than with people. Finally, children identified as **disorganized-disoriented** often appear dazed and confused when with the caregiver. This behavior typically is a result of abuse or neglect.

Keeping in mind that social referencing, temperament, self-regulation, and attachment are all constructs of emotional development, Erik Erikson, a neo-Freudian psychologist, developed eight stages for his theory of psychosocial development in 1959. Like Freud, Erikson was primarily concerned with how personality and behavior were influenced after birth. Erikson's theory basically asserts that a person experiences internal struggles that he or she must then negotiate in order to grow and develop (see Figure 4.1). Each stage involves two opposing emotions. Successfully passing through each stage involves achieving a healthy balance between the two opposing emotions. For example, in Stage 1, which primarily occurs between infancy and 18 months of age, an infant needs to develop a healthy level of trust but also needs to understand when it is helpful not to trust.

According to Erikson (1959), the first stage of psychosocial development, **trust versus mistrust**, is the most critical. During this stage, infants learn whether or not they can trust the people around them. In fact, because of their complete dependence on caregivers, the quality of care that an infant receives is vital to the successful resolution of this stage. When the child cries, does the caregiver consistently respond? When the child is scared, does the caregiver consistently provide comfort? If these needs are consistently met, then an infant develops a healthy balance between trust and mistrust. However, if these needs are not met or are inconsistently met, then mistrust develops and children may believe the world inconsistent and unpredictable. Infants who develop trust feel safe and secure and develop into adults who are able to hope. Table 2.2 on Chapter 2 displays Erikson's stages of psychosocial development throughout the lifespan. Please review the "Trust versus Mistrust" stage as described in the table. Other stages will be discussed in future chapters, as appropriate.

Helping parents and caregivers understand the critical role that they play in a child's social-emotional development is critical in creating a nurturing, supportive environment to allow children to thrive. Guided Practice Exercise 4.1 provides an example of one way that you can begin to educate parents and caregivers about their important role.

While the descriptions above have provided some guidelines to typical infant development, there are individual differences associated with both hereditary and environmental factors. For example, children who have tall parents tend to be taller than the typical child. Environmentally, health and nutrition also play an important role in the differences in infant development. For example, children in more developed areas of the world tend to be taller than children in regions where food is scarce and infectious diseases are more prevalent (Bogin, 2001). Similarly, children who experience chronic poverty are also more likely to experience slower growth (Leathers & Foster, 2004). Ethnic differences can also be found in development. For example, in the United States, African American children typically grow faster and taller than their Caucasian peers, and American Caucasian children tend to be taller and bigger framed than Asian American children.

Guided Practice Exercise 4.1

Design a brochure to educate parents about the social-emotional development of infants. What facts should parents know? What tips could you include to help them respond consistently and appropriately to their baby's needs? How can you convince them that fostering a secure attachment will not lead to spoiling?

Counseling Issues

As you reviewed the characteristics of infancy, and the factors that contribute to healthy development as well as those that could inhibit healthy development, perhaps you began to conceptualize the unique contribution that a counselor could make in providing targeted interventions and prevention services. What follows is a nonexhaustive presentation of the role a counselor and counseling may provide in fostering healthy development. The counselor as educator and provider of support is emphasized throughout the following discussion.

Parent Education-Discipline for the Infant

Parental beliefs about **discipline** have been linked to parenting practices, which in turn have been linked to child outcomes (Harkness & Super, 2006; Sigel & McGillicuddy-DeLisi, 2002). These beliefs are often rooted in cultural and personal beliefs concerning what parents should do to promote their children's development (Keller, 2007; Rubin & Chung, 2006; Sigel & McGillicuddy-DeLisi, 2002). For example, according to Ipsa and colleagues (2004), African-American mothers express stronger beliefs about the use of punishment for infants and have greater concerns about spoiling infants as young as 6 months of age as compared to European American mothers. Therefore, it is critical to explore parental beliefs and cultures surrounding child discipline before suggesting discipline strategies.

Between 20% and 50% of parents are reported to believe that infants, younger than 1 year of age, can be spoiled, and that spoiled infants will later exhibit conduct problems or other negative outcomes if they are not taught to respect authority (Barton & Ratner, 2001). Mothers who use more direct or punitive parenting styles with infants often justify their approach as a way of teaching the infant to respect authority and to avoid spoiling the child (Guzell & Vernon-Feagans, 2004; Smyke, Boris, & Alexander, 2002). Yet providing loving responses to an infant's cries and behaviors actually leads to an increase in independent behaviors when the child is older. One

Photo 4.3 The baby's physical and cognitive developments are stimulated by every activity in which he or she is encouraged to participate in early in life.

Source: Jupiterimages/Creatas/Thinkstock.

study found that mothers who used physical punishment to correct infant behavior believe their infants are capable of intentional negative behavior. They believe this punishment is necessary to avoid spoiling their babies, and they are less likely to demonstrate responsive and stimulating parenting practices with their infants (Burchinal, Skinner, & Reznick, 2010). Mothers who express traditional child-rearing beliefs, concerns about spoiling their infants, or beliefs that their infants act in intentionally negative ways are least likely to engage in positive interactions with their babies (Burchinal et al., 2010).

Counselors can focus on helping parents eliminate the use of physical punishment with children, especially with infants. For parents of very young children, the focus of counseling efforts should be on determining the extent to which parents believe that infants can intentionally misbehave and should focus on removing the negative connotation of spoiling. This focus in counseling has been demonstrated to be successful in helping parents understand that infants do not intentionally misbehave, nor can they be spoiled (Bugental & Happaney, 2000, 2004). By educating parents about typical infant behavior and expectations, counselors can be at the forefront of preventing future child abuse. Case Illustration 4.1 demonstrates how you may face this issue in counseling practice.

Attachment Parenting

Secure attachment, fostered by consistent, predictable relationships, is the foundation for healthy childhood development. Developing a secure attachment has numerous benefits and can be fostered by attachment

CASE ILLUSTRATION 4.1 INFANT DISCIPLINE

Rachel, a young African-American mother, gave birth to a son at the age of 15. She is currently in the 10th grade and the child is now 4 months old. She has been successful in her studies but often makes negative comments about her child to her teachers and classmates. She states that her son is "bad" and "never minds." She often comes to school tired and in a poor mood and blames the child. When interviewed by the school counselor, Rachel discloses that her grandmother helps her with the child and that "he is just bad." When asked what she means by that, Rachel replies that he wakes up during the night; he throws food, drinks, and toys; he always wants attention; and he puts everything in his mouth even though she tells him not to.

Practice Exercise:

As a young mother, Rachel not only faces taking care of an infant but she needs to be taken care of as well. Many of her peers do not have the same responsibilities that she has as a teen parent, so the counselor may want to explore her feelings about that. There may be some built up resentment toward the infant that is contributing to Rachel's view of her son. Additionally, Rachel is still a child and may have needs that are not being met due to the focus on the child.

Rachel is living with her grandmother. Studies indicate that African-American mothers have stronger beliefs about the use of punishment for infants and do not want to spoil their children. Therefore, the counselor may want to explore Rachel's and her grandmother's parental beliefs and culture surrounding child discipline before suggesting discipline strategies.

Once the counselor determines the extent to which Rachel and her grandmother believe that her son can intentionally misbehave, he or she can provide educational materials to help them understand that children this young do not intentionally misbehave and begin to remove the negative connotation of spoiling. Educating Rachel about normal development during infancy may also help her understand what types of behaviors to expect.

parenting, a parenting philosophy based on the principles of the attachment theory. **Attachment parenting** promotes autonomy and independence. Studies demonstrate that securely attached children are more likely to explore their environment (Mercer, 2006), possess more developed consciences (Kochanska & Murray, 2000), and exhibit more empathy and prosocial behaviors (Davidov & Grusec, 2006). Secure attachments also promote emotional availability (Easterbrooks, Biesecker, & Lyons-Ruth, 2000), better moods and emotional regulation (Kerns, Abraham, Schlegelmilch, & Morgan, 2007), reduced levels of stress (Blair, Granger, Willoughby, & Kivilighan, 2006; Waynforth, 2007), and fewer behavior difficulties (van Zeijl et al., 2006). Finally, attachment parenting practices are associated with higher intelligence and academic performance (Landry, Smith, & Swank, 2003, 2006).

Sometimes challenges may arise that interfere with bonding experiences. If either the parent/caregiver or the child is dealing with a problem that interferes with his or her ability to relax, then attachment may be difficult. For example, babies with physical problems, such as compromised nervous systems or other serious health problems, as well as babies with environmental concerns, such as being separated from the primary caretaker at birth or experiencing a series of caretakers, may struggle to bond. Parents may also have issues that interfere with attachment. Parents who are, themselves, products of an insecure attachment, who grew up in abusive or unsafe homes, or have primarily negative memories of their own childhoods, may struggle with bonding. Parents who have emotional problems, such as depression or anxiety, drug or alcohol problems, or who experience high levels of stress may also struggle to offer the nurturing support an infant needs. Guided Practice Exercise 4.2 can help you observe parent/child interactions to begin assessing attachment and the role it plays in parent/child relationships.

Guided Practice Exercise 4.2

When you are out in the community this week, watch for parent/child interactions. Try to find a caregiver/parent with an infant. How does the caregiver respond to the child? Is he or she attentive to the child, or does he or she tend to ignore the child? What does the caregiver do when the infant becomes fussy?

Write a brief synopsis of your observation and include your thoughts based on your reading of this chapter. What did you see that fostered positive attachment, or what did you see that did not?

Counselors can play a critical role in helping new parents to foster a positive attachment. Parents often believe that they may spoil the baby if they are always available. However, it is important to note that the more responsive a parent is to an infant's needs, the less spoiled the baby is as he or she grows. Children with secure attachments tend to be more independent than children who are insecurely attached. Helping parents set up daily routines, encouraging them to respond to baby's cries, and teaching them to follow baby's cues can foster the development of positive attachment. Attachment parenting encourages reciprocity and cooperativeness, being more sensitive, and helps infants manage difficult feelings. Mothers of securely attached infants are more consistent, sensitive, and accepting of their babies when compared to mothers of insecurely attached infants.

There are also criticisms of attachment parenting. The cover and article in the May 2012 *Time* magazine, "Are You Mom Enough?", raised much debate over the attachment parenting philosophy (Pickert, 2012). The arguments that arose were that this parenting philosophy causes mothers to subjugate themselves to their children and to sacrifice everything (working, sex, etc.). However, the other side of the argument is that attachment parenting is the best choice for the development of their children. Some critics are concerned with bed sharing, which has been linked to SIDS; however, Attachment Parenting International tries to address this risk with guidelines for safe bed sharing. Other critics point out that the ability to form healthy attachments is also impacted by peer pressure, relationships during school, dating, and marriage; therefore, early childhood experiences are not the sole indicators of positive attachment. Some believe that attachment parenting can lead to overdependent children or highly stressed parents. However, proponents of attachment parenting disagree with these claims. In the end, most parents try to make the best decisions that they can with their children; however, it is important that counselors remain aware of various parenting philosophies, as well as their benefits and limitations. Even the best philosophy will not be successful if the parent is not able to implement it. Case Illustration 4.2 may help you more clearly see the role of the counselor in helping parents to foster positive attachments with their infants.

Day Care: Quality Matters

Many parents often struggle with the decision of whether or not to place their newborn into a **day care** setting, while many parents simply do not have a choice. Often times, this decision can lead to stress and anxiety as parents try to determine the best setting for their newborn. Counselors can help parents navigate these decisions

CASE ILLUSTRATION 4.2 FOSTERING A POSITIVE ATTACHMENT

After meeting at a local club, Laura and Brent found out that they were going to have a baby after only knowing each other for a few weeks. After much discussion, the couple decided that they would keep the child, but neither was thrilled with the idea of becoming a parent. After the baby, Anthony, was born, Brent had very little to do with his son, and Laura was resentful. Laura does not want to change her lifestyle and continue going to clubs, while leaving Anthony with whoever will keep him. When she comes home, she often feels guilty and lavishes Anthony with attention. Then, she begins to grow tired of being a mother and begins to ignore Anthony. Laura's mother is very concerned about how Anthony is being treated and has convinced Laura to see a counselor.

Practice Exercise:

Counselor's Thoughts and Reactions

Clearly, Laura is struggling with motherhood and her responsibilities to her child. The counselor may benefit from hearing how Laura sees her role as mother, her frustrations with Brent's lack of involvement, her adaptation to such a life-changing event, and whether or not she still wants to keep the child. The pregnancy was not planned; Laura may not have had the chance to explore how her life would be different after having a child.

The counselor also needs to focus on parenting strategies quickly, since attachment forms at such a young age. Laura's inconsistent behavior toward her child may lead to an anxious-resistant or an avoidantly-attached child. The counselor may wish to discuss these concerns and Erikson's stage of trust versus mistrust so that Laura understands how her behavior is hurting the child's attachment. The counselor could also help her explore various options for safe, consistent child care with planned time for Laura to have a social outing. Hopefully, this would allow Laura to enjoy going out with friends without feeling guilty.

by being aware of child care opportunities in the area, understanding the advantages and disadvantages of child care settings, and providing support as parents try to make this decision.

Understandably, the need for day care for infants and children has risen in the past few decades due to the growing number of parents/guardians, especially mothers, entering the workforce. Child care settings may include a day care center or care from a relative or nonrelative in a private home. Whatever the setting, parents need to explore the advantages and disadvantages of each option.

Studies have shown that the overall quality of child care settings is critical to the development of the child. Children placed in high-quality settings demonstrated high achievement and development through middle childhood regardless of their socioeconomic status, as well as increased cognitive and psychosocial skills, because they were exposed to more advanced material (Dearing, McCartney, & Taylor, 2009). On the other hand, children placed in poor quality settings developed psychosocial and emotional problems (Zmiri, Rubin, Akons, Zion, & Shaoul, 2011). Children in these settings may experience extreme separation anxiety, social struggles with peers, poor nutrition, and poor caretaker skills. Therefore, it is critical that counselors work with parents to properly assess various child care options and help them determine the best placement for their child. Counselors and parents should consider the characteristics of the caregiver, staffing ratios and turnovers, environment of the setting, services provided, and personal interactions with the caregiver.

The characteristics of the child caregiver are the most important aspect to consider. Caregivers should be warm, caring, and attentive to the individual needs of each child. Discipline should be positively focused and not punitive. The caregiver should actively communicate and play with children. Good staffing ratios with a low turn-over rate are also important, as are low caregiver-student ratios. The smaller the number of children per adult in the setting, generally the better the child care. At a minimum, the child care setting should have at least one adult for every three to four infants, and one adult for every four to six children under the age of three. Additionally, finding a caregiver with specialized training in early childhood development is extremely beneficial.

The overall environment of the setting should also be assessed. The most frequently noted disadvantages to child care settings are health concerns and the risk of infection (Hedin, Petersson, Cars, Beckman, & Hakansson, 2006; Lu et al., 2004; Nafstad et al., 2004; Zmiri et al., 2011). While children are much more susceptible to infectious diseases in a day care center as opposed to a private home setting, all settings should be checked for signs of mold, water leakage, and damage to floors and walls, as these problems could exacerbate respiratory infections in children. The number of children in the environment should also be assessed, since crowding and lack of hygiene also lead to health problems. A quality environment should not only be clean but should also be welcoming for children to explore and learn. Parents should search for a setting that is neat, clean, orderly, and organized into child activity centers. For parents of newborns, you will want to search for an environment that includes a rocking chair, cribs that are free from blankets and other suffocation hazards, bouncy seats, a tummy time area, and plenty of toys and books. Additionally, when visiting a setting, parents should make sure that babies are individually fed by the caretaker, bottles are not being propped up on the babies, and babies are put to sleep on their backs. For older children, parents should make sure that there are enough developmentally appropriate toys and materials for all of the children to use to discourage aggressive behaviors related to not sharing. Parents of older children should also ask the caregiver about activities planned throughout the day. Parents should search for a setting that encourages imaginative play that enhances a child's social, emotional, physical, and cognitive development. Safety is also of utmost importance. Parents should determine whether the caregiver will be vigilant in his or her supervision of children at all times. Additionally, parents should deter-mine if a caregiver has been trained in child cardiopulmonary resuscitation (CPR) and first aid, as well as if basic sanitary procedures (e.g., washing hands) are being followed. Adequate lighting, temperature, and noise control are also important to assess.

Many quality child care programs also provide comprehensive services for families, such as healthy nutrition, preventative health care, child development monitoring, consultation opportunities with outside specialists, and provision of services for children with disabilities, parent programs, and continual staff development opportunities. Finding a setting that also provides these services can greatly enhance the overall wellness of the child.

Finally, forming a positive relationship between the caregiver and parent, as well as the caregiver and child, is critical for high-quality care. A parent should feel free to visit the setting at any given time and should visit at random times throughout the year. Parents should be notified immediately of any problems or concerns that the caregiver has and should feel comfortable discussing any parental concerns with the caregiver. Finding a caregiver who can give daily reports of the child's behaviors and activities during the day is very helpful. Children in a high-quality day care setting should exhibit happiness and comfort within the setting. This is one of the best indicators of the environment.

High-quality child care environments have the capability of promoting trust, autonomy, and positive well-being in children. Finding the best setting for a child can lead to positive physical, cognitive, and social-emotional growth and development. Counselors can assist with this process by working with parents to assess child care options, which can minimize the amount of stress and anxiety that many parents experience.

Sleep Concerns

Clinical research has found that there is an interaction between sleep and physical, emotional, and behavioral well-being for individuals (Byars, Yeomans-Maldonado, & Noll, 2011). Infants require longer sleep periods than adults do.

Therefore, it is important that normal sleep patterns are established early on after birth in order for both infants and caregivers to have appropriate sleep cycles. Middlemiss (2004) notes that there are several factors that affect sleep (normal sleep cycles as well as sleep disturbances): infant temperament, attachment, physiological states, caregiver presence during the sleep routine, sleeping arrangements, and the continuity of sleep disorders. Maintaining sleeping and waking periods throughout the day is a major developmental milestone for infants. Though normal sleep cycles may be difficult to achieve instantly, there are methods to obtain normal patterns as the infant develops.

Infant sleep has been broken down into four kinds of sleep patterns: awake (eyes opening or opening and closing), active sleep (movements of arms and legs, irregular breathing, and eye movement), quiet sleep (regular breathing patterns, no limb or eye movement), and transitional sleep (anything that does not fall into the previous categories). As infants age, their duration of active sleep compared to quiet sleep increases.

Wakefulness may be due to the need to nurse or feed, being overtired, soiled diapers, or attachment issues. Though these are not all the factors that can contribute to wakefulness, they are probably the most common. Wakefulness, especially at night, can affect caregiver sleep cycles as well. Caregivers may experience fatigue, poor maternal and paternal health, distress, depression, feeding difficulties, and problems in family life (Byars et al., 2011; Lopez-Wagner et al., 2008; Smart & Hiscock, 2007; Thome & Skuladottir, 2005). Often crying is associated with wakefulness, which causes sleep disturbances in both infants and caregivers (St. James-Roberts, 2007). Sleep disturbances have been found to increase with age only if appropriate interventions and sleep management methods are not used (Thome & Skuladottir, 2005). In addition, as children age, they are inclined to participate in problematic behaviors such as watching television, playing video games, using cell phones, or using the Internet that make them alert at night and influence sleep patterns and bedtime behavior (Lopez-Wagner et al., 2008).

For caregivers, sleep is important, not only for their mental well-being but for their ability to care for their child or children. Byars et al., (2011) found that infants with bedtime resistance and daytime sleepiness were associated with parental stress. Therefore, it is imperative that caregivers learn appropriate sleep management methods and interventions in order to allow themselves and their child or children restful sleep.

There are several methods that have been found to be useful when managing sleep in infants. Researchers recommend providing education about infant sleep cycles through parent consultation to promote healthy sleep management for infants (Adachi et al., 2009; Smart & Hiscock, 2007; Thome & Skuladottir, 2005). Caregivers were more likely to have positive results when using these methods than without the use of consultation and education about sleep cycles.

Behavioral approaches have been found to be an appropriate choice for providing sleep management techniques. Extinction, the **Ferber method**, and self-soothing are common strategies for sleep in infants. Extinction is described as extinguishing a behavior (such as infant crying) by removing reinforcing stimulus (such as caregiver attention) in order to gain the desired behavior (Crncec, Matthey, & Nemeth, 2010). There are several different kinds of extinction methods. Unmodified extinction, also known as the "cry-it-out" method, involves the caregiver putting the infant to bed and not attending to him or her until the next day (with the exception of the possibility of illness or danger). However, a recent study has associated this method with increased levels of toxic stress in the infant and is no longer encouraged (Shonkoff et al., 2012). The modified/graduated extinction or the use of the Ferber method is more commonly used and involves brief caregiver comfort when the infant is distressed and slowly reducing caregiver attention by waiting longer periods of time before coming into the room to comfort the infant (Crncec et al., 2010; Kuhn & Weidinger, 2000). Kuhn and Weidinger (2000) describe another extinction approach called extinction with parental presence. In this method, the caregiver stays in the room with the child, preferably in a different bed, until the child falls asleep. The child is aware of his or her caregiver's presence and may be comforted by this fact. Though there have been some criticisms of the latter two sleep strategies, there has not been a significant number of empirical studies that show they affect an infant's mental or emotional well-being (Price, Wake, Ukoumunne, & Hiscock, 2012).

Another method of sleep management involves immediate responding (Crncec et al., 2010). Though there are similarities between extinction and immediate responding, the latter requires caregivers to respond quickly to their infants if they show distress and rocking or nursing their infant until they become drowsy (Crncec et al., 2010). This method does not bring about success as quickly as the extinction methods, in particular the modified extinction method; however, studies have indicated that it is just as successful as the behavioral strategies and may be a more gentle approach for helping an infant sleep.

Positive bedtime routines can also be used when establishing normal sleep patterns. Caregivers reinforce appropriate sleep behavior by establishing relaxing activities intermingled with praise and encouragement. Once a routine is established with reinforcing behaviors from caregivers, the infant will fall asleep faster because of cues given by caregivers. Case Illustration 4.3 and Guided Practice Exercise 4.3 will both help you to further explore the role of the counselor with regard to infant sleep.

CASE ILLUSTRATION 4.3 SLEEPING ARRANGEMENTS AND INTIMACY

Brandon and Sheila are the parents of Maya. Maya is currently 1 year old. Maya has been sleeping in her parents' bed since she was a newborn. Brandon and Sheila are considering transitioning Maya to her own bed. Brandon feels very strongly about Maya being moved into her own room, but Sheila thinks it is easier to let her stay in the bed until Maya decides she wants to use her own bed. Brandon has told the counselor that he and Sheila have not been intimate since the birth of Maya. They have friends who offered to babysit Maya so that the couple could go on a date; however, Sheila does not want to leave their baby and often makes up excuses why they cannot go.

Practice Exercise:

The primary concern between the couple appears to be lack of intimacy, rather than the actual sleeping arrangements for the child. Currently, Brandon views the sleeping arrangement to be the primary reason for the lack of intimacy. However, couples who cosleep with their children can still be very much intimately involved, so the counselor needs to further explore the true reasons behind the lack of intimacy. Additionally, Sheila is not eager to go out on dates with her partner. Perhaps, she feels uncomfortable with her body or perhaps she has a hard time switching from the mother role into the partner role. Perhaps she feels guilty if she is not always available for the baby. The counselor may explore Sheila's feelings regarding her role as a mother versus that of an intimate partner. The counselor may also want to explore the marriage prior to the birth of Maya. What was the intimacy level then? What has changed in the overall relationship (not related to intimacy) between Brandon and Sheila?

Finally, if both partners still want to transition Maya into her own room, then the counselor needs to discuss strategies for a successful transition. Have the parents tried? If so, how did it go? Sheila indicates that she believes it is too soon to move Maya into her own room. So, how is she feeling at night when she puts Maya to bed? Is Maya allowed to come into the parents' bed when she awakens in the middle of the night, or is she put back into her own bed? The couple needs to be reminded that a gradual transition is best, and that the child should not be left alone to cry herself to sleep. This transition may also be taxing on the parents as everyone's sleep is disturbed until the transition is complete. Therefore, the counselor needs to encourage the parents to schedule a time that works well for both of them before beginning this process. For example, initiating this transition during a particularly stressful week at the office is not advisable.

Guided Practice Exercise 4.3

Sleep tends to be a major concern for many new parents. What are your beliefs about cosleeping (having the infant sleep in the same room as the parent(s) versus having the infant sleep in a separate room)? Where do these beliefs come from? How can you work with parents to help them keep their emotional and physical intimacy but also foster a close, secure attachment with their infant?

SUMMARY

- At birth, an infant has poor control of his or her muscles; however, babies are born with certain reflexes, such as the Moro reflex, rooting reflex, and grasp reflex.
- As newborns, babies can discriminate between speech sounds.
- While the brain has grown exponentially during prenatal development, it continues to develop at a rapid pace during the first 3 years of life. It is during this time that a young child's experiences literally shape the neural connections in the brain.
- Supportive relationships help children develop trust, compassion, and empathy.
- Although all infants express universal emotions, the frequency and use of these emotions is influenced by the child's culture, adult-child interactions, and context.
- Researchers and practitioners consider social referencing, temperament, self-regulation, and attachment as constructs of emotional development.
- Healthy nutrition and a supportive environment are critical to the development of an infant.
- Breastfeeding is highly recommended, as is delaying solid foods until after 4 to 6 months of age.
- Because infants are natural explorers, safety is a primary concern.
- Counselors can work with parents with issues such as depression, difficulties with discipline, fostering a secure attachment, decisions regarding child care options, and figuring out a healthy sleep schedule for the entire family.

ADDITIONAL RESOURCES

Websites

http://www.askdrsears.com
http://www.babycenter.com
http://www.cdc.gov/parents/infants/index.html
http://www.nlm.nih.gov/medlineplus/infantandnewborncare.html

Videos

BabyCenter. (2012). *Baby videos*. Retrieved from http://www.babycenter.com/video/baby.
March of Dimes Foundation. (2011). *Baby care 101*. Retrieved from http://www.marchofdimes.com/baby/care.html.

National Association of Child Care Resource & Referral Agencies. (2012). *Watch videos of child care best practices*. Retrieved from http://www.childcareaware.org/parents-and-guardians/helpful-tools/.

Olaf, M. (n.d.). *Child development stages from birth to three years*. Retrieved from http://www.michaelolaf.net/BirthtoThreeDevelopment.html.

Recommended Supplemental Readings

Books

Sears, M., & Sears, W. (2000). *The breastfeeding book*. New York, NY: Little, Brown.

Sears, W., & Sears, M. (2003). *The baby book*. New York, NY: Little, Brown.

Sears, W., Sears, R., Sears, J., & Sears, M. (2005). *The baby sleep book*. New York, NY: Little, Brown.

References

Adachi, T., Chifumi, S., Nishino, N., Ohryoji, F., Hayama, J., & Yamagami, T. (2009). A brief parental education for shaping sleep habits in 4-month-old infants. *Clinical Medicine & Research, 7,* 85–92.

Ainsworth, M. D. S. (1989). Attachment beyond infancy. *American Psychologist, 44,* 709–716.

Ainsworth, M. D. S., Blehar, M. C., Waters, E., & Wall, S., (1978). *Patterns of attachment: A psychological study of the strange situation*. Hillsdale, NJ: Erlbaum.

American Academy of Family Physicians. (2014). *2014 recommended immunization schedules serve as reminder to vaccinate*. Retrieved from http://www.aafp.org/news/health-of-the-public/20140219immunizsched.html.American

Academy of Pediatrics. (2001). The use and misuse of fruit juice in pediatrics. Pediatrics, 107(5), 1210–1213.

American Academy of Pediatrics. (2012). Policy statement. Breastfeeding and the use of human milk. *Pediatrics, 115*(2), 496.

American Academy of Pediatrics. (2014). AAP policy. Retrieved from http://pediatrics.aappublications.org/site/aappolicy/index.xhtml.

American Academy of Pediatrics & American Academy of Periodontics. (1978). Juice in ready-to-use bottles and nursing bottle carries. *AAP News and Comment, 29,* 11.

American Academy of Pediatrics, & Hassink, S. G. (2006). *A parent's guide to childhood obesity: A road map to health*. Elk Grove Village, IL: Author.

American Congress of Obstetricians and Gynecologists. (2014). *Immunization*. Retrieved from http://www.acog.org/About_ACOG/ACOG_Departments/Immunization.

Barton, E. A., & Ratner, H. H. (2001). *Perceptions of "spoiling" and its relations to experience and ethnicity. Occasional Paper Series, 2*. Detroit, MI: Wayne State University, College of Urban, Labor, and Metropolitan Affairs.

Beauchamp, G. K., & Mennella, J. A. (2009). Early flavor learning and its impact on later feeding behavior. *Journal of Pediatric Gastroenterology and Nutrition, 28*(1), S25–30.

Blair, C., Granger, D., Willoughby, M., & Kivlighan, K. (2006). Maternal sensitivity is related to hypothalamic-pituitary-adrenal axis stress reactivity and regulation in response to emotion challenge in 6-month-old infants. *Annals of the New York Academy of Sciences, (1094),* 263–267.

Bogin, B. (2001). *The growth of humanity*. New York, NY: Wiley-Liss.

Bowlby, J. (1969/1982). *Attachment and loss, Vol. 1: Attachment*. New York, NY: Basic Books.

Bowlby, J. (1979). *The making and breaking of affectional bonds*. London, England: Tavistock.

Braungart-Rieker, J. M., Garwood, M. M., Powers, B. P., & Wang, X. (2001). Parental sensitivity, infant affect, and affect regulation: Predictors of later attachment. *Child Development, 72,* 252–270.

Bugental, D. B., & Happaney, K. (2000). Parent–child interaction as a power contest. *Journal of Applied Developmental Psychology, 21,* 267–282.

Bugental, D. B., & Happaney, K. (2004). Predicting infant maltreatment in low-income families: The interactive effects of maternal attributions and child status at birth. *Developmental Psychology, 40,* 234–243.

Burchinal, M., Skinner, D., & Reznick, J. S. (2010). European American and African American mothers' beliefs about parenting and disciplining infants: A mixed-method analysis. *Parenting: Science and Practice, 10*, 79–96.

Byars, K. C., Yeomans-Maldonado, G., & Noll, J. G. (2011). Parental functioning and pediatric sleep disturbance: An examination of factors associated with parenting stress in children clinically referred for evaluation of insomnia. *Sleep Medicine, 12*, 898–905.

Centers for Disease Control and Prevention. (2014a). *Advisory committee on immunization practices (ACIP)*. Retrieved from http://www.cdc.gov/vaccines/acip/index.html.

Centers for Disease Control and Prevention. (2014b*). Possible side-effects from vaccines*. Retrieved from http://www.cdc.gov/vaccines/vac-gen/side-effects.htm#mmr.

Crncec, R., Matthey, S., & Nemeth, D. (2010). Infant sleep problems and emotional health: A review of two behavioral approaches. *Journal of Reproductive and Infant Psychology, 28*, 44–54.

Davidov, M., & Grusec, J. E. (2006). Untangling the links of parental responsiveness to distress and warmth to child outcomes. *Child Development, 77*(1), 44–58.

Dearing, E., McCartney, K., & Taylor, B. A. (2009). Does higher quality early child care promote low-income children's math and reading achievement in middle childhood? *Child Development, 80*, 1329–1349.

Diego, M., Field, T., & Hernandex-Reif, M. (2005). Vagal activity, gastric motility, and weight gain in massaged preterm neonates. *Journal of Pediatrics, 147*(1), 50–55.

Easterbrooks, M. A., Biesecker, G., & Lyons-Ruth, K. (2000). Infancy predictors of emotional availability in middle childhood: The roles of attachment security and maternal depressive symptomatology. *Attachment & Human Development, 2*(2), 170–187.

Erikson, E. H. (1959). *Identity and the life cycle*. New York, NY: International Universities Press.

Guzell, J. R., & Vernon-Feagans, L. (2004). Parental perceived control over caregiving and its relationship to parent–infant interaction. *Child Development, 75*, 134–146.

Halfon, N., Shulman, E., & Hochstein, M. (2001). *Brain development in early childhood*. Retrieved from http://www.healthychild.ucla.edu/Publications/Documents/ halfon.health.dev.pdf.

Harkness, S., & Super, C. M. (2006). Themes and variations: Parental ethno-theories in Western cultures. In K. Rubin & O. B. Chung (Eds.), *Parenting beliefs, behaviors, and parent–child relations: A cross-cultural perspective* (pp. 61–80). London, UK: Psychology Press.

Hedin, K., Petersson, C., Cars, H., Beckman, A., & Hakansson, A. (2006). Infection prevention at day-care centres: Feasibility and possible effects of intervention. *Scandinavian Journal of Primary Health Care, 24*, 44–49.

Hernandez-Reif, M., Diego, M., & Field, T. (2007). Preterm infants show reduced stress behaviors and activity after 5 days of massage therapy. *Infant Behavior and Development, 30*(4), 557–561.

Hoehl, S., Wiese, L., & Striano, T. (2008). Young infants' neural processing of objects is affected by eye gaze direction and emotional expression. *PLOS ONE, 3*(6), e 2389.

Institute of Medicine. (2004). Immunization safety review: Vaccines and Autism. Retrieved from http://www.iom.edu/reports/2004/immunization-safety-review-vaccines-and-autism.aspx.

Ipsa, J. M., Fine, M. A., Halgunseth, L. C., Harper, S., Robinson, J., Boyce, L. . . . Brandy-Smith, C. (2004). Maternal intrusive-ness, maternal warmth, and mother toddler relationship outcomes: Variations across low-income ethnic and acculturation groups. *Child Development, 75*, 1613–1631.

Keller, H. (2007). *Cultures of infancy*. Mahwah, NJ: Erlbaum.

Kerns K. A., Abraham, M. M., Schlegelmilch, A., & Morgan, T. A. (2007). Mother-child attachment in later middle childhood: Assessment approaches and associations with mood and emotion regulation. *Attachment & Human Development, 9*(1), 33–53.

Kisilevsky, B. S., Hains, S. M. J., Brown, C. A., Lee, C. T., Cowperthwaite, B., Stutzman, S. S. . . . Wang, Z. (2009). Fetal sensitivity to properties of maternal speech and language. *Infant Behavior and Development, 32*, 59–71.

Kisilevsky, B. S., Hains, S. M. J., Lee, K., Xie, X., Huang, H., Ye, H. H. . . . Wang, Z. (2003). Effects of experience on fetal voice recognition. *Psychological Science, 14*(3), 220–224.

Kochanska, G., & Murray, K. T. (2000). Mother-child mutually responsive orientation and conscience development: From toddler to early school age. *Child Development, 71*, 417–431.

Kuhl, P. K., Stevens, E., Hayashi, A., Deguchi, T., Kiritani, S., & Iverson, P. (2006). Infants show facilitation for native language phonetic perception between 6 and 12 months. *Developmental Science, 9*, 13–21.

Kuhl, P. K., Tsao, F. M., & Liu, H. M. (2003). Foreign-language experience in infancy: Effects of short-term exposure and social interaction on phonetic learning. *Proceedings of the National Academy of Sciences, 100*, 9096–9101.

Kuhn, B. R., & Weidinger, D. (2000). Interventions for infant and toddler sleep disturbance: A review. *Child & Family Behavior Therapy, 22*, 33–50.

Landry S. H., Smith K. E., & Swank, P. R. (2003). The importance of parenting during early childhood for school-age development. *Developmental Neuropsychology, 24*(2–3), 559–591.

Landry S. H., Smith K. E., & Swank, P. R. (2006). Responsive parenting: Establishing early foundations for social, communication, and independent problem-solving skills. *Developmental Psychology, 42*(4), 627–642.

Leathers, H. D., & Foster, P. (2004). *The world food problem: Tackling the causes of under-nutrition in the Third World.* Boulder, CO: Lynne Rienner.

LeCanuet, J., & Schaal, B. (2002). Sensory performances in the human fetus: A brief summary of research. *Intellectica, 1*(34), 29–56.

Leo, I., & Simion, F. (2009). Face processing at birth: A Thatcher Illusion study. *Developmental Science, 12*(3), 492–498.

Lopez-Wagner, M. C., Hoffman, C. D., Sweeney, D. P., Hodge, D., & Gilliam, J. E. (2008). Sleep problems of parents of typically developing children and parents of children with autism. *The Journal of Genetic Psychology, 169*, 245–259.

Lu, N., Samuels, M. E., Shi, L., Baker, S. L., Glover, S. H., & Sanders, J. M. (2004). Child day care risks of common infectious diseases revisited. *Child: Care, Health, & Development, 30*, 361–368.

McElwain, N. L., Cox, M. J., Burchinal, M. R., & Macfie, J. (2003). Differentiating among insecure mother-infant attachment classifications: A focus on child-friend interaction and exploration during solitary play at 36 months. *Attachment & Human Development, 5*(2), 136–164.

Mercer J. (2006). *Understanding attachment: Parenting, child care, and emotional development.* Westport, CT: Praeger.

Middlemiss, W. (2004). Infant sleep: A review of normative and problematic sleep interventions. *Early Child Development and Care, 174*, 99–122.

Nafstad, P., Jaakkola, J. J. K., Skrondal, A., & Magnus, P. (2004). Day care center characteristics and children's respiratory health. *Indoor Air, 15*, 69–75.

Pickert, K. (2012). Are you mom enough? *Times Magazine, 179*, 20.

Pomares, C. G., Schirrer, J., & Abadie, V. (2002). Analysis of the olfactory capacity of healthy children before language acquisition. *Journal of Developmental Behavior and Pediatrics, 23*, 203–207.

Price, A. M. H., Wake, M., Ukoumunne, O. C., & Hiscock, H. (2012). Five-year follow-up of harms and benefits of behavioral infant sleep intervention: Randomized trial. *Pediatrics, 130*, 209–213.

Price, C. S., Thompson, W. W., Goodson, B., Weintraub, E. S., Croen, L. A., Hinrichsen, V. L. . . . DeStefano, F. (2010). Prenatal and infant exposure to thimerosal from vaccines and immunoglobulins and risk of autism. *Pediatrics, 126*(4), 656–664.

Quinn, P. C., Yahr, J., Kuhn, A., Slater, A. M., & Pascalis, O. (2002). Representation of the gender of human faces by infants: A preference for female. *Perception, 31*, 1109–1121.

Rivera-Gaxiola, M., Silvia-Pereyra, J., & Kuhl, P. K. (2008). Brain potentials to native and non-native speech contrasts in 7- and 11-month-old American infants. *Developmental Science, 8*(2), 162–172.

Rochat, P. (2007). Intentional action arises from early reciprocal exchanges. *Acta Psychology, 124*(1), 8–25.

Rubin, K., & Chung, O. B. (Eds.). (2006). *Parenting beliefs, behaviors, and parent–child relations: A cross-cultural perspective.* London, UK: Psychology Press.

Sangrigoli S., & de Schonen S. (2004a). Effect of visual experience on face processing: A developmental study of inversion and non-native effects. *Developmental Science, 7*, 74–87.

Sangrigoli S., & de Schonen S. (2004b). Recognition of own-race and other-race faces by three-month-old infants. *Journal of Child Psychology and Psychiatry and Allied Disciplines, 45*, 1219–1227.

Schaal, B., Marlier, B., & Soussignan, R. (2000). Human fetuses learn odors from their pregnant mother's diet. *Chemical Senses, 25*, 729–737. Retrieved from http://chemse.oxfordjournalCode = chemse&resid = 25/6/729.

Shonkoff, J. P., Garner, A. S., The Committee on Psychosocial Aspects of Child and Family Health, Committee on Early Childhood, Adoption, and Dependent Care, Section on Developmental and Behavioral Pediatrics, Siegel, B. S., Dobbins, M. I., Earls, M. F. . . . Wood, D. L. (2012). The lifelong effects of early childhood adversity and toxic stress. *American Academy of Pediatrics, 129*(1), e232-e246. doi: 10.1542/peds.2011-2663

Sigel, I. E., & McGillicuddy-DeLisi, A. V. (2002). Parent beliefs are cognitions: The dynamic belief systems model. In M. H. Bornstein (Ed.), *Handbook of parenting* (2nd ed.), pp. 485–508. Mahwah, NJ: Erlbaum.

Smart, J., & Hiscock, H. (2007). Early infant crying and sleeping problems: A pilot study of impact on parental well-being and parent-endorsed strategies for management. *Journal of Pediatrics and Child Health, 43*, 284–290.

Smyke, A. T., Boris, N. W., & Alexander, G. M. (2002). Fear of spoiling in at-risk African American mothers. *Child Psychiatry and Human Development, 32*, 295–307.

Society for Neuroscience. (2009). *Brain facts. A primer on the brain and nervous system.* Retrieved from: http://www.sfn.org/skins/main/pdf/brainfacts/2008/brain_facts.pdf.

St. James-Roberts, I. (2007). Helping parents to manage infant crying and sleeping: A review of the evidence and its implications for services. *Child Abuse Review,16,* 47–69.

Suman, R. P., Udani, R., & Nanavati, R. (2008). Kangaroo mother care for low birth weight infants: A randomized controlled trial. *Indian Journal of Pediatrics, 45*(1), 17–23.

Thiessen, E. D., Hill, E. A., & Saffran, J. R. (2005). Infant-directed speech facilitates word segmentation. *Infancy, 7*(1), 53–71. doi: 10.1207/s15327078in0701_5

Thomas, A., Chess, S., Birch, H., Hertzig, M., & Korn, S, (1963). *Behavioral individuality in early childhood.* New York: New York University Press.

Thomas, M. S. C., & Johnson, M. H. (2008). New advances in understanding sensitive periods in brain development. *Association for Pscyhological Science, 17*(1), 1–5.

Thome, M., & Skuladottir, A. (2005). Changes in sleep problems, parents' distress, and impact of sleep problems from infancy to preschool age for referred and unreferred children. *Scandinavian Journal of Caring Science, 19,* 86–94.

Van Zeijl, J., Mesman, J., Van IJzendoorn, M. H., Bakermans-Kranenburg, M. J., Juffer, F., Stolk, M. N. . . . Alink, L. R. (2006). Attachment-based intervention for enhancing sensitive discipline in mothers of 1- to 3-year-old children at risk for externalizing behavior problems: A randomized controlled trial. *Journal of Consulting and Clinical Psychology, 74*(6), 994–1005.

Wakefield, A. J., Murch, S. H, Anthony, A., Linnell, J., Casson, D. M., Malik, M. . . . Walker-Smith, J. A. (1998). Ileal-lymphoid-nodular hyperplasia, non-specific colitis, and pervasive developmental disorder in children. *Lancet, 351*(9103), 637–41. doi:10.1016/S0140–6736(97)11096–0 (Retracted)

Waynforth, D. (2007). The influence of parent-infant co-sleeping, nursing, and child care on cortisol and SIGA immunity in a sample of British children. *Developmental Psychobiology, 49*(6), 640–648.

Worku, B., & Kassie, A. (2005). Kangaroo mother care: A randomized controlled trail on effectiveness of early kangaroo mother care for the low birth weight infants in Addis Ababa, Ethiopia. *Journal of Tropical Pediatrics, 51*(2), 93–97.

Zmiri, P., Rubin, L., Akons, H., Zion, N., & Shaoul, R. (2011). The effect of day care attendance on infant and toddler's growth. *Acta Paediatrica, 100,* 266–270.

Toddlerhood (Ages 1 to 3)

> You are worried about seeing him spend his early years in doing nothing.
> What?! Is it nothing to be happy? Nothing like to skip, play, and run around all
> day long? Never in his life will he be so busy again.
>
> Jean-Jacques Rousseau

What a beautiful depiction of toddlerhood. More importantly, Rousseau's statement can serve as a needed and valued directive for all those parents who are overly invested in providing their child with the latest technology gadget or educational video game all in hopes of stimulating their advancement. While loving and caring parents do want to do what is best to foster the development of their child, they must be remembered that the work of a toddler is play, and their running, skipping, and imaginative play stimulate and promote development in ways that technology, videos, and flash cards cannot.

This chapter will discuss development during ages one to three focusing on the changes and emerging characteristics of physical, cognitive, and social/emotional development. In addition, the chapter reviews risks to healthy development and the special areas of service for which a counselor's intervention and prevention programming could prove beneficial. Specifically, after reading this chapter, you will be able to

1. describe typical physical, cognitive, and social/emotional development of toddlers;

2. relate various theories of development to toddler development;

3. examine common risks to healthy toddler development;

4. determine areas of counseling that may be needed for parents, including prevention and intervention strategies; and

5. distinguish areas of consultation that can be provided with other health care providers.

Healthy Toddler Development

While the first 12 months of life include vast changes in development, toddlerhood allows us to see the child's personality begin to develop. From an infant who could not lift his own head, the child has grown into a person who runs, responds to your words, and expresses his preferences. While toddlerhood is often referred to as the *terrible 2s,* it is actually a wondrous time to examine the establishment of independence and boundaries.

Physical Development

Compared with infancy development, **physical development** seems to slow during the toddler years, as you can see in Table 5.1. By 2 years of age, the toddler perfects the gross and fine motor skills that emerged during infancy by further developing balance, coordination, and stability. Toys that stimulate a baby's walking and age-appropriate climbing will further develop his balance and coordination. The child is also much better at manipulating objects. By the age of 3 years old, the toddler increases body strength and is able to master challenges such as tricycles and appropriate playground equipment. Additionally, between the ages of 2 and 3, the child should be developmentally ready to begin toilet training, which we will discuss in more detail later in this chapter.

Table 5.1   Toddlerhood 12 to 36 Months Old

Age	Physical	Cognitive	Social/Emotional
12 to 24	Weight is 3Xs birth weight Rate of growth slows Respiration varies with emotional and activity state Chest circumference is larger than head circumference baby fat reduces as child becomes more mobile Body begins to take on a more adult appearance Anterior fontanelle closes (soft spots) Legs may appear bowed, back is swayed, and abdomen protrudes Develops more complex motor skills Is walking and crawling quickly Climbs up and down stairs Turns pages in books Stacks objects Helps feed self Enjoys pushing/pulling toys Uses markers and crayons drawing with whole arm movement	Enjoys hiding objects Looks for hidden objects Puts toys in mouth less often Names many objects Manages 3 or 4 objects during play Has better understanding of shapes and how objects work together Tries to copy how a person makes something work Has increased facial expression understanding Points to objects and familiar people Enjoys rhymes and songs Speech is 25% to 50% intelligible	Is less wary of strangers Helps pick up objects Wants to play Recognizes self in the mirror Throws tantrums when things go wrong or is tired or frustrated Has increasing curiosity about people and environment Pays close attention to keeping self out of unsafe situations Imitates adults Often refuses daily routines Enjoys helping with daily chores or activities Often says " I can do it myself" Parallel and symbolic play

Age	Physical	Cognitive	Social/Emotional
24 to 36	Posture is more erect	Eye-hand movement improves	Shows signs of empathy
	Brain development at 80%	Uses objects for a purpose	Offers kisses and hugs
	Has 16 baby teeth growing out	Can conduct simple classification; sorts toys, clothes, food	Demonstrates physical aggression during frustration
	Balances on one foot		May be impatient or have difficulty with sharing
	Opens door with door knob	Is extremely curious about cause and effect, what happens and where things go	Enjoys helping around home
	Uses feet to make toy move		Offers toys to others
	Climbs up and down on objects		Throws more frequent temper tantrums. Choices are difficult and overwhelming
	Toilet training	Understands family and familiar faces, questions presence and absence, notices changes	
	Grasp is much stronger and controlled		
	Unzips large zippers		Mood changes rapidly
	Unbuttons large buttons	Expresses pain	Shows pride in accomplishments
	Jumps up and down; however, still clumsy	Imaginary play is frequent	Is overly enthusiastic at times
		Can explain and discuss objects or previous events	Is emotionally attached to objects
	Throws underhanded		
	Squats for periods of time	Speech is 65% to 70% intelligible	
	Communication becomes increasingly better through gestures, movements, and words	Asks a lots of questions	
		Listens attentively	
	Can move objects around and begins problem solving	Pretends to read	
	Baby fat disappears and neck appears		
	Tiptoe walking		
	Reaches 50% of height		
	Legs grow faster than arms		
	Jumps off of objects		

Sensory and Perceptual Development. At around 18 months of age, children begin to use their senses to change the way they interact with the environment. For example, a child may adjust his steps depending on the type of surface he is walking on, or he may choose to slide down a steep embankment instead of walking upright. By 36 months, children can more quickly use their senses to adjust their interaction with the environment. For example, a child may quickly realize that he needs to walk more slowly with an open cup of water compared to a lidded cup of water.

Motor Development. Between the ages of 12 and 18 months, a child develops strength, balance, and coordination to walk. By age 2, she or he may be able to climb well, walk up and down stairs while holding on for support, kick a ball, and run short distances. Finally, by the age of 3, a child should be running, jumping, and climbing on age-appropriate playground equipment. Because a 2- to 3- year-old is so active, supervision is critical at this age to prevent accidents.

A baby's fine motor skills also improve during this time. Between 12 and 18 months of age, a baby can pick up small objects and build a simple stack of blocks. By 24 months, a child can mold play-dough, put round and square pegs into holes, and turn rotating handles. At this age, a child may enjoy coloring with crayons and will begin to hold and drink from a cup. By the age of 3, a child should begin to show a preference for one hand over the other. Activities such as large-piece puzzles, big blocks, and musical toys can help further enhance fine motor development. The traditional playing in sand boxes with scoops, measuring cups, and toy trucks will also further develop fine motor muscles and develop early recognition of volume and size.

Language development. While physical growth may seem to slow, language development flourishes during this time. Between the ages of 12 and 18 months, in particular, most children dramatically increase their use of language. The baby develops a greater understanding of words spoken to him or her, but the inability to use expressive language skills may lead to crying, tantrums, and biting, which we will discuss later. Caregivers should listen carefully and allow the child time to express himself or herself. Waiting for approximately 10 seconds may encourage the child to speak more. Caregivers can also model language for the child by describing in simple words what the child is doing as he or she is doing it. Narrating daily activities helps the child associate words with what he or she is doing.

By the age of 24 months, a child may have a familiar vocabulary of about 50 words and may speak in short sentences of one to three words. While he or she may not be able to say all of the words that he or she has learned, he or she can often point to objects when you say the word. By the age of 3, a child may have a vocabulary of between 50 and 250 words. The child will begin to ask "why" a lot. This may become increasingly frustrating for caregivers, but we strongly encourage patiently answering these questions to encourage language development.

Cognitive Development

Toddlers become aware of cause and effect and will often throw objects to see the caregiver's response. This typically becomes a game and will continue as long as the caregiver provides a response. Children become interested in objects that move and begin to prefer action toys. Hide-and-seek is also a wonderful game that toddlers thoroughly enjoy. They become interested in hiding themselves as well as hiding toys. Children also begin their first imitative play activities, often by imitating adult tasks such as caretaking and housekeeping.

By 18 months, children respond to directions, begin to use objects as tools, and can solve simple problems such as using one object to reach another. By 24 months, children become more aware of themselves as individuals. They will begin to identify with their toys and will not want to share them. They will also begin showing preferences. While they may show frustration when they cannot do what they want, they can also be easily redirected. Offering choices, rather than saying "no" can help to minimize tantrums and give them a sense of control. By the age of 3, children begin to develop memories.

Social and Emotional Development

Toddlerhood is a wondrous time but can also be challenging for parents and caregivers. A major theme running through this period of development is the increasing movement toward the child's establishment of **autonomy**, including mastery and control over oneself and one's environment. This push toward independence is both exciting and challenging for child and parent, alike (Erikson, 1963). See Table 2.2 in Chapter 2 (Erikson's Stages of Psychosocial Development) to review the stage of autonomy versus shame and doubt. It is the source of parental laments about the terrible 2s, and yet similarly, parental joy of potty training and various forms of self-care (e.g., feeding).

Counselors can help parents and caregivers understand that this drive for independence is to be seen as a wonderful event rather than a child misbehaving. A child needs to develop himself or herself as separate from the parent, as someone who has individual emotions and thoughts. When parents reframe challenging behaviors into efforts to learn independence, then many misbehaviors are no longer seen as such. During this time, children develop a basic self-concept, which includes experiencing pride for displaying good behavior and embarrassment or distress at displaying bad behavior.

Children's social development begins with an affectionate and trusting relationship with other family members and adults outside of the family, but by the age of 3, children begin to develop relationships with other children. However, children do not begin to actively play with other children until later. At this time, children engage in **parallel play**, which is play in the presence of, rather than in interaction with, other children. Therefore, it is a good idea to have plenty of toys that children can play with so that they do not fight over one toy in particular.

By the age of one, many children will engage in **imitative play**, most often by imitating the caregiver. Children will often choose toys such as a play cell phone, purses, vacuums, pots/pans, and so on to imitate behaviors that they observe Mom or Dad doing. Baby dolls are important for both boys and girls at this age, since they pretend that they are either the mommy or daddy and will engage in caretaking behaviors, such as feeding, washing, and reprimanding them. These actions help the brain develop. During imitative play, children learn adult behaviors by taking on the role of a caregiver, develop empathy and emotional intelligence by caring for the baby doll, and create connections within the brain from imaginative thought. Play is critical to the healthy development of a child.

Photo 5.1   Pretend play is a fun aspect of toddler development.

Risks to Healthy Toddler Development

Unfortunately, not all toddlers experience healthy development. Genetics and environment play a critical role in the development of the human species. This section will describe a few circumstances that can put a child at risk for unhealthy development.

Child Maltreatment

While child maltreatment can occur throughout childhood and adolescence, it most often begins during this stage of development as toddlers begin to assert their independence. Each state supplies its own definitions of child abuse and neglect based on minimum standards set by federal law. The federal **Child Abuse Prevention and Treatment Act (CAPTA)**, reauthorized in 2010, defines child abuse as, at minimum (a) any recent act or failure to act on the part of a parent or caretaker that results in death, serious physical or emotional harm, sexual abuse or exploitation; or (b) an act or failure to act that presents an imminent risk of serious harm. Most states recognize four major types of maltreatment: physical abuse, neglect, sexual abuse, and emotional abuse. Multiple forms of **child maltreatment** are often seen in combination, although in some cases they are found separately.

Keeping in mind that state definitions vary, the following are examples of what most states consider child maltreatment. **Physical abuse** is commonly associated as nonaccidental physical injury inflicted by a parent, caregiver, or other person who is responsible for the child. Injuries range from minor bruises to severe fractures or death as a result of punching, beating, kicking, biting, shaking, throwing, stabbing, hitting, burning, or otherwise harming a child. Hitting can be identified through the use of a stick, strap, hand, or other objects. Such physical discipline as spanking and paddling is not considered abuse as long as it is supported as reasonable and does not cause bodily harm to the child. Any injury, as stated previously, is considered abuse regardless of whether the caregiver intended to harm the child.

Neglect is often defined as failure of a parent, guardian, or other caregiver to provide for a child's basic needs. It can be in the form of physical neglect, medical neglect, educational neglect, or emotional neglect. Physical neglect is most commonly constituted as failure to provide necessary food or shelter or lack of appropriate supervision. Medical neglect is failure to provide necessary medical or mental health treatment. Failure to educate a child or attend to special educational needs is known as educational neglect. Emotional neglect is considered as absence of attention to a child's emotional needs, failure to provide psychological care, or permitting the child to use alcohol or other drugs. Many states have now begun to recognize abandonment and parental substance abuse as forms of neglect. Abandonment is identified when the child has been left alone in circumstances when he or she suffers serious harm, the parent has failed to maintain contact with the child or provide reasonable support for a specified period of time, or if the parent's identity or whereabouts are unknown. In some states, parental substance abuse can also be regarded as maltreatment when a child is prenatally exposed to substances that cause harm to the child. Other instances involving substance abuse as a form of maltreatment include using a controlled substance when supervising a child; manufacturing controlled substances, such as methamphetamines, in the presence of a child; or selling, distributing, or giving illegal drugs or alcohol to a child.

Sexual abuse is defined by CAPTA as the employment, use, persuasion, inducement, enticement, or coercion of any child to engage in, or assist any other person to engage in, any sexually explicit conduct or simulation of such conduct for the purpose of producing a visual depiction of such conduct; or the rape, and in cases of caretaker or interfamilial relationships, statutory rape, molestation, prostitution, or other form of sexual exploitation of children or incest with children. In more general terms, sexual abuse includes activities such as fondling a child's genitals, penetration, incest, rape, sodomy, indecent exposure, and exploitation through prostitution or the production of pornographic materials by a parent or caregiver.

Emotional abuse, also known as **psychological abuse**, is determined as a pattern of behavior that impairs a child's emotional development or sense of self-worth. This form of maltreatment is most always present when other forms are identified, although it is difficult to prove. It may include constant criticism, threats, or rejection, as well as withholding love, support, or guidance.

As a counselor, you will most certainly come into contact with victims of child maltreatment or their families. It is imperative that you have knowledge about the signs and symptoms of the various types of maltreatment and procedures for reporting concerns. Early identification and reporting of abuse reduces further harm to the victim. Children who are abused can suffer a multitude of behavioral and emotional struggles, including depression, anxiety, low self-esteem, substance abuse, eating disorders, and the repetition of the cycle of abuse. As a counselor, you are mandated to report any reasonable suspicion of child abuse. We encourage you to complete the Guided Practice Exercise 5.1 to further help you explore laws and reporting procedures for your state.

Guided Practice Exercise 5.1

Unfortunately, child maltreatment occurs throughout the world; however, the laws regarding child maltreatment vary. Research the laws related to child maltreatment in your area. What is considered maltreatment, and what is not? Who is a mandated reporter? What are the consequences of not reporting? Once you determine the definition of child maltreatment for your area, locate the local hotline number for child abuse reporting, as well as the procedures for reporting. What information should you have when you call? What are the criteria for the acceptance of a report?

Developmental Delays and Learning Disabilities

Unfortunately, some children struggle with developmental milestones and may experience developmental delays, which can lead to learning disabilities later in life. While not all developmental delays and disabilities can be prevented, some conditions can be treated or eliminated with early detection and treatment. Learning ways to recognize, treat, and prevent developmental delays in babies and young children is vital in working with parents to help their children be successful.

Counselors can work with local public health agencies to provide educational programs for women who are pregnant or are considering becoming pregnant. These workshops can provide screening services to determine risk levels and offer information to help a mother improve her health to give the child the best possible start in life. Counselors can work with pregnant mothers to eliminate poor lifestyle habits, including smoking and substance abuse. If taken before and during pregnancy, folic acid can also help prevent neural tube defects or spina bifida.

After birth, counselors can encourage parents to have their child's hearing and vision examined if it was not examined in the hospital after birth. Early treatment and intervention for hearing problems can lessen the impact of this on language development, while early intervention with visual problems may sometimes reverse the problem altogether. Immunizations are also important to discuss with parents. Many may be concerned about the potential side effects, so counselors should encourage them to seek out information and discuss the risks and benefits with their pediatrician. Another issue that parents may want to discuss is metabolic blood screening. The March of Dimes (2013) recommends 31 screenings and provides public information about each of them, which can be helpful for parents.

While learning disabilities are often not diagnosed until a child has been in school for a few years, there are often early signs that parents may notice, which can also lead to earlier interventions. Table 5.2 outlines early risk factors for learning disabilities. It is important to note that while the presence of these early risk factors does not cause a child to have a learning disability, it does indicate a need to monitor the child for possible early intervention.

Table 5.2   Risk Factors for Learning Disabilities

Prenatal Risk Factor	Environmental Risk Factors	Developmental Risk Factor
Family history of learning disabilities	Poverty	Developmental delay with gross motor skills, such as crawling, walking, or jumping
Prenatal injuries affecting neurological development	Injuries or long-term illnesses affecting neurological development	Developmental delay with fine motor skills, such as grasping
Poor prenatal medical care and nutrition	Abuse and neglect	Developmental delay with communication skills, such as struggling with understanding language or inability to use speech
Prenatal injury or delivery complications	Parental substance abuse	Developmental delay with cognitive skills, such as struggling to solve developmentally appropriate problems
Maternal substance abuse or exposure to environmental toxins	Exposure to environmental toxins	Developmental delay with social/emotional skills, such as the inability to interact appropriately with others or show appropriate emotional responses

Counselors should encourage parents to schedule a meeting with the child's teacher after the first few months of preschool to share any concerns and to inquire if the child is on track with development when compared to other children. In the United States, the Individuals with Disabilities Act (IDEA) is a federal law that requires appropriate services be provided for children with disabilities. Infants and toddlers, from birth to 25 months, receive early intervention services under IDEA Part C, while children ages 3 to 21 receive services under IDEA Part B (U.S. Department of Education, n.d.). Public school districts provide screening and assessment for developmental delays so that early intervention can begin.

Furthermore, programs such as Zero to Three (2012), a national nonprofit organization, provide parents, professionals, and policy makers with the knowledge and skills to nurture early child development. This program provides information related to early childhood development, behavior, maltreatment, and public policy. The program also provides information specifically related to military families.

Early Head Start is another program offered in the United States that focuses on healthy early childhood development. This program is available for low-income families and provides services such as home visits, family center activities, center-based child care, and referrals to other community resources. This program also offers prenatal services to encourage a healthy pregnancy and birth.

It is important for counselor to be aware of the services that are provided for parents and their young children. These services can offer additional support to parents who are struggling, answers to parenting questions, and can calm fears related to child development. Remaining vigilant and staying up to date on early childhood laws and regulations and these additional resources is critical if we truly want to help parents nurture healthy toddlers.

Counseling Issues

As noted above, toddlerhood is often characterized as the "terrible 2s" because of the child's struggle for independence. It is often a prime time when families seek out the help of a counselor or a health care provider. This section will provide examples of various concerns that parents may have in regard to rearing healthy toddlers.

Anxiety During Toddlerhood

Anxiety disorders are the most common form of psychopathology in children, and separation anxiety is a common issue for most children and is developmentally normal until the ages of 3 to 4. However, a child with clinical separation anxiety experiences recurrent excessive distress or worry beyond that expected for the child's developmental level. This anxiety results from separation or impending separation from the child's attachment figure. Characteristic features of separation anxiety include severe distress, worry, or fear leading to impairment of functioning. It is also frequently accompanied by somatic symptoms such as headaches, stomachaches, nausea, and vomiting.

While the prevalence rate of all anxiety disorders in children is 8% to 10%, the prevalence rate for separation anxiety is approximately 4.1%, making it the highest occurring anxiety disorder in children (Ehrenreich, Santucci, & Weinrer, 2008). Separation anxiety has also been linked with other disorders such as conduct disorder and depression, therefore making these disorders frequent comorbid conditions of separation anxiety disorder. Studies have also shown that children of parents with panic disorders have a higher risk of developing separation anxiety (Perlmutter, 2000).

As counselors, it is important for us to be aware of the characteristics of separation anxiety as well as different intervention strategies to address the issue. Infants experience numerous emotions. In normal development, infants become familiar with their home environment and feel comfortable when parents or their caregivers are around. When infants are put in situations where something unusual is going on or are unfamiliar with a particular place then they will become fearful. From 8 to 14 months, children become frightened when they meet new people or visit new places. They believe familiar faces and places are safe; therefore, when they are separated from parents, caregivers, or home they feel uneasy or threatened. Separation anxiety, in general, is a normal stage that infants go through and usually ends when the child is around 2 years old. Some toddlers may understand that their parents or caregivers are out of sight but will return later. However, some toddlers may display behaviors that signify higher levels of distress due to separation. There are many symptoms that result from separation anxiety in children, some of these include excessive distress when separated from the primary caregiver, nightmares, reluctance to go to school or other places, reluctance to sleep without the caregiver nearby, repeated physical complaints (stomachaches, dizziness, muscle aches), homesickness, worrying about losing the caregiver, and worrying about harm toward the caregiver. There are no tests for separation anxiety because it is normal; however, if severe separation anxiety persists after age two then an evaluation by a counselor may be needed to see if the child has an anxiety disorder or other condition. Young children with symptoms that improve after age two are considered normal even if some anxiety comes back later in life in stressful situations.

Counselors can work with parents to ease separation anxiety before it becomes a major problem by encouraging parents to help their child feel safe in the home, to trust people other than his or her parents or caregivers, and trust that his or her parents will return. The separation process can be difficult for all persons involved, and it is a process that requires open communication and self-awareness for the parent. Counselors can help parents examine their own thoughts and feelings about the separation process and ask their child about his or her thoughts and feelings. Parents should not ignore their own feelings on separation or their child's feelings. It is important for parents to take baby steps, especially if separation anxiety is a problem. Parents can begin by separating for just a few minutes at a time. For example, by placing the toddler in a safe room or play pen and giving the child a hug or kiss while promising to return, then leaving for a few minutes and giving the child another hug or kiss after returning. Parents can practice this technique multiple times throughout the day until they can build up for longer periods.

Another strategy parents can try is talking about the anxieties. For example, toddlers may struggle with separation anxiety when starting preschool for the first time. Parents should talk to their child about what they like about school and his or her worries. For example, find out if the child is worried that the parent will not come back. Parents should help their child understand that they plan on returning and tell him or her the time. Some children may even be worried that something will happen to their parents while they are gone. Even though parents cannot promise complete safety, they can promise the child they will be extra careful. Parents can also try encouraging a transitional object. A transitional object could be anything the child cherishes such as a favorite stuffed animal or a blanket. Parents can allow their child to take their favorite object with them in order to support feelings of comfort and safety.

It is also important for parents to remember that some children struggle more with anxiety caused by separation than others. Some children may have experienced a loss such as divorce or the death of a loved one or pet, which can cause them to fear that someone or something else will leave them. Other children who struggle with separation anxiety may have attachment issues that last for years. In these types of situations, it is important for parents to seek professional help.

Counselors use many different strategies to help children who are already struggling with separation anxiety issues. The treatment of choice is usually counseling over medications; however, medication may be necessary in severe situations. Most children who have not improved from counseling alone usually have other emotional problems in addition to separation anxiety disorder.

One technique counselors can use for separation anxiety is behavior modification therapy. This intervention directly addresses the symptoms of separation anxiety and is more effective if the behaviors are addressed positively. The child is also rewarded for small accomplishments. For example, this therapy can be used when a child is having issues sleeping in his or her own bed. Instead of withholding dessert from a preschooler who does not want to sleep in his or her own room, give hugs and praises when the child can go near the room. Praises should be continued when the child is able to stay in the room for 5, 10, or 15 minutes alone. This will allow the child to feel some type of success rather than failure.

Cognitive therapy is another technique counselors use to help with separation anxiety. This therapy is used to help children learn how they think. It also allows them to increase their ability to solve problems and focus on positive thoughts. When children focus on more positive feelings, they become open to learning about different ways to deal with anxiety. Some of these include playing games, coloring, listening to music, and so on. Toddlers can even be taught relaxation techniques such as taking deep breaths and counting slowly to 10.

Stranger anxiety is another common childhood anxiety. Typically peaking at 6 to 7 months, stranger anxiety also tends to reappear between the ages of 12 and 24 months. Children often become quiet, verbally protest (crying), or may hide behind a parent when a stranger approaches. It is important to note that children should be somewhat wary of strangers simply because of safety concerns. A child should not willingly walk away with a complete stranger. However, children during this age may also act this way toward people who are not really strangers, such as grandparents, aunts and uncles, and so on. This type of anxiety is very typical and actually indicates a strong bond with the caregiver. To help a child during this phase, parents can prepare the child for a meeting with a stranger by talking about the person, holding the child during moments of distress or staying within arm's length of the child, and making sure that the child is comfortable before leaving him or her with a new babysitter. Counselors can encourage parents to remain calm and show the toddler that he or she is safe. This stage typically only lasts a few months and will pass. However, if a child is displaying more severe discomfort, such as being extremely agitated with a stranger and avoiding all strangers, then the child may be exhibiting signs of stranger terror. Behaviors such as hiding when any unfamiliar person enters the home (even if the person is not trying to interact with the child), being extremely upset in the presence of a stranger even while in a familiar environment, loud screaming and back arching when a stranger attempts to hold or comfort the child, or long periods of extreme stillness and wariness while in the presence of a stranger indicate that the child needs additional help from a pediatrician and counselor. This behavior is not typical of early childhood development and is most often seen in foster children (due to earlier maltreatment) and neglected children. Many of the interventions noted earlier can also be used with stranger terror.

Because anxiety disorders are the most common disorders in children, counselors and parents should be aware of the symptoms as well as prevention and intervention strategies for helping a child. Counselors can work with children, parents, and preschool educators to help alleviate struggles with anxiety for those who suffer. Case Illustration 5.1 can further help you explore how you might respond to parents with a child struggling with separation anxiety.

CASE ILLUSTRATION 5.1 RESPONDING TO SEPARATION ANXIETY

Karen recently weaned her 18-month-old child, Elizabeth, so she planned a special night out for herself and her husband, Justin. However, when the babysitter arrived, Elizabeth cried and cried, and the babysitter had to pull the child off of Karen. The entire time during dinner, Karen could not relax and kept thinking about her child. Finally, she and Justin decided to end the night early and go home. Once they arrived home, the babysitter told them that Elizabeth cried for almost an hour and then fell asleep. Justin and Karen were both disappointed that their plans for a night out did not go as they had hoped, so they planned a night out the following week. The scenario repeated itself. Karen and Justin both feel as though they may not ever get to enjoy an evening out together if this continues.

Practice Exercise:

It is important for Karen and Justin to continue to build their relationship with each other as well as to take care of the needs of Elizabeth. Because Karen recently weaned Elizabeth, the child, as well as the mom, may already be experiencing some anxiety over the end of the nursing relationship. Therefore, they may want to wait a few weeks before leaving Elizabeth with a babysitter until this anxiety has eased. It may also be important for Karen to be mindful of the time spent with Elizabeth. Is she still holding the child as much? Does Elizabeth get moments of undivided attention from her? These things occurred during nursing, so the counselor may want to encourage Karen to continue fostering this close relationship without nursing. Karen and Justin can also seek out a familiar person to babysit during this time of transition, such as a grandparent. Leaving the child with a trusted, familiar adult may help calm Elizabeth's fears. Additionally, explaining to Elizabeth a day in advance that the grandmother will be coming to play while Mommy and Daddy go out for a little while can also help her prepare for the transition. When the moment arrives for Karen and Justin to depart, they should do so fairly quickly. They should not sneak out of the house, as this fosters mistrust, but rather calmly tell Elizabeth that Mommy and Daddy will be back soon, give her kisses and hugs, and walk away. This will help Elizabeth see that there is nothing to worry about. The grandmother can then quickly distract Elizabeth with a fun toy or game.

Photo 5.2 To be able to express yourself emotionally at an early age is part of healthy identity development.

Source: Ryan McVay/Digital Vision/Thinkstock.

Gender Identity Development

Gender identity refers to a child's personal sense of his or her own gender, being either male or female, and typically develops between 18 and 30 months of age. However, gender identity often is encouraged even before a baby is born. Families who know the biological sex of a child before a baby is born tend to begin tailoring their parental planning, such as choosing gender-specific names, picking out clothing, painting the baby's room, and so on. Therefore, people in the child's life have already begun to set up expected gender behaviors. Upon birth, these behaviors typically either begin, for those parents who did not know the sex of the child prior to birth, or continue. During this time, theories of social learning describe different types of parental and environmental influences that help shape the child's gender identity. However, gender development progresses through childhood and is not necessarily set during these early months of life. Evidence suggests that gender identity typically takes place by the ages of 2 to 3; however, it may not be well-defined until 6 years of age (see Table 5.3). While this age range has been accepted for several decades, a final point of gender identity development has still been unproven and may continue throughout life.

Table 5.3   Stages of Gender Identity Development

Age	Stage	Description
8 to 10 months	Child's Awareness	Discovers his or her genitals
1 to 2 years	Physical Difference	Knows the difference between genitals
3 years	Sense of Self	Identifies self by gender
4 years	Child Identity	Understands he or she will always be a boy or girl
4 to 5 years	Gender Stability	Understands gender remains the same across time
6 to 7 years	Gender Constancy	Understands gender is independent of external features

Theories of **social learning** argue that parental behaviors help to shape a child's gender identity. Parents often begin this influence by simply pointing out the differences in genitalia and labeling the body parts correctly (vagina and penis). Clothing, toys, and expectations of play behavior are also encouraged or discouraged according to a child's sex. For example, girls are often encouraged to play more quietly with dolls or stuffed animals, while boys are encouraged to play rough with trucks or blocks. However, it is important to recognize that both boys and girls should be encouraged to cross these gender expectations in play. It is important for girls to play rougher by climbing trees or playing ball and for boys to assume a nurturing role by playing with dolls. Both types of play encourage behaviors that all of our children need.

Gender schema theory was formally introduced by Sandra Bem (1981) as a cognitive theory explaining how individuals become gendered in society and how sex-linked characteristics are maintained by culture. Information related to gender is predominately transmitted through society by schemata that outline a group of beliefs that are feminine and masculine according to the culture. Bem purports that gender identity is influenced by the sex typing that an individual undergoes. She outlines four categories in which an individual may fall: sex-typed, cross-sex typed, androgynous, and undifferentiated. Sex-typed individuals integrate information in accordance with their own gender. For example, a female integrates feminine behaviors and assumes a strong female gender identity. Cross-sex typed individuals may integrate information that is aligned with the opposite gender (female adopting strong masculine behaviors). Androgynous individuals integrate information from both genders, and undifferentiated individuals do not show processing of any sex type.

While the behaviors discussed above are typical of toddlers, some children may demonstrate consistent behaviors that are opposite of their sex, which may lead to the diagnosis of **Gender Identity Disorder** (GID). GID can be defined as an internal conflict where the individual desires to be the opposite sex. Cross-gender behavior in children is very common, but GID is a relatively rare disorder. GID is characterized by powerful and persisting cross-gender identification, with the desire or belief that one is the opposite sex. Individuals diagnosed with GID also prefer stereotypical cross-gender clothing, activities, and playmates and will typically assume the role of the opposite gender in fantasy or make-believe play. Persons with GID also display an aversion to their own genital or sex-typed behavior, activities, or clothing.

Early treatment of GID can help increase the self-esteem of a child as well as peer relationships. A counselor can work with families to understand the flexibility of gender expression during this age period. Generally, the younger the child, the more flexible the gender expression is (Anderson & Reicherzer, 2006). However, while exploring possibilities, it is essential that counselors help the family develop coping strategies and supportive roles that may be needed as the child ages. Treatment for children with GID focuses on treating secondary problems such as depression and anxiety and improving self-esteem. Treatment may also focus on instilling positive identifications with the child's biological gender (Anderson & Reicherzer, 2006).

Sexual Development and Abuse Prevention

Toddlers love to be naked, yet often times parents shy away from discussing sexual development. However, this is actually a very important topic to begin for children as young as toddlers. Parents can begin by providing correct labels for body parts (including vagina and penis), discussing basic bodily functions, and allowing children to explore all of their body parts. Masturbation in young children is normal and should not be punished, but a parent may wish to redirect the child to masturbate in a private setting. A parent's reaction (including voice, word choice, and facial expressions) is the child's greatest lesson regarding sexuality. By not responding with anger, surprise, or disapproving words, the parent can teach the child that this curiosity about his or her body is a normal part of life. Toddlers also tend to be curious not only about their own bodies but about others' bodies as well. Often this is demonstrated through a child's game of playing doctor. Instead of overreacting, parents can ask their child to get dressed and distract him or her with a toy or game. Later the parent may wish to help the child learn more about his or her body (and the bodies of others) through a children's book geared toward toddlers. Completing the Guided Practice Exercise 5.2 can help you begin to identify resources to assist parents with discussing this topic with their young ones.

Guided Practice Exercise 5.2

Sexual development seems to be a hard subject for many parents to discuss with their children. The use of books may help them to feel more comfortable with this topic. Locate and bring to class two books related to sexual development that would be appropriate for parents to read with their children. Discuss why you think these would be good books and strategies for helping parents discuss this topic with their children.

Because of the child's natural curiosity regarding genitalia, it is imperative that parents discuss sexual abuse with their child. However, children must first learn about body parts and functions before they can learn to protect themselves from abuse. Parents can explain that even though touching genitalia may feel good, no one, not even family members or other people they trust, should ever touch him or her in these areas. However, the best prevention of sexual abuse at this age is close adult supervision at all times.

Discipline During Toddlerhood

By the time infants are 12 months old, discipline is a frequent occurrence in many families (Vittrup, Holden, & Buck, 2006). Parents want their children to find happiness, good health, purpose, and confidence once they are grown adults (Flaskerud, 2011). However, many parents struggle with how to help their children achieve these goals.

While there is a multitude of research suggesting disciplinary options that have proven effective, many parents are rarely guided by them because there are multiple other factors influencing their parenting behaviors. Not only are parents forming their own ideas and values about family discipline but individuals such as early childhood educators and counselors are also following this trend. Unfortunately, at times, early childhood educators tend to reflect more on their own upbringing, rather than reflecting on up-to-date research on their training (Smith, 2004). It is critical that those working in the early childhood field, especially counselors, remain current on the research basis for effective parental discipline in order to enhance and maintain a supportive role for families.

Ideally, counselors will work closely with families and develop warm, trusting, and open reciprocal relationships with them. Because of these relationships, early childhood counselors become important agents of change for children and families. When parents are struggling with teaching their young ones the rules on how to communicate and interact with people, places, and things in their physical and social worlds, early childhood counselors can provide a supportive and welcoming environment for parents to turn to and seek assistance. In order to effectively provide discipline, counselors and parents need to understand the functions of the behavior itself. Figure 5.1 demonstrates typical functions of behavior.

It is also important for the counselor to discuss the meaning of discipline with parents and the different options that research suggests for parents to use when disciplining their children. Discipline is the process of teaching children the values and typical behaviors of society. By guiding children's moral, emotional, and physical development, parents will enable their children to take ownership and responsibility for themselves when they are older. There are clear boundaries of what is acceptable and unacceptable behavior, as well as what is right and wrong. Children need to become aware of these boundaries and be able to distinguish amongst them properly.

Many parents use a form of **punishment** when trying to discipline their children. However, discipline is different from punishment in that discipline places emphasis on teaching and making children aware of the consequences of their actions. When an adult uses positive discipline with a child, the parent helps the child understand

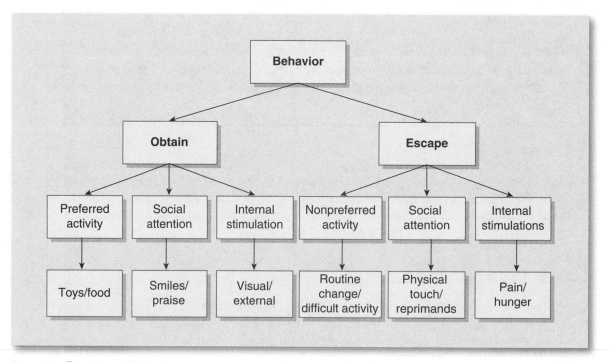

Figure 5.1   Functions of Behavior

why a certain behavior is unacceptable and another behavior is acceptable. If negative discipline is used, the child is usually focused on simple obedience and the avoidance of punishment.

Many parents use physical punishment as their way of disciplining their children. Physical punishment is the use of force to cause pain, but not injury, for the purpose of correction or control. Some individuals may associate physical punishment with abuse, but most authors distinguish physical or corporal punishment from abuse. The primary difference between abusive and nonabusive parents is the frequency and intensity with which parents direct negative behavior toward their child. Depending greatly on cultural values, the line dividing the two concepts may be drawn at different levels and intensities.

The use of corporal punishment by parents is very controversial even though research has clearly demonstrated negative effects on children. While acceptance of physical punishment has declined in America since the 1960s, two thirds of Americans still approve of spanking (Smith, 2012). Internationally, physical punishment is viewed as a violation of human rights. The United Nations Committee on the Rights of the Child issued a directive in 2006 to eliminate legalized violence against children. It has been supported by 192 countries, with only the United States and Somalia failing to ratify it. Thirty countries have banned physical punishment of children in all settings, including the home.

It is important for parents and early childhood educators to be aware of some long-term negative developmental outcomes linked with parental use of physical punishment, as well as what effective discipline looks like. Corporal punishment used by parents may cause disrupted social behavior, delayed cognitive development, poor quality of parent-child relationships, poorer moral internalization including parental values and rules, and increased chances for mental health problems such as depression, anxiety, suicidal ideation, and psychiatric disorders (Smith, 2004).

So what is effective discipline? This is a question many parents ask when they have young children. Being an effective parental discipliner unfortunately has no magic universal recipe, but there are research findings that are useful in showing parents practices that are linked with positive outcomes. The research literature demonstrates six principles or characteristics of effective discipline, which are described in Table 5.4 (Smith, 2004).

Additional forms of maintaining appropriate behavior can also include using behavior charts and time out. However, these must be implemented appropriately in order to be effective, and parents may sometimes struggle with being consistent. See Tables 5.5 and 5.6 for directions for using behavior charts and time-out.

Table 5.4 Effective Discipline

Principle of Effective Discipline	Description
Parental warmth and involvement	Parents are responsive to children demonstrating attention, care, and affection while fostering a reciprocal relationship.
Clear communication and expectations	Parents set clear, achievable goals for behavioral expectations.
Induction and explanation	Parents explain why behaviors are appropriate or inappropriate and set up logical consequences for inappropriate behaviors.
Rules, boundaries, and demands	Parents design rules that are easy to understand and are fair and equitable for the child's developmental level.
Consistency and consequences	Parents are consistent with reinforcement. Positive consequences can strengthen appropriate behaviors, while mild punishment (time-out or privilege withdrawal) can discourage inappropriate behaviors.
Context and structure	Parents model appropriate behavior.

Table 5.5   Effective Time-Out Strategies

Prior to initial use of time-out for discipline, role play what time-out will look like so that the child understands. Parents might consider using a doll, stuffed animal, or puppet for demonstrating what time-out looks like. Demonstrate that time-out includes being quiet and sitting in one spot.
Decide on a specific length of time (general rule is 1 minute times the child's age; therefore, a 2-year-old, would sit in time out for 2 minutes maximum); use a timer if needed.
The time-out area should be in a boring place with limited entertainment (as much as possible).
Child should be directed to time-out immediately after inappropriate behavior occurs.
Do not interact with the child while they are in time-out. If the child gets up, then place the child back in the spot, but do not look at or talk to the child.
When time-out is over, discuss the inappropriate behavior with the child, emphasize the appropriate behavior that you would like to see, and give him or her a hug to express unconditional love.
If inappropriate behavior continues, then place child back in time-out.
Consistency is a major issue and is often why parents struggle with this intervention.

Table 5.6   Using Behavior Charts

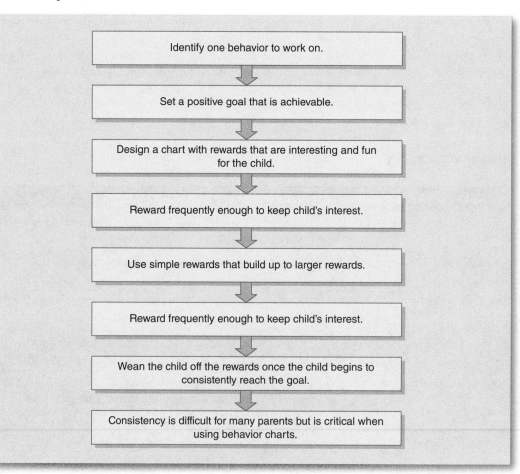

Table 5.7   Temper Tantrums

Temper Tantrums Behavior Prevention	
Be consistent with rules and expectations.	Do not compromise on rules or expectations for behavior. When you change these, a child becomes confused and does not know when the rules apply.
Identify any specific triggers that are preliminary to tantrums, and try to reduce or avoid them as much as possible.	Triggers may include being hungry or sleepy, having to sit still for prolonged periods of time, or excitement in the environment around him or her.
Provide opportunities throughout the day to help the child express his or her thoughts and feelings.	Help the child learn feeling words (happy, mad, sad, etc.) as well as appropriate methods for displaying emotions.
Provide positive reinforcement when the child is following rules or displaying appropriate behaviors.	Positive reinforcement should be consistent and ongoing.
Develop a plan for how you handle temper tantrums in a variety of situations and environments.	Consider different scenarios, and develop a plan for how you will react. Having a plan will help you remain calm during the temper tantrum.
Intervention	
Consider the reason for the tantrum.	Reasons could be seeking attention, inability to communicate, emotional frustration, exhaustion, or fear.
Get down on the child's eye level and convey unconditional support for his or her emotions.	Bend down and look the child in the eye. Convey that you understand how he or she is feeling, but that this behavior is not acceptable.
Clarify rules, and stay calm.	Explain rules and consequences to the child in a calm voice. Do not give in.
Keep in mind that tantrums are scary for the child.	Learning to experience emotions is uncharted territory for toddlers.

Taming Temper Tantrums. Toddlerhood is often known for the terrible 2s and the terrifying 3s. Triest (2006) reported that toddlers and preschoolers spend 20% to 35% of their day in transition between activities, which creates a prime environment for **temper tantrums**. The presence of tantrums is frequently exhibited after the child is attempting to say, express, understand, react, or convey something that another person does not understand. When children tend to fall short of adequate communication with others in their environment, signs of frustration might be exhibited in the form of temper tantrums. Children have their own unique understanding of the world around them, and adults in their lives can help them to learn to handle disappointments, fear, and irritants with healthy and effective communication. Understanding that children see the world in extreme intensities can assist caregivers with empathy and endurance when handling tantrums. Teaching children to verbalize frustrations can aid in prevention of further tantrums. If the child does not have adequate pragmatics, teaching sign language or an alternate form of communication to convey a message may help the child to feel secure and in control. However, some temper tantrums are inevitable and parents may struggle with how to respond appropriately. Table 5.7 provides strategies to assist parents with preventing temper tantrums as well as for responding to a temper tantrum.

Biting. While not all toddlers bite, **biting** is a typical normal behavior for many toddlers. Toddlers bite as a small form of aggression that is typically displayed when the child is feeling frustrated. When parents or caregivers use the biting opportunity to teach self-control, the behavior tends to diminish more quickly. Biting also seems to decrease as a toddler matures and can better express himself or herself. As counselors, it is important to remind parents that that a child who begins to bite is attempting to communicate in some way, and he or she is not just exhibiting bad behavior. Figure 5.2 provides some precautions or preventions to take if this behavior does arise.

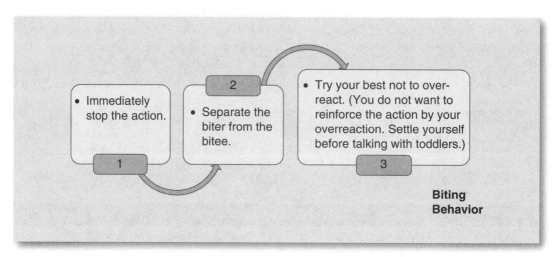

Figure 5.2   Responding to Toddler Biting Behavior

Source: Sparrow, J. (2008).

CASE ILLUSTRATION 5.2 TODDLER BITING

After staying home for 2 years with her son, Michael, Kim decides to go back to work. During the first week Michael is in day care, Kim receives a phone call from the day care saying that Michael is having a problem biting other children in the class. She has never seen her child bite another child, so she does not believe the worker. The next week, she receives another phone call saying that parents were complaining about Michael biting their children. The worker stated that if he does not stop the biting, he will be expelled from the day care so that the other children are not in danger. Finally, Kim realizes that her son is biting other children, but she does not know what to do about it.

Practice Exercise:

Toddlers typically begin biting because they cannot adequately express their frustrations. The key to helping Kim will be determining what is frustrating Michael and then helping him to express these frustrations in a more positive manner. The counselor may wish to observe Michael in the day care setting so the counselor can clearly see the events leading up to the biting behavior. Once the antecedent events are determined, then the counselor can work with Michael and the day care employees to eliminate or reduce the frustrating events (if possible) and help him express his frustrations in a healthier manner.

Parenting is a very difficult task and can sometimes seem overwhelming to many individuals. Spending time getting to know a child and what they need as an individual is a great place to begin. Once a parent has an idea of how their specific child reacts to certain situations or experiences, the parent can move forward in discovering the best discipline method to use. Reviewing the example case provided in Case Illustration 5.2 can give you a clearer idea of the behavioral struggles that parents may experience and how a counselor can assist.

Sleep During Toddlerhood

Circadian rhythms, or the sleep-wake cycle, begin to develop at about 6 weeks. The sleep-wake cycle is regulated by light and darkness and is the primary activity of the brain during early development. These rhythms take time to develop, resulting in irregular sleep schedules of newborns; but, by 3 to 6 months, most infants have a regular sleep-wake cycle. Sleep is especially important for children because it directly impacts mental and physical development. By age 2, most children have spent more time asleep than awake and approximately 40% of childhood is spent sleeping. Toddlers need about 12 to 14 hours of sleep per 24-hour period. However, the increase in toddlers' motor, cognitive, and social abilities can interfere with sleep. A drive for independence and need for autonomy may also inhibit a proper daily sleep routine. In addition to sleep disturbances, their ability to get out of bed, separation anxiety, and development of their imagination are also factors that can lead to sleep problems. Daytime sleepiness and behavior problems may signal poor sleep habits.

Around 18 months, a child's nap time is typically once a day and lasts only about 1 to 3 hours. Parents should not allow naps too close to bedtime as this may delay sleep at night. A constant bedtime routine and maintenance of a daily sleep schedule could help prevent sleep problems in toddlers. Limits should be consistent, communicated, and enforced. Toddlers may also be encouraged with the use of a security object such as a blanket or stuffed animal. The bedroom environment should also be the same every night, as well as throughout the night.

For parents who are attempting to transition their toddler to sleep alone, TVs, computers, and any other electronic devices should be removed from the child's room to create an environment that is conducive to sleep. Light from these devices as well as their protected stimuli make it much more difficult to fall asleep. Establishing a bedtime routine psychologically prepares toddlers for sleep and also reduces their nighttime anxiety. Parents may encourage a schedule such as taking a warm bath at a designated time every evening, followed by dressing in pajamas, then teeth brushing, and reading good-night stories. This consistent routine will lower stress levels and create steps that are anticipated by the toddler and are associated with bedtime. Parents are also responsible for creating a sense of security during sleep and should be prepared to calm fears and ease the transition from sleep to waking to make the event as stress-free as possible.

Television and Video Games

While the American Academy of Pediatrics (AAP) does not recommend any television viewing for children under the age of 2, the Kaiser Family Foundation (2006) found that 74% of all infants and toddlers have watched TV before the age of 2. More alarming is that 43% of children under the age of 2 watch TV every day, and 18% watch videos or DVDs every day. The AAP reports that there is no proof that media for children under the age of 2, even media marketed as educational, is beneficial. In fact, studies actually suggest that media use, even background television exposure, harms children's language development (Lapierre, Piotrowski, & Linebarger, 2012). Guidelines in North America, Canada, and Australia urge parents to limit screen time, including other technology tools such as IPads, Kindles, cell phones, and so on. Parents should also encourage no screen time in the bedroom. Infants' and toddlers' vocabulary growth is directly related to how much time parents spend talking to them rather than hearing a person on television speak. Additionally, television viewing for children under the age of 3 has been associated with irregular sleep schedules, which can affect a child's mood, behavior, and concentration. As can be expected, children who live in homes with high media use are likely to spend less time being read to and looking at books. This could result in more time needed to be able to learn how to read in comparison with children who live in households with low media use. Table 5.8 includes recommendations for media exposure for toddlers. Additionally, the Guided Practice Exercise 5.3 provides an opportunity for you to develop a proactive counseling tool for use in your own community. We encourage you to further explore how tools like this one can be used.

Table 5.8 Media Viewing for Toddlers

Avoid media use for children under age 2.
If media is viewed by toddlers, then parents should be present to watch with the children and use the opportunity to increase conversation.
Adult content should be avoided, even if the toddler is not actively watching, because it distracts both the parent and child from engaging with each other.
When parents are consumed with household duties and cannot actively play with their child, they can encourage free play instead of relying on television to keep the toddler occupied. Independent play allows children to think creatively, problem solve, and accomplish new tasks.

Guided Practice Exercise 5.3

Pediatrician offices often have television monitors in the waiting rooms to entertain both the parents and children. These monitors can also be used to disseminate important parenting and health-related information to families. Design a PowerPoint presentation or a video that could be displayed on a monitor to educate parents about the dangers of screen time for children. Be sure to include recommended guidelines as well as practical strategies for parents to use for limiting the screen time that their child is exposed to.

Social Skills

It is very important for toddlers to develop good **social skills**, because the skills they develop at this age will influence how they interact with peers and adults later in life. When children are between the ages of 2 and 3 years old, they are able to make friends and initiate play themselves. However, some toddlers struggle with social development. About 10% of toddlers have social development problems that are serious enough to cause distress. While reasons vary, many toddlers struggle with social skills due to autism, speech problems, temperament, or a nonsupportive caregiver, as well as many others factors.

There are several strategies for counselors to use when working with toddlers on social skills. Symbols, such as gesturing and speaking, can be early predictors of how toddlers' social skills will develop. Counselors can ask the toddler's parent(s) how often the child points or speaks. Toddlers who have a higher frequency of pointing at objects will have better development of social-emotional concepts later, such as being talkative or having a bigger vocabulary (Vallotton & Ayoub, 2010). If the child is not gesturing or trying to speak a lot, then the counselor will have a good idea that the toddler is having trouble with social skills.

At this age, it is important for counselors to involve play in a session with a toddler. Mathieson and Banerjee (2010) found that peer play between the ages of 2 and 3 is critical in developing social skills in children. When children engage in play at this age, they learn basic social skills like compromise and mutual support (Mathieson & Banerjee, 2010). Also, if the counselor and toddler play with toys, the counselor can see how well the child shares. Manners can also be taught when playing is involved (McCoy, 2006). For example, if the toddler wants to play with a certain toy, the toddler must ask nicely to play with it.

Another tool for counselors to use with toddlers is children's music. If the counselor plays a song that the toddler knows, or is familiar with, then the toddler may start to dance and sing. Music can help with social skills in toddlers because it gives children a chance to express themselves through dancing and singing. Singing is also a way for the child to develop or improve their language skills (Forrester, 2010). Playing age-appropriate music in the home or in the car is an easy way parents can get their toddler to start dancing and singing, which can help improve his or her language.

Helping a child feed himself or herself is also a way to build social skills in toddlers. If the parent and toddler

Photo 5.3 Playtime and sharing toys are the first steps to gaining positive social skills.

Source: Jupiterimages/liquidlibrary/Thinkstock.

have an enjoyable experience while the parent is feeding the child, this can increase social skills, because the parent is interacting with the child. In order for this to work, the parent must be responsive to the child and interact in a cooperative way with the child. If this is successful, then the child will eventually learn to feed himself or herself and gain other social skills, such as knowing how to properly interact with another person (Spegman & Houck, 2005).

Some easy things parents can do in the home to promote social development can be as simple as letting the toddler play dress-up. This will allow the toddler to pretend to be someone else. Another easy thing that parents can do to promote social skills in toddlers is to use manners with the child every day. If the child wants a cookie, then the child should be able to ask nicely for a cookie. This will also help promote language development. Taking turns with a toddler is also important in developing social skills. A parent could ask to use a crayon the child has and then explain why it is important to share and take turns (McCoy, 2006).

Parents really have the control as to how well their toddler's social skills develop. Parents are able to praise good social skills, such as sharing, or offer alternatives for not using good social skills, such as hitting. The hope is that the toddler will enjoy the praise and continue to develop those good social skills. Toddlers and other children will often model what they see their parents do, so it is important for the parents to be the model for good social skills. If a toddler sees mom and dad hitting each other, then the toddler will just assume it is okay for that kind

Photo 5.4   Even very young children can communicate with each other.

Source: iStockphoto.com/kate_sept2004.

of behavior to occur. If a child sees the parents asking nicely for something, then the child is more likely to ask nicely the next time he or she wants something.

Toilet Training

Some parents look forward to the day of no more diapers but find that toilet training is more difficult than they anticipated. The key to successful toilet training is to know when the child is both physically and socially ready and to take it in stride. Parents who push their toddler to be toilet trained too early only set themselves up for struggles.

Physical Development. A child should be able to get his or her pants up and down quickly before potty training. This skill is difficult, so have the toddler practice dressing and undressing. Playing dress-up is a fun way to encourage this skill. Additionally, children must be able to physically hold their urine or bowel movements. If a child is not physically able to do this, then he or she is not ready to be toilet trained.

Social Readiness. Be supportive throughout the toilet-training stage. Do not punish a child for accidents and encourage him or her to seek out your help when needed. Bowel movements and urinating should not be referred to as *gross* or *dirty* because this could lead to a feeling of shame. Instead, parents should focus on this as being a normal part of life. Additionally, both the ability and the desire to imitate others will speed toilet training. Many children learn by watching peers, siblings, parents, or a doll go through the process. Encourage parents to allow children into the bathroom so that the parent can model appropriate methods for using the toilet.

Sometimes children can develop fears during toilet training. Do not discount these fears! The loud flushing sound of the toilet, automatic toilets, and falling into a toilet can all be very frightening to a toddler. Some toddlers even struggle when watching their bowel movement disappear down the toilet, as if it is part of them. Encourage parents to be empathetic and understanding when responding to these fears. The toilet-training process should be fun for the toddler. Parents can encourage appropriate toileting behaviors by offering enthusiastic praise and modeling appropriate behaviors. If a child is struggling, then perhaps the process was started too early. In this case, simply step back and wait a little longer before trying again. Case Illustration 5.3 provides an example of how toilet training struggles can be addressed by a counselor.

CASE ILLUSTRATION 5.3 ISSUES WITH TOILET TRAINING

Aniya is 2 and one half years old and goes to day care while her parents are working. In order to move to the 3-year-old class, Aniya must be potty trained. While both the day care teacher and her parents are working on this, Aniya refuses to use the toilet and continuously has accidents in her clothes.

Practice Exercise:

As a counselor, the first priority is to determine if Aniya is physically capable of holding her urine and bowel movements. By asking the parents questions about her developmental history, the counselor may be able to determine whether this is an issue or not. If Aniya seems to be physically able to hold her urine and bowel movements, then the next step is to determine a positive approach for potty training. At this point, Aniya may already have negative thoughts about using the toilet since both her parents and teachers have already been trying to potty train her. It will be important to ensure that negative comments and actions are not part of the potty-training plan and that Aniya is not made to feel guilty about her accidents. It may be necessary to put toilet training on hold for few weeks so that Aniya's negative perception can wane. During this time, the parents should allow Aniya into the restroom with them so that they can model appropriate bathroom behavior. Once a few weeks have passed, the counselor may design a behavior chart to encourage potty training. Depending on Aniya's interests, a reward chart can be designed for both home and day care. Additionally, asking Aniya throughout the day to use the toilet and reminding her of the reward chart may help her get into the habit of using the toilet.

SUMMARY

- Children learn best through one-on-one playful interactions with a loving and caring adult.
- The primary developmental task between ages 1 and 3 involves the development of autonomy.
- Child maltreatment most often begins during this stage of development as toddlers begin to assert their independence.
- At this time, children engage in parallel play, which is play in the presence of, rather than in interaction with, other children.
- Learning ways to recognize, treat, and prevent developmental delays in babies and young children can be vital in working with parents to help their children be successful.
- Separation anxiety is a common issue for most children and is developmentally normal until the ages of 3 to 4.
- Gender identity typically develops between 18 and 30 months of age.

> ➢ Sexual development and abuse prevention is an important topic to begin discussing with toddlers.
> ➢ It is critical that counselors remain current on the research basis for effective parental discipline in order to enhance and maintain a supportive role for families.
> ➢ Toddlers need about 12 to 14 hours of sleep per 24-hour period.
> ➢ The AAP does not recommend any screen viewing for children under the age of 2.
> ➢ It is very important for toddlers to develop good social skills, because the skills they develop at this age will influence how they interact with peers and adults later in life.
> ➢ The key to successful toilet training is to know when the child is both physically and socially ready and to take any setbacks in stride.

ADDITIONAL RESOURCES

Websites

Grief counseling for Children. http://www.recover-from-grief.com/grief-counseling-for-children.html.
Temper Tantrums - Topic Overview. http://children.webmd.com/tc/temper-tantrums-topic-overview.
Infant and Toddler Health. http://www.mayoclinic.com/health/potty-training/CC00060.
Gender Identity Disorder. http://www.webmd.com/sex/gender-identity-disorder.
Association for Play Therapy (APT) Approved Providers-Training Directory. http://www.a4pt.org/ps.index.cfm?ID = 2113.

Videos

APT Play Therapy Channel. http://www.youtube.com/user/Assn4PlayTherapy
Child-Centered Play Therapy Preview. http://www.youtube.com/watch?v = JIMWOOIR_9g
Play Therapy Session. Jungian Analytical Play Therapy: A Clinical Session. http://www.youtube.com/watch?v = 6u00rgXn8Tc
Portable Play Session. http://www.youtube.com/watch?v = ng9KnNq_5Fw

RECOMMENDED SUPPLEMENTAL READINGS

Books

Karp, H. (2008). *The happiest toddler on the block: How to eliminate tantrums and raise a patient, respectful, and cooperative one-to-four-year-old* (Rev. ed.). New York, NY: Bantam.
Pantley, E. (2007). *The no-cry discipline solution: Gentle ways to encourage good behavior without whining, tantrums, and tears.* New York, NY: McGraw Hill.
Sears, M. (1995). *The discipline book: How to have a better-behaved child from birth to age ten.* New York, NY: Little, Brown.
Stavinoha, P. L. (2008). *Stress-free potty training: A commonsense guide to finding the right approach for your child.* New York, NY: American Management Association.

REFERENCES

Anderson, J., & Reicherzer, S. (2006). *Ethics and the gender continuum: A lifespan approach.* Retrieved from http://counselingout-fitters.com/Reicherzer.htm
Bem, S. L. (1981). Gender schema theory: A cognitive account of sex typing. *Psychological Review, 88,* 354–364

Early head start. (2011). *Early Head Start*. Retrieved from http://earlyheadstart.us/.

Ehrenreich, J. T., Santucci, L. C., & Weinrer, C. L. (2008). Separation anxiety disorder in youth: Phenomenology, assessment, and treatment. *Psicologia Conductual, 16*(3), 389–412. Retrieved from http://www.ncbi.nlm.nih.gov/pubmed/19966943.

Erikson, E. (1963). *Childhood and society* (2nd ed.). New York, NY: Norton Press.

Flaskerud, J.H. (2011). Discipline and effective parenting. *Issues in Mental Health Nursing, 32*(1), 82–84. doi:10.3109/01612840.2010.498078

Forrester, M. A. (2010). Emerging musicality during the pre-school years: A case study of one child. *Psychology of Music, 38*, 131–158.

Kaiser Family Foundation. (2006). *The media family: Electronic media in the lives of infants, toddlers, preschoolers and their parents*. Retrieved from http://www.kff.org/entmedia/7500.cfm.

Lapierre, M. A., Piotrowski, J. T., & Linebarger, D. L. (2012). Background television in the homes of US children. *Pediatrics, 130*(5), 839–846. doi: 10.1542/peds.2011–2581

March of Dimes Foundation. (2013). *Newborn screening*. Retrieved from http://www.marchofdimes.com/baby/bringhome_newbornscreening.html.

Mathieson, K., & Banerjee, R. (2010). Pre-school peer play: The beginnings of social competence. *Educational and Child Psychology, 27*, 9–20.

McCoy, J. (2006). *Parenting 24/7: Games for learning*. Retrieved from http://parenting247.0rg/article.cfm?contentid=1148&agegroup=2.

Perlmutter, Susan. (2000). *Childhood anxiety disorders*. Retrieved from http://www.acnp.org/g4/gn401000163/ch159.html.

Smith, A. B. (2004). How do infants and toddlers learn the rules? *International Journal of Early Childhood, 36*(2), 27–42.

Smith, B. L. (2012). The case against spanking. *Monitor on Psychology, 43*(4), 60.

Sparrow, J. (2008). Why babies bite. *Scholastic Parent & Child, 15*(8), 34.

Spegman, A., & Houck, G. M. (2005). Assessing the feeding/eating interaction as a context for the development of social competence in toddlers. *Issues in Comprehensive Pediatric Nursing, 28*, 213–236.

Triest, R. (2006). Triumph over toddlers' tantrums. *Behavior Analysis Digest, 18*(3), 11.

U.S. Department of Education. (n.d.). *Building the legacy: IDEA 2004*. Retrieved from http://idea.ed.gov/.

Vallotton, C. D., & Ayoub, C. C. (2010). Symbols build communication and thought: The role of gestures and words in the development of engagement skills and social-emotional concepts during toddlerhood. *Social Development, 19*(3), 601–626.

Vittrup, B., Holden, G. W., & Buck, J. (2006). Attitudes predict the use of physical punishment: A prospective study of the emergence of disciplinary practices. *Pediatrics, 117*(6), 2055–2064. doi: 10.1542/peds.2005–2204

Zero to Three: National Center for Infants, Toddlers, and Families. (2012). *Early experiences matter*. Retrieved from http://www.zerotothree.org/.

Preschool: Early School Age (Ages 3 to 6)

It is easier to build strong children than to repair broken men.

Fredrick Douglass

As every bird must leave a nest, so too must our children venture out into the world beyond the security of home and family. The new experiences that await them as they engage in formal learning and expanded peer interactions will stimulate growth. These same experiences, however, can be a challenge to their health and well-being. This period of development presents new struggles and new challenges. Developing resilience, positive peer relationships, and self-control are just a few of the challenges confronting the early school-aged child.

It is our hope, as it is with their parents, that they enter these new experiences, this new world, strong, and that they will find others who care and will continue to foster the knowledge, skills, and strength needed for their continued healthy development

This chapter explores the physical, cognitive, and social/emotional development occurring during this period of early childhood, along with the risks to healthy development encountered, and specific counseling issues that often arise during this time of development. Specifically, after reading this chapter, you will be able to

1. understand the physical, cognitive, and social and emotional development of preschool children;

2. compare various theories of human development and how they relate to development during the preschool years;

3. assess common risks to healthy development during the preschool years;

4. apply counseling skills that may be needed for parents and children, including prevention and intervention strategies; and

5. identify areas of consultation that can be provided with other health care providers.

Healthy Preschool Development

Physical Development

By the age of 3, most basic gross motor abilities have emerged, but the child continues to practice and perfect these skills through increasingly challenging and complex situations. Preschool children have better balance than toddlers, so they are able to jump, go downstairs one foot at a time, flip forward, and get dressed by themselves (although they may still need a little help, especially with buttoning and snapping). With this improved ability in motor skills, preschoolers become more independent and often seek risks to determine if they have the ability to do a task, such as climb the rock wall at the playground. Fine motor skills also improve during the preschool years with the child being able to grasp crayons or pencils with just fingers instead of his or her fist, cutting on a line with scissors, stringing small beads, and picking up small objects. During the preschool years, parents may also notice that their child becomes leaner. The change seems more drastic due to the child growing taller, but children are also more active during this time.

To encourage physical development, caregivers can provide numerous opportunities to further develop gross and fine motor skills. First, make sure the child gets plenty of sleep and nutrition to fuel his or her development and activity. Provide opportunities to play outside with running, climbing, and swinging. Toys such as hula hoops, large balls, and tricycles are also great for large motor skills. To further develop fine motor skills, create projects with the preschool child using child safety scissors, gluing, painting, and plastic building blocks (e.g., Legos). All of these activities can help the preschooler physically develop.

It is important to keep in mind that not all preschoolers will develop on the same timeline; however, there are a few areas that may create concerns for caregivers. If a preschooler is awkward and clumsy (much more than peers), has significant trouble with buttons or zippers, has difficulty using small objects, such as Lego building blocks or puzzle pieces, or has difficulty coloring or writing on the paper, then the caregiver may want to talk to a pediatrician. While the child may simply be developing slower than his or her peers, the earlier a problem can be diagnosed, then the earlier interventions can begin to obtain better outcomes.

Photo 6.1 **Outdoor play is very important for children's physical development.**

Cognitive Development

The brain undergoes dramatic changes again during this time period. Neurological connections allow for increased language development, better hand-eye coordination, better motor control, and of course increased cognitive ability. According the Piaget (1952) preschoolers are in the **pre-operational stage** of cognitive development, which typically lasts until the age of 7. Please refer to Piaget's Stages of Cognitive Development, Table 2.3 in Chapter 2.

During this stage, thinking is more symbolic and **egocentric**; preschoolers have a difficult time understanding others' points of view. For example, asking a child "how do you think that made him feel when you hit him" may not be an effective strategy for the preschooler when compared to children who are in the concrete operational stage of cognitive development, which begins around the age of 8. The child may be able to answer the question correctly but may not internalize the point that when you hit someone it hurts them, and therefore we should do that. Problem solving is still illogical. However, one of the most important cognitive shifts seen during this age is the development of **symbolic thought**, or the ability to symbolically represent concrete objects, actions, and events (Piaget, 1952). During this time, parents and caregivers will begin to see a significant increase in make-believe play. For example, children may use a broom as a horse or a wooden block as a car. For example, they might use pots and pans as drums or boxes as spaceships.

According to Vgotsky's (1978) sociocultural theory of cognitive development, the social world plays a critical role in facilitating the child's cognitive development. Children generally internalize thought processes that occur through interactions in the social environment. Because of his emphasis on the social role, language plays a primary role in developing intellectual abilities. He also emphasized that the child's culture determines the nature of learning; and therefore, no child will develop in the same manner. Instead, Vgotsky proposed that a child learns by those around him or her. His concept of the **zone of proximal development** emphasizes that people in the child's life influence the child's cognitive abilities. As a caregiver or preschool teacher, understanding the level of current abilities of the preschool child is critical. Once this level is assessed, then the adult introduces material that is just beyond the capabilities of the child but that the child can do with guidance. The adult provides the guidance until the child can practice the skill independently. In recent years, this concept has resulted in scaffolding, an instructional method where the teacher adjusts the type of support offered to the child to suit the child's abilities and then withdraws support as the child becomes more skilled. For example, consider a set of training wheels on a bicycle. The training wheels are adjustable and temporary and provide the young child with support while needed. This scaffold allows the learner to practice the necessary skills needed to ride a bicycle, and when ready, the scaffold will be removed. Scaffolding may include breaking a large task down into smaller parts, verbalizing cognitive processes, working in peer groups, or prompting. As the child begins to learn and work independently, part of the scaffolding is removed. Another example would be learning how to zip a jacket. A parent may first demonstrate how the zipper goes together and how the zipper works. He or she would show the child how to insert the pin into the slider, then how to hold the bottom of the zipper while pulling up on the zipper. Then the parent would help the child to do this and would encourage independent practice, with help as needed, until the child mastered zipping up the jacket.

Photo 6.2 & 6.3 Activities like dressing up and playing store are typical for preschoolers.

Source: iStockphoto.com/StefanoLunardi (Photo 6.2); Courtesy of the author (Photo 6.3).

Structure and routine are very important for younger children during this stage of development. While three-year-olds have a good short-term memory, they have difficult time recalling information over long periods of time. While this enables them to repeatedly enjoy the same book over and over again, knowing what to expect and being able to predict what they will be doing calms them.

As children age during this stage of development, they begin to develop problem-solving skills. Four-and 5-year-olds think about cause-and-effect relationships and express these thoughts to others. During this time, they begin to understand the difference between private thoughts and public expressions. Four-year-old children actively manipulate their environment and construct meaning from their world. However, they are still very egocentric and see the world through their own point of view. Their thinking is still concrete. For example, if a child has a gentle dog, then he assumes that all dogs are gentle. Memory skills begin to strengthen around this age. While the child still may not be able to remember 2 weeks ago, with some prompting, events from previous days can be recalled. Significant events, however, are more easily remembered, such as a birthday party, vacation, or so on.

Five-year-old children are filled with questions about how things work, where things come from, and so on. They have a desire to learn about the world around them. Most of their play centers on pretending, but they are able to make distinctions between when they are pretending and when they are not. While they are still egocentric in their thinking, children of this age begin to be more aware of how others feel and their points of view (Siegler, 1997). Children are fascinated with magic and continue to enjoy imaginative play.

Moral Development

Preschoolers are emerging into the world of moral thought as they consider what is right and what is wrong. Jean Piaget (1952) was perhaps the first to delve into the thought processes behind a child's moral decision making. Through his studies, Piaget was more interested in how a decision was made rather than the decision itself. He observed children playing games, told stories involving moral situations, and questioned them. According to Piaget, preschoolers are in a stage referred to as **morality of constraint**. During this stage, children tend to think of actions as either always being right or always being wrong. People are either good or they are bad—always. Behavior is deemed right or wrong according to whether or not it results in punishment. Rules must remain the same and cannot be changed. Preschoolers think of right and wrong in terms of absolutes, how much physical damage was done, whether an act will evoke punishment, what the rules are, and their own perspective.

CASE ILLUSTRATION 6.1 MORAL DEVELOPMENT

"That's mine. I don't want to share! They are all mine. I need them!" shouted Grace as she tried to bundle up all six of her baby dolls in her arms. "We need to share with Brenna. She came over to play with you today," responds Mom. "She can play with something else but not my babies! And not that, and not that either. These are all mine," responds Grace.

Is Grace spoiled? Is she purposefully being mean? Not necessarily. Children during the preschool years are egocentric and only see the world through their own point of view. They do not quite understand how others view the situation or how their actions impact the feelings and thoughts of others.

Preschool children are also very egocentric, which can be tied to their difficulty in taking another person's perspective or thinking about how another person feels. During the stage of Morality of Constraint, the preschool child sees only his or her point of view. It is not until middle childhood that the child can begin seeing others' points of views (Selman, 1980). Furthermore, preschoolers tend to think of an act regardless of whether or not it is accidental. For example, let's consider two children, Eva and Alex, playing. If Eva is spinning around in circles and accidentally bumps into Alex, then Alex will perceive Eva as being wrong, even though it was an accident. Preschoolers also look to adults as being in authority regardless of whether or not the adult has earned respect. Because the person is an adult, the preschool child believes he or she must be obeyed. This is one factor that makes the preschool child vulnerable to abuse.

Several decades later, Lawrence Kohlberg began a lifelong study of human moral development. In his studies, Kohlberg (1984) asked children to respond to a series of moral dilemmas. Like Piaget, he was interested in the process that the child used to make the decision. Based upon their reasoning, Kohlberg developed stages of moral development that he believed were hierarchical: **preconventional thought, conventional thought,** and **postconventional thought.** Like Piaget, he also believed that moral development was directly linked to cognitive development; however, he also believed that if a person was regularly exposed to reasoning at a slightly higher cognitive level, then moral development could be advanced. Table 6.1 provides a summary of Kohlberg's stages of moral development.

Preschool children are in the preconventional thought level. When they make their moral decisions, Kohlberg predicted that those decisions will be based on avoiding punishment and satisfying their own desires. The next level, conventional thought, focuses primarily on listening to others and doing what is helpful. The emphasis and desire is on being a good boy or girl. While this level is beyond that of the preschool child, Kohlberg suggests that because this is the next level, children should be exposed to moral thinking at this level in order to facilitate growth. For example, take the cases of Eva and Alex or Grace and Brenna mentioned earlier. In both of these situations, parents could point out how the other child feels. For Alex, the parent could explain that Eva did not mean to bump into him, that she was only playing and accidentally bumped into him. The parent could remind Alex of a time when he did something similar that was an accident. For Grace, the parent could remind her of how Brenna may be feeling and how it would feel if Brenna did not share her toys. This dialogue between parents and children fosters the development of the next stage of moral thought.

Table 6.1   Kohlberg's Stages of Moral Development

Preconventional Stage	Obedience or Punishment	All young children begin at this stage. Rules are seen as fixed and absolute. Obeying the rules is important because it means avoiding punishment.
	Self-Interest	Decisions are made based on what the child receives. For example, behavior is chosen that leads to a reward.
Conventional Stage	Interpersonal Accord and Conformity	Being moral is being a good person in your own eyes as well as others'. What the majority thinks is deemed as being right.
	Authority and Social Order Obedience	Laws are unquestionably accepted and followed. Being good means doing one's duty and showing respect for authority.
Postconventional Stage	Social Contract	Individuals can hold different opinions. Laws are regarded as social contracts rather than rigid dictums. Although laws should be respected, individual rights can sometimes supersede these laws if they become too restrictive or destructive.
	Universal Ethical Principles	Moral action is determined by inner conscience and may or may not be in agreement with public opinion or society's laws. Moral reasoning is based on abstract reasoning using universal ethical principles.

While Kohlberg's theory remains strong, there are several criticisms. Some researchers note that these beliefs hold true for Western culture, but that some Eastern cultures may not base their decisions on the same justice criterion that was posed by Kohlberg (1984). Carol Gilligan (1982) also was offended by Kohlberg's assertion that males tended to think in higher moral stages than females. Her research led her to conclude that females think about moral dilemmas differently than males, but that one is not better. Females are typically less concerned with justice and more concerned with caring and preserving relationships when making a decision.

Counselors working with children, caregivers, and parents are in a prime position to foster moral development. By helping children deal with problems appropriately, discussing moral dilemmas, and exploring the concept of intention and motive, counselors can help children navigate the daily moral decisions that they face. Table 6.2 provides several ideas for further fostering this development.

Social and Emotional Development

Social development of the preschool child is critical as it sets the foundations for a child's interaction with both adults and other children. According to Erikson (1963), the primary task for the preschool child is to develop initiative, or develop self-confidence in performing tasks, as can be seen in a different variation (from Table 2.2 in Chapter 2) of Erikson's Stages of Psychosocial Development in Table 6.3.

Developing initiative can be accomplished by allowing children to create their own play activities and through encouragement. During this stage, preschool children may be seen as being curious and continually trying new things; however, many interpret this stage as the child being intrusive and taking charge. It is important to note that parenting behavior that encourages these behaviors can foster purpose and direction in the child, while parents who

Table 6.2   Fostering Moral Development

Deal with problems appropriately.	Determine if a discipline problem involves a moral concern or a social concern. If the problem is of a moral nature then sit down with the child and discuss the behavior. Help the child reason through the moral decision.
Allow children to experience moral conflict.	Schedule lots of free time to allow children the opportunity to work through natural moral dilemmas.
Discuss moral dilemmas.	Read stories involving moral dilemmas, and talk through the decision making process.
Encourage children to change the rules.	Play games in various ways. Teach children that it is okay to change the rules sometimes.
Involve children in making some classroom rules.	Emphasize decisions that are good for the entire group.
Encourage dramatic play and role-playing.	Encourage play that enables children to see other people's perspectives.
Explore the concepts of intention and motive.	Use stories and puppets to explore intentional actions versus accidental actions.
Praise moral behavior.	Recognize children for being kind, fair, and helpful.
Use real dilemmas.	Use everyday classroom situations to discuss moral decisions.

Table 6.3   Erikson's Stages of Psychological Development

Psychosocial Crisis State	Life State	Age range and other descriptions
Trust vs. Mistrust	Infancy	0–1½ yrs., baby birth to walking
Autonomy vs. Shame	Early Childhood	1–3 yrs., toddler, toilet training, doubt
Initiative vs. Guilt	Play Age	3–5 yrs., preschool, nursery
Industry vs. Inferiority	School Age	6–12 yrs., early school
Identity vs. Role Confusion	Adolescence	13–18 yrs., puberty, teens
Intimacy vs. Isolation	Young Adult	19–40 yrs., courting, parenting
Generativity vs. Stagnation	Adulthood	30–65 yrs. Middle adulthood, family
Integrity vs. Despair	Old Adulthood Age	65 yrs. and over, grand/great-grandparenting

consistently disapprove of their child's play and efforts at performance tasks can lead to feelings of guilt for the child and ultimately inhibition. Because the child now understands the concepts of *right* and *wrong*, this disapproval from caregivers may lead to feelings of guilt, which can lead to poor self-assessments and impact the development of self-esteem. For example, a parent may fuss at his or her child for getting dirty while playing outside. If the parent *consistently* fusses at the child for getting dirty, then the child will begin to feel guilty and will not actively play outdoors. On the other hand, if this disapproval is rare (given it was an inappropriate time for the child to get dirty),

then the child will explore his or her outside world and fulfill his or her curiosity. Parents often make comments to children that they do not necessarily realize may inhibit play. For example, saying that things are gross or icky (like mud), responding with a squeal of fear at the sight of the child holding a bug or frog, or even groaning when the child has mud on his boots can all lead to inhibited play and diminished curiosity.

Developing a positive self-concept and self-esteem is an important goal during the preschool years. **Self-concept**, or a child's consistent perceptions about himself or herself, despite variations in behavior, forms rapidly during the preschool years. However, children do not develop a positive self-concept by simply being told they are good at tasks; they must take initiative, experience a challenge, and succeed. Then they begin to internalize feelings of competence and sense that they are capable. It is important for caregivers to provide activities that children may find a bit challenging but that they can successfully accomplish.

Preschoolers are also developing skills in self-control of their emotions and behaviors. By this stage of development, most children have developed their language enough to verbally express their feelings; however, their emotional states are very situation-specific and can change rapidly. For example, a three-year-old may laugh hysterically at a character on a television show and then immediately burst into tears when someone changes the channel. While most three-year-olds can

Photo 6.4   Playtime is essential for early school age.

Source: Katy McDonnell/Digital Vision/Thinkstock.

recognize their emotions as happy, mad, or sad, they still have a difficult time regulating these emotions. However, as preschoolers become older and acquire more cognitive and language skills, they are more able to internalize and regulate their emotions. It is important to remember that preschoolers often act out their emotions. Therefore, when they are angry, they may act out aggressively. When they are happy, they may jump up and down. As a counselor working with preschoolers or their parents, helping a child express his or her emotions in a healthy behavioral manner can decrease negative outbursts. For example, a caregiver might provide a bean bag or pillow for the child to hit when he or she is angry. As the child grows older, though, he or she is more able to verbally express emotions and temper tantrums begin to decrease (Mayo Foundation for Medical Education and Research, 2010). A five-year-old child begins to separate his or her feelings from behaviors. He or she is able to delay desires; for example, he or she will wait his or her turn or ask for a toy rather than taking it.

During this time, preschoolers also begin to expand their social relationships outside the family and develop more cooperative play skills with peers. Magical thinking and fantasies are common during this age, which lead to an increase in dramatic play. Three-year-olds may still not be good at sharing, but they are increasing their skills with cooperative play and may even create imaginary friends. They mostly participate in parallel play, where two 3-year-olds will play side by side but not necessarily with each other. Even though they are playing independently, they are still aware of the other child and will begin to take turns and mimic each other's behaviors. By the age of 4, preschoolers become more adept at sharing, although at times it can still be a struggle. Their imagination is more creative, and they seek approval from both peers and adults. During this time, children may engage in associative play, which is similar to parallel play, but the children are involved with what others are doing. For example, they may develop a city with wooden blocks. Each child builds his or her own section of the city, but overall they are working together to build a larger project. By the age of 5, children often have a wide group of friends and start truly playing together. They understand rules, interact mostly with peers of their own gender, and exhibit concern for the feelings of others. Cooperative skills help to build positive relationships and friendships as well as the ability to work constructively with peers or adults. Children who struggle with peer relationships are at an increased risk of social isolation as they enter school (Masten et al., 2005). It is especially important for caregivers and preschool teachers to pay attention to children who are struggling with relationships and help them develop more positive relationship skills. Table 6.4 provides additional strategies that you might employ as a counselor working with preschoolers or their caregivers.

Importance of Play. Parents today are surrounded with a wide array of options for preschool activities and classes. However, it is important to keep in mind that children must have time for free play, and overscheduling a child can lead to increased behavioral concerns. Rather than signing a child up for random activities or activities based on your own or another child's interests, parents should consider the child's personal interests. For example, is the child drawn to art, gym, sports, or music? Instead of signing up for all four types of activities, choose one or two. This will allow enough time for unstructured play.

Play is defined by Piaget as a "happy display of known actions" or an open-minded experience that should be minimally scripted, if at all, and completely spontaneous (Ortlieb, 2010). From a young age, parents and guardians encourage children to play; however, the meaning has a deeper significance than most attribute. In the past 80 years, researchers have explored the ramifications of play and the possibilities it holds in the overall development of young minds. In 1932, Parten observed that social play increases with age and described six categories of social play: unoccupied behavior, onlooker behavior, solitary play, parallel play, associative play, and cooperative play. While the first two categories are considered to be nonplay behavior, the last three involve social participation. Table 6.5 provides a description of each of these categories. Researchers continue to refer to Parten's categories of developmental levels of social play as they try to understand how young children progress from playing by themselves to playing with others. It is important to note that solitary play does not always indicate shyness or peer rejection, which can sometimes be assumed, but it can actually be constructive and has been related to happier moods and increased alertness in children (Katz & Buchholtz, 1999). Some children simply realize that some tasks are best accomplished alone or he or she may need some time alone (Katz & Buchholtz, 1999). Luckey and

Table 6.4 Strategies for Promoting Social/Emotional Development

Developing Self-Concept	• Provide opportunities for children to share personal information • Provide appropriate levels of challenging work that children are able to be successful with • Plan opportunities for each child to demonstrate his or her abilities • Provide tasks that children can accomplish (putting forks on table, putting on pants, etc.) • Provide specific feedback (you did a great job putting all the forks on the table)
Developing Self-Control	• Establish warm, caring relationships with children, especially those with behavioral concerns • Set clear limits for unacceptable behavior, and provide correction in a caring, warm manner • Provide attention when the child is behaving appropriately, not just when he or she is misbehaving • Encourage children to express their emotions verbally • Model self-control by using self-talk (I am so frustrated because I cannot get this to work)
Developing Social Relationships	• Provide opportunities for children to work and play together • Develop empathy by asking children how others are feeling and if they have felt the same way • Model caring behavior • Teach positive social skills

Fabes (2005) hypothesize that children may experience peace of mind, self-regulation, and control over their environment during solitary play. Social play, however, becomes much more evident during the preschool years due to an increase in social contacts and exposure.

Socio-dramatic play is considered to be the most advanced form of social and symbolic play. Children engage in imitation, drama, and fantasy play together that often involves role-playing in which children imitate real-life

Table 6.5   Developmental Levels of Social Play

Category of Social Play	Description
Unoccupied behavior	The child does not play but occupies himself or herself with watching anything that may be of momentary interest; may just stand around or follow teacher.
Onlooker behavior	Child spends most of the time watching other children play; may talk to children being observed, but does not join in playing.
Solitary play	Child plays along and makes effort to join other children; pursues own activity regardless of what others are doing.
Parallel play	Child plays independently, but the activity chosen brings him or her close to other children; may play with similar toys but does not include others in play.
Associative play	Child plays with other children; communication centers on common activity; borrows or loans play materials; all members engage in similar activity.
Cooperative play	Child in a group that is organized for a purpose (i.e., making something, attaining a competitive goal, imitating adult life, formal games, etc.).

people and experiences they have had themselves. As children take on roles in socio-dramatic play, they are able to act out relationships and experience the emotions of the person in the role they are playing. As children externalize their feelings through play, they begin to develop a sense of mastery and control. Once negative emotions have been resolved, children can then move on to other types of expression in their play. Freud (1955) proposed that play can be cathartic. Children use play to understand traumatic experiences and may re-create an unpleasant experience repeatedly to assimilate it and diminish the intensity of emotions (Frost, 1992; Schaefer, 1993). Play can be a powerful tool for counselors when trying to help a preschool child who does not yet have the language to fully express his or her thoughts and emotions.

Studies have also demonstrated an increase in language development, social-emotional development, as well as an overall increase in integrative learning behaviors in the classroom. Pizzo and Bruce (2010) examined an intervention of play to encourage language development. They found that as pretend play and symbolic play increased, so did the overall language of preschoolers with disabilities. Sometimes in minimally delayed children, a child may have difficulty expressing feelings or thoughts, in which case there are ways to use play in different forms to encourage knowledge of language. An example of this is for the counselor or parent to sit down with the child and talk through the activities of the day in great detail while drawing out a series of pictures that exemplify the various activities. In doing this, the child is able to reflect on the day as well as learn one-on-one from an adult who is summarizing what he or she recalls.

As we have previously discussed, social interaction is a key component of any child's development; play can offer a boost to the preschooler who is struggling with social development (Webster-Stratton & Reid, 2003). The inclusion of symbolic play with dolls or other objects can encourage an increase in comfort when interacting with peers and adults other than the care provider. Puppets are also a great tool to practice appropriate social interactions as well as provide praise for the child for using positive social strategies because preschool children are into fantasy play. Additionally, when encountering children who may have suffered abuse or are dealing with a sensitive home situation, a doll house or doll family can be used to help the child demonstrate his or her perceived notion of correct social interactions in a more relaxed environment than an interview. Guided Practice Exercise 6.1 can help you further explore the importance of play when counseling preschool children.

Guided Practice Exercise 6.1

Counseling preschool children is vastly different than counseling adolescents and adults. They do not have the language ability for traditional talk therapy, so preschool counselors often use a variety of counseling modalities. Visit a counselor who works with preschool children. Develop a list of questions to ask him or her. You might like to consider the biggest challenges, best theoretical approaches, group counseling, child abuse reporting, and so on for this age group. Were the responses what you expected? Write a description of what you learned from your visit.

During this stage of development, preschoolers struggle for more independence. However, it is important to realize that this struggle may lead to increased anxiety. Keeping a daily routine and being as consistent as possible can help to ease this anxiety. While times of the day cannot always be the same for each day of the week, the order of activities can remain fairly consistent. For example, a nightly routine might be eating supper, playing a game, taking a bath, reading a book, and then going to bed. These activities might begin at 5:00 one night but then may need to begin around 6:00 the next night due to other obligations. While the caregiver does not need to vary dramatically in times, a little variation is okay as long as the routine is fairly consistent. The Guided Practice Exercise 6.2 can help you explore the impact of routines and when those routines are broken. Additionally, Table 6.6 the National Association for the Education of Young Children's (NAEYC) Ten Signs of a Great Preschool, provides a summary of the developmental milestones that preschoolers experience to consider as we talk about risks to healthy preschool development.

Guided Practice Exercise 6.2

Interview a parent of a preschool child. What routines have they established? How do they feel about these routines? How do they manage times when the routine cannot be followed (during holidays, vacations, etc.)? How does their child react to the routine and when the routine is not followed?

Risks to Healthy Preschool Development

Children are often faced with a variety of risks that are beyond their control. From family hindrances like alcoholism, abuse, divorce, and poverty to unforeseen challenges like natural disasters, medical illness, death and traumatic events, children are often faced with adversity.

Children who manage to fare well despite these traumatic events are viewed as being resilient or stress-resistant. Some children, however, are not so resilient. It is not unusual to have these children manifest the ill-effects of the trauma behaviorally by way of conflicts with peers, personality regression, or withdrawal, or academically through lower grades, disinterest in school, or truancy. Symptoms of trauma can take on physical form with a child exhibiting hygienic digression, self-harm, or weight fluctuation. Emotionally, children may

Table 6.6   NAEYC Ten Signs of a Great Preschool

Signs of Great Preschool	Spend most of their time playing and working with materials or other children.
	Access to various activities throughout the day (assorted building blocks, props for pretend play, picture books, paints, games, etc.); children should not be doing the same thing at the same time.
	Teachers work individually with children throughout the day.
	Classroom is decorated with children's original work.
	Learn numbers and alphabet in the context of their everyday experiences—meaningful activities such as cooking, serving snacks, discovering plants, and so on occur naturally.
	Have long periods of time to play and explore—worksheets are used minimally, if at all.
	Have an opportunity to play outside every day.
	Teachers read books to children individually or in small groups throughout the day.
	Curriculum is adapted for individuals to learn at their own pace.
	Children and parents look forward to school—children are happy to attend.

display extreme anger or frustration. Therefore, it is imperative that counselors become aware of environmental factors that place children at risk as well as protective factors that can be fostered to strengthen resilience (Masten, Best & Garmezy, 1990).

Fostering Resilience

One of the more familiar and widely accepted definitions of **resilience** is "the process of, capacity for, or outcome of successful adaptation despite challenging or threatening circumstances" (Masten et al., 1990). This definition implies the possession of multiple skills that are both internally and externally based. We believe that these skills can be learned and strengthened in individuals who may be at risk. For more information see Table 6.8 Fostering Resilience.

Protective factors alter a person's response to an environmental threat. They can arise from within the child, such as a child's intelligence and ability to regulate behavior, while others are based on external influences, such as competent parents, effective schooling, and the availability of support networks. These factors, however, must be viewed in the context of developmental level as well as cultural expectations and norms. For example, while some cognitive strategies have been found to serve as protective factors, some children may be developmentally too young to employ them. Further, for some children, from some cultures, reliance on faith and spirituality may be a stronger protective factor, whereas for others this may not be of great value. Because we believe that many protective factors can be taught, we encourage counselors to understand which factors promote resiliency. After reviewing the literature, Alvord and Grados (2005) identified six factors, which are discussed below: (a) proactive orientation; (b) self-regulation; (c) proactive parenting; (d) connections and attachments;(e) school achievement and involvement, IQ, and special talents; and (f) community. Furthermore,

Table 6.7   Preschool Age 36 to 60 Months

Physical	Cognitive	Social/Emotional
• Growth slows 3–4 inches per year • Uses physical activity to develop gross and fine motor movement • Body is adult-like in proportion • Visual tracking is well developed • Baby teeth begin to be replaced with permanent teeth • Significant increase in muscle mass • Body may appear lanky • Needs 1,600 calories a day	• Understands shapes that are the same in size and color • Counts to 20 • Recognizes numbers 1–10 • Relates clock time to daily routine • Identifies coins • Eager to learn • Understands concepts of half, less, and more • Asks: What? When? Where? Why? How? • Knows alphabet • Knows a calendar and what it's used for • Understands 1st, 2nd, 3rd • Does not understand ethical or moral behavior • Eager to please	• Enjoys role-play and make-believe • Establishes close relationships • Outgoing and friendly • Sulks over being left out • Often appears selfish • 1 or 2 focused friendships • Likes entertaining people • Better self-control of emotions • Needs comfort & reassurance • Uses language over tantrums • Talks self through simple problem solving • Increasing fear of the unknown

consider Table 6.8 that describes various interventions that can be implemented to strengthen these protective factors.

A primary characteristic defining resiliency is having a proactive orientation, or the ability to take initiative in your life and to believe in your effectiveness. Protective factors, such as having a positive level of self-efficacy and self-esteem, positive future expectations, good coping skills, personal control, problem-solving abilities, initiative, optimistic thinking, and internal motivation all increase a child's ability to be resilient. Resilient children also take positive action; they seek out opportunities to better their lives. Preschool children who demonstrate confidence in themselves and have a good outlook on life typically have a proactive orientation. Self-control, such as gaining control over emotions and behavior, is also one of the most fundamental protective factors for developing resilience. However, it is important to remember that preschool children are still working on their self-control. By the end of the preschool years, though, children who are resilient should demonstrate more self-control. Additionally, children with parents who practice **authoritative parenting** demonstrate more resilience. Authoritative parents are responsive and have high, realistic expectations. They provide warm and loving support, a cognitively stimulating environment, and rational, consistent rules and behavioral expectations. Outside of the family, the ability to develop friendships and get along with peers is also paramount for forming connections. However, it is important to note, that children must be active in creating and maintaining supportive relationships. In other words, they must learn the skills necessary to maintain these relationships. Teachers and parents can help children learn positive social skills and then observe their play with others to determine if the child has the skills to actively apply what they have learned.

Children who share, are compliant with social rules, and are positive with peers are more likely to be able to do this. Active engagement in academics and extracurricular activities as well as cognitive ability is also correlated with resiliency in children. Children's areas of competence should be highlighted by parents and teachers

Table 6.8   Fostering Resilience

Individual /Group Counseling

- Teach problem-solving and social skills
- Help child to determine which situations are controllable and which are not
- Encourage healthy display of emotions
- Help child identify personal strengths
- Teach child that mistakes are okay and can be learned from
- Teach cognitive strategies such as thought stopping
- Teach optimistic thinking
- Teach relaxation and self-control techniques

Parent Training

- Teach problem-solvling skills
- Encourage healthy display of emotions within the home
- Identify positive family experiences, such as a family night
- Encourage parents to assign small, meaningful tasks to children that can be accomplished (such as helping with dishes, feeding the pet, etc.)
- Teach authoritative parenting skills
- Encourage a routine and setting realistic expectations for the child

School-Based Interventions

- Teach problem-solving and social skills
- Teach appropriate display of emotions
- Encourage activities that allow children to demonstrate competence and encourage strengths
- Teach cognitive strategies, such as thought stopping
- Teach relaxation and self-control techniques

Community-Based Interventions

- Target unsafe neighborhoods and begin community-wide clean-up program
- Begin or improve recreational programs
- Provide support services for families, such as afterschool programs, family workshops, etc.
- Locate community leaders to serve as mentors

to reinforce a sense of accomplishment. When a preschooler is successful at writing his or her letters or numbers, parents and teachers should provide praise. Additionally, when a child has mastered the climbing wall at the playground, parents should provide encouragement and praise. On the other hand, when a child cannot climb the wall, he or she should not be discouraged by the family member. The child needs encouragement to continue trying or perhaps he or she is not physically talented and a different type of activity should be praised. Finally, community factors, such as having positive role models outside of the family, recreational facilities and programs, and safe neighborhoods have also been associated with having a protective influence on children. Enrolling a preschooler in a positive preschool environment or placing the child on a t-ball team with a good, nurturing coach can increase resiliency.

Considering these six areas of protective factors, counselors can begin to assess at-risk children to determine which areas can be strengthened. Case Illustration 6.2 will help you do this as well as hypothesize about what interventions can possibly be implemented to help a child develop resiliency skills.

CASE ILLUSTRATION 6.2 FOSTERING RESILIENCE

Wesley is struggling in kindergarten. The teacher has requested a parent conference in January because of his poor academic performance and behavioral concerns. Wesley's family is also struggling at home. His mother does not have a job, and his father is working two jobs to keep the family going. Wesley appears to be tired and hungry at school. When the teacher contacted Wesley's mother about scheduling a conference, she told the teacher that she was too busy with the other children to come by and that his father would be working so he could not come either. After numerous attempts to schedule a conference, the teacher is at a loss as to what she can do.

Practice Exercise

1. In this scenario, it is apparent that Wesley is at risk for failure and behavioral problems at school. Because the mother seems nonresponsive to scheduling a teacher conference, the school counselor can begin implementing strategies in the school environment to strengthen Wesley's protective factors, as well as contact the school-based therapist (through community counseling) to reach out to the family. At the school, Wesley's teacher could begin by pointing out Wesley's strengths and continuing to build on those. By giving him meaningful tasks to complete in the classroom, the teacher can begin to build his feelings of self-efficacy. For example, his teacher may consider allowing him to be the line leader or the lunch monitor if he meets behavioral expectations for the morning. He or she may ask him to hand out class papers and then provide praise for a job well done. The counselor may also include Wesley in small-group counseling to foster positive social skills and allow him to connect with peers. During these sessions, the counselor can focus on the appropriate display of emotions, problem-solving skills, and cognitive restructuring.

2. The school-based therapist will need to visit the parents in the home environment to assess other risk factors to which Wesley may be exposed. During this visit, the therapist could discuss

(Continued)

(Contineud)

opportunities for parenting classes, job skills training, and resources within the community. It will be important to find resources for the parents for day care during these trainings, and often this is provided on-site. The therapist will also need to stress skills in authoritative parenting in order to assist the family with creating a more positive home environment.

Poor Social Skills

Establishing friendships with other children is one of the major developmental tasks of preschool (Shonkoff & Phillips, 2000). Friends can help children feel better about themselves, build self-confidence, and adapt more easily to child care settings. However, when children experience problems in developing social skills, difficulties can emerge, such as behavior problems, struggles with future relationships, and psychological concerns. Children who experience these deficits are also found to be more likely to experience problems transitioning into kindergarten and being unprepared academically as well as manifesting a number of social and behavioral problems in school. Additionally, up to 50% of children who struggle with social skills development may exhibit a more significant clinical disorder when they are older if an intervention does not take place (McCabe & Altamura, 2011). It is critical that children who struggle with social skills development be identified early so that interventions can be implemented.

During this time, children should become self-aware, develop self-concept or self-perception, and understand emotional expression. The preschool child should be able to demonstrate an increased ability to understand others and become better able to regulate his or her emotions. Preschoolers should also show empathy toward others. During this time, the child also discovers abilities, attributes, behaviors, attitudes, and values that make him or her different from others. They will start to identify and express their emotions as well as interpret other children's emotions through facial expressions and voice tone. Each of these steps is very important in a preschooler's social development process.

Children with special needs, however, may not experience these steps. They are at an increased risk for difficulties related to social-emotional development. Many of these preschoolers lack the social and language skills needed to initiate and maintain friendships. For example, children with an **autism spectrum disorder** have an impaired ability to relate socially to others. They prefer solitary, repetitive activities. These children will need additional support to participate in social activities. On the contrary, children diagnosed with **attention deficit hyperactivity disorder (ADHD)** may be quite social; however, their impulsivity, temper outbursts, and bossiness may interfere with developing friendships.

Thankfully there are numerous empirically proven strategies for counselors to help preschool children who struggle with social development. Parent training programs have been the single most successful treatment approach for reducing behavioral problems in young children as well as increasing social skills. Various parenting programs have even resulted in clinically significant and long term improvements for more than two thirds of young children treated for more serious problems such as **conduct disorder** and **oppositional defiant disorder**.

Oppositional Defiant Disorder (ODD) can look very similar to a child who is simply misbehaving; however, the difference can be seen when comparing the child's behaviors to those of his peers. Children with ODD often exhibit signs such as refusing to follow adults' requests (both at home and at preschool), constantly arguing with adults, being angry and resentful of others, blaming others for their own mistakes, having few or no friends, being in constant trouble at preschool, seeking revenge, deliberately irritating others, and being easily annoyed. The primary emphasis of treatment for ODD is primarily the use of social learning theories that emphasize the crucial role that parenting style and discipline effectiveness play in determining a child's social competence (Schroeder & Gordon, 2002).

Children diagnosed with conduct disorder (CD) have great difficulty following rules and behaving in a socially acceptable manner. They typically display behaviors such as aggression toward people and animals, destruction of property, deceitfulness, lying, stealing, and serious violation of rules. Many factors contribute to this diagnosis, including brain damage, child abuse or neglect, genetic vulnerability, school failures, and traumatic life experiences. Many children with conduct disorder may also have coexisting conditions such as mood disorders, anxiety, posttraumatic stress disorder (PTSD), ADHD, and learning problems. Research indicates that children with conduct disorder are likely to have ongoing problems if they and their families do not receive early, comprehensive treatment that includes behavioral therapy for both the child and the caregivers and may include medication.

The Preschool Environment. Preschool environments are another location that can have a vast impact on the development of preschoolers' social development. In the preschool environment, children are given an opportunity to engage in imaginative play and are able to further develop social skills learned from their families at home. However, in today's high-pressure world, some preschools may be overemphasizing academic materials more than social skills and play. It is important for parents and caregivers to adequately research various preschool environments to ensure that a preschool environment is the right fit for the child. While parents certainly want their child to be ready for kindergarten, it is critical to remember the developmental stages that a child goes through before being ready to do K-12 academic work. Young children learn best through hands-on, playful activities. Caregivers should be wary of preschools with too many academic worksheets. For example, while parents often feel great seeing a page where their child has written the letter *B* numerous times, the child may have been extremely frustrated completing the assignment if his or her fine motor skills were not ready. Having a child draw the letter in the sand with a stick may be a better choice. The preschool environment should also be noisy! Children need to squeal in delight, dance to a rhythm, and get their wiggles out. While some circle time is needed, preschool children should not be expected to sit still and quiet for long periods of time. Most importantly, preschools should be fun. Separation anxiety is normal for a child during the first few weeks, but if a child still does not want to go to preschool after a month, then perhaps the preschool environment is not the best fit for the child. Caregivers should make periodic stops at random times during the day to see what the children are doing. Table 6.6 provides a description of the top ten signs, according to the National Association for the Education of Young Children (NAEYC), of a good preschool environment.

To encourage positive social skill development, some preschools implement schoolwide programs, such as **Positive Behavioral Support (PBS)** or the **Early Screening Project**. PBS is an empirically based approach to eliminate challenging behaviors and replace them with positive social skills. This intervention can be targeted to a specific child or can address an entire school. While the children are the direct beneficiaries of this approach, PBS seeks to change the environment, such as creating a more pleasant physical environment for teachers and children as well as individualized instruction and reinforcement. The program requires the use of **functional behavioral assessment (FBA)** and ongoing monitoring of the impact of the program. Therefore, the needs of the child are constantly being assessed and appropriate interventions designed.

The Early Screening Project uses a similar approach to monitoring children at a preschool level. This project proactively screens and identifies preschool children who are experiencing adjustment problems. Children with the highest risks of developing behavioral disorders are identified early, and interventions are implemented sooner. Screening for the Early Screening Project includes several stages of assessment, ranging from teacher ratings of behavior to direct observations of behavior.

Skills training programs can also be extremely useful by promoting social interventions that are designed to teach children social skills to promote social acceptance. These interventions use coaching procedures that include four skills that consist of leading peers, asking questions of peers, making comments to peers, and supporting peers. The skills are based on a **cognitive-social learning counseling model** in which children receive instruction in social skill concepts and are encouraged to perform skill behaviors and monitor and evaluate their reactions with other children their age. This approach is modeled throughout the day and can be easily tailored to fit each child's level of social competence. To further promote effective social skill development, preschools may also send parenting materials home that include parenting tips, videos that model effective parenting, and learning activities to complete with a child at home. Guided Practice Exercise 6.3 will help you evaluate a preschool setting, while Case Illustration 6.3 can further help you understand the counselor's role in helping preschool children with social skills.

Guided Practice Exercise 6.3

As you have noted in your readings, having a positive preschool environment is vital to the healthy development of a child. Visit a preschool classroom. Write a description of what you observed. What did you see that would foster healthy development? How did the teachers manage behavior? What could be improved?

CASE ILLUSTRATION 6.3 SOCIAL SKILLS

Ty is in a preschool classroom with 11 other students. While Ty seems to be right on target for academic development, he struggles with peer relationships. Many of his peers refer to him as being "mean," and very few children continue to play with him for very long. The teacher and assistant teacher have observed him hitting, yelling, and saying mean things to the other children. When they talk about this with him, he does not see anything wrong with what he does. The teachers are concerned about his behavior and his lack of friends.

Practice Exercise

1. Parent training programs have been the single most successful treatment approach for reducing behavioral problems in young children as well as increasing social skills. It will be important for the counselor to emphasize the crucial role that parenting style and discipline effectiveness play in determining a child's social competence. Therefore, the counselor should invite Ty's parents to either small-group counseling that focuses on these skills or provide individual training for his family.

2. Because the child is currently in preschool, the teachers can also work to improve Ty's social skills. Teachers can send parenting materials home that include parenting tips, videos that model effective parenting, and learning activities to complete with Ty at home. Another intervention that the teachers may wish to consider is the PBS model or the Early Screening Project if other children in the class are experiencing similar problems.

3. The counselor can include Ty in either small-group counseling or individual counseling that focuses on using coaching procedures that includes leading peers, asking questions of peers, making comments to peers, and supporting peers. These skills are based on a cognitive-social learning counseling model in which children receive instruction in social skill concepts and are encouraged to perform skill behaviors and monitor and evaluate their reactions with other children their age.

Pros and Cons of Technology

While many would not consider technology as a possible risk to healthy development, the use of computers, phones, and apps also have disadvantages to the developing skills of the preschool child. Some studies have indicated that the use of technology can have several advantages, such as an early introduction to educational skills, spatial and logical skills, and problem-solving skills. Other studies have shown that the use of technology can prepare children for future computer use, increase self-esteem and self-confidence, stimulate language comprehension, and improve long-term memory and manual dexterity. However, experts also point out that there are disadvantages for the preschool child. Some cite concerns for children's physical developments, while others express psychological and developmental concerns. If preschoolers are spending a great amount of time sitting in front of technology, then they are not actively playing. Preschoolers need to run, jump, slide, and so on to help their bodies fully develop. Additionally, preschoolers do not learn to interact with other people or develop socio-dramatic play when they are simply focusing on the piece of technology equipment in front of them. Therefore, caregivers should be cognizant of the amount of time that children are exposed to technology. Additionally, programs should offer opportunities to many different solutions and should be interactive. Finally, computer time should always be monitored.

The NAEYC (Technology and Interactive Media as Tools in Early Childhood Programs Serving Children from Birth through Age 8: A joint position statement issued by the National Association for the Education of Young Children and the Fred Rogers Center for Early Learning and Children's Media at Saint Vincent College (http://www .naeyc.org/content/technology-and-young-children) provides guidelines for preschool teachers to keep in mind when using technology in the classroom. They encourage teachers to allow children to freely explore touch screens that include developmentally appropriate interactive media experiences that are designed to allow children to experience feelings of success. Additionally, the NAEYC encourages the use of the traditional mouse and keyboard. The organization also provides creative ideas for implementing technology in the classroom. One example is to take pictures of creations made by children and have them create a storybook with their recorded voices as the narrative. As you can see, technology can be another creative avenue for students to get hands-on experience, but care givers must be sure to allow plenty of physical activity and other creative outlets as well.

Counseling Issues

While preschoolers and parents can, of course, present many issues for counseling, this section will cover the predominant concerns that parents and caregivers often present when seeking counseling services.

Preschool Age Temper Tantrums

The expression of a child's physical, mental, or emotional frustration in the challenges of the moment can manifest in a tantrum. Tantrums are a part of the normal development of children and typically occur in children who are unable to express their frustrations in words. Preschool temper tantrums typically appear between the ages of 2 and 3 and begin to decline by age 4 (Wilder, Chen, Atwell, Pritchard, & Weinstein, 2006).

Temper tantrums in preschool children are exacerbated by inconsistent discipline, parents being too overbearing or too protective, lack of parental attention, interference with play, parental marital or emotional problems, sibling rivalry, illness, hunger, thirst, speech problems, and too much criticism. Children typically exhibit tantrums with a particular person in a particular place. Another major cause of preschool tantrums involves transitions, both major and minor. Children beginning preschool experience a major transition that can be an unwanted interruption in a comfortable routine, and children tend to lack the skills to deal with major transitions. Adults must remember that every experience for children is a new experience; change makes adults nervous, but they know from experience that they will get through it, whereas, children do not. Additionally, even small classroom transitions from one activity to another can result in a tantrum. Classroom transition tantrums usually result from a child being moved away from a task that the child is enjoying or being moved to a task that he or she dislikes.

When working with children exhibiting tantrum behavior or their parents, it is important to remember that the children are not throwing tantrums on purpose. They are not trying to frustrate or embarrass their parents; children are simply reacting to the world around them and their own lack of ability to communicate effectively. However, there are many things a parent or counselor can do in working with young children to minimize temper tantrums.

According to Wilder, et al., (2006) constant temper tantrums are often a product of inconsistent parenting. Further, the pattern can become circular with hundreds of daily occurrences: the child is attacked, criticized, or yelled at; as skills increase, tantrums should become less common. However, if tantrums persist into elementary school, it could be an indicator of a more serious physical or psychological problem. Table 6.9 describes various strategies for taming temper tantrums.

Table 6.9   Taming Temper Tantrums of Preschoolers

Set a good example
• Encourage parents to examine their own behavior when frustrated or angry. It is critically important for parents to remain calm when a child is having a temper tantrum.
Plan ahead
• Parents need to consider what the child will be doing throughout the day. If the child will go on errands, then do the errands early in the morning. If the child will be sitting in a waiting room, then bring along toys and books.
Distract or redirect the child
• Sometimes a child can be distracted at the beginning of a tantrum.
Discipline should be prompt and brief
• Immediately implement consequences, but do not make the consequence too lengthy. For example, a child can be immediately removed from the setting or physically held until the tantrum ends.
Try to discover what led to the tantrum
• If reasons can be identified, then parents can work to eliminate or reduce antecedents.
Model appropriate behaviors, and teach emotion words
• Do not make the child feel guilty for expressing frustration or anger. Instead discuss with the child that the emotion is okay but the behavior is not. Model appropriate behaviors and teach the child words to describe how he or she is feeling.
Be realistic in your expectations
• Keep in mind the child's age. A 3-year-old child cannot express anger in the same way that a 10-year-old child can.
Reward appropriate behavior
• Praise the child each time he or she demonstrates appropriate behavior for frustration or anger.
Be consistent
• Parents must be consistent in their reaction to a tantrum. This is the only way a child knows what to expect.

Discipline

Behavior problems are prevalent in every child, but behavior problems in preschool children will most likely determine their future socialization skills as they get older. Examples of behaviors that demonstrate appropriate social/emotional development for children in preschool include following rules, playing cooperatively, internalizing parental standards, interacting appropriately with adults and peers, using language to express feelings, and using words to control impulses. When this development is delayed or impaired, disruptive behavior, including temper tantrums, excessive whining or crying, demanding attention, noncompliance, defiance, aggressive acts against self or others, stealing, lying, destruction of property, or delinquency may occur. While all preschoolers demonstrate some of these behaviors at times, most do not display these enough to interfere with daily functioning (Sullivan, 2002). Early aggressive and oppositional behaviors, if left untreated, are likely to persist over time or develop into more severe and potentially debilitating behavioral or emotional problems; therefore, it is imperative that interventions are applied as early as possible.

Some parents, as well as teachers, worry that their preschoolers exhibit signs of too much disruptive behavior. Teachers reported that children's challenging behavior was their greatest concern, with 10% to 20% of preschool-age children engaging in significant challenging behavior (Carter, Van Norman, & Tredwell, 2011). Preschool children with behavior problems are more likely to experience school discipline, failure, and drop out; encounter the juvenile justice system; or experience peer rejection, unemployment, psychiatric illness, divorce, fatal accidents, or early death (Carter et al., 2011).

To encourage positive behavioral actions, a counselor, parent, or teacher may wish to employ **behavior management** strategies. Behavior management is similar to behavior modification but is less intense. Behavior management encourages children to choose behaviors that are socially acceptable through nonpunitive measures. For example, parents may design a reward system in which children earn tokens for desired behaviors and lose tokens for undesired behaviors. These tokens can then be traded in for various privileges, such as extra television time or ice cream.

Counselors can provide parents and teachers with suggestions for implementing behavior management strategies in the home or school environment. Once a problem behavior has been identified, parents and teachers should sit down and describe the problem behavior to the child in a firm but nonconfrontational tone. They should explain why the behavior is a problem, and then discuss the consequences if the behavior continues. They should model the appropriate behavior for the child so that he or she can clearly see what is expected. If the child displays appropriate behavior, then they provide lots of praise and encouragement; however, if the behavior continues, then they must implement the consequences stated earlier. It is important for parents and caregivers to realize that they must implement the stated consequence, so they must really think about an appropriate consequence before stating it! Finally, they must remember to be patient. Changing behavior takes time and requires consistent responses. Table 6.10 further describes these steps for effective behavior management.

Behavior modification is more intense than behavior management and can be used for preschoolers who need to change specific behaviors when behavior management does not work. Behavior modification includes identifying a specific target behavior and implementing positive and negative reinforcement to adapt, reduce, or extinguish a problem behavior. This is also often referred to as **applied behavior analysis**.

When applying behavior modification, it is important to target only one behavior at a time. As a counselor, make sure that the behavior is observable and easily measured. Once the behavior has been identified, the counselor will measure the current frequency of behavior to determine a baseline. To get an accurate frequency, you want to get at least three data points that are consistent (increasing, decreasing, or remaining constant). If the frequency levels are up, down, up again, then you cannot determine a pattern. While you are collecting baseline data, you also want to write down what happened just before the behavior (antecedent) and what happened immediately afterward (consequence). Once the behavior is fully understood, then the counselor can design an intervention strategy to strengthen the desired behaviors and weaken the problem behavior. Keep in mind that praise and consequences must be implemented immediately and consistently. As the treatment continues, the

Table 6.10   Behavior Management

Talk about the problem behavior	Describe the problem behavior in a firm, nonconfrontational tone. Explain why the behavior is a problem. For example, say "Yelling in the grocery store is not appropriate because it disturbs the other customers" instead of "Stop throwing a fit."
Explain the consequences	Clearly state the consequences of the behavior if it continues. Be specific. Say "If you continue to yell, then we go to the car for a time-out."
Model the desired behavior	Demonstrate the desired behavior. "See, Mommy is not yelling or crying. I am talking in a quiet voice so I do not disturb the other customers."
Encourage and reinforce the child's positive behavior OR Implement consequences	If the child is compliant, then offer praise and encouragement. "I am so proud of you for getting quieter. The other customers and I really appreciate it." If the child remains noncompliant, then implement the consequences. "You are still yelling, so we are going to the car for a time-out until you can calm down."
Be patient and consistent	Remember that changing behavior takes time and patience. The intervention must be implemented consistently each and every time the inappropriate behavior is displayed.
Plan ahead	Plan ahead for situations that you think might elicit negative behavior. For example, if you know that your child is going to have a hard time leaving a friend's house, then begin preparing the child before you even go. Discuss the time limit of the visit, and then remind him or her throughout the visit that you will be leaving. Offer praise and encouragement when he or she does not respond negatively.

counselor will continue to evaluate the effectiveness of the intervention by continued behavior observations and data collection. Case Illustration 6.4 and Guided Practice Exercise 6.4 will help you further explore behavioral interventions with preschool children.

CASE ILLUSTRATION 6.4 DISCIPLINE

Thomas and Jill have their daughter Ella Claire in preschool. They are constantly getting notes sent home from the teacher telling them that Ella Claire does not follow rules, does not play with other students fairly, lies, and is continuously demanding attention. They understand the teacher's frustration because they also see the same behaviors at home. They have not been able to correct these behaviors at home, so they are at a loss as to what to do.

Practice Exercise

1. In this scenario, Ella Claire is consistently displaying the same behaviors both at home and at school. The counselor will therefore need to work on a behavioral intervention that can be easily implemented in both settings. The first step is to interview both the teacher and the parents to

determine what has been tried in the past, what has worked, and what has not worked. The counselor will also want to explore any underlying reason behind the behavior, which may need to be addressed before focusing on the behavior. The counselor will then need to observe Ella Claire in both the school environment and home environment if possible. This will allow the counselor to see the antecedents and consequences of the behavior. Once the interview and behavioral observation has occurred, it may be necessary to narrow down the target behaviors, since the teacher initially presented so many. Finally, the counselor can develop a behavior management plan. Because this plan will be implemented in two settings it will be important to emphasize that both parties must be consistent in order to fully help Ella Claire. Rules and expectations should be clearly explained to Ella Claire, and rewards should be given promptly if expectations are met.

Guided Practice Exercise 6.4

Create a behavior modification plan for a specific preschool behavior (e.g., tantruming, hitting/kicking/getting out of seat, etc.). Be sure to include a clearly defined target behavior, methods for collecting baseline data, and description of the antecedents and consequences. Describe a research-based intervention strategy for this behavior and how you will evaluate the effectiveness of the intervention.

It is important for parents, caregivers, and teachers to keep in mind that all preschoolers will display inappropriate behaviors at times. Preschoolers lack the language needed to accurately tell us exactly what is frustrating them, bothering them, or making them angry, so they act out. If we keep this in mind, and try to understand what they are trying to tell us, then we can begin to work with them to effectively communicate their needs.

SUMMARY

➢ With an improved ability in motor skills, preschoolers become more independent and often seek risks to determine if they have the ability to do a task.
➢ Preschoolers' thinking is concrete and egocentric, while problem solving is still illogical.
➢ Social development of the preschool child is critical, as it sets the foundation for a child's interaction with both adults and other children.
➢ Supporting resilience should be based on preventative measures in early childhood along with interventions once risk is presented.
➢ It is critical that children who struggle with social skills development be identified early so that interventions can be implemented.
➢ During this time, children should become self-aware, develop self-concept or self-perception, and understand emotional expression.

➢ Parent training programs have been the single most successful treatment approach for reducing behavioral problems in young children as well as increasing social skills.
➢ Play is vital to the healthy development of a child.
➢ Preschool temper tantrums typically appear between the ages of 2 and 3 and begin to decline by age 4. However, constant temper tantrums are often a product of inconsistent parenting.
➢ Behavior problems are prevalent in every child, but consistent behavior problems in preschool children will most likely determine their future socialization skills as they get older.

ADDITIONAL RESOURCES

Websites

Bright Horizons Child Care. http://www.brighthorizons.com.
American Academy of Pediatricians. http://www.healthychildren.org.
APA Resilience Guide for Parents. http://www.apa.org/helpcenter/resilience.aspx.

Videos

Child Therapy with the Experts: 11-DVD Series. http://www.psychotherapy.net/video/child-therapy-series.
Behavior Modification Demonstration. http://www.teachertube.com/video/behavior-modification-video-145213.
Making Child Therapy Work. http://robinwalker.hypermart.net/makingchildtherapywork/73920EC3D24E4A64B396.php.

RECOMMENDED SUPPLEMENTAL READINGS

Books

Bracken, B. A., & Nagle, R. J. (2006). *Psychoeducational assessment of preschool children* (4th ed.). Hillsdale, NJ: Lawrence Erlbaum.
Hirsh-Pasek, K., Michnick Golinkoff, R., Berk, L. E., & Singer, D. (2008). *A mandate for playful learning in preschool: Presenting the evidence.* New York, NY: Oxford University Press.
Kaiser, B., & Rasminsky, J. S. (2011). *Challenging behavior in young children: Understanding, preventing, and responding effectively* (3rd ed.). Upper Saddle River, NJ: Pearson.

REFERENCES

Alvord, M. K., & Grados, J. J. (2005). Enhancing resilience in children: A proactive approach. *Professional Psychology: Research and Practice, 36*(3), 238–245. doi: 10.1037/0735–7028.36.3.238
Carter, D. R., Van Norman, R. K., & Tredwell, C. (2011). "Program-wide positive behavior support in preschool: Lessons for getting started." *Early Childhood Education Journal, 38*(5), 349–355.
Erikson, E. (1963). *Childhood and society* (2nd ed.). New York, NY: Norton.
Freud, S. (1955). Beyond the pleasure principle. In J. Strachey (Ed.), *The standard edition of the complete psychological works of Sigmund Freud, Vol. XIX* (pp. 141–154). London, UK: Hogarth.
Frost, J. L. (1992). *Play and playscapes.* Albany, NY: Delmar.
Gilligan, C. (1982). *In a different voice: Psychological theory and women's development.* Cambridge, MA: Harvard University Press.

Katz, J. C., & Buchholtz, E. S. (1999). "I did it myself": The necessity of solo play for preschoolers. *Early Child Development and Care, 155,* 39–50.

Kohlberg, L. (1984). *Essays on moral development, volume II: The psychology of moral development.* San Francisco, CA: Harper & Row.

Luckey, A. J., & Fabes, R. A. (2005). Understanding nonsocial play in early childhood. *Early Childhood Education Journal, 33*(2), 67–72.

Masten, A. S., Best, K. M., & Garmezy, N. (1990). Resilience and development: Contributions from the study of children who overcome adversity. *Development and Psychopathology, 2,* 425–444.

Masten, A. S., Roisman, G. I., Long, J. D., Burt, K. B., Obradovic, J., & Riley, J. R. (2005). Developmental cascades: Linking academic achievement and externalizing and internalizing symptoms over 20 years. *Developmental Psychology, 41*(5), 733–746.

Mayo Foundation for Medical Education and Research. (2010). *Temper tantrums: How to keep the peace.* Retrieved from http://www.mayoclinic.com/health/tantrum/HQ01622.

McCabe, P. C., & Altamura, M. (2011). Empirically valid strategies to improve social and emotional competence of preschool children. *Psychology in the Schools, 48*(5), 513–540. doi:10.1002/pits.20570

National Association for the Education of Young Children. (n.d.). *Technology and young children.* Retrieved from http://www.naeyc.org/content/technology-and-young-children/preschoolers-and-kindergartners.

Ortlieb, E. T. (2010). The pursuit of play within the curriculum. *Journal of Instructional Psychology, 37*(3), 241–246.

Parten, M. (1932). Social participation among preschool children. *Journal of Abnormal and Social Psychology, 28*(3), 136–147. doi:10.1037/h0074524

Piaget, J. (1952). *The moral judgment of the child.* New York, NY: Free Press.

Pizzo, L., & Bruce, S. M. (2010). Language and play in students with multiple disabilities and visual impairments or deaf-blindness. *Journal of Visual Impairment & Blindness, 104*(5), 287–297.

Schaefer, C. E. (Ed.). (1993). *The therapeutic powers of play.* Northvale, NJ: Jason Aronson.

Schroeder, C. S., & Gordon, B. N. (2002). Assessment and treatment of childhood problems (2nd ed.). New York, NY: The Guilford Press.

Selman, R. (1980). *The growth of interpersonal understanding: Developmental and clinical analysis.* New York, NY: Academic Press.

Shonkoff, J. P., & Phillips, D. A. (Eds.). (2000). *From neurons to neighborhoods: The science of early childhood development.* Washington, DC: National Academy Press.

Siegler, R. S. (1997). Beyond competence—Toward development. *Cognitive Development, 12,* 323–332. doi: http://dx.doi.org/10.1016/S0885-2014(97)90004-6

Sullivan, D. (2002). Easing into preschool. *Parenting, 16*(7), 104–108.

Vgotsky, L. S. (1978). *Mind and society: The development of higher psychological processes.* Cambridge, MA: Harvard University Press.

Webster-Stratton, C., & Reid, M. (2003). Treating conduct problems and strengthening social and emotional competence in young children: The dinosaur treatment program. *Journal of Emotional and Behavioral Disorders, 11*(3), 130–143. doi:10.1177/10634266030110030101

Wilder, D. A., Chen, L., Atwell, J., Pritchard, J., & Weinstein, P. (2006). Brief functional analysis and treatment of tantrums associated with transitions in preschool children. *Journal of Applied Behavior Analysis, 39(1):*103–107.

Middle Childhood
(Ages 6 to 12)

The essence of childhood, of course, is play, which my friends and I did
endlessly on streets that we reluctantly shared with traffic.

Bill Cosby

What may be most insightful about Dr. Cosby's quote is not the emphasis on play but the description of his reluctance to share the road, now turned playground, with traffic. The middle-aged child clearly has one foot in childhood and one foot dangling at a precipice of self-discovery, adult-like independence. This is a period marked by rapid behavioral and cognitive development. It is a period in which the child begins to transition toward young adult ideals and developing expectations of the world around them. Often at this stage, the expectations are rigid and egocentric, taking form in such things as reluctance to accept others' views of the world, or at least views of the purpose for a street.

This chapter will review the interesting and exciting changes that mark this period of development. After reading this chapter, you will be able to

1. describe the physical, cognitive, social, and emotional development of middle childhood;

2. apply developmental theories to counseling practices as they relate to middle childhood;

3. identify risks to the development during middle childhood;

4. understand factors that can impact middle childhood; and

5. discuss cultural differences and their impact on development during middle childhood.

Healthy Middle Childhood Development

Physical Development and Growth Patterns

The rapid growth observed during early childhood begins to slow during middle childhood. At age 6, the average weight of a child is 48 to 49 pounds, and the average height is 42 inches. Children have reached approximately

80 pounds and about 58 inches in height by the age of 11 years old. Accordingly, variations around these averages may exist; however, the numbers used in this book are based on the average percentile for height and weight during middle childhood. The average weight gain between the ages of 6 and 12 is about 5 to 7 pounds per year. Boys and girls also grow approximately 2 inches in height per year. Children continue to become less stocky and more slender until the adolescent growth spurt is reached around age 12. However, individual differences in height and weight are far more pronounced in middle childhood than those seen in the years of early childhood. Additionally, boys tend to be slightly taller and heavier than girls through the age of 10. At this age, girls begin their adolescent growth spurt and may surpass their male peers in both height and weight. At the age of 11, females begin to develop more fatty tissue, whereas males gain significantly more muscle tissue. For girls, this growth spurt is linked to puberty, which in turn begins the development of secondary sex characteristics during late middle childhood. The male adolescent growth spurt does not typically occur until the age of 14. See Table 7.1 for more information on Healthy Middle Childhood Development.

Table 7.1   Healthy Middle Childhood Development

Ages	Physical Development	Cognitive Development	Social Development	Emotional Development
6–8	Dresses self Has complete sphincter control Has refined motor skills Coordination increases Prints letters Ties shoes	Adheres to logic Develops a personal sense of right and wrong Vocabulary is expanding dramatically Identifies right and left	Has rules for games No sexual feelings Competence is important	Development is at about 75% Emotional display of confusion (working toward separating emotions and personal association)
8–10	Skips with alternating feet Boys are heavier than girls Rides bike Draws recognizable body parts (head, arms, feet)	No hypotheticals (ifs) Mnemonic strategies Law of conservation achieved	Self-identity is very important Identification of sexes/gender Being team member is a focal point	Setting the stage for pre-adolescence and hormonal changes that affect emotions
10–12	Adult growth spurts (girls before boys) Sexual maturity is beginning Primary and secondary sex characteristics are forming	Systematic problem solving Deals with past, future, and present Can handle hypotheticals	Identity and conformity with peers is key Participation in organized sports diminishes Cross-sex relationships form	Adopts personal speech pattern Communication becomes focus of relationships

Source: http://www.thebody.com

Nutrition and Obesity

The average body weight doubles during middle childhood development. Children must eat far more than they did in preschool years in order to fuel such a vast amount of growth over a relatively short amount of time. The average 6- to 11-year old requires approximately 2,000 calories per day to sustain proper growth. However, proper nutrition involves far more than mere calories. Unfortunately, childhood obesity is steadily on the rise in the United States (American Heart Association, 2012). Today, about one in three U.S. children are overweight. That number is nearly triple the number reported in 1963. In fact, childhood obesity is now the number one health concern among parents in the United States, topping drug abuse and smoking (American Heart Association, 2012). Children are now at an increased risk for developing diabetes, increased blood cholesterol level, and high blood pressure, all of which have customarily been seen only in adults before this time.

While there are many contributing factors to this increase in obesity, part can be attributed to the high fat and high sugar content found in foods that are eaten on a regular basis., foods which until recently have been easily and readily accessible within our schools (Bauer, Yang, & Austin, 2004). Children with poor eating habits as well as an inactive lifestyle are likely to carry these behaviors over into adulthood, resulting in a host of health problems. Recently, efforts to combat childhood obesity have come to the forefront. In 2012, First Lady Michelle Obama launched "Let's Move: America's Move to Raise a Healthier Generation." The campaign combats the epidemic of childhood obesity using a comprehensive approach that uses effective strategies and collaboration between both the public and private sector resources.

Accordingly, portion sizes in general have grown larger over time. Many of the less expensive and more popular foods, such as pizza, burgers, and french fries, have increased in both density and portion size (Bauer et al., 2004). Although, recently, such entities such as McDonald's restaurants have been offering healthier alternatives on their menus, most people continue with the old habit of eating the not-so-healthy fast food. In addition, the federal government has put in place laws requiring corporations to label foods and display nutritional information on menus. Adding to the problem at hand, children are less interested in physical play. This trend has been attributed to advances in technology and the popularity of television and video games. Cecil-Karb and Grogan-Kaylor (2009) found that parents sometimes have a strong influence over children's reduction in physical activity. For example, parents who perceive their neighborhoods as unsafe are less likely to allow their children to play outdoors. Obese children are more likely to face social rejection by peers during middle childhood, which could lead to low self-esteem. It is during this stage of development that children place great value on how other children perceive them.

Implications of Obesity in Childhood

While the risk of obesity to a child's physical health and well-being are well documented, so too is the damage that obesity can do to a child's social and emotional well-being. For example, Storch, Milsom, DeBraganza, Lewin, Geffken, & Silverstein (2007) reported that childhood peer victimization (i.e., bullying) is increasingly recognized as a serious and widespread occurrence during childhood today. Studies have shown that children dislike an obese build, hold negative attitudes toward obesity, and express a fear of becoming fat. Estimates indicate that the percentage of children who are targets of overt or relational acts of aggression may be as high as 17%. In addition, peer victimization has been linked to high levels of depression, loneliness, social anxiety, and lower social status. Indications also show that low self-esteem is positively correlated with weight-based teasing in middle childhood. Many overweight children avoid taking part in physical activity to avoid teasing (Bauer et al., 2004; Storch et al., 2007).

Addressing the psychological barriers to physical activity may be paramount in successful therapeutic treatment of obesity in children and adolescents. Accordingly, clinicians are advised to consult with parents to increase adherence to physical activity recommendations. Specialized group interventions in schools may target bullying

Photo 7.1   Participating in recreational activities with friends and family members develops positive social interaction skills.

Source: David Sacks/Digital Vision/Thinkstock.

in the environment in which it is most likely to occur. Such interventions must include staff training in dealing with aggressors and victims. The primary focus should be on the development of an antibully school climate (Storch et al., 2007).

The "Cure" as Bad as the Problem

Some children, as young as age 5, have indicated concerns over being fat and having less than perfect body images. And while much research on body image and excessive worry about being overweight has been targeted to the adolescent, children as young as age 8 have been reported taking part in unhealthy dieting and eating behaviors. Many have reported skipping meals, episodic binging and purging, and use of laxatives or diet pills. These eating behaviors could place children at risk for stunted growth and malnutrition during these critical developmental years of life. As a counselor, you will be faced with issues related to childhood obesity. We encourage you to complete Guided Practice Exercise 7.1 to further help you in assisting students and parents in handling childhood obesity.

Guided Practice Exercise 7.1 Childhood Obesity

Create a flyer for parents informing them of the risks of childhood obesity. Include some resources for parents to use if their child is obese or becomes obese. Also, provide ways to prevent obesity.

Cognitive Development

As the period of middle childhood progresses, cognitive development results in the improvement of many different brain processes. Children now have an expanded working memory, which allows them to take in and manage more information at one time. Not only do children process the information given to them more quickly, they also have gained the ability to store this information in order to expand their knowledge base. While much of the increase in cognitive functioning is thought to be a result of engagement in formal schooling, it is important to note that middle childhood is a period of continuous **neurophysiologic** changes. Many of the changes occur within the **prefrontal cortex**, which is the brain center responsible for attention, working memory, behavioral monitoring and self-regulation, reasoning, information processing, goal-setting, and inhibition (Nuru-Jeter, Sarsour, Jutte, & Boyce, 2010)

During middle childhood, thought processes develop into what Piaget classified as the concrete operational stage. The new form of thinking, referred to as *concrete operational thought* develops typically around age 6 or 7 years old. Prior to the concrete operational stage, children operate strictly through behavioral actions. As children enter into this stage of thinking, the ability to operate or carry out an action can be done through thought as well as through behaviors. While thought processes become more complex during this stage, children have not reached the point of using logic and hypothetical reasoning to think and operate, as adolescents and adults do.

Children develop conceptual skills during this middle childhood period, specifically those of conservation, classification, and computational skills. Conservation involves the child realizing that just because the shape or form of an object changes, that object doesn't simply appear or disappear. A child who has the skill of conservation understands that two balls of play-dough that are the same exact size are still the same exact size after one of the balls is flattened out. Classification skills develop as the child learns to classify in not only groups but subgroups as well. Computational skills develop in the form of children understanding that numbers remain constant. Prior to the concrete operational stage, numbers are understood in a nominal form, strictly used for naming (i.e., 3 is the number of the table where the child sits). The development of thought processes in middle childhood allows the skills of using numbers in ordinal forms as well as quantity forms. The child's active functioning in his or her surroundings, particularly the school setting, allows the child to gain understanding of these stated concepts as well as practical application of the skills to help in development and skill mastery.

Memory

Memory function in middle childhood is very similar to that of adult memory in terms of organization and memorization strategies. Memory capacity is a good indicator of overall cognitive ability. A typical 6-year-old is capable of working with two pieces of information simultaneously. Additionally, the ability to recall a series of digits significantly improves throughout the course of middle childhood. Children at this age are capable of retaining approximately seven pieces of information in short-term memory at one time. Children in middle childhood are also more likely to use the method of rehearsal in order to store information into long-term memory. During this period of development, children acquire the skills to accurately retrieve and recall information from memory. **Metamemory** and **metacognition** also develop during middle childhood. For example, children are now more aware of and able to assess their own memory function. They are also more aware of various techniques for storing and retrieving information. Metacognition equips children with the skills needed to practice self-monitoring or self-instruction techniques. Once children are able to be aware of their own thinking, they can begin to work on monitoring their own behavior and attention.

Influence of Social Factors

As noted above, cognitive functioning is in part the outgrowth of the neurophysiological changes occurring in the brain, it is highly affected by the conditions of one's social environment. Chronic stress has been found to significantly affect cognitive development by interrupting prefrontal cortex functioning. It has been noted that economic strife may add to the level of stress in children and adolescents, resulting in higher levels of depression and a lower sense of self-worth (Kutash & Duchnowski, 2004).

Threats to Healthy Development

Cognitive development can be effected by a child's socioeconomic status. School children who are classified as living in concentrated poverty are more likely to "lack access to regular medical care, live in a household headed by a single mother, become a victim of a crime, have a parent who never finished high school, become pregnant, and drop out of school" (Lee, 2005). The national poverty level assesses if a family is poor by their annual income; however, poverty should not just be characterized by dollar signs. A child in poverty suffers due to a lack of "emotional stability, mental skills, spiritual guidance, physical health and mobility, support systems, role models, and knowledge of hidden rules" (Payne, 2005). As children in middle school, living in poverty enter the school system and begin developing their self-identity and comparing themselves to their middle class classmates, they become very susceptible to developing low self-esteem, which can trigger a downward spiral. As you can see, socioeconomic status (SES) plays an important role in middle childhood cognitive development. As a counselor, it is crucial that you are knowledgeable about the SES of students in your school district. We encourage you to complete Guided Practice Exercise 7.2 to assist you in developing this knowledge.

Guided Practice Exercise 7.2 Socioeconomic Status

Since SES plays a major role in childhood learning, decide on a place that you would want to teach. Look up the stats regarding SES for that school. What is the school's free and reduced lunch rate? How many students are considered homeless? How do these rates compare to the rest of the state?

Social Development

Middle childhood is marked by a vast expansion of the child's social world. Children become more sophisticated in their language abilities, thus opening a world of opportunities in the social arena. The beginning of formal schooling exposes children to the influence of many variables other than the primary caregiver(s), such as teachers and peers. This period marks the beginning of a shift in the relationship between parent and child.

Middle childhood is a period of developing deeper social relationships, which allows for a deeper understanding of oneself and the surrounding world. Friendships develop between children who share similar interests and enjoy playing together. The development of the friend group provides a way for children to expand their perspective. The relationships and friendships developed during middle childhood help children learn how to consider other perspectives. Instead of looking at the world from only their point of view, they now take in their surroundings and react according to how their friends act. This is the point when peer pressure becomes an acting determinant of behaviors for most children. Not only are they gaining an awareness of how others around them behave; children are beginning to notice the reactions of others to their personal behaviors. This social awareness often results in

Photo 7.2   Friendship and socialization are important growing-up factors in middle childhood.

Source: iStockphoto.com/GlobalStock.

differing levels of self-esteem, social anxiety, and self-acceptance for children. For example, children who are not invited to social events, such as birthday parties or celebrations, may experience painful feelings of exclusion. In addition, sitting alone during lunch or being selected last for a team event can cause the same reactions.

Social Inclusion and Self-Esteem

The middle childhood years mark a time of growing autonomy as children leave their parents and forge their own identity and position in their social groupings. They begin to learn from the outside world, "match themselves against the expectations of others, compare their performance with that of their peers and develop customary ways of responding to challenges" (Eccles, 1999). Parental opinions are influential, but their peers' opinions are more important. They become very self-aware and self-conscience about their appearance, abilities, and behavior in relation to others.

Middle childhood, more so than any other developmental stage, is characterized by a strong desire to be included and to belong (Lease, Musgrove, & Axelrod, 2002). Peer acceptance during middle childhood plays an important role in short-term and long-term adjustment and coping. Members of this age group begin to establish a concept of self, as well as begin to navigate the scene of sophisticated social interaction. Children during this period learn how to effectively communicate within a group, gain problem-solving skills, and begin to understand norms for acceptance and rejection. The majority of conversation between these preteens is spent learning about social rules and norms (Lease et al., 2002). Additionally, time is spent acquiring self-presentation skills in hopes of gaining status and inclusion. This could include more recent methods of social interaction, such as social media and texting.

Middle childhood is a period often defined by the need for peer approval. Children attempt to imitate the behaviors, personalities, conversation styles, and dress of their peers in order to feel as if they fit in or belong. Conformity is very much a pressure faced by all children as they search for their role during middle childhood.

How well children succeed at learning the social rules and self-presentational strategies has a large impact on the development of **social self-concept**, as do social successes and failures (Lease et al., 2002).

Social self-concept includes beliefs about one's own self-desirability, self-efficacy, and social competence. Preadolescents are highly concerned about social status within their peer group (Lease et al., 2002). In addition, having friends is crucial to children's social and emotional well-being. Positive feelings of self-worth are related to lowered anxiety and rejection, as well as heightened social competence.

Social Hierarchy

As in general society and adult interactions, the middle child will find himself or herself operating within a social world that has established social hierarchies. Those with social dominance and increased social status have greater influence over peer group function. In contrast, low social dominance in children is marked by the inability or low motivation to acquire control or resources. Thus, peer group members often overlook these individuals.

Children who use prosocial strategies (i.e., leadership qualities) to achieve dominance are generally more liked by their peers. However, combinations in types of social dominance have been shown to ultimately determine likability and popularity in middle childhood. This may be due to the fact that higher status pre-adolescents are more socially sophisticated. In addition, popularity seems to be linked to higher intelligence, increased athleticism, and physical attractiveness. These children also likely play a large role in establishing social norms within peer groups. While those deemed as *popular* students do not employ coercive strategies to gain social dominance (Lease et al., 2002), others have relied on such coercive strategies such as bullying as a way of exerting influence.

Often, bullying occurs within same demographic groups. Since differences in physical characteristics, such as hair and skin color, along with school factors like academic performance and ability, serve as targets for bullying, one might assume that there would be an increased occurrence of bullying across ethnic groups. Research, (e.g., Merrell-James, 2006) suggests that the majority of bullying often occurs in intraracial environments. As a counselor, it is important to recognize that intraracial bullying often occurs in schools and develop a zero-tolerance policy for verbal bullying in your school that is adequately enforced. In addition, the counselors could provide prevention activities, such as groups for students, classroom guidance activities, and workshops for parents.

While the form that bullying takes appears to vary according to gender, with females more likely to use gossip and rumors as coercive strategies and males more likely to exhibit physical aggression, the impact is, or can be, just as damaging for the victims.

Friendship

Friendship in middle childhood fosters self-efficacy development, social development, and social awareness and helps children understand how to work with other members of society (Jacobson & Brudsal, 2012). Selman & Schultz (1990) explained friendship development as taking place in approximated stages. During middle childhood, children can move between stages 0, 1, and 2. There are a total of 5 stages, each defined by the approximate age of children in that group, the forms that their shared experience take on while in that stage, the social perspective-taking tendencies of that stage, and their interpersonal negotiation strategies. Table 7.2, Selman's Stages of Friendship and Levels of Perspective-Taking Skills, outlines the different stages of friendship and levels of perspective-taking skills.

While having friends is important for all children, the nature of friendships seems to differ according to gender. Boys, for example, tend to prefer larger and loosely organized friendship circles, whereas girls seem to prefer fewer, more exclusive friendships.

Table 7.2   Selman's Stages of Friendship and Levels of Perspective-Taking Skills

Stage	Approximate Age	Forms of Shared Experience	Social Perspective-Taking	Interpersonal Negotiation Strategies
0	3 to 6 years	Unreflective imitation or enmeshment	Undifferentiated/Egocentric	Physical force; impulsive fight or flight
1	5 to 9 years	Unreflective sharing of expressive enthusiasm	Differentiated/Subjective	One-way, unilateral power; orders or obedience
2	8 to 12 years	Reflective sharing of similar perceptions or experiences	Reciprocal/Self-Reflective	Cooperative exchange; reciprocity; persuasion or deference
3	10 to 15 years	Empathic sharing of beliefs and values	Mutual/Third-Person	Mutual compromise
4	Late teen/adulthood	Interdependent sharing of vulnerabilities and self	Intimate/In-Depth/Societal	Collaborative integration of relationship dynamics

Source: Adopted from Selman, 1980.

It is clear that friendship is crucial to the developmental process in middle childhood. Bowker, Rubin, Burgess, Booth-LaForce, & Rose-Krasnor (2006) investigated the importance of best-friend relationships during middle childhood. Although some children have the same best friend throughout middle childhood, others have numerous best friends. Research suggests that it is not necessarily the stability of one consistent best friend that is important but the stability of having a friend or buddy at all times during this developmental period. Results of this study went on to suggest that having different best friends instead of the same best friend can lead to higher levels of positive adjustment, and that the loss of a best friend without their being replaced by a new best friend can lead to increased difficulties with adjustment during middle childhood (Bowker et al., 2006).

The presence of friendships, regardless of quantity or exclusivity, tends to increase self-esteem, promotes adjustment, and reduces social anxiety. Similarly, the absence of friendships in middle childhood can result in problem behaviors, low academic achievement, and emotional difficulties within students. Research has shown that peer rejection and neglect during middle childhood can result in short-term and long-term behavioral and emotional problems (Hoglund, Lalonde, & Leadbeater, 2008).

Effects of Social Anxiety

There is also a strong link between friendship quality and risk for social anxiety. Unfortunately, these implications have been found to be stronger for females during middle childhood. For example, negative friendship qualities such as conflict and betrayal place children at higher risk for development of social anxiety (Greco & Morris, 2005).

Whereas social anxiety could be the result of negative friendship, research also shows that social anxiety contributes to the lack of positive relationships. For example, those with social anxiety often lack social skills necessary for engagement (Greco & Morris, 2005). Further, the tendency toward avoidance and withdrawal, which are hallmark indicators of social anxiety, may hinder the development of crucial social skills during middle childhood due to lack of exposure. Case Illustration 7.1 will assist you in gaining the knowledge you will need to work with these clients.

Additional Factors

Peers are one of the many factors across the early stages of life that affect an individual's self-esteem. In addition, early attachment with parents is one factor that may greatly impact a child's self-concept (Booth-LaForce, Oh, Kim, Ribin, Rose-Krasnor, & Burgess, 2006). Children in preadolescence adopt an internal working model of experiences with parents. Children are likely to view themselves as a product of how they have been cared for or neglected by their caregivers. Studies have shown that children who view their parents as trustworthy and dependable feel that they are more worthy of trust and love, thus positively impacting self-esteem (Minzi, 2010). This view of self carries over into other relationships as well, affecting the quality and foundation of each relationship.

In addition, children with supportive primary caregivers are more likely to hold positive expectations regarding social situations and have greater opportunities to learn social skills. Using the caregiver as a secure base for social exploration, the secure parent-child attachment results in socially competent behavior with peer interactions. Consequently, children who are insecurely attached are at risk for developing social problems, such as anxiety, avoidance, or aggression (Minzi, 2010). Security with the mother results in higher social competence, while security with the father results in lower aggression (Booth-Laforce et al., 2006). However, secure attachment with both parents is related to more a positive self-concept.

Gender Identity and Self-Esteem

During middle childhood, children develop their gender identity, which can affect self-esteem. Gender identity is defined as "an individual's knowledge of his or her membership into a gender category or identification of oneself as male of female" (Xie, 2010). Gender typicality and gender contentment are positively related to peer acceptance and higher self-esteem. Gender typicality is a self-perceived sense of similarity to members of one's own gender group, whereas gender contentment is one's satisfaction with his or her own gender. Individuals who feel pressure to conform to gender stereotypes are more likely to have low gender typicality and low gender contentment, resulting in lower psychological adjustment and internalizing problems (Xie, 2010).

The multifactorial gender theory suggests that gender identity not only includes one's identification with a chosen gender but also involves ones' personal and public esteem of their gender, as well as the effect of gender stereotypes (Xie, 2010). Each culture, with its own view of gender status, gender socialization, and stereotypes, may influence gender identity development. For example, in cultures where males have higher status, males have reported greater pressure to conform to gender stereotypes. This pressure often leads to more negative psychological adjustment, as well as affects one's gender typicality and gender contentment (Xie, 2010). Middle childhood is a time period in which fitting in is of upmost importance to a child's self-esteem. Thus, above all, gender typicality is the most predictive correlate of adjustment and self-esteem in middle childhood (Xie, 2010). This implies that parents, counselors, and mental health professionals should help children become more comfortable with their own gender category but also encourage them to explore cross-gender activities (Xie, 2010).

CASE ILLUSTRATION 7.1 ADJUSTING TO NEW SCHOOL

Annie moved with her family from China to the United States when she was 7 years old. Her family emigrated so that they could be close to other family members and for the educational opportunities for their children. Once Annie's family moved, her parents found employment very quickly, and Annie had to go to school. Currently, Annie is in the third grade, and her older brother, Andrew, is in the eighth grade. Andrew is an academically advanced student and gets along with his peers very well. Annie, however, is very shy and reserved. She also has a heavy Chinese accent that is hard to comprehend. This makes her not want to answer questions in class or talk with the other students. Although the school Annie attends is very multicultural, Annie seems to get teased the most, even by the students of Chinese descent. The students make fun of her speech and the items she wears. Even though Annie has not made friends in her class, she has made friends at church. She seems to have a lot in common with her friends from church, and she wishes that she had friends like them in her class at school.

Mrs. Natsis, Annie's teacher, assigns a group project for the week. Annie is put in a group with her classmate Jill, a leader in the class and a popular girl in school. Jill has called Annie at night to work on the project and is nice to her; however, Jill teases Annie while at school. Annie does not understand why Jill is nice to her on the phone but mean to her at school.

Mrs. Natsis begins to observe and realize that Annie is not participating in the group project. From the teacher's perspective, she believes that Annie is "too reserved" and does not see her receiving a passing grade for the assignment. She also mentions that Annie does not participate in class by answering questions. Hoping she will help Annie do better in school, she refers her to the school's student support team, whose role is to evaluate students with special needs.

Practice Exercise: The following exercise questions are design to make you reflect after reading the Case Illustration 7.1 and for the purpose of class discussion.

1. Should the teacher call on her since she is not going to answer questions independently?

2. Is there anyone in her class that she could make friends with?

3. Can you give her ways to deal with the students making fun of her? To let her know that what they are saying is not right, and that she needs to tell the teacher or counselor when she hears it?

4. It is positive that she has made friends at church—do any of those friends go to school with her—does she have anything in common with the students at school?

5. Ask Jill why she is acting that way to Annie.

6. Could Jill and Annie be friends?

7. Should the teacher have referred Annie to the school counselor even though she is not a student of special needs, but she just does not understand the culture in the United States?

Moral Development

Children in middle childhood are active in the self-development process. An important aspect of self-development is the development of morals or values. During the years of middle childhood, children establish their own set of beliefs that help actively justify their behaviors. Children's moral development is influenced by both parents and friends, each playing a very important role in the rate of moral growth and development. The influence that parents have on a child's moral development is much different than the influence had by the child's peers (Walker, Hennig, & Krettenauer, 2000). As cognitive processes become more advanced, children take their understanding of the differences in right and wrong a step further, now evaluating situations and determining the way in which they choose to behave. A person's moral beliefs are somewhat of a guiding factor throughout daily life. Middle childhood provides the initial opportunities for children to practice their beliefs and act based on their personal morals.

Kohlberg constructed a theory of moral development that consists of three levels, each having two stages within each level. The three levels are preconventional reasoning, conventional reasoning, and postconventional reasoning. During middle childhood, moral development is somewhere between the preconventional and conventional reasoning stages. During the preconventional reasoning stage, children do not internalize moral values and their moral reasoning is controlled by rewards and punishment. The conventional reasoning stage is the middle stage of moral development. During this stage, children begin to abide by certain standards, but these standards are set by others around them (Santrock, 2007). Kohlberg's stages are further defined in Table 7.3, Kohlberg's Stages of Moral Development, below.

Piaget constructed a stage theory of moral development. In this theory, children around ages 4 to 7 are in the first stage of moral development known as heteronomous morality. During this stage, children perceive justice and rules as unchangeable and beyond the control of people. Children who are heteronomous thinkers see rules that are broken to result in immediate punishment tied to that rule. The second stage of moral development is autonomous morality. This stage is usually entered into around age 10, and children gain the ability to understand that

Table 7.3   Kohlberg's Stages of Moral Development

Level	Stage	Age	Social Orientation/ Focus	Focus
Preconventional	1	Up to 10–13 Years	Obedience and punishment	Self
Preconventional	2	Up to 10–13 Years	Individualism, instrumentalism, and exchange	Self
Conventional	3	Beginning of middle school, up to middle age.	"Good boy/girl"	Significant others
Conventional	4	Beginning of middle school, up to middle age.	Law and order	Significant others
Postconventional	5	Few reach this level, most not prior to middle age.	Social contract	Justice, dignity for all life, and common good
Postconventional	6	Few reach this level, most not prior to middle age.	Principled conscience	Justice, dignity for all, and common good

Source: http://www.csudh.edu/dearhabermas/kohlberg01bk.htm

rules and laws are created by people and consequences are not so black and white but instead are something to be considered along with the intentions of the person (Santrock, 2007). For example, a child during this stage might cheat on a test or lie to a parent or teacher. Thus, dealing with the consequences as they go through this stage of development could be challenging. Table 7.4 Piaget's Stages of Moral Development further explains Piaget's stages of moral development.

Emotional Development

It is necessary to understand some of the factors regarding middle childhood and emotional development. According to estimates by practitioners, researchers, and policy makers, currently, one in five children has a diagnosable mental illness. Additionally, one in 10 children has a serious emotional disturbance that negatively affects functioning (Kutash & Duchnowski, 2004; Mellin, 2009). Unfortunately, an astounding 70% of children and adolescents, who are in need of mental health services, reportedly never receive the treatment needed for healthy functioning (Kutash & Duchnowski, 2004; Mellin, 2009). Disruptive behaviors, mood disorders, and adjustment disorders are the most frequent diagnoses seen among children today. Much of the literature addressing children and adolescents with emotional disturbances has identified the majority of consumers to be mostly male with low to average intelligence, with most falling about 2 years behind their peers in academic performance. In addition, many individuals who are classified in this category show symptoms associated with oppositional defiance or conduct disorders. Antipsychotic medications are prescribed at a rate of six times higher than they were a decade ago; however, an astounding 86% of children who are prescribed antipsychotic medication do not have a psychotic disorder (Mellin, 2009).

Parenting Styles

Differing styles and trends in parenting often lead to various emotional outcomes during middle childhood. In the early 1990s, a new type of intelligence, known as **emotional intelligence**, was coined in the field of human science.

Table 7.4   Piaget's Stages of Moral Development

Stage	Age	Child's View of Morality	Child's View of Rules	Child's View of Punishment
Premoral	0 to 3 yrs.	Child has little to no concept of morality.	Child has little to no concept of rules.	Child has little to no concept of punishment.
Heteronomous Morality	4 to 10 yrs.	Moral reasoning is governed by external rules. Outcomes are seen as more important than intentions.	Rules are beyond the control of people; they are fixed and can't be changed; they are created by older adult.	Expiatory punishment; no attempt to fit the punishment to the crime.
Autonomous Morality	10 yrs. and up	Child has more flexible view of morality. Intentions are considered more than outcomes.	Rules are created by people; they are more flexible and can change.	Reciprocal punishment; attempts to fit the punishment to the crime.

Source: Adapted from www.psychology4a.com/develop10.htm

Emotional intelligence may be a predictor of future success, as research has confirmed a positive relationship between high emotional intelligence and positive developmental outcomes. Emotional intelligence may lead to an overall sense of well-being, academic achievement, adaptive coping, and physical and psychological health. Individuals who are emotionally healthy are capable of understanding and regulating their emotions, which in turn guides behavior. Different parenting styles model different methods of displaying and communicating emotion and coping for children. Four types of parenting styles have been identified and are typically discussed in literature. The variety of parenting styles can have direct impact on children and their emotional development.

Authoritative parents often use developmentally appropriate demands. They are affectionate and responsive to their children. This type of parenting is usually marked by open communication. Authoritative parents also gain control of their children in a developmentally appropriate fashion and only when necessary.

Authoritarian parents are highly demanding and use a high level of control in handling their children. These parents usually show little affection toward their children and have closed communication between one another.

Permissive parenting is marked by very few rules and regulations over their children. These parents make very few demands and exercise little control over their children. This parenting style is often associated with a high level of responsiveness and affection from parent to child.

Neglectful parents make very few demands of their children and are often uninvolved in their children's lives. This style of parenting is marked by little control, low level of affection, and little to no communication between parent and child.

Authoritative parenting styles yield the most positive emotional outcomes in children. These children have persistently scored higher in measures of adjustment, resilience, attachment, academic achievement, and social competence. Many children of authoritative parents have been found to have lower externalizing behavior and higher levels of self-regulation skills. Many of the outcomes associated with such positive parenting traits have been found to extend well into adulthood with few diminishing effects. Negative parental demands include practices such as psychological control, inconsistent or punitive discipline, and harsh disciplining. These types of parenting practices are found to correspond with internalizing and externalizing problems, personality disorders, lower prosocial behavior, and anxiety. Extend your knowledge about different parenting styles by completing Guided Practice Exercise 7.3.

Guided Practice Exercise 7.3 Parenting Styles

1. What are the four parenting styles?

2. Compare and contrast each:
   - Which one were your parents?
   - Which one do you see yourself being?
   - Which one do you see as best and worst?

Counseling Issues

In response to the crisis in youth mental health, counselors need to be competent in reference to the identification of several factors to guide service delivery, which include culturally specific and sensitive interventions, contextually

Photo 7.3   Counselors need to understand the unique needs of clients from different ages.

Source: Stockbyte/Stockbyte/Thinkstock.

based practices that are geared toward individual needs, practices that are family driven and community centered, strengths-focused and resilience-focused interventions, and practices that are coordinated across various mental health and related systems (Mellin, 2009). Today, many practitioners are moving their interventions for children and adolescents from controlled settings to ordinary school settings. Recent literature has shown the importance of school contexts in development as well as the vast potential for improving mental health through implementing services within the school context (Kutash & Dutchnowski, 2004; Masten, 2003). Schools have many avenues to foster some of the most powerful systems for teaching social adaptation, building self-efficacy, and problem-solving skills. The school grounds have recently come to the forefront of theory in developmental psychopathology, resilience, and prevention research. Research has shown that 70% of children who receive mental health services are doing so within the context of school systems (Kutash & Duchnowaski, 2004). Children who receive mental health services at school may also receive the services at home as well. When children receive services at home and in the school setting, school counselors are able to collaborate with the mental health professional as well as with the parents on what issues are being seen in the school setting and how they can be addressed at home also. It keeps all the parties that are involved with the student on the same page and if further issues arise, all three parties are in contact and responsive services can be provided in the school and at home simultaneously. Children at this age might need to speak with a counselor for a variety of issues. Case Illustration 7.2 is an example of one such problem that might occur and that is common today among children of military parents.

CASE ILLUSTRATION 7.2 DEALING WITH MILITARY DEPLOYMENT

Elaina has always been an *A* student. Now, she is in the sixth grade, and her grades are beginning to drop. She is very quiet in class and has started to realize that if she keeps to herself and is quiet, she will not get called on in class. It is almost as if she fades away with the scene and she likes it. She has completely disengaged from the school. She is compliant and easily overlooked by her teacher. Since

(Continued)

(Continued)

she is obedient and not disruptive, the teacher does not believe she needs counseling. Elaina's teacher recently told Elaina's mother that if Elaina does not start paying attention in class, she is afraid she will fail the sixth grade. This is very unusual to the mother because Elaina has never had academic problems in school. The teacher shows the mother where she has had multiple homework assignments she has not turned in for a grade and asks if she thinks Elaina believes it is cool not to make good grades. She also asks Elaina's mom if there is anything going on at home that would make Elaina so disengaged. Elaina's mom mentions that her husband recently was deployed. She says that she thinks this may have something to do with Elaina's actions.

Practice Exercise: The following exercise statements and questions are design to make you reflect after reading the Case Illustration 7.2 and for the purpose of class discussion.

1.   Elaina should receive individual counseling to talk about her father leaving—how does it make her feel? What are her thoughts about him not being at home?

2.   Grades are not on Elaina's mind. What can the counselor do to help her to get her grades back up? How can the counselor get Elaina to think about school while at school and home while at home?

3.   The counselor should talk with Mother about Elaina doing her homework. Can Mother help her with her homework? Could her teacher send home daily e-mails telling Mom what homework there is to do so that Elaina cannot say that she does not have any homework?

4.   When is Elaina going to get to see her father again? Is there any chance they could Skype him while he is away?

5.   Could the counselor talk to the teacher and let her know that Elaina needs to be called on more in class to keep her engaged?

6.   Elaina needs to know that she could possibly fail. What would happen if she failed? Would her dad be proud of her? Does she want her dad to be proud of her?

Current Counseling Trends

Currently, in the school setting, counseling can be brief, particularly if there is only one counselor for 600 or more students. Time constraints, along with psychological testing and noncounseling duties, often leave little time to be spent on individual counseling. Not only do counselors provide classroom guidance and individual and group counseling for students but they also provide behavior interventions for students exhibiting a significant number of behavioral issues within the school setting. Behavioral interventions can be in the form of group counseling, individual counseling, and check-in/check-out methods. Solution-focused brief counseling is advantageous in the school setting as it works toward a solution to the problem. Solution-focused counseling can be incorporated into a group setting or individual counseling. Instead of revisiting the past and what occurred prior to the problem, the student focuses on the present and works toward a solution. If the student needs more intense therapy, school counselors usually refer the parents to an outside or community agency or private practice.

Additionally, choice theory has also been seen as being effective when working with middle childhood and pre-adolescent children in the school setting. Choice Theory can be used as a preventative and remedial intervention for dealing with students who have repetitive behavioral issues in the school setting (Walter, Lambie, & Ngazimbi, 2008). During middle childhood, at-risk students often feel as if their need for belonging has not been met, and the importance of school begins to decline (Davis & Lambie, 2005). When using Choice Theory during middle childhood, students began to see how their own choices and actions affect their behavioral outcomes in all aspects of life. This is related to their natural drive toward independence and responsibility, cognitive capabilities, and moral reasoning during this stage of development.

Corey (2004) suggests that using choice theory with reality therapy techniques in a group setting can be very effective for children during middle childhood. During group counseling, students begin to see and hear how different choices made by others in the same situation produced a more responsible outcome for the student (Walter et al., 2008). Reality therapy techniques are incorporated to focus on changing the current behavior exhibited by the student so that his or her needs are met more effectively (Glasser, 2001). Therefore, students in the group begin to realize that by making more responsible and appropriate choices, other areas of their life will benefit from the choices made, and additionally, their needs are met more effectively in all aspects of life.

Cultural Diversity Issues

Because demographics in the United States are constantly shifting, it is crucial for counselors and educators to understand and respect the diverse cultural, racial, ethnic, and national backgrounds of children, learned from their parents, and how each of these facets can impact a child's development during middle childhood (Coll & Szalacha, 2004). At a pivotal point in self-development, children from all ethnicities face the pressures of social comparison, wavering self-esteem levels, and a desire for social acceptance. Because of these developments, it is crucial that children from diverse backgrounds are encouraged to establish their multicultural identity. During middle childhood, behaviors and thoughts are easily influenced by the child's environment. It is important that the role of counselor be used to encourage multicultural exploration throughout the school's population. Students, parents, and teachers should be informed on the multicultural diversity that exists around them or that they represent within their school environment. As is often the case, individuals in minority groups choose to take on a strong ethnic role, proudly being part of a smaller part of a large society. The connection to this group, and the sense of social acceptance and belonging that comes as a result of their cultural awareness, also proves to raise self-esteem levels. The downfall of this is that although strong cultural ties provide positive outcomes, children in middle childhood rarely will go against the social norms of their surroundings to seek out their racial identity (Merrell-James, 2006). It is pertinent that the role of a professional counselor be used to provide the opportunities for students of all cultural backgrounds to gain this identity. Encouraging the exploration of different cultures, races, and minority groups allows for children to experience a more complex understanding of differing perspectives that exist around them. Additionally, the encouragement of multicultural awareness and forming of identities increases the social competence of all students regardless of their being a part of a minority group or not.

While middle childhood can provide a positive environment for multicultural students who are encouraged to explore and connect to their multicultural identity, this is often not the environment that is home to students from diverse backgrounds. Middle childhood often exposes children of color and immigrant backgrounds to racism, discrimination, and exclusion for the first time. All children, especially during middle childhood, should acquire specific developmental competencies; however, children from different cultures, backgrounds, or ethnicities may not acquire specific competencies in the same manner (Coll & Szalacha, 2004). During middle childhood, students from culturally diverse backgrounds, tend to acquire negative attitudes toward school, teachers, and academic achievement (Coll & Szalacha, 2004). Segregation, discrimination, and racism toward culturally diverse students are often the causes of negative attitudes. When students from various backgrounds are segregated or excluded from the mainstream students, they start to mistrust individuals from the dominant culture that surrounds them. This, in turn, may affect a student's relationships with his or her peers or teachers, which can decrease his or her motivation to achieve academically (Coll & Szalacha, 2004).

Developmental outcomes of culturally diverse children during middle childhood are also affected by the lack of resources within the school to address the needs of culturally diverse students (Coll & Szalacha, 2004). Bilingual students, along with their parents, may struggle to communicate with school faculty and staff if the school does not have a translator. Communication between the school personnel and a culturally diverse student is essential when trying to meet the needs of the student. If the parents of a culturally diverse student cannot understand the reasoning of specific interventions being incorporated into their child's education, the interventions will become less effective, placing the child at a greater developmental risk (Coll & Szalacha, 2004). Lastly, through effective communication, school counselors, community agencies, and culturally diverse families can mutually define the problem of the student, underlying causes of the problem, and the course of action for appropriate cultural interventions (Coll & Szalacha, 2004). Through collaboration, the parents are assured the interventions are appropriately aligned with cultural goals and values as well as the purpose of the intervention within the dominant culture. The student becomes the ultimate beneficiary of interventions and makes significant gains in developmental competencies (Coll & Szalacha, 2004).

Middle childhood is a period of continuous change and transformation for all children, regardless of their cultural background or minority status. Social development proves challenging for almost all children in some form or another, students from diverse cultures being no exception. Children become aware of ethnic stigmas at a very young age, and these stigmas can lead to academic anxiety and low intrinsic motivation (Gillen-O'Neel, Ruble, & Fuligni, 2011). School counselors should encourage teachers to create learning environments that consider the difficulties faced by children of minority status in the classroom. The current focus of education is that of educating all children. In order to assure the education of all students occurs, regardless of their ethnic background, teachers and educators must reach beyond traditional teaching methods and employ instructional methods to create a classroom environment that will foster learning and encourage participation of all students. As counselors, it is crucial to advocate for the students from multicultural backgrounds by encouraging the educators to recognize their own personal biases, seek out instructional methods to reach all students, and provide support for the multicultural awareness of the school as a whole. Case Illustration 7.3 can further help you explore the challenges you might face as a counselor when working with culturally diverse students.

CASE ILLUSTRATION 7.3 ISSUES WITH BEING A GIFTED STUDENT

In second grade, Jon was accepted into the gifted program at school. Now, Jon is in fourth grade, and he is starting to show signs of depression. He is academically advanced; however, he struggles at paying attention in class and getting along with his peers. His teacher, Ms. Warnock, believes he is not as socially advanced as he is academically, and that it is putting him at a disadvantage in class. She has referred him to the school counselor, Mr. Coulter, to see if he can work with him on finding a social niche and lifting his depression.

When talking with Mr. Coulter, Jon mentions that no one in the class likes him because he is so much smarter than everyone else. Jon believes that he needs to start making lower grades so that he will fit in with everyone else. He also talks about the material they are learning in class and bring ups why he doesn't pay attention. He says that it is boring because he already knows how to do it since his parents taught him. Therefore, he finishes his work quickly and then has nothing to do. He wishes the teacher would teach him something that he did not already know.

Practice Exercise: The following exercise statements and questions are design to make you reflect after reading the Case Illustration 7.3 and for the purpose of class discussion.

1. Has the teacher thought of having something extra for him to do when he finishes his work?

2. The counselor needs to talk with Jon about paying attention in class—does he possibly have ADHD/ADD?

3. Jon needs to know that being gifted is not a fault. He can make good grades and keep them to himself instead of letting the entire class know that he makes good grades. How can the counselor help him understand this?

4. If he is diagnosed with depression, he could have a 504 plan, but the teacher needs to make some type of accommodations for him since he is finishing his work early and is bored. Since he knows some of the work already, could he teach some of it to the class?

5. Jon needs to make a friend in his class. How could the counselor help him do that?

6. The counselor could start a social skills group and get his parents to sign a permission slip saying he could be in it. How could this help his poor socialization skills and help him meet new people and make friends?

7. What does Jon like to do? Is there a club he could join? Could he tutor students who need help?

A Time of Wonder

This period of middle childhood is certainly one of excitement, concern, enjoyment, anxiety, and most certainly change. During this developmental period, the middle childhood, children begin the transition that will take them to adulthood. They realize that they need to function more independently as they move toward adolescence. They begin to make better decisions and social choices. They begin to establish their own society and social grouping while continuing to rely on parents and peers as they make their way to early adolescence.

Counselors can play an important role not just in directly supporting the individual through this developmental period but by assisting parents, teachers, and extended family through educational programming and psychological support. Working as a team, as a community of caregivers, we can all help make the transition to early adolescence go much smoother.

SUMMARY

➤ Middle childhood, the period after early childhood, approximately from age 6 to 12, is the elementary school period.
➤ Emotional development is very important during this stage, as it has a direct effect on coping and problem-solving skills.
➤ Social development can directly impact emotional development, but counselors need to remember these are highly individualized.

➤ The brain undergoes two major growth spurts during middle childhood.
➤ According to Piaget, middle childhood is marked by specific developmental milestones that directly impact a child's social cognition.
➤ Peer acceptance during middle childhood plays an important role in a child's self-esteem.
➤ Children develop characteristics of social self-concept and social anxiety during this stage, which can have an effect on their self-identity.
➤ Many counselors are moving their interventions for children and adolescences from controlled settings to school settings.
➤ Solution-focused brief counseling is an effective counseling theory within the school setting.
➤ More research should be done on the comparison of developmental competencies of children of color and immigrant families along with children of the dominant culture (Coll & Szalacha, 2004).

ADDITIONAL RESOURCES

Journals

Developmental Psychology
Journal of Abnormal Child Psychology
Journal of Clinical Child and Adolescent Psychology
Journal of Cognition and Development
Journal of Experimental Child Psychology
Journal of Nutrition Education & Behavior

Websites

Challenges of Middle Childhood. http://www.education.com/reference/article/Ref_Development_Ages/.
Early and Middle Childhood. http://www.healthypeople.gov/2020/topicsobjectives2020/ebr.aspx?topicId = 10.
Middle Childhood (9 to 11 years of age). http://www.cdc.gov/ncbddd/childdevelopment/positiveparenting/middle2.html.
Middle Childhood. http://www.wellsphere.com/wellpage/middle-childhood.
Physical, Cognitive and Psychological Development. http://www.livestrong.com/article/5417-need-stages-middle-childhood-development/.

Videos

Lifespan Development—Middle Childhood Development. http://www.youtube.com/watch?v = swG2DQpNs-k.
Lifespan Development—Middle Childhood—Intellectual Development Intelligence and Creativity. http://www.youtube.com/watch?v = 1vib6gwIP14&feature = relmfu
Lifespan Development—Middle Childhood—Personality Development. http://www.youtube.com/watch?v = oRB2yGQu-9g&feature = relmfu
Lifespan Development—Middle Childhood—Social Development. http://www.youtube.com/watch?v = Flhr7gxLp5U&feature = relmfu

Books

Blake, R. R., & Blake, B. (2012). *Becoming a teacher: Using narrative as reflective practice. A cross-disciplinary approach. Counterpoints: Studies in the postmodern theory of education* (Vol. 411). New York, NY: Peter Lang.
Geffner, R. A., Loring, M., & Young, C. (2001). *Bullying behavior: Current issues, research, and interventions.* Binghamton, NY: The Haworth Press.

Giannetti, C. C., & Sagarese, M. (1997). *The roller-coaster years: Raising your child through the maddening yet magical middle school years. A comprehensive guide for parents of 10- to 15-year-olds.* New York, NY: Bantam Doubleday Dell.

Henn-Reinke, K., & Chesner, G. A. (2006). *Developing voice through the Language Arts.* Thousand Oaks:, CA: SAGE.

Recommended Supplemental Readings

Chen, B., & Chang, L. (2012). Adaptive insecure attachment and resource control strategies during middle childhood. *International Journal of Behavioral Development, 36*(5), 389–397. doi:10.1177/0165025412445440

Colle, L., & Del Giudice, M. (2011). Patterns of attachment and emotional competence in middle childhood. *Social Development, 20*(1), 51–72. doi:10.1111/j.1467–9507.2010.00576.x

Kushner, S., Tackett, J., & Bagby, R. R. (2012). The structure of internalizing disorders in middle childhood and evidence for personality correlates. *Journal of Psychopathology & Behavioral Assessment, 34*(1), 22–34. doi:10.1007/s10862-011–9263-4

Lancy, D., & Grove, M. (2011). Getting noticed. Middle childhood in cross-cultural perspective. *Human Nature, 22(3).* Hawthorne, N.Y., pp. 281–302.

Rogers, L., Zosuls, K., Halim, M., Ruble, D., Hughes, D., & Fuligni, A. (2012). Meaning making in middle childhood: An exploration of the meaning of ethnic identity. *Cultural Diversity & Ethnic Minority Psychology, 18*(2), 99–108.

References

American Heart Association. (2012). *Overweight in children.* Retrieved from http://www.heart.org/HEARTORG/GettingHealthy/WeightManagement/Obesity/Overweight-in-Children_UCM_304054_Article.jsp

Bauer, K. W., Yang, Y. W., & Austin, S. B. (2004). How can we stay healthy when you're throwing all of this in front of us? Findings from focus groups and interviews in middle schools on environmental influences on nutrition and physical activity. *Health Education and Behavior, 31(1),* 34–46.

Booth-LaForce, C., Oh, W., Kim, A. H., Ribin, K. H., Rose-Krasnor, L., & Burgess, K., (2006). Attachment, self-worth, and peer-group functioning in middle childhood. *Attachment and Human Development, 8(4),* 309–325.

Bowker, J. C. W., Rubin, K. H., Burgess, K. B., Booth-LaForce, C., & Rose-Krasnor, L. (2006). Behavioral characteristics associated with stable and fluid best friendship patterns in middle childhood. *Merrill-Palmer Quarterly, 52*(4), 671–693.

Cecil-Karb, R., & Grogan-Kaylor, A. (2009). Childhood body mass index in community context: Neighborhood safety, television viewing, and growth trajectories of BMI. *Health Social Work, 34(3),* 169–177.

Coll, C. G., & Szalacha, L. A. (2004). Children of immigrant families. *The Future of Children, 14*(2), 81–97.

Corey, G. (2004). *Theory and practice of group counseling* (6th ed.). Belmont, CA: Brooks/Cole.

Davis, K. M., & Lambie, G. W. (2005). Family engagement: A collaborative, systemic approach for middle school counselors. *Professional School Counseling, 9,* 144–151.

Eccles, J. S. (1999). The development of children ages 6 to 14. *The Future of Children, 9*(2), 30–44. Retrieved from http://www.princeton.edu/futureofchildren/pubilcations/docs/09_02_02.pdf.

Gillen-O'Neel, C., Ruble, D. N., & Fuligni, A. J. (2011). Ethnic stigma, academic anxiety, and intrinsic motivation in middle childhood. *Child Development, 82*(5), 1470–1485.

Glasser, W. (2001). *Counseling with choice theory: The new reality therapy.* New York, NY: Haper Collins.

Greco, L. A., & Morris, T. L. (2005). Factors influencing the link between social anxiety and peer acceptance: Contributions of social skills and close friendships during middle childhood. *Behavior Therapy, 36,* 197–205.

Hoglund, W. L. G., Lalonde, C. E., & Leadbeater, B. J. (2008). Social-cognitive competence, peer rejection and neglect, and behavioral and emotional problems in middle childhood. *Social Development, 17*(3), 528–553.

Jacobson, L. T., & Brudsal, C. A. (2012). Academic performance in middle school: Friendship influences. *Global Journal of Community Psychology Practice, 2*(3), 1–12. Retrieved from http://www.gjcpp.org/.

Kutash, K., & Duchnowski, A. J. (2004). The mental health needs of youth with emotional and behavioral disabilities placed in special education programs in urban schools. *Journal of Child and Family Studies, 13(2),* 235–248.

Lease, A. M., Musgrove, K. T., & Axelrod, J. L., (2002). Dimensions of social status in preadolescent peer groups: Likability, perceived popularity, and social dominance. *Social Development, 11(4),* 508–533.

Lee, C. C. (2005). Urban School Counseling: Context, Characteristics, and Competencies. *Professional School Counseling, 8*(3), 184–188.

Masten, A. S. (2003). Commentary: Developmental psychopathology as a unifying context for mental health and education models, research, and practice in schools. *School Psychology Reviews, 32*(2), 169–173.

Mellin, E. A. (2009). Responding to the crisis in children's mental health: Potential roles for the counseling profession. *Journal of Counseling and Development, 87,* 501–506.

Merrell-James, R. (2006). Intra-racial bullying: An issue of multicultural counseling. *Persistently Safe Schools 2006: Collaborating with Students, Families, and Communities,* 283–294.

Minzi, C. D. R. (2010). Gender and cultural patterns of mothers' and fathers' attachments and links with children's self-competence, depression, and loneliness in middle and late childhood. *Early Childhood Development and Care, 180*(1–2).

Nuru-Jeter. A. M., Sarsour, K., Jutte, D. P., & Boyce, W. T. (2010). Socioeconomic predictors of health and development in middle childhood: Variations by socioeconomic status measure and race. *Issues in Comprehensive Pediatric Nursing, 33,* 59–81.

Payne, Ruby K. (2005). *A framework for understanding poverty.* Highlands, TX: Process, Inc.

Santrock, J. W. (2007). *Child Development.* New York, NY: McGraw-Hill.

Selman, R. L. (1980). *The growth of interpersonal understanding.* New York, NY: Academic Press.

Selman, R. L., & Schultz, L. H. (1990). *Making a friend in youth: Developmental theory and pair therapy.* Chicago, IL University of Chicago Press.

Storch, E. A., Milsom, V. A., DeBraganza, N., Lewin, A. B., Geffken, G. R., & Silverstein, J. H. (2007). Peer victimization, psychosocial adjustment, and physical activity in overweight and at-risk-for-overweight youth. *Journal of Pediatric Psychology, 32*(1), 80–89.

Walker, L. J., Hennig, K. H., & Krettenauer, T. (2000). Parent and peer contexts for children's moral reasoning development. *Child Development, 71*(4), 1033–1048.

Walter, S. M., Lambie, G. W., & Ngazimbi, E. E. (2008). A choice theory counseling group succeeds with middle school students who displayed disciplinary problems. *Middle School Journal, 40*(2), 4–12.

Xie, L. Y. (2010). Multidimensional gender identity and psychological adjustment in middle childhood: A study in China. *Sex Roles, 62,* 100–113.

PART III

Early Adolescence
(Ages 13 to 18)

Mother Nature is providential. She gives us twelve years to develop a love for our children
before turning them into teenagers.

William Galvin

The teen years are times of storm and stress for those going through this developmental period and for all who love them. Changing bodies, changing minds, challenging what should be, and the ever present drama of social life are the hallmarks of this time of development. These changes are wonderful and empowering. However, when emerging all at the same time, within the same person, these changes can be quite tumultuous.

This chapter will discuss the many changes encountered during this period of development along with the challenges they present. As will be explained, today's teens are experiencing puberty and hormonal changes at an earlier age and are dealing with more elevated emotional and environmental stressors than ever before. With rising concerns surrounding obesity, drugs, alcohol, sexually transmitted diseases, contraception, and rising mental health problems, teens in early adolescence are confronted with life impacting decisions unknown by many generations that preceded them.

The stage of early adolescence is a very critical stage, and hopefully, each child has or will enter this period of development with the love and support of parents, family, peers, and professionals, such as a counselor. These years are an exciting time of many varied and rapid changes. But, this can be a confusing time for the child and parents, and both must get used to the new person the child is becoming. After reading this chapter you will be able to

1. describe the physical, cognitive, social, and emotional developments of early adolescence;

2. identify the what and how of counseling intervention and prevention services as relating to early adolescent needs;

3. identify risks to human development during early adolescence; and

4. describe the impact of culture and cultural difference on adolescent development.

Healthy Early Adolescence Development

Physical Development

Adolescence is a time most clearly demarcated by the onset of puberty. This starting point, or onset of puberty has been occurring at earlier ages with boys beginning puberty at around 9.5 to 12 years of age and females around 13 years old (Downing & Bellis, 2009).

While most are aware of the secondary sexual changes that make their appearances (e.g. breast buds, body hair, etc.), it is the endocrinological and neurological changes that have the greatest impact on the changes being encountered by the early adolescent.

Beginning with the release of a hormone called gonadotropin-releasing hormone (GnRH) by the **hypothalamus** that signals the **pituitary gland** to release two more hormones—luteinizing hormone (LH) and follicle-stimulating hormone (FSH), the process of puberty and sexual development takes flight. Additionally, the **adrenal gland** responds to the changes signaled by the hypothalamus and pituitary glands and begins to effect digestion, energy, immune system, energy, and sleep.

There is a degree of individual variation in terms of the timing with which these processes begin. However, while variation and individual differences is normative, timing is important especially when the arrival of puberty is far in advance of one's social group and the complete development of cognitive and emotional capabilities to handle the emerging new characteristics. Those who begin puberty at an earlier age often experience increased anxiety, concern with body shape, concern with their weight, and inappropriate adaptive styles, including the development of eating disorders (Downing & Bellis, 2009). Further, those who experience early puberty are often-times more likely to engage in damaging behaviors, such as developing dependence on alcohol, engaging more sexual partners by age 16, and being in relationships with older individuals (Downing & Bellis, 2009).

Girls' Physical Changes

While there are individual differences when girls begin puberty, as previously noted, in general, girls are starting to reach puberty at an earlier age. There are many speculations as to why early onset of puberty is taking place, ranging from genetic contributions to environmental factors including the presence of genetically modified foods and hormone inclusion in products such as milk and cheese.

Table 7.1 Healthy Middle Childhood Development in the previous chapter (Chapter 7), provides a brief description of the physical changes typically encountered during this phase of development, up to age 12. What is noteworthy is the psychological impact that these changes can have, a point that will be discussed later within this chapter. Whether it is a sense of embarrassment, or perhaps empowerment, the physical changes that occur can support or shake a girl's self-concept and esteem. Whether it is the fact that a girl's growth spurt happens typically 2 years before that of a boy (around the age of 10 or 11) lending to her height superiority, or the fact that she has a body that is different from her peers' (e.g., having or failing to have developing breasts) and most certainly different from the ideals set forth in popular media, these changes can drastically affect her sense of psychological well-being.

Boys' Physical Changes

As with females, the first signs of puberty are found within the activation of primary and secondary sex characteristics. For the male, **spermarche**, typically occurs late in the pubertal process, generally around the age of 14 and is accompanied by growth of testes and penis, appearances of facial and body hair, and an increase in height and muscle development. As is true throughout each period of development, the timing of these changes will reflect individual variation. The fact that physical changes in a boy occur at various rates can lead to many feeling awkward for a period of time. This can cause many boys to suffer from low self-esteem and dissatisfaction with body image. Case Illustration 8.1 will increase your counseling knowledge and skills to better equip you for dealing with this type of client.

CASE ILLUSTRATION 8.1 BODY IMAGE

Instructions: Below you will find a brief description of a 13-year-old client, Andrew. After reading the vignette, reflect upon the questions posed and discuss your responses with a colleague or classmate.

Body Image

Andrew has come to the counselor because he is 13, and he is still the same size as he was when he was 11. He does not understand why his body is not changing like all of his friends'. He says that he is not strong, not tall, and his voice has not begun to deepen. He also mentions not being able to shave because he has no hair. He wants to know why he is not changing like everyone else. He says that it is not fair that all the girls like his friends but not him because he has not changed yet.

Practice Exercise:

1. What is Andrew missing or not understanding?

2. What, other than telling Andrew to "wait; it will all work out," could you, as a counselor, do to assist him at this time of insecurity?

3. What role, if any, could his parents and his peers play in providing the support he needs?

4. What prevention programming might a school counselor employ, perhaps in the form of class-room guidance units?

Cognitive Development

During the developmental stage of adolescence, several cognitive processes begin to change. Adolescents are more likely to be able to think abstractly, consider hypothetical situations, engage in advanced information-processing strategies, reflect on self, and try to solve problems (Wigfield, Lutz, & Wagner, 2005). In addition, the reasoning and decision-making skills also become more advanced. However, the issue of adolescents being more likely to engage in risky behavior often leads some to question how advanced the cognitive abilities of adolescents really are (Wigfield, Lutz, & Wagner, 2005).

Social Development

During adolescence, there are many changes that occur with adolescents' relationships with their parents and peers. While in middle childhood, children are more likely to be attached to their parents while transitioning to the world of peers, by adolescent age, the transition is in full swing with the teen rebelling, exhibiting detachment, and often experiencing parent-child conflict. Since adolescents can now fully think logically, they begin to want a more logical

Photo 8.1   Today's communication technology contributes to developing friendships.

Source: Jupiterimages/Photos.com/Thinkstock.

reasoning for everything. Furthermore, adolescents start to think egocentrically. Therefore, everything revolves around the adolescent. Ultimately, the adolescent begins to feel as if the parent has become more harsh, controlling, and irrational because of the difference in thoughts, views, and beliefs. Although adolescents become more detached from their parents, they become more attached to their peers. They begin to listen to and value their peers' opinions more than their parents'. They want to fit in with their peers and know what the current fad is for the week. Adolescents believe that their peers define who they are. Often peers form in groups depending on a subject of interest. For example, adolescents may form a group if they all like cars or fashion. Not only do peers become a major part of an adolescent's life, but also opposite-sex relationships become important. At this age, adolescents start to become attracted to the opposite sex and start dating. By the age of 15, adolescents are able to receive a driver's permit and by sixteen, they are able to have a license. If able to get a car, adolescents begin to have more freedom. Many adolescents begin to do more and more things on their own without parental support.

As adolescents are transitioning from elementary to middle school and high school, they often are faced with the challenges of being separated from the classroom-instilled friendships commonly experienced in the earlier school years and must develop friends and social groups on other terms. While some adolescents seem to naturally excel in social aspects, other students experience difficulty finding their place within the social world of their school. The desire to fit into a specific social group or to identify with any group of students can lead to stress, anxiety, and depression in adolescents. It is important for adolescents to establish friendships in order to feel a sense of identity and belonging, and counselors who work with students should help foster identity development in adolescents. Additionally, counselors should be aware of the confusion adolescents often face as they are experiencing more self-awareness than they have previously, facing physical changes, and attempting to define their social role. Friendships in the early adolescent years are not only important as a way to help adolescents with identity development and have a sense of belonging, but friendship also allows students to learn the realms of society and how their role within society might look.

Emotional Development

It is discussed by Vandell, Burchinal, Vandergrift, Belsky, & Steinberg (2010) that although some believe that the effects of early childhood fade over time, that may not always be the case. Some children exhibit the effects of childhood experiences during adolescence or even adulthood. Many people grow up in unhealthy environments such as being physically, emotionally, or sexually abused; having alcoholic or drug addict caretakers; having an incarcerated household member; having a household member who is chronically depressed, suicidal, institutional-ized, or mentally ill; having a mother who is being treated violently; not having parents or having only one parent; and/or being emotionally or physically neglected. These factors can affect adolescents while in school by not allow-ing them to concentrate or focus. Some of these factors can lead to early sexual activity. Some can also lead ado-lescents to believe it is the right thing to do, which ultimately harms the adolescent, or potentially lead the adolescent to harm someone else. (See Guided Practice Exercise 8.1)

Guided Practice Exercise 8.1 Gender-Based Developmental Differences

If possible, visit a middle school (grades 7 and 8), and gather data that would help you discuss the following:

1. What differences were you able to discern along the lines of physical, cognitive, social, and emotional development between girls and boys?

2. To what degree did you note variations in development—even within the same grade or age grouping?

Discuss these differences as a class with your fellow students and professor.

Moral Development

Conscience and morality are defined as the "development, maintenance, and application of generalizable, internal stan-dards of conduct for one's behavior" (Kochanska, 2006). Moral self-relevance or identity is defined as the degree to which individuals perceive moral qualities (for example, honesty, and kindness; Gibbs, 2010). The question is how or when does this moral development take place? Moral behavior (conduct) is assumed to reflect the adolescent's internal monitor of behavior and the adolescent's ability to comply with this internal monitor (Kochanska, 2006). Moral behavior is often tied to emotions, such as empathy, kindness, sympathy, guilt, shame, and self-consciousness (Laible, Eye, & Carlo, 2008).

Positive feelings such as empathy, kindness, and sympathy are assumed to promote moral behavior and con-duct. Links have been made between sympathy and prosocial behavior in research (Eisenberg, Fabes, & Spinrad, 2006). Negative feelings, such as shame and guilt, are often the result of poor behavior choices. Shame causes negative emotions that surround the adolescent and may cause the adolescent to associate himself or herself with being bad or not good enough (Eisenberg, 2000). Guilt is thought to affect behavior by the adolescent wanting to mend the situation or correct the behavior (Laible et al., 2008).

In addition to emotions, adolescents' moral development is influenced by their embrace of moral values. In adolescence, these values are already considered to be part of the adolescent's self-concept as opposed to compli-ance to parents' rules (Laible et al., 2008).

Self-Concept and Self-Esteem in Early Adolescence

Early adolescence is a time of development in which specific forms of competence take on special value to the development of one's self-concept and esteem. Harter (1999) identified five areas of competence in 8- to 13-year-olds, including academic competence, athletic competence, likeability by peers, physical appearance, and behavior. While it can be assumed that competence in each area contributes to positive self-concept and esteem, research has demonstrated that self-esteem is affected by competence in areas that are viewed as important by the adolescent. For example, consider two adolescents who think of themselves as highly academically competent but not very competent in the area of physical appearance. Both adolescents have similar self-concepts. However, if one adolescent places a much higher value on academic competence, he or she will have higher self-esteem than the other adolescent who may place more value on physical attractiveness. Counselors, teachers, and those working with children and adolescents can help them improve their self-esteem by encouraging them to focus on, explore, and value their areas of higher competency.

Adolescent Identity Development

During adolescence, according to Erik Erikson (1968), the main task of each individual is to achieve a state of identity through working out the crisis of *identity versus role confusion*. While young children begin to form their identities, adolescence is a time marked by new identity formation (Kroger, Martinussen, & Marcia, 2010).

According to Erikson, several things happen during adolescent identity development. Erikson described a situation causing adolescents to make significant life decisions with the term identity crisis. As adolescents form their identities, they must give up, or repudiate, some possibilities while accepting others. Many adolescents choose to experiment with a variety of identities without committing to any one during a period of moratorium, while others experience premature foreclosure and commit to an identity before fully exploring themselves (Erikson, 1968).

Marcia (1966) explains four different identity statuses that adolescents experience as they form vocational, ideological, spiritual, and sexual identities. Adolescents who experience *identity confusion* have not experienced an identity crisis and have not committed to an identity. Those experiencing *identity foreclosure* have committed to an identity without exploring themselves, often because the identity has been forced upon them by an authority such as a parent or religious institution. Adolescents described by *identity moratorium* experience numerous

Photo 8.2   Early adolescence is a period of exploration for self-identity and sexuality.

Source: iStockphoto.com/101dalmations.

crises and try on many identities but have not committed to an identity. Finally, those who have attained *identity achievement* have experienced an identity crisis, have explored many aspects of their identities, and have committed to an identity. Valde (1995) suggests adding a fifth identity status, *identity closure,* which accounts for many individuals' experiences of reforming their identities during late adolescence and adulthood. Adolescents do not progress through the statuses in a neat order but may skip some statuses or return to statuses that they experienced earlier. By late adolescence, most individuals have reached *identity achievement.*

Counseling Issues

There are many counseling issues that develop during early adolescence, most of which are directly or indirectly connected to issues of self-concept, esteem, and peer inclusion. Some adolescents may develop eating disorders or become involved in bullying situations. Others, in addition, may become involved in risk-taking behaviors and be influenced by peer pressure. Counselors working with students must be aware of the issues that are faced by early adolescents and have a firm grasp on how adolescents are impacted by these issues in order to effectively provide support to these students. Having an understanding of the concepts and causes of the issues that commonly affect adolescents allows counselors to assist students in navigating through the turmoil that often results when these years of change and exploration begin.

Eating Disorders

Body image and weight management become very important concerns to adolescents, especially during early adolescence when weight concerns and abnormal eating patterns begin to emerge (Hutchinson, Rapee & Taylor, 2009). Dieting is a widely recognized risk factor for the development of eating disorders during adolescence and is defined by Rasmus, Anna-Lisa, Mauri, Riittakerttu, and Bjorkqvist (2010) as "intentional and sustained restriction of caloric intake for the purposes of weight loss or weight maintenance." The drive for thinness and dieting is a common behavior for female adolescents. Researchers and therapists alike have been looking for reasons why abnormal eating habits and weight concerns emerge during this age for several years. Hutchinson, Rapee, and Taylor (2009) concluded one factor may be a negative mood experienced by the adolescent. The negative mood an adolescent experiences is oftentimes dealt with by engaging in binge eating or other compensating behaviors. Hutchinson et al. (2009) suggest that having an unrealistic desire to be thin, oftentimes leads to a decreased self-esteem and negative mood. As a result of the decreased self-esteem and negative mood, one may engage in bulimic behaviors as mentioned earlier. Therefore, it is suggested that there is a vicious cycle adolescents are involved in, and this should be made known to counselors and teachers so that proper preventions can be put into place.

In addition to negative mood, factors such as family, media, and peer groups have been shown to have an effect on eating behaviors with adolescents. According to Hutchinson et al. (2009), developmental theorist say peers play a significant role in eating behaviors in early adolescence. Other research states that the concerns adolescents hold about their weight are a result of pressure from their peers to be thin. Oftentimes, this pressure results in abnormal eating behaviors for adolescents.

In addition, peers have an effect on adolescent's' bodily perceptions and eating behaviors through socialization. This is done by hanging out with people who constantly talk about thinness and dieting, which can shape one's attitude about the subjects, resulting in dieting or bulimic behaviors. Also, teasing effects adolescents' perceived body image leading to negative mood, dieting, and bulimic behaviors. Adolescents may receive reinforcement from their peers by being thin or dieting, and this could further motivate the behavior. Punishment by peers for not complying with these norms of behavior may also result in the adolescent engaging in dieting and bulimic behavior as well as a negative self-image (Hutchinson et al., 2009).

There are negative effects to an adolescent's physical and mental health as a result of dieting. Dieting can affect one's metabolism and puts one at an increased risk for weight gain in the future (Isomaa, Isomaa, Marttunen, Kaltiala-Heino, & Bjorkqvist, 2010). The mental health effects of dieting during adolescence can be depression, anxiety, and lower self-esteem. Adolescents who engage in dieting are also more likely to engage in unhealthy eating that may affect their physical development, as well as be less likely to engage in physical activity. Adolescents who diet may also engage in more physical activities but not receive the proper amount of nutrients from eating, and this could affect their health. (Isomaa et al., 2010).

However, not all adolescent dieting is negative, and in many cases, it is harmless. Therefore, it is important for a teacher or counselor to try and determine an adolescent's reason for dieting in order to assess if they are at risk for developing extreme dieting or bulimic behaviors. It is also important to assess for depressed mood in adolescents that can be a factor in leading to extreme eating behaviors.

Peer Pressure

Peer influence and peer acceptance, is very important in early adolescence. This is because adolescence is a time when individuals begin distancing themselves from their parents and looking to their peers to help define who they are (Ward, Lundberg, Ellis, & Berrett 2010). Many adolescents voluntarily follow peer leaders who influence them to engage in antisocial and unhealthy behavior such as illegal acts and substance abuse (Steinberg, 2008). Why youth choose one peer leader over alternatives remains unclear, and despite its importance, this followership question has been largely unexplored. Professionals serving youth need to understand the adolescent followership phenomenon, so they can be able to focus their energy toward youth who are likely candidates to be peer leaders. Past research has suggested that the social exchange theory may explain adolescent peer followership (Ward et al., 2010; Steinberg, 2008). One constant across social science research is the correlation between the behaviors of adolescents and their peers (Vargas, 2011).

Photo 8.3   Engaging in risky behaviors like alcohol and substance abuse are very serious issues during early adolescence.

Source: BananaStock/BananaStock/Thinkstock.

While it could speculated that peers with positive values, choices, and behaviors can positively affect an early adolescent, the sad truth and statistics highlight the negative effects. For example, the abuse of drugs and alcohol occurs more when supported by a peer group; automobile accidents are more serious or fatal when in the presence of their peers; and even the potential to commit crimes increases when engaged with peers supporting such activities (O'Brien, Albert, Chein, & Steinberg, 2011). Overall, research has highlighted the fact that adolescents tend to engage in more risk-taking behavior when in the presence of their peers (O'Brien et al., 2011). As a counselor, you will be working with students and parents dealing with peer pressure and the positive and negative outcomes of such pressure. Case Illustration 8.2 can assist you in gaining knowledge on how to use your counseling skills to help individuals.

CASE ILLUSTRATION 8.2 MATT AND HIS PEERS

Instructions: Below you will find a brief description of Matt and his peer relationships. After reading the vignette, reflect upon the questions posed, and discuss your responses with a colleague or classmate

Matt and His Peers

In middle school, Matt was a straight-*A* student. He did not have many school friends, but he was very involved in scouts where most of his friends were. By ninth grade, Matt began to be picked on by the students at the school for still being in scouts. Wanting to fit in at school, Matt quit the scouts to try and make friends at school. After he quit, his grades slowly started to drop. All of a sudden, Matt was a *C* student and still did not have many friends at the school. He started playing video games instead of doing his work or hanging out with other students. He socially isolated himself because he thought no one wanted to be his friend at school.

However, when Matt reached tenth grade, he begged his parents for a car, and they bought him one. His parents believed that this would get him out of the house and help him meet people to hang out with, and they were right. Since Matt was older than most in his grade, he was one of the only ones in his class to have a car. He started making friends very quickly because people wanted rides, but he did not care. He started hanging out with the wrong crowd at the school and began to smoke, drink, curse, and slack more in school. His math teacher called home because she was worried about him since he was failing the class. His parents did not know what to do with him. He finally had friends, and they did not want him to lose that since he had been in the house for so long.

One weekend, Matt wanted to drive his friends to a concert in another town. His parents were very skeptical but told him that he could drive if he would do better in math the next week. Obviously, Matt agreed and went to pick up his friends. The concert was 30 minutes away so the boys decided to spend the night at one of the other guy's camp houses. After the concert, all the boys went to the camp house and had a huge party. The neighbors called the police, and all the boys were arrested for underage drinking and smoking. Matt's parents were the first to be called since Matt was the one who had the car that got them to the house. Extremely disappointed in Matt, they went to pick him up and talk to him. On the way home, Matt convinced his parents that he had no clue no one would be at the house to supervise, so they gave him the benefit of the doubt. However, a month later, Matt's mom found more alcohol and cigarettes in Matt's car. Both parents finally decided that they needed to seek help.

(Continued)

(Continued)

Practice Exercise:

1. The parents seem very lenient and easily believed Matt. Although Matt has never had many friends, they still should put boundaries on him with his new friends—they can't just let him run free. They also should have punished him for the party instead of listening to him tell a lie and letting him get away with it. They should have taken the incident more seriously, and then they wouldn't have been so shocked to find alcohol and cigarettes in Matt's car. Should the parents be surprised about Matt's behavior? Should Matt have more open communication with his parents about his behavior and potential peer pressure?

2. Matt needs to choose his friends wisely. Does he want to be friends with the people who are going to use him, or does he want to be friends with people that genuinely want to be friends with him too?

3. Talk to Matt about the drug and alcohol use. How will it affect him in the long run and right now? Does he want to continue on the path of destruction or be the scout he really is?

4. Does Matt really not have friends? What is wrong with the scout friends he has? Does he need to be in a social skills group to teach him how to properly make and keep friends?

5. Are there one or two people at school that he wants to be friends with—should the counselor help by getting him involved in clubs, activities, sports, and so on?

Guided Practice Exercise 8.2 Peer Pressure

Come up with something to try and talk your class into doing. It can be anything. One by one, stand up and try to convince your classmates to do this thing with you. Then, take a poll of how many peers would have done it with you. After the class has completed this, answer these questions individually or as a class:

1. How easy do you think it is to give in to peer pressure?

2. What makes something easier or harder to turn down?

3. What are some ways to teach others how not to give in to peer pressure?

Not all interaction between adolescents and their peers is negative. One benefit of peer interaction is that adolescents are more likely to engage in physical activity when amongst their peers than individually (Fitzgerald, Fitzgerald, & Aherne, 2012).

Non-Suicidal Self-Injury Tendencies

While the prevalence of self-injurious behaviors has been noted since the 1970s, there has been an influx of research efforts over the past 2 decades. What is now being called Non-Suicidal Self-Injury (NSSI) has had many names over the years, such as self-wounding, parasuicide, deliberate self-harm, or self-mutilation. David Klonsky

(2006) defined NSSI as deliberate self-injury that is intentional and directly injures the body tissue without suicidal intent. Such intentional self-injurious acts could include, but are not limited to, cutting or scratching, head-banging, burning or branding, interfering with wound healing by picking, and self-poisoning.

Recent studies indicate that between 15% and 3% of all adolescents have participated in NSSI acts. In general, individual studies find that that NSSI is more common in females than in males. Additionally, the methods of self-injury vary between genders; females tend to use methods related to cutting or scratching, while males are more prone to self-harm by burning or branding. The highest rates of NSSI are reported between the ages of 12 and 25 years old, with a peak around 16 to 17 years old.

Reasons for engaging in self-injurious acts vary from person to person, but recent research has noted that the function of the behaviors goes beyond what was previously thought as seeking attention and can serve many functions for a particular individual. While the motivation of attention seeking still exists, other such proposed functions may include an alternative to suicide, to express displeasure with oneself, to feel in control of a situation, to alleviate the tension of negative mood, or even to incite an enjoyable mood.

The proportion of the population touched by NSSI and the devastating potential effects of NSSI calls for more research and understanding of both the conditions that lead to such behavior as well as those steps that can be taken to prevent them, and when necessary, intervene. It is an area that counselors will need to continue to follow.

Bullying Behavior

Bullying is a severe problem in several countries. The estimated rates of bullying and victimization range from 10% to 30% of students suffering from bullying in Australia, Canada, Japan, and the United States (Konishi &

Table 8.1   High School Students Who Were Electronically Bullied in the Past Year, by Sex and Race/Ethnicity

Source: Adapted from http://apps.nccd.cdc.gov/youthonline.

Hymel, 2009). Bullying has been defined by Espelage, Bosworth, and Simon (2000) as behaviors that are intentional and cause psychological and physical harm to the recipient. It is important there be an understanding of the factors that contribute to bullying behavior and how to reduce the behavior during early adolescence (Konishi & Hymel, 2009). As technology continues to develop, bullying has also developed into another form known as cyber bullying. See Table 8.1, High School Students Who Were Electronically Bullied in the Past Year.

Some factors explored by researchers are family warmth, family hostility, low parental support, low teacher support, and family physical discipline, which contribute to bullying behavior (Espelage et al., 2000). Also, the effect of peers is also examined to be a factor that contributes to the occurrence of bullying or aggression by an adolescent. Benson and Buehler (2012) stated that mere talk of deviant behaviors among a group of peers has been shown to be a factor in future deviant behavior and aggression. They also found that those adolescents whose morals are not present to the degree of other adolescents' morals are oftentimes more prone to physical aggression during adolescence. Some even speculate that those adolescents who are experiencing stress from other areas of life sometimes use aggression and bullying as an outlet.

Konishi and Hymel (2009) noted ways in which adolescents may respond to being bullied. One way is through direct action by directly confronting it with the intention of ending the conflict. The other proposed way to deal with the situation is to deal with the emotions that are caused by the bullying situations. Research suggests that adults hold a major influence on adolescents' aggressive actions and that bullying can be significantly reduced for adolescents that spend time with adults who teach them nonviolent ways to handle stress and conflict (Espelage et al., 2000). It is important for adolescents to have adequate time with adults whether it is parents, teachers, counselors, or mentors. Guided Practice Exercise 8.3 can help you further understand bullying and bullying behavior.

Guided Practice Exercise 8.3 Bullying

Visit a middle school (grades 6 through 8) or high school and interview the school counselor regarding the following. Share your findings with your classmates and instructor.

1. Does bullying occur at this school? Has the frequency changed over the past few years?

2. What form does bullying most often take (i.e., physical confrontation, gang, cyber, etc.)?

3. What if anything serves as a trigger or identifying target/characteristic for those bullied?

4. What if anything has the counselor found that has reduced the bullying and has increased the resilience of those bullied?

Sex Risks and Pregnancy

The arousal of one's sexual potential in combination with an increase of natural curiosity and explorative nature can be a dangerous combination, one that is by definition the experience of the adolescent. Not only are adolescents ready to explore their limits but they also have other factors that contribute to trying out their sexual development. This development encompasses natural curiosity, hormonal roller coasters, and the taboo nature of sex before marriage and the consequences of unwanted pregnancy.

Although many parents and others within society would like to believe that teenagers are not engaging in sexual behaviors, the truth is many are involved. Even more alarming is the fact that these adolescents are not just engaging in sexual behaviors, but many are taking unnecessary sexual risks of another nature. It is society's norm to encourage abstinence before marriage. Churches, learning institutions, and even governmental funding promote the idea that sex before marriage is wrong and risky. Parents and older adults often communicate that they do not want teenagers to experiment with sex, but they fail to explain why they feel this way and the consequences this behavior may have not only morally but also personally in terms of health and social responsibilities. However, the problem appears to be that there are too few explicit conversations, between teenagers and their parents or older guardians, about safe-sex education and what options adolescents may consider to protect themselves from taking risks.

Despite the recent decline in teen pregnancy rates in the United States, pregnancy and birth rates for youth in this country continue to be among the highest of all developed countries, largely because of differences in opinions about contraceptive use and cultural-social norms (Boonstra, 2002; Moore et al., 2001). Despite dramatic increases over the past 2 decades in the reported use of contraceptives (especially condoms) by teens at first intercourse, contraceptive use at most recent sexual intercourse has declined (Terry-Humen, Manlove, & Moore, 2000). While an estimated 34% of teen girls ages 15 to 19 report that they did not use contraceptives the first time they had intercourse, 31% report that they did not use contraceptives the last time they had intercourse. These figures are higher for Hispanic females, 47% of whom report that they used contraceptives at their last intercourse. Thus, a substantial number of sexually active teen girls from all socio-economic and cultural backgrounds remain at risk for unintended pregnancy (Terry-Humen et al., 2001). In addition, research such as that of Levy, Vaughan, and Knight (2002) highlights the role of alcohol and drug use in increasing the rates of unprotected sexual activity. These authors found that teens who scored positive on the CRAFFT, a screening for alcohol and drug use, were more likely to have sexual contact after drinking alcohol, using drugs, when drunk or high, with a partner who had used alcohol or drugs, without use of a condom, and with multiple different partners. At this stage of development, adolescents have a certain amount of independence, and it is unrealistic to think that an adult will always be around to monitor their behavior. But if there is an established trust between the teen and the adult, it is likely that the teen will feel comfortable speaking about his or her sexual thoughts or feelings before actual interactions occur. The best ways to approach adolescent sexuality are to build and maintain an open line of communication, to promote abstinence until maturity, and to encourage safe sex practices in case adolescents choose to engage. See Table 8.2, Percentage of Students in Grades 9 through 12 who Report Sexual Activity.

Table 8.2   Percentage of Students in Grades 9 through 12 Who Report Sexual Activity

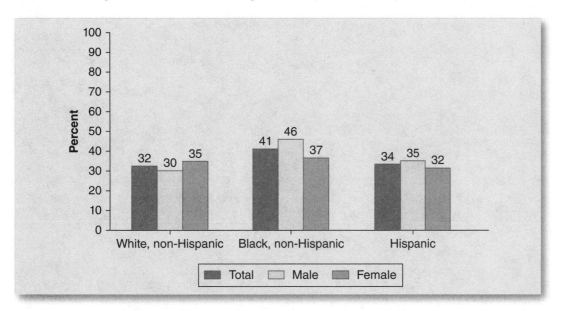

Source: U.S. Department of Health and Human Services. (2012). Youth risk behavior surveillance: United States 2011. MMWR Surveillance Summaries, *61*(4), Table 65.

Sexually Transmitted Diseases

The United States ranks at the top of the list for sexually transmitted diseases. In 2008, the latest year for which statistics are available, the U.S. pregnancy rate among girls between 15 and 19 was 67.8 per 1,000, according to the National Campaign to Prevent Teen and Unwanted Pregnancy (2013). The rate has steadily declined since 1991, when it was 117 per 1,000 teens between the same ages. U.S. teen birth rates have also declined. In 2010, according to the Centers for Disease Control and Prevention (CDC, 2010), the rate was 34.3 births per 1,000 teens, compared with 61.8 births per 1,000 teens in 1991. Fewer babies were born to teenagers in 2010 than in any year since 1946. Still, the teen birth rate in the United States remains nine times higher than in other developed countries, according to the CDC.

Adolescents who demonstrate personality characteristics that promote risky behaviors are part of an environment that enhances the likelihood of risks. They are more likely to participate in risky behaviors and are prone to engage in risky sexual behavior (Moilanen, Crockett, Raffaelli, & Jones, 2010). The CDC noted that counselors working with this age group should educate adolescents regarding prevention, abstinence, vaccination, monogamy, condoms, and having a small number of sex partners. In addition, counselors should be knowledgeable about the types of sexual transmitted diseases such as chlamydia, gonorrhea, hepatitis, herpes, HIV/AIDS, HPV, PID, and syphilis.

Risk-Taking Behaviors

Adolescent risk behaviors are a significant issue that can contribute to a reduced quality of life (Dunn, Kitts, Lewis, Goodrow, & Sherzer, 2011). Risk behavior is more common among adolescents than older adults (O'Brien et al., 2011). Adolescents are more likely to engage in binge drinking, to smoke cigarettes, and to engage in criminal behavior.

Adolescents engage in driving under the influence of alcohol, which leads to more serious and fatal automobile crashes (O'Brien et al., 2011). Results from the CDC state that 72.5% of high school students had one drink of alcohol in their lifetime, and 41.8% had one drink in the last 30 days. In addition, 46.3% of students had tried cigarettes, with 19.5% doing so in the last 30 days. When it comes to marijuana, 36.8% of students had used it in their lifetime, with 20.8% using in the last 30 days. In addition, 46% of students reported having had sex in

Table 8.3   Reported Drinking Patterns Among 8th-, 10th-, and 12th-Grade Students

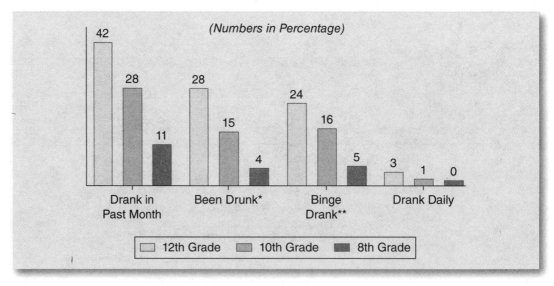

Source: Adapted from http://www.centurycouncil.org/underage-drinking/statistics.

their lifetime. The statistics were reported from the Youth Risk Behavior Survey conducted by the CDC (CDC, 2011; Kann et al., 2009). See Table 8.3 Reported Drinking Patterns Among 8th- 10th- and 12th-Grade Students.

Several theories have been proposed as to why adolescents engage in risky behaviors (Arnett & Balle-Jensen, 1993; Gibbons & Gerrard, 1995; Jessor, 1991). One theory stresses the need for excitement, fun, and novel and intense sensations that override the potential dangers involved in a particular activity (Arnett & Balle-Jensen, 1993). Another theory stresses that many of these risk behaviors occur in a group context and involve peer acceptance and status in the group (Jessor, 1991). A third theory emphasizes that adolescent risk taking is a form of modeling and romanticizing adult behavior (Gibbons & Gerrard, 1995). In other words, adolescents engage in some behaviors, such as cigarette smoking and sex, to identify with their parents and other adults. In considering these theories, it should be kept in mind that teenagers are not all alike and that they may have different reasons for engaging in the same risk behavior (Jaffe, 1998).

Adolescents may also have multiple reasons for engaging in a particular risk behavior. For example, given the use of sexuality to market just about every product imaginable, it is no wonder that adolescents are so curious and tempted to experiment without thinking about consequences. At the same time, research shows that many youths experience significant peer pressure to engage in sexual behavior. In a national survey of 12- to 18-year-olds, 61% of the girls and 23% of the boys said that they thought that pressure from a partner was "often" a reason that teenagers have sex, and 43% of boys and 38% of girls said they thought that fear of being teased by others about being a virgin was often a reason (Kaiser Family Foundation, 2002).

Overall, many experts conclude that risk taking in adolescence is "normal" (Dryfoos, 1998; Hamburg, 1997; Roth & Brooks-Gunn, 2000) and that the key is to provide guidance in decision making and to encourage the adolescent to channel the positive developmental aspects of this energy into less dangerous and more constructive "risky" pursuits.

Dunn et al. (2011) noted the more risk factors at home an adolescent has, the more likely he or she will engage in risk-taking behaviors. Some risk factors at home include poor family communication, peer pressure, and lack of family support. In support, adolescents who had positive adult role models in their lives were less likely to use alcohol, tobacco, and other drugs. The study supports the idea that strong family communication leads to less use of these substances (Dunn et al., 2011).

Evans et al. (2004) noted peer values regarding risky behaviors such as low adult support and low empathetic relationships with youth were associated with risky sexual behaviors. When these aspects were strengthened, less adolescent sexual behavior occurred. These factors can be important when working with adolescents.

Significant relationships have been found between an adolescent not using alcohol and the availability of peer help, high parental expectations, and positive peer relationships. It is reported that an adolescent who had any one of these characteristics in his or her life was 1.2 to 3.5 times less likely to abuse alcohol. An adolescent who did not have any of these factors in his or her life was more likely to abuse alcohol (Dunn et al., 2011). Parental support and positive peer influence effect whether or not adolescents will or will not use marijuana. Adolescents with these factors in their lives were 1.5 to 3.0 times less likely to use the drug. However, according to Dunn et al. (2011), this was evident only with adolescents when reporting on the last 30 days.

Interestingly enough, Chein, Albert, O'Brien, Uckert, and Steinberg (2010) state that the presence of peers actually has an influence on the brain. The presence of peers activates the "**ventral striatum and orbitofrontal cortex**" as the adolescents make decisions that concern risk-taking behaviors. Empirical proof of the influence of peers on risk-taking behaviors is important in counseling. Counselors understand the context of when risk-taking behaviors are more likely to occur and plan behavioral interventions accordingly. Adolescents are shown to respond more to rewards than punishments in the context of risk-taking behaviors and peer influence. Behavioral interventions should be structured with this information in mind.

Current Trends

Just as trends affect each stage of development, during early adolescence the effects can be powerful with regard to their socialization and development. As noted earlier, most early adolescents value their peers' opinions more than anyone else's. Many trends have evolved during the last few years such as clothing trends. Some adolescents like Converse shoes, Vans shoes, Rainbow flip flops, and other name brand items. However, this year has brought about some newer trends such as colored skinny jeans, Piko shirts, pastel colors, chevron prints, and a variety of jewelry items.

Technology is another trend that has overcome this age group. Smart phone apps such as Instagram, Twitter, Vine, SnapChat, Pinterest, and Facebook are very popular along with the phone itself. In addition, television shows like *Pretty Little Liars*, *The Walking Dead*, *Duck Dynasty*, and *Awkward* have early adolescents glued to their electronic devices. Also, many in this age range use abbreviations like lol, nbd, and jk along with shortening words. For example, people have changed the word probably to probs, precious to presh, crazy to cray, and totally to totes. One of the biggest sayings for this group has been the abbreviation YOLO, or you only live once. It is clear more research needs to be conducted regarding media influences on youth cognition, given adolescents spend an average of 8.5 hours per day engaged with media (Benson, Elmore, Kupersmidt, Parker, & Scull, 2009).

Cultural Diversity Issues

Developing a sense of ethnic identity is an important task for many adolescents, and numerous studies have found that having a strong ethnic identity contributes to high self-esteem among ethnic minority adolescents (Carlson, Uppal, & Prosser, 2000). Ethnic identity includes the shared values, traditions, and practices of a cultural group. Identifying with the holidays, music, rituals, clothing, history, and heroic figures associated with one's culture helps build a sense of belonging and positive identity. For many of these youth, adolescence may be the first time that they consciously confront and reflect upon their ethnicity (Spencer & Dornbusch, 1990). This awareness can involve both positive and negative experiences.

During early adolescence, there is a heightened awareness of social status and how groups of people are viewed by others. Adolescents spend a great deal of time evaluating their racial, cultural, and ethnic identities, along with varying sexual orientations. They examine concepts such as stereotyping, discrimination, exclusion, racial remarks, and language barriers. Some young people have had more exposure to different cultures than others. In addition, some have had more parental education about prejudice and discrimination. These factors can contribute to the development of early adolescents' views of multicultural differences.

Adolescents with a strong ethnic identity tend to have higher self-esteem than do those who do not identify as strongly with an ethnic group. Professional counselors can advise parents of this fact, encouraging them to discuss and practice aspects of their own ethnic identity (e.g., history, culture, traditions) at home to help their child develop a strong ethnic identity (Phinney, Cantu, & Kurtz, 1997; Thornton, Chatters, Taylor, & Allen, 1990).

As a school counselor working with multicultural adolescents, it is important to work with these students to encourage their development of an ethnic identity. Self-esteem levels often are very low during the adolescent years, especially for students who lack a specific group to consider an in-group to join. The same is especially true for adolescents from diverse cultural backgrounds. Ethnic minorities often lack a large group of friends in schools with whom they can share the same multicultural experiences and foster their development and raise their overall self-esteem. It is important for adolescents from diverse cultural and ethnic backgrounds to have a strong culture and ethnic identity (Verkuyten, 2009).

All adolescents struggle to find their in-group and face pressures from those around them to look, act, or think a certain way. Often, the adolescent years turn into a constant aim to please in order to be accepted or fit in. As a school counselor working with multiculturally diverse students, it is important to be aware that the aim to please and fit in is often more difficult for them than it is for majority students. Many times, students from different cultural backgrounds experience a pull in two different directions. While at school, socially acceptable behavior looks one way, but while at home, it looks completely different. These students are not to a state, developmentally speaking, to make their own values and establish their own beliefs completely independent of those instilled in them by their families and cultures. It is important to be aware of students' cultural traditions, family functions, and religious beliefs in order to provide them with the support needed to take on these challenging situations.

For many in the United States, becoming aware of racism and gaining an understanding of the manifestations of social injustice is an inevitable and important part of building a sense of ethnic identity. Professionals who work with cultural and ethnic minority youth can help them to make sense of the discrimination they may face and to build the confidence and skills necessary to overcome these obstacles (Boyd-Franklin & Franklin, 2000; Oyserman, Gant, & Ager, 1995). Professionals can also help Caucasian youth to understand and be aware of racism and discrimination and the impact on other youth who are from multicultural backgrounds.

A Time of Storm and Stress, as Well as Wonder and Awe

Early adolescence includes a time of major change in cognitive, social, and emotional development along with the formation of self-concept. It is during this time that changes occur in academic achievement, physical aptitude, relationships, and behavior.

Parents and adolescents are confronted with challenges such as negotiating issues of body changes, presence of drugs and alcohol, opportunity for sexual engagement, and the ever increasing stress as a result of peer inclusion or exclusion. Counselors will need to be knowledgeable in dealing with elevated emotional and social factors during early adolescence and to be able to provide support and education to the teen and the parents.

CASE ILLUSTRATION 8.3 ALCOHOL AND EARLY ADOLESCENCE

Instructions: Below you will find a brief description of Lacy and her experience with alcohol. After reading the vignette, reflect upon the questions posed and discuss your responses with a colleague or classmates.

Alcohol and Early Adolescence

Lacy's parents have always been alcoholics, and Lacy knows the effects alcohol can have on the body. However, after beginning to fail in school and watching her older sister attempt suicide, Lacy has begun to drink. She claims that the alcohol makes her forget about everything that is going on. She recently told her friends that she sees herself going down the path her parents made and set for her. She has low self-esteem and hates herself for beginning to drink because she knows how it makes her parents disappointed. She does not want to follow in her parents' footsteps, so she talks to her favorite teacher at school and tells her what is going on. The teacher refers her to the school counselor and also tells her that she will work with her to improve her grades.

Practice Exercise:

1. What are the factors impacting Lacy's decision to drink?

2. What are the potential, multidimensional impacts of her decisions?

3. What intervention or prevention strategies may be or have been useful here?

SUMMARY

➢ Early adolescence, the period typically between ages 12 and 18, is the middle to high school period.
➢ During early adolescence, many physical and cognitive changes occur.
➢ This is the age of pubertal onset; boys begin puberty around 9.5 to 12 years of age and girls begin puberty around age 13.
➢ Girls' height spurt occurs around 10 to 11 years old, whereas, boys' height spurt occurs around 12 to 13 years old.
➢ During this time, adolescents begin to develop a self-concept, individual beliefs about their roles and abilities.
➢ Self-esteem is at the lowest point as one enters early adolescence but increases as one enters seventh grade.
➢ Social behaviors change, such as detaching from parents and gravitating to peers, which can cause some conflict.
➢ Some, during this stage, exhibit the emotional effects of childhood experiences, these factors can affect the development of early adolescence emotions.
➢ Counseling issues may include eating disorders, peer pressure, bullying behavior, sex risks, and risk-taking behaviors.

ADDITIONAL RESOURCES

Journals

Journal of Youth and Adolescence
Journal of Adolescence
Journal of Abnormal Child Psychology
Journal of Autism and Developmental Disorders
International Journal of Psychological Studies

Websites

Center on Early Adolescence https://www.earlyadolescence.org/.
Eli Newberger, M.D., Pediatrician. http://www.elinewberger.com/earlyadol.html.
FOCUS Adolescence Services. Early Adolescent. http://www.focusas.com/Adolescence-Early.html.
eHow Characteristics of Early Adolescence http://www.ehow.com/list_6883604_characteristics-early-adolescents.html.
Early Adolescence: Understanding the 10 to 15 Year Old. http://www.amazon.com/Early-Adolescence-Understanding-The-Year/dp/0738207527.

Videos

Child Development 101: Early Adolescence. http://www.youtube.com/watch?v = KbrP32yZlRc.
Puberty: Guide for Parents—Early and Late Development. http://www.youtube.com/watch?v = n8dHPKD5ePA.

Books

Cowie, H. (2012). *From birth to sixteen: Children's health, social, emotional and linguistic development.* New York, NY: Routledge, Taylor & Francis.
Howe, A., & Richards, V. (2011). *Bridging the transition from primary to secondary school.* New York, NY: Routledge, Taylor & Francis.

Pajares, F., & Urdan, T. (2002). *Academic motivation of adolescents. Adolescence and education series.* New York, NY: Psychology Press.

Vagle, M. D. (2012). *Not a Stage! A critical re-conception of young adolescent education. Adolescent cultures, school and society* (Vol. 60). New York, NY: Peter Lang.

RECOMMENDED SUPPLEMENTAL READINGS

Baghdadli, A., Assouline, B., Sonie, S., Pernon, E., Darrou, C., Michelon, C., & Pry, R. (2012). Developmental trajectories of adaptive behaviors from early childhood to adolescence in a cohort of 152 children with Autism Spectrum Disorders. *Journal of Autism and Developmental Disorders, 42*(7), 1314–1325.

Bowkea, J. C., Markovic, A., Cogswell, A., & Raja, R. (2012). Moderating effects of aggression on the associations between social withdrawal subtypes and peer difficulties during early adolescence. *Journal of Youth and Adolescence, 41*(8), 995–1007.

Hubley, A. M., & Arim, R. G. (2012). Subjective age in early adolescence: Relationships with chronological age, pubertal timing, desired age, and problem behaviors. *Journal of Adolescence, 35*(2), 357–366.

Kamkar, K., Doyle, A., & Markiewicz, D. (2012). Insecure attachment to parents and depressive symptoms in early adolescence: Mediating roles of attributions and self-esteem. *International Journal of Psychological Studies, 4*(2), 3–18. doi:10.5539/ijps.v4n2p3

Monshouwer, K. K., Harakeh, Z. Z., Lugtig, P. P., Huizink, A. A., Creemers, H. E., Reijneveld, S. A. . . . Vollebergh, W. M. (2012). Predicting transitions in low and high levels of risk behavior from early to middle adolescence: The TRAILS study. *Journal of Abnormal Child Psychology, 40*(6), 923–931.

REFERENCES

Arnett, J., & Balle-Jensen, L. (1993). Cultural bases of risk behavior. *Child Development, 64,* 1842–1855.

Benson, M. J., & Buehler, C. (2012). Family process and peer deviance influences on adolescent aggression: Longitudinal effects across early and middle adolescence. *Child Development, 83*(4), 1213–1228.

Benson, J. W., Elmore, K. C., Kupersmidt, J. B., Parker, A. E., & Scull, T. M. (2009). Adolescents' media-related cognitions and substance use. *Journal of Youth Adolescence,* 281–298.

Boonstra, H. (2002). Teen pregnancy: Trends and lessons learned. *The Guttmacher Report on Public Policy, 5,* 7–10.

Boyd-Franklin, N., & Franklin, A. J. (2000). *Boys into men: Raising our African American teenage sons.* New York, NY: Dutton.

Carlson, C., Uppal, S, & Prosser, E. C. (2000). Ethnic differences in processes contributing to the self-esteem of early adolescent girls. *Journal of Early Adolescence, 20,* 44–68.

Centers for Disease Control and Prevention. (2010). *Teen birth rates drop, but disparities persist.* Atlanta, GA: National Center for Chronic Disease Prevention and Health Promotion, Division of Reproductive Health.

Centers for Disease Control and Prevention. (2011). Sexual risk behavior: HIV, STD, & teen pregnancy prevention. Youth risk behavior surveillance. *MMWR 2012;*61(SS-4).

Chein, J. Albert, D., O'Brien, L, Uckert, K., & Steinburg, L. (2010). Peers increase adolescent risk taking by enhancing activity in the brain's reward circuitry. *Developmental Science,14*(2), 1–10.

Downing, J., & Bellis, M. (2009). Early pubertal onset and its relationship with sexual risk taking, substance use and anti-social behavior: A preliminary cross-sectional study. *Bio Med Central Public Health, 9,* 436. 1–11.

Dunn, M. S., Kitts, C., Lewis, S., Goodrow, B., & Scherzer, G. D. (2011). Effects of youth assets on adolescent alcohol, tobacco, marijuana use, and sexual behavior. *Journal of Alcohol and Drug Education,* 23–40.

Dryfoos, J. G. (1998). *Safe passage: Making it through adolescence in a risky society.* New York, NY: Oxford University Press.

Eisenberg, N. (2000). Emotion, regulation, and moral development. *Annual Review of Psychology, 51,* 665–697.

Eisenberg, N., Fabes, R. A., & Spinrad, T. (2006). Prosocial development. In N. Eisenberg, W. Damon, & R. Lerner (Eds.), *Handbook of child pscyhology: Vol. 3, Social, emotional, and personality development* (6th ed., Vol. 3). Hoboken, NJ: Wiley.

Erikson, E. (1968). *Identity, youth, and crisis.* New York, NY: W. W. Norton.

Espelage, D. L., Bosworth, K., & Simon, T. R. (2000). Examining the early social context of bullying behaviors in early adolescence. *Journal of Counseling and Development, 78,* 326–333.

Evans, A. E., Sanderson, M., Griffin, S., Reininger, B., Vincent, M. L., Parra-Medi, D. . . . Taylor, D. (2004). An exploration of the relationship between youth assets and engagement in risky sexual behaviors. *Journal of Adolescent Health, 35*:424.e21-424.e30.

Fitzgerald, A., Fitzgerald, N, & Aherne, C. (2012). Do peers matter? A review of peer and/or friends' influence on physical activity among American adolescents. *Journal of Adolescence, 35*, 941–958.

Gibbs, J. C. (2010). *Moral development and reality: Beyond the theories of Kohlberg and Hoffman* (2nd ed.). Boston, MA: Pearson, Allyn and Bacon.

Gibbons, F. X., & Gerrard, M. (1995). Predicting young adults' health risk behavior. *Journal of Personality and Social Psychology, 69*, 505–517.

Hamburg, D. A. (1997). Toward a strategy for healthy adolescent development. *American Journal of Psychiatry, 154*, 7–12.

Harter, S. (1999). *The construction of the self: developmental and sociocultural foundations* (2nd ed.). New York, NY: Guilford.

Hutchinson, D. M. Rapee, R. M., & Taylor, A. (2009). Body dissatisfaction and eating disturbances in early adolescence: A structural modeling investigation examining negative affect and peer factors. *The Journal of Early Adolescence, 30*(4), 489–517.

Isomaa, R., Isomaa, A, Marttunen, M., Kaltiala-Heino, R., & Bjorkqvist, K. (2010). Psychiatric symptoms and their recognition in adolescents institutionalized for behavior problems. *European Eating Disorders Review, 18*(4), 296–303.

Jaffe, M. L. (1998). *Adolescence*. New York, NY: Wiley.

Jessor, R. (1991). Risk behavior in adolescence: A psychosocial framework for understanding and action. *Journal of Adolescent Health, 12*, 597–605.

Kaiser Family Foundation. (2002). *Teens, sex, and TV. Survey snapshot. Publication #3229*. Menlo Park, CA: Author.

Kann, L., Kinchen, S. A., Williams, B. I., Ross, J. G., Lowry, R., Grunbaum, J. A., & Kolbe, L.J. (2009). *Youth risk behavior surveillance, United States,* (Vol. 49, pp. 1–96). Atlanta, GA: Centers for Disease Control and Prevention.

Klonsky, E. D. (2006). The functions of deliberate self-injury: A review of the evidence. *Clinical Psychology Review, 27*(2007), 226–239.

Kochanska, G. N. (2006). Children's conscience and self-regulation. *Journal of Personality, 74*, 1587–1617.

Konishi, C., & Hymel, S. (2009). Bullying and stress in early adolescence: The role of coping and social support. *The Journal of Early Adolescence, 29*(3), 333–356.

Kroger, J., Martinussen, M., & Marcia, J. E. (2010). Identity status change during adolescence and young adulthood: A meta-analysis. *Journal of Adolescence, 33*(5), 683–698. doi:8.1016/j.adolescence.2009.11.002

Laible, D., Eye, J., & Carlo, G. (2008). Dimensions of conscience in mid-adolescence: Links with social behavior, parenting, and temperament. *Journal of Youth and Adolescence, 37*, 875–887.

Levy, S., Vaughan, B. L., & Knight, J. R. (2002). Office-based intervention for adolescent substance abuse. *Pediatric Clinics of North America, 49*(2), 329–43.

Marcia, J. E. (1966). Development and validation of ego identity status. *Journal of Personality and Social Psychology, 5*, 551–558.

Moilanen, K. L. Crockett, L. J., Raffaelli, M., & Jones, B. L. (2010). Trajectories of sexual risk from middle adolescence to early adulthood. *Journal of Research on Adolescence, 20*(1), 114–139.

Moore, K., Manlove, J., Terry-Humen, M., Williams, S., Papillo, A., & Scarpa, J. (2001). *Child trends facts at a glance*. Washington, DC: Child Trends.

National Campaign to Prevent Teen and Unplanned Pregnancy (2013). *Teen pregnancy*. Retrieved from: thenationalcampaign.org.

O'Brien, L., Albert, D., Chein, J., & Steinberg, L. (2011). Adolescents prefer more immediate rewards when in the presence of their peers. *Journal of Research on Adolescence, 21*(4), 747–753.

Oyserman, D., Gant, L., & Ager, J. (1995). A socially contextualized model of African American identity: Possible selves and school persistence. *Journal of Personality and Social Psychology, 69*, 1216–1232.

Phinney, J. S., Cantu, C. L., & Kurtz, D. A. (1997). Ethnic and American identity as predictors of self-esteem among African American, Latino, and White adolescents. *Journal of Youth and Adolescence, 26*, 165–186.

Rasmus, I., Anna-Lisa, I., Mauri, M., Riittakerttu, K., & Bjorkqvist, K. (2010). Psychological distress and risk for eating disorders in subgroups of dieters. *European Eating Disorders, 18*, 296–303.

Roth, J., & Brooks-Gunn, J. (2000). What do adolescents need for health development? Implications for youth policy. *Social Policy Report, XIV*, 3–19.

Spencer, M., & Dornbusch, S. M. (1990). Challenges in studying minority youths. In S.S. Feldman & G.R. Elliot (Eds.), *At the threshold: The developing adolescent* (pp. 123–146). Cambridge, MA: Harvard University Press.

Steinberg, L. (2008). A social neuroscience perspective on adolescent risk-taking. *Developmental Review, 28*, 78–106.

Terry-Humen, E., Manlove, J., & Moore, K. (2001). *Births outside of marriage: Perception vs. reality.* Child Trends research brief. Washington, DC: Child Trends.

Thornton, M., Chatters, L., Taylor, R., & Allen, W. (1990). Socio-demographic and environmental correlates of racial socialization by Black parents. *Child Development, 61*, 401–409.

Valde, G. (1995). Identity closure: A fifth identity status. *The Journal of Genetic Psychology: Research and Theory on Human Development, 157*(3), 245–254.

Vandell, D. L., Burchinal, M., Vangergrift, N., Belskey, & Steinburg, L. (2010). Do effects of early child care extend to age 15 years? Results from the NICHD study of early child care and youth development. *Child Development, 81* (3), 737–756.

Vargas, R. (2011). Being in "bad" company: Power dependence and status in adolescent susceptibility to peer pressure. *Social Psychology Quarterly*, 310–332.

Verkuyten, M. (2009). Self-esteem and multiculturalism: An examination among ethnic minority and majority groups in the Netherlands. *Journal of Research in Personality, 43*, 419–427.

Ward, P., Lundberg, N., Ellis, G., & Berrett, K. (2010). Adolescent peer followership: A self-determination theory perspective. *Journal of Park and Recreation Administration, 28*, 3, 20–35.

Wigfield, A., Lutz, S., & Wagner, L. A. (2005). Early adolescents' development across the middle school years: Implications for school counselors. *Professional School Counseling, 9*(2), 112–119.

Late Adolescence (Ages 19 to 25)

A child becomes an adult when he realizes that he has a right not only to be right,
but also to be wrong.

Thomas S. Szasz

The ability to not only know and embrace but express that one might be wrong, requires not only the sense of self-worth not to be threatened by such admittance but also the cognitive abilities to step out of one's egocentric view of life to allow for an alternative perspective. The strength of ego, the change in cognition, and the motivation to be more socially engaged are the elements supporting Dr. Szasz's prescription for adulthood.

This current chapter will review the developmental changes, opportunities, and challenges confronted during the period called late adolescence. This period, which is sometimes referred to as *emerging adulthood*, is a particularly important stage of development as it sets the tone for lasting development throughout the lifespan.

Although most people who have reached this stage have left adolescence, they are seldom prepared to make the transition into adulthood, with its accompanying decisions and responsibilities. As adolescents enter the stage of late adolescence, usually upon completion of high school, decisions and challenges become focused on a new set of choices: education or vocational training, possible entrance into the labor market, further emotional and physical separation from parents, and the possibility of marriage and children.

It is during this phase of life that a person will undergo a substantial amount of change in a short period of time. With so many changes taking place and decisions being made, there are many stressors in an individual's life that influence the path he or she chooses. Although paths will be different, there is continuity in the biological, cognitive, and emotional development of these individuals.

After completing this chapter, you will be able to

1. describe the physical, cognitive, social, and emotional development of late adolescence;

2. identify theories of development as related to late adolescence;

3. understand the risks and stressors to development that may be encountered during late adolescence;

4. understand the role of culture and cultural differences in development through this period of late adolescence; and

5. apply developmental theory to counseling practices.

Healthy Late Adolescence Development

Although teens experience emotions intensely, which is a consequence of brain development for most, the teen years are not filled with angst and confusion. Rather, this time is experienced as one of concentrated social, emotional, and cognitive development. With the support of good family and social network, most emerge from the teen years ready to move forward toward greater social and economic independence. The late adolescence years are often referred to as *peak potential years*. Young adults often have excellent health, energy, and ideal physical capabilities. There is optimal use of strength, coordination, reaction time, senses (taste, touch, smell, hearing, and vision), fine motor skills, and sexual responses. However, males and females peak at different times, and even within the same sex, individuals will mature at different rates. Because individuals come in all different shapes and sizes, and society tends to judge one on physical attributes, these differences will be relevant to the individual. This may lead to a time of self-doubt, low self-esteem, or depression or anxiety about one's appearance and stage of physical maturity. For better understanding, reflect on your own state of well-being, and be prepared to explain to a peer.

Healthy Lifestyle

Late adolescents are typically able to establish lifestyle choices that will establish long-term influences. There is a perception that young adults who choose to exercise regularly and partake in a healthy diet tend to adopt other positive health habits such as avoiding the unhealthy habits of smoking and alcohol and drug use. In a study published in the *American Journal of Public Health* (Maturo, Solveig, & Cunningham, 2013), researchers indicate that young adults who have little or no involvement in physical activity are associated with cigarette smoking, marijuana use, poor dietary habits, television viewing, failure to wear a seat belt, and perception of low academic performance.

According to the Centers for Disease Control and Prevention (CDC, 2008), young adults need at minimum 2 hours and 30 minutes of moderate exercise (or 1 hour and 15 minutes of vigorous intensity) every week in addition to muscle strengthening activities 2 or more days a week that include all major muscle groups. Maintaining a regular fitness schedule will help reduce the risk of many chronic diseases, establish better sleeping patterns, and improve overall health and fitness. In 2008, 76% of late adolescents reported excellent or very good health (Aud, KewalRamani, & Frohlich, 2011). American Indian/Alaskan, White, and Asian individuals reported the highest level of health, and Hispanic individuals reported the lowest (Aud et al., 2011). Over half of these late adolescents reported a healthy weight, with a greater number of females than males reporting a healthy weight (Aud et al., 2011).

The most common health problems of young adulthood include asthma, diabetes, depression and other mental problems, hypertension (high blood pressure), and ulcers. Two additional categories of health concerns during young adulthood are disabilities and sexually transmitted diseases (STDs), with one in two sexually active people acquiring an STD condition by the age of 25 (It's Your Sex Life, 2012).

The CDC (2011) indicates that alcohol consumption among persons aged 12 to 20 years old contributes to the three leading causes of death among this age group in the United States: unintentional injury, homicide, and suicide. Drinking alcohol is associated with other health-risk behaviors, including high-risk sexual behavior, smoking, and physical fighting.

The Brain

Significant changes in the brain structure continue after age 18. According to a study by Bennett and Baird (2006), the brain's structure continues to change, specifically in the areas related to emotion and cognition, during later adolescence. These findings may indicate that as an individual continues to experience opportunities to mature and grow, his or her brain will also continue to adapt, not reaching full maturity until the mid-20s.

In a study produced by the National Institutes of Health, Steinberg (2008) determined that **risk-taking behaviors** decline between adolescence and adulthood. "Risk-taking declines between adolescence and adulthood because of changes in the brain's cognitive control system—changes which improve individuals' capacity for self-regulation" (Steinberg, 2008, pp.78). The changes are primarily found in the prefrontal cortex, which is the epicenter of self-regulation, in addition to the **lateral prefrontal lobe**, **parietal cortices**, and parts of the **anterior cingulate cortex (ACC)**, which are all highly interconnected. As the brain matures, the neural connections between the prefrontal cortex and the limbic system begin to disappear allowing the individual to reduce the influence of peers. This results in the continued enhancement of abilities to organize, plan, coordinate emotions, enhance cognitions, and engage in long-term planning and self-regulation (Steinberg, 2008, pp.91). The cerebral cortex is in a vital period of development during late adolescence (Crews, He, & Hodge, 2006). The cortex is sensitive to environmental changes in synaptic strength. The synaptic receptors and frontal cortical area experience a great amount of change during this time (Crews et al., 2006).

There are also changes between the cortical (gray matter) and subcortical (white matter) regions of the brain. As the gray matter decreases with age, the white matter will continue to increase into an individual's 20s, continually influencing the coordination of cognition and affect (Casey, Tottenham, Liston, Durston, 2005; Keating, 2004). This permits individuals to better function socially and emotionally, using reasoning and decision-making skills based on social and emotional information rather than impulsivity.

Individuals of this group tend not to get the recommended hours of sleep. This can result in negative effects on the brain. Travis et al. (2008) found that the frontal areas of the brain, which are responsible for planning and guiding, lead to better decision making when the right amount of sleep is obtained. Eliasson, Lettieri, and Eliasson (2009) noted that the amount of sleep was not as important as the timing of sleeping and waking. Earlier sleep and wake times correlated with higher grade point averages. Higher performing students tended to nap more frequently than those who did not perform as great (Eliasson et al., 2009). Sleep is an important factor in the success of individuals in this stage of development.

Cognitive Development

Cognitive development, or the way individuals process data, make meaning, think, learn, reason, and remember, begins to expand the individual's perspective from one so self-centered or egocentric to that of multiple perspectives. During this period, individuals start to understand the long-term implications of their decisions and also begin to see as them as not so clear-cut.

Those in the late adolescence phase are typically thought of as adults within Western society, with the ability to problem solve and cope with ambiguity the same as those with much more experience; however, their cognitive development more closely resembles that of someone in early adolescence. Because of this, many young people perceive life from a more optimistic or idealistic perspective. They may perceive life in an unrealistic manner in which love conquers all, those in authority are always honest and trustworthy, and invincibility is taken for granted. Young people lack the experiences that life gives to a person only with age and time. As a result, their worldview may be very true or false, black or white, and they may find the gray areas very hard to navigate. **Perry's Theory of epistemic cognition** states that individuals move from **dualistic thinking**, where information can be understood as right or wrong, to **relativistic thinking**, which is characterized by the awareness of multiple truths (Berk, 2007).

This is not to say that all young adults are incapable of logical thought patterns, systematic reasoning, and adequate assessment of abstract concepts. But rather, it is the developmental phase when young people begin to question authority, the rules, and put into practice adult autonomy skills. By doing so, young adults are able to assess normal developmental tasks, enabling them to use coping skills, problem-solving skills, and deductive reasoning. Complex cognitive functions such as impulse control, goal setting, motivation, interactions with others, reasoning, and evaluation of rewards and punishments are all maturing during this stage of development (Crews et al., 2006).

Individuals in this stage of development have typically surpassed Piaget's formal operations into a stage known as **postformal thought**, which involves more complex decision making that takes into consideration situational circumstances and integrates emotion with logic (Kail, Cavanaugh, & Ateah, 2006).

As previously described in Chapter 2, Piaget posited that young adults are in the formal **operational stage of cognitive development** (age 12 and older) focusing on logic, abstract thought, and problem solving. It is during this phase that young adults use logic to resolve hypothetical situations, attempting to answer the *what if* questions within their lives. This ability to utilize deductive logic requires the capability to take an unknown and decipher the appropriate answer. Deductive reasoning is also used in math and science skills.

It is also within this phase of development that young adults begin to see the world in shades of gray, rather than the concrete scope they once held. A child assumes that a rule handed down by an authority figure is fixed, unwavering, and finite. Rather than referring solely to their childhood experiences and beliefs, young adults begin to question and assess all possible alternatives, outcomes, and consequences, devising a course of action that is well thought out. It is through the deciphering of abstract thought that young adults are able to create a systematic way of solving problems, rather than reverting to trial-and-error methodology. Honing problem-solving skills allows for a young adult to quickly assess and organize a solution in order to resolve the issue at hand (Piaget, 1965).

Another aspect of late adolescence cognitive development is moral development and judgment. **Lawrence Kohlberg** modified Piaget's work, stating that moral development, reasoning, and judgment take longer to develop than Piaget believed. As a result, Kohlberg identified six stages of moral reasoning grouped into three major levels. The first three stages share many similarities with Piaget's work with children; whereas the final three stages expand beyond children and adolescents and into young adults (Kohlberg & Turiel, 1971).

Gilligan took a different approach as she attached gender as a fundamental role in ethical thinking (Donleavy, 2007). She felt that females tend to emphasize caring when cognitively handling ethical decisions whereas males emphasize justice. Furthermore, Gilligan asserts that moral development is based on individuality for males and connectedness for females (Donleavy, 2007). See Table 9.1 Gilligan's Stages of the Ethic of Care.

Stage four of Kohlberg's theory, Maintaining the Social Order, states that an individual will maintain rules and regulations, not because they are a child and an authority figure has directed them to do so but because the

Table 9.1   Gilligan's Stages of the Ethic of Care

Gilligan's Stages of the Ethic of Care	
Stage	**Goal**
Preconventional	*Goal is individual survival*
Transition is from selfishness to responsibility to others	
Conventional	*Self-sacrifice is goodness*
Transition is from goodness to truth that he or she is a person, too	
Postconventional	*Principle of nonviolence: do not hurt others or self*

Source: Adopted from C. Gilligan, Theories of Life Stage and Human Development.

individual has a greater concern for society as a whole. The individual is fully integrated as a member of society and bases his or her ethical decision making on a collectivist perspective regarding the greater good of society. This perspective far exceeds the grasp of a child's understanding (Crain, 1985).

Emotional and Social Development

Although the stereotype of adolescence emphasizes emotional outbursts and mood swings, in truth, the teen years are a quest for emotional and social competence, one typically found by late adolescence. Emotional competence is the ability to perceive, assess, and manage one's own emotions. Social competence is the capacity to be sensitive and effective in relating to other people.

Emotional and social development work in concert: through relating to others, you gain insights into yourself. The skills necessary for managing emotions and successful relationships have been called *emotional intelligence* and include self-awareness, social awareness, self-management, and the ability to get along with others and make friends. Social and emotional development depends on establishing and maintaining healthy, rewarding relationships based on cooperation, effective communication, and the ability to resolve conflict and resist inappropriate peer pressure.

Intimate Relationships

According to **Erik Erickson's psychosocial stages of development**, a later adolescent has the basic conflict of **intimacy** versus isolation. Erickson states that young adults need to form intimate, loving relationships with other people during this phase of their lives. The success of these relationships leads to stronger more resilient relationships in middle and late adulthood, whereas failure results in fear of loneliness, isolation, and abandonment

Photo 9.1   Beginning and finishing college education are significant life events for young adults.

Source: iStockphoto.com/akajeff.

(Harder, 2012). Intimacy requires sacrifice of the self and full commitment to another person. An individual must sacrifice some independence in order to foster the growth of the intimate relationship. Gender has been found to be a predictor of intimacy. For females, intimacy and identity processes may be fused, as they tend to seek values and closeness and develop their identity based on their intimacy. Females may take longer to develop their sense of identity in early adolescence, but they catch up with males by middle adolescence and move ahead of them in the intimacy domain during emerging adulthood (Montgomery, 2005).

This is similar to the findings of Montgomery (2005), where she indicates that intimacy is critical in the transition from adolescence to adulthood. However, Montgomery states that in order for an individual to experience mature, genuine intimacy with another person, he or she must first establish a true sense of himself or herself. This may include the formation of an identity as an adult, while balancing his or her role as a member of the family, in addition to an identity as an adult in the work/school environment. As a counselor, you will be faced with late adolescent clients trying to navigate through this relationship conundrum. Case Illustration 9.1 will assist you in gaining the knowledge you need to work with these clients with relationship issues.

The adult identity is heightened by the awareness of the need for the individual to know who he or she is and what he or she stands for in addition to a quest for independence. With growth comes a change in communication. A young adult no longer wishes to be spoken to or addressed as a child but rather as the adult he or she is attempting to become. When this wish is not fulfilled, a young adult may revert to his or her early adolescent communication style, which means no communication at all.

CASE ILLUSTRATION 9.1 RELATIONSHIP ISSUES

Noah and Allie have been together for 6 months. They fell in love the night they met and have been in a relationship ever since. After discussing their past, Allie realized that Noah had been with many girls. She has never had a serious relationship, and she has always wanted to abstain from intimacy until her marriage to the man she loved. However, Noah's past did not faze her when he was telling her about his multiple intimate relationships. Now, 6 months later, Noah wants to move their relationship to a more intimate level. Allie continues to tell him that she wants to wait, but she can tell that her decision is putting a damper on their relationship. Noah told Allie that he could not be with her anymore if she was not physically attracted to him. Allie tried to explain that she was not ready for sexual intimacy yet. Noah did not understand, so he stormed out the door saying, "How can you be with someone if you aren't attracted to them in a physical way?" Allie has come to the counselor because she is confused about her feelings for Noah and does not know what to do with the relationship.

Practice Exercise:

1. Do you expect Allie to stay in the relationship with Noah?

2. How would you guide Allie to have clear communication with Noah about her feelings to wait until marriage for intimacy?

3. Would you discuss with Allie and Noah the risks of STDs and benefits to be checked for STDs?

4. Would you discuss with Allie the possible consequences of breaking up the relationship even after agreeing to be intimate with Noah to please him?

5. If given the opportunity, what would be your strategy to talk to both Allie and Noah in a counseling setting?

It is through the attempt to create the adult identity that the individual will discover a new level of independence and self-reliance. Parents/guardians can assist in this transition by developing a plan that enables the adolescent to learn and understand the importance of responsibility. This can be as simple as requiring them to pay a bill, expecting them to be on time, or as complex as allowing them to live out the consequences for their actions. As the role of responsibility shifts from parent/guardian to young adult, there will be moments of stress and anxiety in addition to the possible sense of loss and detachment. To help ease these possible side effects, communication between parent/guardian and child will help each party understand and recognize the difficulties associated with the transition to adulthood. This can help foster conditions that encourage growth or at least discourage digressional functioning.

Social Cognition

Late adolescents face significant changes in many of their social relationships, creating the opportunity for exploration and development of their own identity. Familial relationships can serve as important assets to those who have had positive experiences and established healthy attachments during the adolescent years. Family can serve as emotional and financial support as well as important role models. However, while families can serve as a protective factor for many, they can also serve as a significant risk factor for late adolescents who lack that family stability and support (Zarrett & Eccles, 2006). Peer relationships are also an important factor for emerging adults, or late adolescents. While peer relationships tend to trump all responsibilities and relationships in early adolescence, as they grow, mature, and become more self-assured and independent, the significant impact of peers tends to decline.

Social Clock Theory

Early models of late adolescent development sometimes assumed that intimate relationships, such as marriage, were essential to maturing into adulthood. However, a growing number of individuals are choosing to marry later

Photo 9.2   Entering the workforce during the late adolescence years is a positive experience for becoming a responsible adult.

Source: iStockphoto.com/sturti.

in life or to remain single. According to the U.S. Bureau of the Census (2010), the median age of marriage in the United States is 28 for men and 26 for women, as compared to 22 and 20 in the 1960s. Yet, although trends are changing, the internal calendar of goals society places upon individuals remains the same.

The foundation of the social clock theory states that individuals should achieve specific coming-of-age goals at various points in life. Graduation, job, marriage, childbirth, building a family, and buying a home are all examples of societal assumptions associated with this theory. When an individual does not take on the traditional role in society, he or she may face pressure to conform or explain why he or she is not conforming.

Some individuals who do not conform to these social norms are viewed negatively, as if they are abnormal or something is wrong with them (DePaulo, 2004). This negative perception is especially true of those who do not choose to leave home. This can result in especially tense households, but if the move is done at the right time, it can result in strong emotional growth.

Emotional Development

Observing the emotional development of young adults involves watching the transition from Erikson's Identity vs. Role Confusion stage to Intimacy vs. Isolation stage play out (see Chapter 5 for more information). Witnessing the situational decisions made that construct emotional development is illuminating. Each decision, whether to go out to the fraternity party, attend the movie night, or make a stop at the local bar to socialize with new coworkers, is one step further in development. Transitioning from one life role to another and from Erikson's forming identity stage to Erikson's intimacy stage is not a clean-cut process but a gradual shift. Young adults encounter new areas in which they create their identity and fulfill their need for intimacy due to the life change prompted by the end of their secondary education, whether choosing to enter the work force, attend postsecondary schooling, or a combination of both. For many young adults, this transition marks the first time they are confronted with making their own decisions without scaffolding from parents. The choice is theirs alone. The desire to fit in and be accepted transfers from one stage of emotional development to another. Meeting new people is standard for young adults. Those enrolled in college are surrounded by new people in classes and can choose to enhance this exposure by becoming involved with social clubs, sororities and fraternities, student government, or residence hall participation.

Young adults have a different professionally based environment in which to emotionally develop. By meeting new people, young adults work on establishing an identity while fostering intimate relationships. Personal boundaries need to be established, which usually means they need to be explored and pushed. Because this is new and uncomfortable, many young adults turn to alcohol and drug use as a social catalyst. Engaging in the party scene is the perceived norm, especially in college life. Stereotypes associated with aspects of college environments, such as partying in fraternities and sororities, perpetuate the use of alcohol and drugs in college. Young professionals often meet for drinks after work or gather at monthly meetings to forge bonds of friendship in commiserating about work. Either way, new acquaintances are made. Friendships are strengthened or tested during these social engagements.

When these social gatherings are positive experiences, reminiscing about shared experiences and inside jokes, they facilitate emotional development. Healthy and reciprocal friendships can blossom in a short period when positive group dynamics and mutual aid are present. Embarking on the search for personal identity with intimate friends assists emotional development. Many college students experience an abbreviated time span in intimate relationship formation due to the intensity and frequency of social engagements. Having the freedom to make personal choices allows for personal control over social interactions. Young adults entering the work force experience the same freedom of choice but may not experience the intensity of social situations, therefore extending the amount of time needed for establishing intimacy. If the experiences are negative, emotional development may be hindered, and young adults may become more isolated, relying on alcohol and drug use as an escape instead of a social catalyst.

Career Development

During late adolescence, an individual will begin the decision-making process of determining a career path and defining goals. There are many avenues an individual can take. This includes entering the job market directly, military, college or trade school, or selecting to remain out of the career environment. There are also pressures to conform to family or society expectations. This can result in an uncertain and confusing time for some individuals. It is during this time that an individual should explore and experiment, empowering him or her to approach the exploration with a positive attitude and promote positive outcomes. The ultimate goal is for the individual to take actions that will enrich his or her career options.

There are many factors to take into consideration when selecting a career. First, the individual may want to consider what his or her natural or special abilities are. From these natural set of skills or traits, is there a viable career choice that will result in a desired profession? Second, are there special environmental factors or conditions that should be recognized as important influences in the individual's life? For example, Astin (1970) states that external factors such as socioeconomic status (SES), scholastic aptitude, and even marital-familial status all influenced how the women in her study chose a career path. Lastly, learning experiences can give guidance to a potential career path. What one is able to derive from past experiences and performances can result in a set of skills that can further develop into a career path. Success of goals and career investments can result in healthy emotional development and high self-esteem. As a counselor, you will need to be knowledgeable in issues dealing with late adolescence and career decision making. We encourage you to complete Case Illustration 9.2 to assist you in developing this knowledge. In addition, Guided Practice 9.1 will strengthen your skills when working with career counseling.

CASE ILLUSTRATION 9.2 COLLEGE DECISIONS

Rob is a second year college student and is having a really hard time. He is majoring in agriculture because his dad made him. His dad told him that one day he will run the family farm, so he needs to know all the farming business. He does not like farming. He actually hates it, but he does not know how to change his major without disappointing his father. He also thinks that if he changes his major and his dad finds out, then he will not receive any money to pay for college. Since he does not want to disappoint his father, he decides he will drop out at the end of the semester. He does not want to do another semester of work that he is not interested in, but he wants to at least complete the semester he is in. When Rob talks to his friends about what he is thinking, they tell him it is a ridiculous idea. One of his friends advised him to consult with a counselor to see what other options could be considered.

Practice Exercise:

1. Would you advise Rob to drop out or to change his major?

2. Do you expect difficulty in explaining to the father the best possible option for Rob's education?

3. If you had the opportunity to talk to Rob's father, what would be your strategy for helping them to maintain a positive father-son relationship?

4. What do you think are the real motives for Rob's situation, and how is this situation affecting him?

> **Guided Practice Exercise 9.1 Career Development**
>
> Go to the U.S. Bureau of Labor Statistic's Occupational Outlook Handbook online at http://www.bls .gov/ooh/fastest-growing.htm. Research your profession. What is the work environment, job outlook, education level, and pay? Then go to ONET from that website. What are the tasks, skills, knowledge, abilities, work activities, work styles, and work values of your profession?

Alcohol and Drug Use: A Particular Challenge

A normative activity. Drinking alcohol is considered a normal social behavior in Western countries. For most people, alcohol is used as a form of recreation or a method of relaxation. According to a study conducted by the U.S. Department of Health and Human Services in 2007 among adults aged 18 to 25, an estimated 57.1% of females and 65.3% of males reported currently drinking alcohol. These rates are similar to those reported in 2006 (57.9% and 65.9%, respectively) (U.S. Department of Health and Human Services, 2007). Individuals who begin drinking before the age of 14 are at higher risk for developing alcohol abuse disorders (Zeigler et al., 2004). During late adolescence, individuals tend to engage in underage drinking. Participation in underage drinking leads to more severe immediate consequences such as alcohol poisoning, neurodegeneration, and impairments in functional brain activity (Zeigler et al., 2004). Underage drinking, is associated with many neurological risks as well. Brain damage and neurocognitive deficits can result from underage drinking, which can lead to deficiencies in learning and intellectual development. This can continue to affect individuals throughout adulthood. Memory is negatively affected by frequent alcohol use in this group of individuals (Zeigler et al., 2004). Dalwani et al. (2011) found that less spatial working memory is present in individuals who frequently abuse alcohol. Other substance abuse patterns can lead to neurocognitive deficits as well. Dalwani et al. found that individuals with substance abuse disorders had less gray matter volume among areas related to behavioral inhibition, impulsivity, and empathy. More gray matter was present in the areas related to self-referential processing. Furthermore, individuals with substance abuse disorders are found to have increased risk for conduct disorders (Dalwani et al., 2011). This could be due to the amount of gray matter in related areas. Late adolescents are also at high risk for developing addiction disorders due to the effect heavy alcohol consumption has on cortical development (Crews et al., 2006). Consuming alcohol in large quantities impairs higher executive functions, which promotes impulsive behaviors, thus increasing risk for addiction disorders (Crews et al., 2006).

The Inclusion of Drugs

McCabe, Knight, Teter, and Wechsler (2005) found that nonmedical prescription drug use at colleges and universities is becoming increasingly prevalent. Students who are White, male, members of the Greek system, and have lower grade point averages tend to participate in nonmedical prescription drug use most frequently (McCabe et al., 2005). The health and safety consequences related to alcohol, tobacco, and other drug use, remain significant among the age group between 18 and 24. The behaviors of college students place them at high risk for driving under the influence, unprotected sex, sexual assault, physical injury, and death resulting from substance use. Rates of heavy episodic (or binge) drinking have continued to be high, and the misuse of additional substances, specifically prescription medications, has increased sharply in the past decade on college campuses, which consequently increased overall risk factors associated with substance use in this population (Hingson, Zha, & Weitzman 2009). Individuals who engage in nonmedical prescription drug use are more likely to report using alcohol, cigarettes, marijuana, ecstasy, and cocaine and participate in other risky behavior. Individuals using prescription drugs for nonmedical use should be monitored to determine the best intervention strategies, as this group is at high risk for dangerous behaviors (McCabe et al., 2005).

The danger is that late adolescents have the highest rate of drinking, taking pills, and smoking marijuana. This, in part, can be due to the amount of time spent with peers, going away to college, and becoming the legal age to purchase alcohol and other drugs. The legal age to buy, possess, and consume alcohol in the United States is 21 years old. However, cases have shown many young adults are not waiting until this age to begin experimenting with alcohol. Additionally, in most states, marijuana is illegal for people of any age to buy, posses, or consume. However, this legislation is far from convincing young adults to avoid the consumption of marijuana. Both of these substances have been linked to increased risky behaviors and decreased cognition and motor coordination (Parks, Collins, & Derrick, 2012). Specifically, the rate of risky sexual behaviors, such as promiscuity and irregular condom use, is increased when the person is under the influence of alcohol and/or marijuana (Orchowski & Barnett, 2011; Parks et al., 2012). Without the use of protection during sex, both partners take a chance at causing an unplanned pregnancy or contracting a sexually transmitted infection. Because alcohol and marijuana are so widely available, many young adults are at risk of overconsumption, which can lead to the possibility of risky behavior. Guided Practice 9.2 will help you better understand the resources that are available to assist you with these counseling issues.

Guided Practice Exercise 9.2 Alcohol and Drug Use

There are numerous agencies that will help and support people with alcohol and drug addictions. Research and make a list of these agencies within your community for future reference. Review them in class and write down others that students found to your list.

Alcohol Use in High School and College

Increased autonomy, decreased parental supervision, and peer pressure are all factors that affect young adults making the transition from high school to college. Orchowski and Barnett's (2011) research provides evidence that the rate of heavy drinking episodes increases from high school to college. While these are all reasons for general alcohol consumption to rise, the specific activity of "pregaming" is currently on the rise. *Pregaming* is the act of consuming significant amounts of alcohol in a short span of time before even arriving at the main event (Haas, Smith, Kagan, & Theodore, 2012). Those under the age of 21 use pregaming as a way of becoming intoxicated before they arrive at a venue that will not serve them due to their age. Individuals of legal drinking age also pregame but do it for a multitude of other reasons such as already having lowered inhibitions early on in the main event. Much of the research on pregaming indicates that this act increases the risk of alcohol poisoning and blackouts (Haas et al., 2012). Additionally, the transition time from high school to college is pinpointed as a high-risk period for problematic drinking. As you can see, counselors will need to have knowledge and skills to assist older adolescent clients dealing with alcohol and drug abuse during the transition to college and from college to career. Case Illustration 9.3 will be helpful in your counselor training to address this issue.

Preventative Intervention

Due to the fact that many students are drinking and consuming marijuana during their high school careers, education and interventions concentrated on the use of alcohol and drugs need to begin sooner rather than later. Specific subjects, including the dangers of pregaming or the increased chance of risky behavior, should be addressed as students enter high school, not after. Creating a more specific, tailored program for high school students may make the risks of drug and alcohol use more applicable to their lives. Increasing the student's knowledge of the risks involved with misuse of alcohol and marijuana could improve his or her chances of making more informed choices in the future (Parks et al., 2012).

Counseling is an essential part of comprehensive care for this age group in dealing with alcohol and drug abuse. Counselors help identify, prioritize, and work on problems and recovery issues. They can help clients in the late adolescence stage develop specific skills, such as coping with alcohol or other drug cravings, refusing offers from others, challenging their faulty thoughts, coping with negative effects, and improving interpersonal behaviors.

CASE ILLUSTRATION 9.3 ALCOHOL ADDICTION

Candice began drinking when she was in the ninth grade. It was never a problem for her because in high school she only drank when a big event was occurring. When she started college, she began drinking more. She blames it on the college scene and says that drinking in college is "normal," so she never considered herself an alcoholic, though she drank four out of seven days each week. She said there was always something going on that dealt with alcohol, and everyone else was drinking just as much as she, so it did not bother her. Now that she is out of college and has gotten a good job at a local bank, she is starting to realize how much she relies on alcohol. Her friends no longer drink as they used to; however, she is still drinking. She did not think it was a problem until she began needing a drink to finish the workday. She also started noticing that she was drinking every night, even if no one was drinking with her. She now believes that she is an alcoholic and wants to get help.

Practice Exercise:

1. Would you refer Candice to an AA group?

2. Is it the right time for her to join a counseling group for recovering alcoholics?

3. Would it be beneficial for Candice to keep a log of her drinking?

4. Have you discussed with Candice the health and safety risks of alcohol abuse?

College: A Unique Arena for Emerging Adulthood

Photo 9.3   Late adolescents' personality factors of self-identity, likeability, and sociability are indicators of age-appropriate development.

Source: John Howard/Digital Vision/Thinkstock.

Important Factors

A young adult's transition from high school to college can be simultaneously filled with great excitement and apprehension. Many factors come into play when discussing this major life change. The same factors can make this transition smooth or rocky for the student. Personal factors such as race, gender, academic ethic, presence of high school and college advisors, and academic instructors all play a significant role in the success of a student's transition from secondary to postsecondary education (Zhang & Smith, 2011). Predictably, high academic ethic and achievement correlate with a positive transition from a high school to college setting. Furthermore, student interactions with teachers and professors are related to the student's grade point average (Zhang & Smith, 2011). Thus, discussions and interactions between instructors and student should be highly encouraged to aid in raising a student's grade point average.

However, student interactions and accomplishments in high school are not the only factors that can relate to a successful transition to college. Race and gender also play a part in the success of a student's transition. According to Zhang and Smith (2011), mothers of African American students provide more assistance and support than that of Caucasian mothers. However, African American females are the most likely out of both races and genders to be first-generation college students. Maternal assistance and support may be greatly needed when becoming the first person out of the family to attend a higher education institution. It seems facilitating a smooth transition from high school to college depends on numerous factors that are both in and out of the student's control.

Academic Transition

The latter part of a student's high school career through the first few semesters of his or her college career is an essential time frame during the transition from secondary to postsecondary institutions. Currently, many high school students are ill-prepared for the transition to college (Cleary, Walter, & Jackson, 2011; Hoffman, Vargas, & Santos, 2008). One of the main issues with facilitating a continuous transition is the lack of quality curriculum during high school. It is unlikely that a student who receives low academic scores will be able to succeed in a higher institution (Zhang & Smith, 2011). Many secondary schools have begun implementing programs to ensure academic success and aid in transitioning students to a postsecondary career. Due to its affordability and convenience, concurrent enrollment platforms are used by many students to obtain economical college credit while still pursuing a high school diploma. Although program models may vary, the overall procedure of concurrent enrollment is to prepare students for college curriculum by offering a variety of college-level classes while the student is still in high school. Some programs, called Early College Schools, offer low-cost, sometimes tuition-free, courses that translate to a two-year degree by the time the student graduates from secondary school (Hoffman et al., 2008). Blending high school and college course work often blurs the intimidating line between the two. Creating a streamlined pathway between secondary and postsecondary institutions may be the direction other high schools take in order to better fit the students' needs.

Psychological Transition

Adding to the stress of being academically prepared for college, students are often emotionally unprepared for the social and environmental changes that the transition to college may bring. Disbanded social groups, movement away from home, adaptation to a new environment, and adoption of new methods of studying can place young adults at risk of developing a mental illness or trigger the reoccurrence of a psychiatric condition (Cleary et al., 2011). Research shows that the occurrence of mental illness and the rate of suicide is higher in young adults who are pursuing higher education than those who are not (Cleary et al., 2011). Due to a number of factors including peer pressure and newly absent parental guidance, alcohol and drug misuse or abuse can easily become an enemy to a student's battle against poor mental health.

Graduates: Returning Home After College and Choosing Not to Go to College

Late adolescence is a time of decision making for many. Adolescents are starting the transition from dependence into adulthood and are gaining more autonomy. Typically, this period is marked by adolescents going to college, entering the workforce, becoming financially independent, getting married, and moving out of their parents' homes, but this life change is far from uniform. Some young people quickly and smoothly make the shift into adulthood while others take more time; still others leave but later return home (Qian, 2012). In recent years, these trends are becoming less and less used as markers of entering adulthood. In 2012, 36% of the nation's young adults ages 18 to 31 were living in their parents' homes, according to a new Pew Research Center analysis of U.S. Census Bureau data.

The number of late adolescents never leaving home or returning home after college has increased drastically due to a number of factors, including the fall in the economy in recent years, lack of employment opportunities available, a rising number of young adults being enrolled in college, and a decline in the number of individuals getting married (Fry, 2013). The level of coresidence is much higher among males than females. The reason for this difference has been related to the differing gender roles men and women are faced with as well as the fact that females typically reach developmental and life milestones quicker than males do (Boyd & Norris, 1999; Fry, 2013; Qian, 2012). Additionally, there is some evidence that the increase in living at home has been concentrated among less-educated young adults, supporting the theory that those with no education following high school are more likely to reside at home than those who do continue their education (Fry, 2013; Qian, 2012). Finally, individuals of minority status are much more likely to continue or return to residence with their parents than individuals of majority status, a fact most likely attributed to the lack of resources and opportunities presented to lower SES individuals (Qian, 2012).

Other issues also impact the readiness of individuals to establish their independence. Regardless of their sex, race, education level, or SES status, many late adolescents emerging into adulthood often experience great uncertainty and instability as they play out their different life course options (Qian, 2012). As a counselor, it is important that you are aware of the growing trend of coresidence. Additionally, it is crucial for counselors to be knowledgeable in the concerns and needs of late adolescents and young adults entering into periods of gained autonomy and increased independence in life so that you can provide the support and assistance needed in these times.

Risky Behaviors

Risky behavior of youth is seen as an area that is largely ignored (Gruber, 2001). These behaviors have a negative impact on the life of youth and can prevent youth from reaching their full potential (de Guzman & Bosch, 2007). The effects of these behaviors do not occur in isolation and can also affect the lives of others involved in the youth's life such as those of their parents, family, and friends/peers (de Guzman & Bosch, 2007). According to Gruber (2001), the majority of youths engage in drinking, sex, and drugs before the age of 19. Research also shows that 40% of preventable deaths in the United States have been linked to behaviors that compromise the health of individuals.

A report by the CDC in 2012 revealed that teenagers and young adults are seen as being at a high risk for STDs in the United States, with half of all incidences of HIV infections occurring in individuals below the age of 25 (Markowitz, Kaestner, & Grossman, 2005). Data from the CDC Youth Risk Behavior Surveillance System indicate that in 2011 the six leading causes of death among youth and young adults in the United States were linked to injury-causing behaviors; tobacco; alcohol, drug, and substance use behaviors; risky sexual behaviors; poor dietary practices; and physical inactivity (CDC, 2012). According to the CDC, these behaviors are established in childhood and extend into an individual's adulthood. De Guzman & Bosch (2007) have collapsed youth risk behaviors into three main categories: self-injurious behaviors (violence and suicide, underage drinking, driving under the influence, fighting and aggression, suicide, etc.); substance use (illicit drug use, smoking of cigarettes, marijuana and other harmful inhalants, abuse of prescription and over the counter medication, etc.); and risky sexual behaviors (early initiation of sexual intercourse, unprotected intercourse, multiple sexual partners, and sex while under the influence of drugs or alcohol).

Multiple factors are associated with risk-taking behavior in young adults. These factors are individual (low self-esteem, negative peer influence, peer rejection, low educational aspirations); familial (high levels of interparental conflict, high levels of violence in the home, physically punitive parental discipline, poor parent-child communication, lack of family support, and parents who also engage in risky behaviors); and extra-familial (low SES, negative school climate, unsafe neighborhoods) in nature (Criss, Petit, Bates, Dodge, & Lapp, 2000). Positive well-being is regarded as an important characteristic that can help adolescents make the transition to young adulthood without compromising their health in the process.

According to data obtained from the first three waves of the National Longitudinal Study on Adolescent Health (Harris, Halpern, Haberstick, & Smolen, 2013), positive well-being (happiness, self-esteem, optimism) in adolescence is also associated with positive psychological health and fewer risky behaviors in adulthood. In addition, the data revealed that characteristics such as happiness, enjoyment of life, and hopefulness about the future had stronger correlations with healthy living. Counseling interventions aimed at addressing risky behaviors are seen as an underused resource that can be employed to address a variety of prevalent health-related and risky behaviors such substance use and dependence, risky sexual behavior, and poor dietary practices and physical inactivity (Whitlock, Orleans, Pender, Allan, 2002). Intensive groups aimed at tobacco cessation have also seen some success (Fiore, 2000; Hollis, 2000). Some literature also suggests that counseling and HIV prevention counseling aids behavior change in young adults (Kanekar, 2011; Reynolds, Beauvais, Lugina, Gmach, & Thomsen, 2010). HIV prevention counseling in particular focuses on a variety of biopsychosocial issues that may impact young adults (Kanekar, 2011).

Sexual Activity

In today's young people's popular culture and social networks, it is common to hear new terms related to sexual partnerships. For some, this type of jargon becomes part of the way they communicate among peers, and terms may include *hooking up*, *friends with benefits*, *one timer*, and *casual acquaintances* referring to sexual partners.

According to research, sexual intercourse usually happens first in a committed relationship, but 25% of the time it first occurs with a friend, stranger, or someone the person is dating or occasionally dating (Elo, King, & Furstenburg, 1999; Manning, Longmore, & Giordano, 2000).

Differences in sexual activity are related to gender and sexual values, with more women tending to abstain from sexual intercourse than men outside of a monogamous relationship. Freshman college students who had more conservative sexual values tended to be less sexually active, with females tending to be more conservative than males (Balkin, Perepiczka, Whitely, & Kimbrough, 2009).

Hooking up, as defined by Paul and Hayes (2002) is "a sexual encounter which may or may not include sexual intercourse, usually occurring on only one occasion between two people who are strangers or brief acquaintances." Another study defines *hooking up* as two people who meet at a bar or party and agree to engage in some form of sexual behavior with no plans for future sexual activity (Lambert, Kahn, & Apple, 2003). *Hooking up* includes many behaviors: kissing, nongenital touching, oral sex, manual stimulation of genitals, and intercourse (Kalish & Kimmel, 2011). Students in the college culture who frequently engage in hooking up tend to be younger, White, and less religious (Kalish, 2007). Approximately 75% to 80% of college students reported "hooking up" with someone for some form of sexual activity for one night (Kalish & Kimmel, 2011).

Friends with benefits are described as friends who engage in sexual activity without a monogamous relationship or commitment (Furman & Shaffer, 2011). To be a friend with benefits, sexual activity will normally have occurred more than once, and friends with benefits are no different from other friends except for the sexual activity. The typical friend with benefits may engage in fewer activities than those with friends who do not revolve around sexual activity (Furman & Shaffer, 2011).

Eating Disorders

The symptoms of anorexia nervosa and other eating disorders usually first appear during early or middle adolescence (Lock & Gowers, 2005). Eating disorders have been associated with both internalizing and externalizing disorders, thus representing a variety of developmental issues (Bodell, Joiner, & Ialongo, 2012). Impulsivity in childhood is associated with disordered eating in both Caucasian American and African American adolescents, suggesting that impulsivity may be the greatest risk factor among externalizing behaviors for bulimia (Bodell et al., 2012; Wonderlich, Connolly, & Stice, 2004). While most studies on eating disorders are focused on the prevalence in the Caucasian American population, research has shown that African American females have equal or higher rates of bulimic symptoms compared with Caucasian American women (Bodell et al., 2012). Even given the prevalence rates of eating disorders, effective treatment options for eating disorders are lacking (Lock & Gowers, 2005). Research has shown that adolescents with anorexia nervosa benefit from outpatient family therapy following an inpatient treatment program (Dare & Eisler, 2000).

While cognitive behavioral therapy has proven to be the therapy of choice for treating bulimia in adults, family therapy has shown to be effective for treating adolescents with bulimia and adolescents with anorexia (Dare & Eisler, 2000). There are two main options in offering treatment to adolescents with eating disorders: outpatient and/or inpatient care. Outpatient family therapy is effective for a majority of adolescents with anorexia nervosa and is by far the most studied treatment module for adolescents with anorexia nervosa (Dare & Eisler, 2000; Lock & Gowers, 2005). One tradition is to offer outpatient treatment following an inpatient treatment. Inpatient care provides a protective buffer from anxious and worried family members and friends. The second tradition is outpatient family therapy with no inpatient treatment (Dare & Eisler, 2000). Outpatient treatment has been found to be as successful as inpatient care for those who did not require emergency services (Lock & Gowers, 2005). Thus, solely outpatient treatment has shown to be effective because the adolescent is less likely to go through a relapse period of an aversion to eating, which is common in adolescents that complete inpatient treatment (Dare & Eisler, 2000). Completing Guided Practice Exercise 9.3 will increase your knowledge and help better prepare you for working with clients with eating disorders.

Guided Practice Exercise 9.3 Eating Disorders

Make a PowerPoint presentation about one eating disorder, and be prepared to present it to your class for class discussion. Make sure you include what the eating disorder is, the percentage of people suffering from the disease, signs and symptoms, medical complications, causes, treatment, and any other pertinent information concerning the eating disorder. Be sure to cite your resources.

Counseling Issues

Many health risk behaviors are more prevalent in late adolescence than in any other developmental period (Centers for Disease Control and Prevention, 2011). Alcohol and drug abuse, eating disorders, and risky sexual behaviors are among the most common counseling issues for this phase of life. It is also during this time when individuals will see the onset of several chronic health conditions including severe to moderate substance use disorders, depression, and obesity as a result of their risky behaviors. Counselors must be mindful in addressing these potential health risk behaviors, as the behaviors established now are likely to become a lifestyle rather than just a passing phase of life.

Counselors should also be aware of multicultural issues that can arise within this group during this developmental period. Counselors should always be aware of characteristics of the culture the client is associated with, as they can be quite different from the prevalent American culture. Individuals in this stage can be influenced quite easily, and they tend to develop stereotypes. Hu and Kuh (2003) recommend that college-aged students take part in interactional diversity, as this positively effects social interactions with other cultures. Individuals who have previously experienced inequality tend to have a better understanding of the daily impact inequality has on individuals (Einfeld & Collins, 2008). First-year students tend to encounter a greater amount of diversity than upperclassmen (Hu & Kuh, 2003). This could be due to the fact that first-year students are actively seeking new friendships, whereas upperclassmen already have established social relationships. Counselors should strive to understand the interpersonal skills of clients in this developmental stage for effective interactions with multicultural clients. This includes aspects of empathy, patience, attachment, trust, and respect (Einfeld & Collins, 2008). Understanding the importance of these life values can help counselors approach the counseling environment in the most beneficial way possible for the client.

Current Counseling Trends

Technology is a major trend during early adolescence but even more prevalent with individuals in the late adolescence phase. Social networking, such as Facebook and Twitter, continues to be an important part of their lifestyle. Facebook tends to be an important factor in maintaining social capital, whereas "social networks have value" among older adolescents (Ellison, Steinfield, & Lampe, 2007). This age group tends to place great emphasis on social capital, and intense Facebook use has been found to predict social capital. Facebook helps individuals to maintain contact with high school friends as well as recently developing friendships (Ellison et al., 2007). Counselors need to be cognizant of areas of social networking, such as peer counseling, online chat services, and other online social networking. Research has shown that implicating social media as a means to increase engagement on college campuses has been quite effective (Junco, Heiberger, & Loken, 2010). Engaging these individuals via methods with which they are familiar has been shown to increase academic and social development (Junco et al., 2010). Though social media has received negative stigma, counselors could embrace the opportunity to use it to their advantage when trying to reach this group of individuals.

Cultural Diversity Issues

It is critical that professionals educate themselves about the different cultural and ethnic groups with whom they work in order to provide competent services and to relate effectively one-on-one with adolescents. The population of adolescents in the United States is becoming increasingly racially and ethnically diverse, with 37% of adolescents ages 10 to 19 today being Hispanic or members of non-White racial groups. This population diversity is projected to increase in the decades ahead.

Late adolescence and young adulthood marks the start of one's exploration of independence. The teen years allow for more individualistic thinking exploration, it is not until late adolescence and young adulthood that most individuals are truly free of the values, beliefs, and traditions set forth by their families and able to establish their own sense of cultural identity. Certain cultures instill such strict values and beliefs into children and teens growing up that it is only natural for those beliefs and values to be carried into adulthood. Regardless of the decision to continue following the beliefs instilled or the taking of the opportunity to take on other beliefs and traditions, this period of development is an important transition, especially for those of diverse cultural backgrounds.

Many young adults struggle with establishing their own identity. This case holds true for young adults of different cultural backgrounds as well. Not only is it crucial for them to develop their individual identity during this period of growth, it is important that they embark on this journey with a strong sense of cultural or ethnic identity. According to Syed (2013), identity exploration and identity confusion, above ethnic identity, are predictive of an individual's multicultural ideology. Syed went on to conclude that it is important to understand how individuals gain a multicultural view of the world in order to recognize the need for self-cultural understanding before attempting to understand the beliefs and values of someone else.

Many individuals are faced with the challenge of leaving the comfortable environment of home and school that they have grown up in. It is at this point where some individuals go to college and others enter the workforce. At the same time, casual dating and friendship building is a large focus of individuals, while others seek to pursue a more serious relationship with a long-term partner. Regardless of which path is chosen, this time marks the removal from the often-sheltered and highly observed traditions that have surrounded them in their homes as well as the departure from a school in which the majority of their friendships more than likely stemmed from. This time of change can prove to be challenging as it is the first time many individuals from diverse cultural backgrounds have been given the opportunity to explore different friendships, consider other beliefs, and determine their own desires for relationships and behaviors. Although cultural values and traditions that mark a person's ethnic identity are typically carried with them to some extent, culturally diverse young adults must begin establishing the relationships and connecting with the people and organizations they choose that will likely determine the direction in which the next years of life will go. While friendships occur between all ethnicities, individuals from diverse backgrounds tend to become friends with individuals who share similar ethnic beliefs and levels of commitment to their ethnicity (Syed & Juan, 2012).

Regardless of the decision to begin a college career, enter into the workforce, engage in new friendships, or pursue a serious romantic relationship, young adulthood proves to be challenging and often overwhelming. This period in life presents a wide range of decisions that individuals are faced with, and often they are left confused and somewhat hopeless without specific direction. These struggles and stressors are faced by individuals from all cultural backgrounds; however, it is important to realize that individuals identifying with an ethnic minority might face additional stress such as acculturative stress. This stress increases the feelings of hopelessness and vulnerability often faced by young adults because the individuals are also facing difficulties adapting to how different individuals around them interact within a specific culture. Polanco-Roman and Miranda (2013) found that this acculturative stress can be predictive of suicidal ideation among young adults. This fact is something that counselors working with young adults should be aware of, being careful to pick up on behaviors that show the individual to feel hopeless, confused, or depressed. Counselors should work with individuals in their late adolescent years, encouraging the exploration and development of cultural identity, because a strong ethnic identity has shown to buffer against suicidal thoughts and depression that tends to surface during young adulthood (Polanco-Roman & Miranda, 2013). Although the transition from late adolescence into early adulthood is often difficult, a firm grasp of individual and ethnic identity can help individuals from an array of diverse cultural backgrounds maneuver through challenging life experiences.

It is important to remember that later adolescence is a phase of life full of transition, decision making, and uncertainty. Individuals are no longer children but rather seen as adults with adult privileges and responsibilities. They are expected to make wise decisions that will affect the remainder of their lives, although they are not cognitively able to process the information they are given in an optimal manner. Emotionally, they are in between a child and an adult and still developing biologically and cognitively, though they are legally and socially considered adults. Many will struggle with the uncertainty of who they are, who they want to be, and what they want for their futures. This is expected at this stage and can be fostered by mentors, teachers, family, and counselors to become the opportunities they need to safely explore their world. Patience and understanding is needed in order to successfully navigate this phase of life.

The factors contributing to the physical, social, emotional, and psychological development are complex and often have their roots in the early adolescence and childhood years. Zarrett & Eccles (2006) have outlined some specific qualities that are seen as "critical" for healthy development. These qualities include an intrinsic belief in self and the abilities to make a difference in the world, master difficult tasks, and maintain social connectedness. These emerging adults should be able to regulate their emotions, develop healthy attachments, and problem solve, and these abilities will be important as they enter the labor market, prepare to separate from their families of origin, and begin their lives as independent adults.

SUMMARY

- The age period from 18 to 24 years old has been labeled *emerging adulthood*, as individuals have often left the dependency of childhood but have not yet assumed adult responsibilities.
- There is both continuity and change in the transition from high school to college; the transition can involve positive and negative features.
- Positive features of adolescents' maturity include feeling more grownup, increased freedom, and exploration of new ideas; negative features include increased stress and more depression.
- Physical development reaches its peak and begins to decline in early adulthood; peak physical status is often reached between 19 and 26 years of age.
- There are some hidden dangers in the peaks of performance and health in early adulthood, and the negative effects done to one's body may not show up until later in early or middle adulthood.
- Cognitive development/cognitive stages have many developmental changes that can be confusing to the adolescent and the parents.
- Perry's theory of epistemic cognition notes that individuals in this stage move from dualistic thinking to relativistic thinking (right or wrong to relativistic thinking).
- Piaget thought that young adults were quantitatively advanced in their thinking (they have more knowledge than younger adolescents); however, they are qualitatively similar to older young adults.
- Lawrence Kohlberg modified Piaget's work, stating that moral development, reasoning, and judgment take longer to develop than Piaget believed.
- According to Erik Erickson's psychosocial stages of development, a late adolescent has the basic conflict of intimacy versus isolation in intimate relationships.

ADDITIONAL RESOURCES

Journals

Journal of Adolescence
Journal of Adult Development
Journal of Clinical Child & Adolescent Psychology
Journal of Research on Adolescence

Websites

Centers for Disease Control and Prevention, Adolescent and Metal Health. http://www.bls.gov/ces/.
National Institute on Alcohol Abuse and Alcoholism, Alcohol Facts and Statistics. http://www.niaaa.nih.gov/alcohol-health/overview-alcohol-consumption/alcohol-facts-and-statistics
U.S. Department of Labor, Employment Statistics. http://www.bls.gov/ces/.

Videos

The Adolescent Brain. http://www.youtube.com/watch?v = 7GSVja_AO-Q&feature = related.
Adolescent Brain Development, Part I & II. http://www.youtube.com/watch?v = Hl-5vtERj8&feature = relmfu.
Adolescent Brain Development, Part III. http://www.youtube.com/watch?v = inKprzgu56g&feature = relmfu.

Books

Bachman, J. G., Wadsworth, K. N., O'Malley, P. M., Johnston, L. D., & Schulenberg, J. E. (1997). *Smoking, drinking, and drug use in young adulthood: The impacts of new freedoms and new responsibilities. Research monographs in adolescence (RMA)*. Mahwah, NJ: Psychology Press.

Harter, S. (1999). *The construction of the self: A developmental perspective*. New York, NY: Guildford Press.

Holmes, G. R. (1995). *Helping teenagers into adulthood: A guide for the next generation*. Wet Westport, CT: Praeger.

Micucci, J. A. (1998). *The adolescent in family therapy: Breaking the cycle of conflict and control*. Guilford Family Therapy Series. New York, NY: Guildford Press.

RECOMMENDED SUPPLEMENTAL READINGS

Bakker, M. P., Ormel, J., Verhulst, F. C., & Oldehinkel, A. J. (2012). Childhood family instability and mental health problems during late adolescence: A test of two mediation models: The TRAILS Study. *Journal of Clinical Child & Adolescent Psychology, 41*(2), 166–176. doi:10.1080/15374416.2012.651990

Hawkins, M., Villagonzalo, K., Sanson, A., Toumbourou, J., Letcher, P., & Olsson, C. (2012). Associations between positive development in late adolescence and social, health, and behavioral outcomes in young adulthood. *Journal of Adult Development, 19*(2), 88–99. doi:10.1007/s10804-011-9137-8

Johnson, D. P., Whisman, M. A., Corley, R. P., Hewitt, J. K., & Rhee, S. (2012). Association between depressive symptoms and negative dependent life events from late childhood to adolescence. *Journal of Abnormal Child Psychology, 40*(8), 1385–1400.

Letcher, P., Sanson, A., Smart, D., & Toumbourou, J. W. (2012). Precursors and correlates of anxiety trajectories from late childhood to late adolescence. *Journal of Clinical Child & Adolescent Psychology, 41*(4), 417–432. doi:10.1080/15374416.2012.680189.

Poteat, V., & Anderson, C. J. (2012). Developmental changes in sexual prejudice from early to late adolescence: The effects of gender, race, and ideology on different patterns of change. *Developmental Psychology, 48*(5), 1403–1415. doi:10.1037/a0026906

Shaw, L. A., Amsel, E., & Schillo, J. (2011). Risk taking in late adolescence: Relations between sociomoral reasoning, risk stance, and behavior. *Journal of Research on Adolescence, 21*(4), 881–894.

REFERENCES

Astin, H. (1970). *Personal and environmental factors in career decisions of young women*. Washington, DC: Bureau of Social Science Research. Retrieved from http://www.eric.ed.gov/PDFS/ED038731.pdf

Aud, S., KewalRamani, A., & Frohlich, L. (2011). *America's youth: Transition to adulthood*. Washington, DC: U.S. Government Printing Office.

Balkin, R. S., Perepiczka, M., Whitely, R., & Kimbrough, S. (2009). The relationship of sexual values and emotional awareness to sexual activity in young adulthood. *Adult-span Journal, 8* (1), 17–28.

Bennett, C., & Baird, A., (2006). Anatomical changes in the emerging adult brain. *Human Brain Mapping, 27*, 766–777.

Berk, L. (2007). *Development through the lifespan* (4th ed.). Boston. MA: Allyn & Bacon.

Bodell, L. P., Joiner, T. E., & Ialongo, N. S. (2012). Longitudinal association between childhood impulsivity and bulimic symptoms in African American adolescent girls. *Journal of Consulting and Clinical Psychology, 80*(2), 313–316. doi:10.1037/a002709

Boyd, M., & Norris, D. (1999). The crowded nest: Young adults at home. *Canadian Social Trends, 11*(008), 1–4.

Casey B. J., Tottenham N., Liston C., & Durston S. (2005). Imaging the developing brain: What have we learned about cognitive development? *Trends in Cognitive Science, 9*, 104–110.

Centers for Disease Control and Prevention. (2008). How much physical activity do adults need? *2008 Physical Activity Guidelines for Americans*. Retrieved from http://www.cdc.gov/physicalactivity/everyone/guidelines/adults.html.

Centers for Disease Control and Prevention. (2011). *Void substance abuse*. Retrieved from http://www.cdc.gov/family/college/.

Centers for Disease Control and Prevention. (2012). Youth Risk Behavior Surveillance-United States, 2011. *Morbidity and Mortality CDC Weekly Report, 61*(4), 1–168.

Cleary, M., Walter, G., & Jackson, D. (2011). "Not always smooth sailing": Mental health issues associated with the transition from high school to college. *Issues in Mental Health Nursing. 32,* 250–254. doi: 10.3109/01612840.2010054906

Crain, W. C., (1985). Kohlberg's stages of moral development. *Theories of Development,* 118–136. Cranbury, NJ: Prentice-Hall.

Crews, F., He, J., & Hodge, C. (2006). Adolescent cortical development: A critical period of vulnerability for addiction. *Pharmacology, Biochemistry, and Behavior, 86,* 189–199. doi: 10.1016/j.pbb.2006.12.001

Criss, M. M., Petit, G. S., Bates, J. E., Dodge, K. A., & Lapp, A. L. (2000). Family adversity, positive peer relationships, and children externalizing behavior: A longitudinal perspective on risk and resilience. *Child Development, 73* (4), 1220–1237.

Dalwani, M., Sakai, J. T., Mikulich-Gilbertson, S. K., Tanabe, J., Raymond, K., McWilliams, S. K., & Crowley, T. J. (2011). Reduced cortical gray matter in male adolescents with substance and conduct problems. *Drug and Alcohol Dependence, 118,* 295–305. doi: 10.1016/j.drugalcdep.2011.04.006

Dare, C., & Eisler, I. (2000). A multi-family group day treatment program for adolescent eating disorder. *European Eating Disorders Review, 8*(1), 4–18.

de Guzman, M. R., & Bosch, K. R. (2007). *High-risk behaviors among youth.* Retrieved from http://www.ianrpubs.unl.edu/epublic/live/g1715/build/g1715.pdf.

DePaulo, B. (2004). The scientific study of people who are single: An annotated bibliography. *The Spectrum Institute.* Retrieved from http://www.unmarriedamerica.org/Spectrum/Bibliography/contents-page.htm.

Donleavy, G.D. (2007). No man's land: Exploring the space between Gilligan and Kohlberg. *Journal of Business Ethics, 80,* 807–822. doi: 10.1007/s10551-007-9470-9

Einfeld, A., & Collins, D. (2008). The relationships between service-learning, social justice, multicultural competence, and civic engagement. *Journal of College Student Development, 49*(2), 95–109.

Eliasson, A. H., Lettieri, C. J., & Eliasson, A. H. (2009). Early to bed, early to rise! Sleep habits and academic performance in college students. *Sleep Breath, 14,* 71–75. doi: 10.1007/s11325-009-0282-2

Ellison, N. B., Steinfield, C., & Lampe, C. (2007). The benefits of Facebook "friends:" Social capital and college students' use of online social networking sites. *Journal of Computer-Mediated Communication, 12,* 1143–1168. doi: 10.1111.j.1083.2007.00367.x

Elo, I. T., King R. B., & Furstenburg, F. F., Jr. (1999). Adolescent females: Their sexual partners and the fathers of their children. *Journal of Marriage and the Family, 61,* 64–74.

Fiore, M. C. (2000). A clinical practice guideline for treating tobacco use and dependence: A U.S. Public Health Service report. *JAMA: Journal of the American Medical Association, 283*(24), 3244–3255.

Fry, R. (2013). *A rising share of young adults live in their parents' home.* Washington, DC: Pew Research Center. Retrieved from http://www.pewsocialtrends.org/2013/08/a-rising-share-of-young-adults-live-in-their-parents-home.

Furman, W., & Shaffer, L. (2011). Romantic partners, friends, friends with benefits, and casual acquaintances as sexual partners. *Journal of Sex Research, 48*(6), 554–564.

Gruber, J. (2001). *Risky behavior among youths: An economic analysis.* Cambridge, MA: MIT Press.

Haas, A., Smith, S., Kagan, K., & Theodore, J. (2012). Pre-college pre-gaming: Practices, risk factors, and relationship to other indices of problematic drinking during the transition from high school to college. *Psychology of Addictive Behaviors, 26*(4), 931–938.

Harder, A. F. (2012). The developmental stages of Erik Erickson. Bellingham, WA: L.T. Creations. Retrieved from http://www.support4change.com/index.php?option=com_content&view=article&id=47&Itemid=108.

Harris, K. M., Halpern, C. T., Haberstick, B. C., & Smolen, A. (2013). The national longitudinal study of adolescent health. *Twin Research and Human Genetics, 16*(1), 391–308.

Hingson, R. W., Zha, W., & Weitzman, E. R. (2009). Magnitude of and trends in alcohol-related mortality and morbidity among U.S. college students ages 18–24, 1998–2005. *Journal of Studies on Alcohol and Drugs* (Suppl. 16):12–20, 2009 Retrieved from http://www.ncbi.nlm.nih.gov/pmc/articles/PMC2701090/.

Hoffman, N., Vargas, J., & Santos, J. (2008). Blending high school and college: Rethinking the transition. *New Directions for Higher Education, 144,* 15–25. doi: 10.1002/he.322

Hollis J, F. (2000). Population impact of clinician efforts to reduce tobacco use. *[Monograph]. Smoking and Tobacco Control, 12,* 129–154

Hu, S., & Kuh, G. D. (2003). Diversity experiences and college student learning and personal development. *Journal of College Student Development, 44*(3), 320–334. doi: 10.1353/csd.2003.0026

"It's your sex life." (2012). Retrieved from http://www.itsyoursexlife.com/gyt/.

Junco, R., Heiberger, G., & Loken, E. (2010). The effect of Twitter on college student engagement and grades. *Journal of Computer Assisted Learning,* 1–14. doi: 10.1111/j.1365-2729.2010.00387.x

Kail, R., Cavanaugh, J., & Ateah, C. (2006). Emerging adulthood (Canadian ed.). In custom edition of *Human development: A life-span view*. Scarborough, Ontario: Thomson.

Kalish, R. (2007). *Perceived norms and hook ups among college students: Evidence from the College Social Life Survey*. Unpublished manuscript. Department of Sociology, Stony Brook University, New York.

Kalish, R., & Kimmel, M. (2011). Hooking up: Hot hetero sex or the new numb normative? *Australian Feminist Studies, 26*(67), 137–151.

Kanekar, A. S. (2011). HIV/AIDS counseling skills and strategies: Can testing and counseling curb the epidemic? *International Journal of Preventive Medicine, 2*(1), 10–14.

Keating, D. (2004). Cognitive and brain development. In R. Lerner & L. Steinberg (Ed.), *Handbook of adolescent psychology, 2*, 45–84. New York, NY: Wiley.

Kohlberg, L., & Turiel, E. (1971). Moral development and moral education. In G. Lesser (Ed.), *Psychology and educational practice*. Chicago, IL: Scott Foresman.

Lambert, T. A., Kahn, A. S., & Apple, K. J. (2003). Pluralistic ignorance and hooking up. *Journal of Sex Research, 40,* 129–133.

Lock, J., & Gowers, S. (2005). Effective interventions for adolescents with anorexia nervosa. *Journal of Mental Health, 14*(6), 599–610. doi:10.1080/09638230500400324

Manning, W. D., Longmore, M. A., & Giordano, P. C. (2000). The relationship context of contraceptive use at first intercourse. *Family Planning Perspectives, 32,* 104–110.

Markowitz, S., Kaestner, R., & Grossman, M. (2005). An investigation of the effects of alcohol consumption and alcohol policies on youth risky sexual behaviors. *American Economic Review, 95*(2), 263–266.

Maturo C. C., Solveig, A., & S. A. Cunningham. (2013). Influence of friends on young adult's physical activity: A Review. *American Journal of Public Health,103*(7), e23–238.

Montgomery, M. (2005). Psychosocial intimacy and identity: From early adolescence to emerging adulthood. *Journal of Adolescent Research, 2*(3), 346–374.

McCabe, S. E., Knight, J. R., Teter, C. J., & Wechsler, H. (2005). Non-medical use of prescription stimulants among US college students: Prevalence and correlates from a national survey. *Addiction, 99,* 96–106. doi: 10.0000/j.1360–0443.2004.00944.x

National Institute on Alcohol Abuse and Alcoholism (NIAAA). (2006). Alcohol Alert, No. 67 "Underage drinking." Retrieved from http://pubs.niaaa.nih.gov/publications/AA67/AA67.htm.

Orchowski, L., & Barnett, N. (2011). Alcohol-related sexual consequences during the transition from high school to college. *Addictive Behaviors. 37*(3), 256–263. doi:10.1016/j.addbeh.209.10.010

Parks, K., Collins R., & Derrick J. (2012). The influence of marijuana and alcohol use on condom use behavior: Findings from a sample of young adult female bar drinkers. *Psychology of Addictive Behaviors, 26*(4), 888–894.

Paul, E. L., & Hayes, A. (2002). The casualties of 'casual' sex: A qualitative exploration of the phenomenology of college students' hookups. *Journal of Social and Personal Relationships, 19*(5), 639–663.

Pew Research Center. (2012). *Young, underemployed and optimistic*. Washington, DC: Pew Research Center. Retrieved from http://www.pewsocialtrends.org/files/2012/02/young-underemployed-and-optimistic.pdf.

Piaget, J. (1965). *The moral judgment of the child*. New York, NY: Free Press.

Polanco-Roman, L., & Miranda, R. (2013). Culturally related stress, hopelessness, and vulnerability to depressive symptoms and suicidal ideation in emerging adulthood. *Behavior Therapy, 44,* 75–87.

Qian, Z. (2012). *During the great recession, more young adults lived with parents*. Census Brief prepared for Project US2010. Retrieved from http://www.s4brown.edu/ us2010.

Reynolds, H. W, Beauvais, H. J., Lugina, H. I., Gmach, R. D., & Thomsen, S. C. (2010). A survey of risks for unintended pregnancy and HIV among youth attending voluntary counseling and testing (VCT) services in nine centers in Urban Haiti and Tanzania. *Vulnerable Children and Youth Studies, 5*(1), 66–78.

Steinberg, L. (2008). A social neuroscience perspective on adolescent risk-taking. *Development Review 28*(1), 78–106. doi:10.1016/j.dr.2007.08.002

Syed, M. (2013). Identity exploration, identity confusion, and openness as predictors of multicultural ideology. *International Journal of Intercultural Relations, 37,* 491–496.

Syed, M., & Juan, M. J. D. (2012). Birds of an ethnic feather? Ethnic identity homophily among college-age friends. *Journal of Adolescence, 35,* 1505–1514.

Travis, F., Haaga, D. A., Hagelin, J., Tanner, M., Nidich, S., Gaylord-King, C., & Schneider, R.H. (2008). Effects of transcendental meditation practice on brain functioning and stress reactivity in college students. *International Journal of Psychophysiology, 71,*170–176. doi: 10.1016/j.ijpsych0.2008.09.007

U.S. Bureau of the Census. (2010). *Median age at first marriage*. Retrieved from http://www.census.gov/http://wps.ablongman .com/ab_duggan_career_1/55/14211/3638138.cw/index.

U.S. Department of Health and Human Services. (2007). The Surgeon General's call to action to prevent and reduce underage drinking: A guide to action for families. Washington, DC: U.S. Department of Health and Human Services, Office of the Surgeon General.

Whitlock, E. P., Orleans, C. T., Pender, N., & Allan, J. (2002). Evaluating primary care behavioral counseling interventions: An evidence-based approach. American Journal of Preventive Medicine, 22(4), 267–284.

Wonderlich, S. A., Connolly, K. M., & Stice, E. (2004). Impulsivity as a risk factor for eating disorder behavior: Assessment implications with adolescents. *International Journal of Eating Disorders, 36,* 172–182. doi:10.1002/eat.20033

Zarrett, N., & Eccles, J. (2006). The passage to adulthood: Challenges of late adolescence. *New Directions for Youth Development, 111,* 13–28. doi: 10.1002/yd.179

Zeigler, D. W., Wang, C. C., Yoast, R.A., Dickinson, B. D., McCaffree, M. A., Robinowitz, C. B., & Sterling, M. L. (2004). The neurocognitive effects of alcohol on adolescents and college students. *Preventative Methods, 40,* 23–32. doi: 10.1016/j .ypmed.2004.04.044

Zhang, P., & Smith, W. (2011). From high school to college: The transition experiences of black and white students. *Journal of Black Studies. 42*(5), 828–845. doi:10.1177/0021934710376171

Early Adulthood (Ages 26 to 35)

10

To be a healthy person, you have to be sympathetic to the child you once were and maintain the continuity between you as a child and you as an adult.

Maurice Sendak

Early adulthood, ages 26 to 35, includes developmental struggles that are often shared by both young and old. Most individuals are concerned with developing more mature friendships and intimate relationships, repositioning family ties, selecting a long-term career, considering the future, and establishing a secure personal identity. During this time of life, individuals make more choices than in any other phase of life. Individuals often increase financial and emotional investments and become more focused on advancing their careers and gaining personal stability through marriage and child rearing. When decisions are made in tune with beliefs and the person's social world, then life can be full and rewarding. However, when these decisions do not align, struggles may occur.

Young adults do not go through emerging adulthood alone and often require substantial support from their families to successfully accomplish the many developmental tasks of this period. Not all young adults share the same pathways through early adulthood. There is diversity in the paths of young adults, reflecting not only variation due to structural factors such as socioeconomic status, gender, race, culture, and ethnicity but also individual differences in social, cognitive, and emotional development and adjustment, which are shaped in part by early and ongoing family dynamics. Today's families are increasingly complex due to nonmarital childbearing, divorce, cohabitation, remarriage, and same-sex marriage as well as the health and well-being of their members. Young adults' ability to draw on family resources varies according to the characteristics of their families of origin. Individual and group differences in the family can cause a lack of resources available to young adults, which may be especially pronounced in the early adult period, given the growth of income inequality over the last several decades and the severity of the current socioeconomic challenges. Counseling this age group often focuses on the family contexts of early adulthood, emphasizing the importance of both the family and new and highly variable types of family experiences that occur in early adulthood (Arnett, 2004)

This chapter will discuss human development during the early adulthood stage. We will explore physical, cognitive, social, and emotional development as well as specific counseling issues that often arise during this time of development. Specifically, after reading this chapter, you will be able to

1. consider the physical, cognitive, and social/emotional development of early adulthood;

2. apply various theories of development as related to development during early adulthood;

3. assess common risks to healthy development during early adulthood; and

4. prepare for areas of counseling that may be needed during early adulthood, including prevention and intervention strategies.

Healthy Early Adulthood Development

The four types of development are physical, cognitive, social, and emotional development. Each individual develops differently. When considering development during early adulthood, it is essential to examine the influence of structural constraints on the individual's sociocultural environment, which is the choices and engagement in activities that promote future options, opportunities, and trajectories, during the adolescent period. It is also critical to understand what assets and needs are essential for keeping individuals in early adulthood on healthy, productive pathways into adulthood. We have learned from Erik Erikson (1968), how he asserted that tasks of adolescence are played out in a complex set of social contexts and in both cultural and historical settings. These complexities have an impact on development in later adulthood.

According to Jeffrey Arnett (2006), there are five key features that characterize emerging adulthood:

1. *Identity exploration, especially in love and work.* Emerging adulthood is the time during which key changes in identity take place for many individuals.

2. *Instability.* Residential changes peak during early adulthood, a time during which there also is often instability in love, work, and education.

Photo 10.1   Entering the workforce can be a stressful adjustment and a daunting task during early adulthood.

Source: Creatas Images/Creatas/Thinkstock.

3. *Self-focused.* According to Arnett (2006, p. 10), emerging adults "are self-focused in the sense that they have little in the way of social obligations, little in the way of duties and commitments to others, which leaves them with a great deal of autonomy in running their own lives."

4. *Feeling in-between.* Many emerging adults don't consider themselves adolescents or full-fledged adults.

5. *The age of possibilities, a time when individuals have an opportunity to transform their lives.* Arnett (2006) describes two ways in which emerging adulthood is the age of possibilities: (1) many emerging adults are optimistic about their future; and (2) for emerging adults who have experienced difficult times while growing up, emerging adulthood presents an opportunity to chart their life course in a more positive direction.

Recent research studies indicate that these five aspects characterize not only individuals in the United States as they make the transition from adolescence to early adulthood but also their counterparts in European countries and Australia (Arnett, 2012). Although emerging adulthood does not characterize development in all cultures, it does appear to occur in cultures that postpone assuming adult roles and responsibilities (Kins & Beyers, 2010). Criticism of the concept of emerging adulthood is that it applies mainly to privileged adolescents and is not always a self-determined choice for many young people, especially those in limiting socioeconomic conditions (Cote & Bynner, 2008).

In reference to early adulthood development, one of the theories that has made significant contributions to the field of counseling is Erik Erikson's psychosocial development sixth stage, intimacy versus isolation. This stage takes place during early adulthood between the ages of approximately 19 and 40. During this period of time, the major conflict centers on forming intimate, loving relationships with other people. While psychosocial theory is often presented as a series of neatly defined, sequential steps, it is important to remember that each stage contributes to the next. For example, Erikson believed that having a fully formed sense of self (established during the identity versus confusion stage) is essential to being able to form intimate relationships. Studies have demonstrated that those with a poor sense of self tend to have less committed relationships and are more likely to suffer emotional isolation, loneliness, and depression. Erikson also believed that it was vital that people develop close, committed relationships with other people during early adulthood. Success leads to strong relationships, while failure results in loneliness and isolation (Erikson, 1968).

Physical Development

Early adulthood is, for most people, the time of peak physical capacity. The body reaches full height by the late teens, and physical strength increases into the late 20s and early 30s (Whitbourne, 2001). Manual agility and coordination, and sensory capacities such as vision and hearing, are also at their peak. However, change is imminent, even in these basic capacities. Some decline in the perception of high-pitched tones is found by the late 20s (Whitbourne, 2001), and manual dexterity begins to reduce in the mid-30s.

Physical development includes biological aging, physical changes, health, and fitness. By early adulthood, the body has completed its physical growth and begins to enter **senescence**. Senescence is "genetically influenced decline in the functioning of organs and systems that are universal in all members of our species" (Berk, 2010, p. 329).

Development takes on new meaning in early adulthood because the process is no longer defined by physical and cognitive growth spurts. Early adulthood, which encompasses the majority of a person's life-forming and productive lifespan, is marked instead by considerable psychosocial gains that are coupled with steady but slow physical decline. **Age clocks**, or the internal sense of timing of physical and social events, determine the various life stages through which young adults pass. Although people age at different rates, the majority of Americans, reinforced by social norms, go through a series of predictable periods. Perhaps one of the best-known stage theories of adult development is that offered by Daniel Levinson.

According to Levinson, the ages of 17 to 45 encompass *early adulthood,* which he divides into the *novice phase* (17–33) and the *culminating phase* (33–45). Levinson further divides the novice phase into the stages of *early adult transition* (17–21), *entering the adult world* (22–28), and *age-30 transition* (28–33). The *culminating phase* (33–45) consists of the *settling down* (33–40) and *midlife transition* (40–45) stages. As with any stage theory, these stages are only a guide for the development that normally occurs along a continuum of the lifespan. Not everyone progresses through each stage at exactly the same age.

The young adult years are often referred to as the peak years. Young adults experience excellent health, vigor, and physical functioning. Young adults have not yet been subjected to age-related physical deterioration, such as wrinkles, weakened body systems, and reduced lung and heart capacities. Their strength, coordination, reaction time, sensation (sight, hearing, taste, smell, and touch), fine motor skills, and sexual response are at a maximum.

Additionally, both young men and women enjoy the benefits of society's emphasis on youthfulness. They typically look and feel attractive and sexually appealing. Young men may have healthy skin, all or most of their hair, and well-defined muscles. Young women may have soft and supple skin, a small waistline, healthy hair, and toned legs, thighs, and buttocks. Early in adulthood, neither gender has truly suffered from any double standards of aging; mainly, the misconception that aging men are distinguished, but aging women are over the hill. With good looks, great health, and plenty of energy, young adults dream and plan their future. Adults in their 20s and 30s set many goals that they intend to accomplish—from finishing graduate school, to getting married and raising children, to becoming financially stable before age 40. Early adulthood is a time when nothing seems impossible; with the right attitude and enough persistence and energy, most young adults think that anything can be achieved.

Physical Changes

Up until this point, each stage in life has demonstrated tremendous physical changes. While physical changes do occur throughout adulthood, they do not occur at near the rate of those in childhood and adolescence. Remember that during adolescence, youth experience dramatic changes in the shapes of their bodies, an increase in gonadal hormones (reproductive cells gametes, e.g., in testis or ovary), and changes in brain structure. Another major biological change during this period between puberty and early adulthood is in the frontal lobes of the brain, responsible for such functions as self-control, judgment, emotional regulation, organization, and planning (Begley, 2000). These changes in turn fuel major shifts in young adults' physical and cognitive capacities and their social and achievement-related needs. During early adulthood, the primary task consists of managing these biological and cognitive shifts and the subsequent influences these have on behavior, mood, and social relationships. How young adults cope with these hormonal and cognitive changes will ultimately influence their well-being in middle and later adulthood as multiple additional tasks and responsibilities are imposed on them.

While mortality rates of this age group are typically very low, health and fitness is still an important factor of physical development during early adulthood. For most people, these years are the prime of life. Early adulthood is a time when individuals are generally in good health, with biological function and physical performance peaking between the ages of 20 to 35. Economically advantaged, well-educated individuals usually have good health over most of their lives, but lower-income individuals with limited education often do not have good health mainly due to their living conditions and habits (Berk, 2010). Many young adults have a large increase in weight due to sedentary lifestyles and diets high in sugar and fat. Regular exercise "reduces body fat, builds muscle, helps prevent disease, and enhances psychological well-being" (Berk, 2010, p. 362). Unfortunately obesity is increasing among U.S. adults and is linked to an increased risk of hypertension, diabetes, and cardiovascular disease. Additionally, diseases such as testicular cancer, cervical cancer, and Hodgkin's lymphoma are a threat to this age group. In underdeveloped countries, HIV/AIDS has also significantly increased mortality of those in early adulthood.

In general, individuals in early adulthood feel robust and energetic, although it is not unusual to see fluctuations around stressful periods such as establishing intimate relationships and managing education or job responsibilities. On the other hand, people in this age group are also legally able to engage in many social activities including the use of damaging substances, such as alcohol and tobacco, and many can obtain access to illegal stimulants or narcotics. The two most common substances that are abused during early adulthood are cigarettes and alcohol (Santrock, 2009). Furthermore, young adults also have an increasing responsibility for organizing their own eating habits and exercise regimes. Not surprisingly, the health status and prospects of emerging young adults are dependent more than ever before on their own behavioral choices.

Cognitive Development

By the beginning of early adulthood, most people are capable of the levels of reasoning that we would expect for normal functioning in adult society. Although there are wide individual differences in attainment, most young adults are able to deal with cognitive tasks in a more abstract way than before and to attain solutions to problems by comparing possible explanations. Does this mean that cognitive development has reached a plateau? Piaget and others argued that thinking stabilized at the end of the teen years, but increasing evidence suggests that we continue to develop cognitively throughout our lifespan. Many theorists suggest that the nature of thinking changes qualitatively during early adulthood, with adults exhibiting postformal thought. Postformal thought acknowledges that the world sometimes lacks pure right and wrong solutions, so adults must draw upon prior experiences to solve problems. Therefore, while formal-operational thinking is absolute; post-formal thinking is more complex and involves making decisions based on situational contexts and circumstances and integrating emotion with logic.

Cognitive skill development over the early adolescent years enables youth to become increasingly capable of managing their own learning and problem solving while also facilitating their identity formation and maturation of moral reasoning. This skill is demonstrated as the individual reaches later adulthood and into the late 30s. There are distinct increases in early adults' capacities to think abstractly, consider multiple dimensions of problems, process information and stimuli more efficiently, and reflect on the self and life experience (Keating, 1990).

The successful development of these cognitive skills relates to a youth's ability to be resourceful, an important skill for successful pursuit of educational and occupational goals (Heckhausen, 1999). It has also been linked to early adulthood individuals' greater investments in understanding their own and others' internal psychological states and the resulting behavioral shift in focus on their developing close and intimate friendships. As young people consider what possibilities are available to them, they are more capable of reflecting on their own abilities, interests, desires, and needs. Overall, early adults are able to come to a deeper understanding of the social and cultural settings in which they live. In fact, research has found an increase in their commitments to civic involvement when such cognitive developments are coupled with prosocial values and opportunities to think and discuss issues of tolerance and human interaction with others. In a culture that stresses personal choice in life planning, these concerns and interests set the stage for personal and social identity formation and ultimately influence educational, occupational, recreational, and marital and family choices (Furstenberg, Rumbaut, & Settersten, 2005). This is a very important factor when counseling needs arise and needs to be taken into consideration for effective counseling interventions.

Schaie and Willis's Stage Theory of Cognition (2000) (see Table 10.1) has proven to be very relative when considering the developmental stages entering early adulthood and beyond. This theory uses findings from research on adult intellectual development to formulate seven adult stages: acquisitive, achieving, responsible, executive, reorganizational, reintegrative, and legacy creating. Individuals in early adulthood are typically identified in the stages of achieving and responsible.

In early adulthood, for example, people typically switch their focus from the acquisition of knowledge to the application of knowledge, as they use what they know to pursue careers and develop their families. This is referred to as the achieving stage. It represents most prominently the application of intelligence in situations that have profound consequences for achieving long-term goals. The kind of intelligence exhibited in such situations is similar to that employed in educational tasks, but it requires careful attention to the possible consequences of the problem-solving process.

Table 10.1   Schaie & Willis's Stage Theory of Adult Cognitive Development

Acquisitive Stage	Encompasses all of childhood and adolescence; main developmental task is to acquire information
Achieving Stage	Intelligence is applied to specific situations involving attainment of long-term goals regarding careers, family, and societal contributions
Responsible Stage	Major concerns of middle-aged adults relate to their personal situations, including protecting and nourishing their spouses, families, & and careers
Executive Stage	Period in middle adulthood when people take broader perspective than earlier, including concerns about the world
Reorganizational Stage	Occurs past adulthood when adults enter retirement and need to reorganize their lives around activities not related to work
Reintegrative Stage	Period in late adulthood during which the focus in on tasks that have personal meaning
Legacy Creating Stage	During the last stage of life when adults enjoy telling their life stories and begin distributing their possessions

Young adults who have mastered the cognitive skills required for monitoring their own behavior and, as a consequence, have attained a certain degree of personal independence will next move into a stage that requires the application of cognitive skills in situations involving social responsibility. Typically, the responsible stage occurs when a family is established and the needs of spouse and offspring must be met. Similar extensions of adult cognitive skills are required as responsibilities for others are acquired on the job and in the community. Some individuals' responsibilities become exceedingly complex. Such individuals like presidents of business firms, deans of academic institutions, officials of churches, and a number of other positions need to understand the structure and the dynamic forces of organizations. They must monitor organizational activities not only on a temporal dimension (past, present, and future) but also up and down the hierarchy that defines the organization. They need to know not only the future plans of the organization but also whether policy decisions are being adequately translated into action at lower levels of responsibility. Attainment of the executive stage, as a variation on the responsibility stage, depends on exposure to opportunities that allow the development and practice of the relevant skills (Avolio, 1991; Smith, Staudinger, & Baltes, 1994).

Social/Emotional Development

According to Erikson (1968), the primary conflict for individuals ages 18 to 40 is intimacy versus isolation. While this struggle begins during later adolescence and was discussed in Chapter 11, the struggle continues during this period of life as well. Additionally, Freud argued that a healthy adult is one who can love and also work. Therefore, finding personal relationships as well as work environments that are satisfying are important during this time of life. We will talk about both of these in greater detail throughout this chapter.

Levinson (1978) extended some of Erikson's ideas but drew also on social psychological theory to explain the relationship between the developing individual and the demands of society. He emphasized social role requirements at different life stages and the interaction between personal growth and relationships. He maintained that all normally developing adults progress through the same stages, in the same sequence, and at roughly the same pace. Early adulthood begins with the substage of early adult transition (approximately 17–22 years old), in which

Photo 10. 2   Enduring relationships are built on trust and respect.

Source: BananaStock/BananaStock/Thinkstock.

young people are working toward autonomy from their parents and formulating a dream of what they hope to become in life. The dream is important because it guides their efforts and choices in both the occupational and personal spheres. Think for a moment: Do you have your own dream, or did you have one during this phase of life, and how does/did it relate to your current occupation and plans? The next substage is the period of entering the adult world (22–28 years old) and is organized around forging a pathway at work and attaining a special personal relationship. This is followed by the age 30 transition (28–33 years old), in which people undergo a moderate degree of self-questioning—reviewing their dreams, the choices they have made, and the problems in their lives. At this point, social and emotional development should be more under the person's control.

However, early adults face some formidable developmental tasks. As previously indicated, many people at the beginning of this stage are concerned with launching their careers. They may be studying to gain the critical qualifications or training at the entry level of a job or an organization. Some will not be so lucky. In many countries, youth unemployment rates have been very high during the last century and appear set to continue. Studying for course work, employment, and unemployment all present their own unique stresses. At the same time, young adults tend to be finding their way through the world of romance, which can also lead to stress and anguish. All of this happens alongside changes in relationships with parents and the increasing expectation that the young person will take responsibility for his or her own life—including, perhaps, a shift to a new home.

It would be an unusual young person who proceeded through these developmental tasks without at least occasionally wondering who he or she is, or who he or she is becoming, and how he or she is faring compared to his or her peers. For most people, facing these issues brings a range of emotional reactions and signs of maturity. These situations usually provide an opportunity or need for professional counseling to clarify or set new directions to follow the pathways of early adulthood that will lead into later adulthood and middle age.

According to developmental models such as Erikson's, Schaie's, and Levinson's, individuals in their early adulthood are developing a sense of personal identity along with a need for closeness to others. They have also progressed through the biological developments of adolescence and are now fully matured sexual beings. Therefore, finding and developing relationships with an intimate partner, or series of partners, becomes a priority for many young adults during this stage. These relationships will be discussed in more depth later in the chapter.

Moral Development

In early adulthood, many are still in the conventional stage of Kohlberg's theory of morality development. As mentioned in Chapter 10, this stage typically begins in adolescence and unfortunately the majority of adults will stop there. During this stage, adults believe in conforming to stereotypical behaviors and values of their culture. Most acts are done in an effort to belong to the group. Respect for rules and laws is valued. Authority figures are seldom questioned.

While most adults remain at this stage, life crises often present opportunities for moral growth. These include loss of a job, relocation, death of a significant other, and other unforeseen tragedies. Because adulthood is often a time when these events occur, some adults continue to move beyond the conventional stage of moral development. For those that are able to move beyond this stage, Kohlberg believed that the postconventional stage colud be reached. In this stage, the individual values dignity for all life, believing all individuals have natural or inalienable rights and liberties that come before societal needs. Ethical decisions are made based on situational information rather than concrete rules for specific behaviors. In other words, there are no set consequences for a specific action; rather, a person in the postconventional stage will consider the reasons behind the action for each individual person. Adults in this stage also believe that the freedom of the individual should be limited only when that freedom infringes upon someone else's freedom.

Risks to Healthy Early Adulthood Development

Erikson argued that maintaining a firm sense of identity was critical to having successful intimate relationships. Studies repeatedly demonstrate that those who lack a strong sense of identity have less satisfactory relationships. Because the development of intimate relationships is critical to life happiness at this phase of life, a lack of these relationships can be a risk for healthy early adulthood development. In fact, studies suggest that individuals who do not have satisfactory personal relationships tend to be more isolated, lonely, and depressed.

Photo 10.3   Depression is a common problem among young adults.

Source: David DeLossy/Photodisk/Thinkstock.

Depression

It is not uncommon for an individual who is approaching the age of 30 to perceive life as becoming more serious. Sometimes individuals may begin to consider where they are in life at this point and may end up tearing up the life structure that they put together thus far and starting anew. If this transition becomes difficult, depression may be a result.

Depression is a major concern for individuals in their 20s to mid-30s. Of those people diagnosed with major depression, most are diagnosed at this age.

Individuals who have previously experienced depression or had an eating disorder are at higher risk of developing depression during this time (Johnson, Cohen, & Kasen, 2009), and women are more likely than men to experience depression, with 1 in 4 women requiring treatment at some point, compared with 1 in 10 men. However, these statistics may be more the result of men not seeking services for depression and not the actual occurrence of depression. Men, however, are much more likely to commit suicide, which is the largest killer of men under the age of 40. While many think of depression as a person sleeping all day, a person who is depressed may also be unable to sleep and experience feelings of restlessness. It is important for counselors to be aware of all of the signs and symptoms of depression. For more information see Figure10.1 Symptoms of Depression

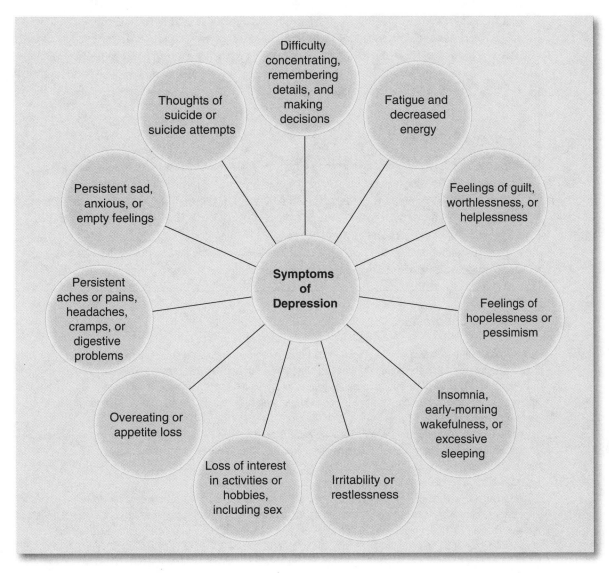

Figure 10.1 Symptoms of Depression

CASE ILLUSTRATION 10.1 DEPRESSION

After 3 years of marriage, Kesha and Tommy got a divorce. Tommy felt as if there was no hope for their marriage; whereas, Kesha thought they would always stay together. While married, Tommy and Kesha had a son and were financially stable. However, now that they are divorced, Kesha is financially

(Continued)

(Continued)

unstable. After a couple of months of dealing with bills, Kesha has found herself depressed. She not only is depressed about her financial situation but also from the guilt of being a single parent. She feels as if her son will never be able to experience life with a father as she did. Kesha has been going to work, then coming home and just wanting to sleep. She wants to spend time with her son, but she just does not feel like doing anything. She told her sister that she just wants to sleep to make everything go away.

Practice Exercise:

As a counselor, it will be important to assess the extent of Kesha's depression and refer to a medical doctor or psychiatrist for medication, if appropriate. The counselor may wish to explore issues such as what makes Kesha happy, how she felt during the marriage, options for her son to have active father involvement or another adult to serve in this role, and so on. Cognitive-behavioral therapy can help Kesha reframe her thoughts and focus on her new life with her son. Because Kesha is also financially insecure, it will be important to help her explore stable job positions and find additional resources to assist as needed. Discuss your response to this scenario with your colleagues or professor.

Body Image Concerns

Body image refers to how a person experiences his or her embodiment, since we all live embodied lives. Body image is more than a mental picture of what one looks like; our body image consists of our personal relationship with our body. This involves our perception, beliefs, thoughts, feelings, and actions that pertain to our physical appearance. In other words, body image is not a simple, singular aspect of the person. It is something quite complex and multifaceted.

While there is no uniform agreement among experts on the exact definition of body image, there is little disagreement that body image is a multidimensional construct. Most counselors use the term *body image* to describe our internalized sense of what we look like. This can be thought of as a mental representation or map of our body against which we judge our external appearance (Cash & Pruzinsky, 2002).

We recognize our image as our *self* when we are children and as we grow into adults. However, when our appearance changes suddenly, perhaps after an accident or as a result of disease, it can be very disconcerting, and it takes quite a long time before we see ourselves once more when looking in the mirror. Body image can also be studied in terms of what we look like in the eyes of an observer. What other people see and what we think they can are like two sides of a coin, as they both contribute to how we feel about our looks. For example, we might receive positive or negative feedback about our appearance that might influence the way we think and feel. Equally, the way we act and feel about our appearance will have an impact on others. For example, if a young adult keeps his or her head down and does not make eye contact, due to concerns about his or her looks, then others will think the young adult is not interested in socializing with them. People could be critical and reject the young adult, not because of his or her appearance but because of his or her actions. Body image can therefore be positive or negative and can vary over time. It is just one aspect of the way we feel about ourselves.

Having a negative body image can create other problems in living. This is very true during the adolescent years and equally significant in early adulthood. In fact, body image perception stays with the person for most of the person's lifespan. We all want to look our best, but a healthy body is not always linked to appearance. Actually, healthy bodies come in all shapes and sizes, as we well know. Having a positive body image means that you see yourself in a positive way; you feel comfortable in your body; and you feel good about the way you look. It is common to see young adults struggling with changing their body; instead of changing the way they think about their bodies.

Body image development is affected by cultural images and the influence of family, peers, the media, and others. Concern about our appearance and our body image is quite normal and understandable. Again, we all want to look our best, and while a positive body image contributes to enhanced psychological adjustment (less depression, positive self-worth, life satisfaction, less interpersonal anxiety, fewer eating disorders), a negative body image can lead to serious eating and exercise disorders. These distortions in our thinking contribute to a negative body image, low self-esteem, and low self-concept (Cash, Phillips, Santos, & Hrabosky, 2004).

Concerns with appearance are not just an aberration of modern Western culture. Every period of history has had its own standards of what is and is not beautiful, and every contemporary society has its own distinctive concept of the ideal physical attributes of a person. Due to the influence of the mass and social media, we as a society have become accustomed to a uniform standard of beauty and a set ideal body image (Sarwer, Grossbart, & Diddie, 2003). At the same time, healthy lifestyle choices are also key to improving body image. Indeed, attractive people (as defined by our culture) have distinct advantages in our society. According to many studies, attractive children are more popular, with both classmates and teachers. Teachers give higher evaluations to the work of attractive children and have higher expectations of them. Individuals, during their early adulthood years, who are more attractive have a better chance of getting jobs and of receiving higher salaries.

It is well known that body dissatisfaction contributes significantly in the development and maintenance of eating pathology and disorders in all ages of the population. Children and youth with negative body images and eating disorders are very common nowadays, but these negative unhealthy attitudes and behaviors do not stop at adolescence and most likely continue into early and middle adulthood and even into later adulthood. Despite the growing numbers of individuals suffering from poor body image, unfortunately there are a limited number of scientifically sound measurements developed for the use in the evaluation, prevention, and treatment of body image concerns associated with mental and physical illnesses (Weinshenker, 2002).

During the stage of early adulthood, the concern of one's appearance and body image becomes important to one's psychological well-being as competition for partners and jobs, as well as acceptance by peers, becomes more central. Unfortunately, body image dissatisfaction is a common psychological problem affecting many Westernized societies due to the heavy influence of the media's portrayal of the perfect body. Therefore, it is critical that counselors understand the implications of body image in reference to the etiology and development of body image disturbances as well as effective prevention strategies.

As previously indicated, being dissatisfied with your physical appearance may be no problem at all, or it may be a very big problem. The difference is determined by the impact or consequences of the person's body image in everyday life (Williams, 2004). The question to ask clients in counseling therapy is, Does your body image influence your feelings about yourself, your social interactions, your eating and exercise behaviors, your sexuality, and so on? The ultimate goal of counseling is to enhance the client's quality of life by helping to improve his or her body image acceptance.

Substance Abuse

One of the current uniqueness features in reference to human development is the transition to emerging early adulthood, which has become expanded in the number of years (ages 26–35) due to shifts of modernization in society. Some of the changes that have been observed during this age span are that marriage and parenthood have begun later due to career responsibilities, lifestyles, and delayed or extended education and professional development. This transition period, is referred to as *emerging adulthood,* and most young adults who are in this transition period are deeply ambivalent about entering marriage and parenthood; mainly, they are reluctant to end the exceptional freedom and lifestyle they have experienced in the previous stage of development. Today, individuals in early adulthood see marriage, home responsibilities, and children as obligations that they would like to avoid or try at a later date (Arnett, 2005). This delay provides more opportunities to experiment or engage in habit-forming behaviors such as the excessive use of alcohol and drugs.

Substance abuse is identified as a paramount public health problem due to its linkage with subsequent negative health and social outcomes. Research has documented the association between adverse childhood experience and substance abuse (Dube, Felitti, Dong, Chapman, Glies, & Anda, 2003; Sartor, Lynskey, Heath, Jocob, & True, 2006). However, the determinants of the onset of substance use and progression to substance abuse are not well known. Not much empirical evidence shows whether there are different factors related to the onset of use and drug dependence in a developmental framework. The goal of many studies has been to identify antecedent factors in childhood and adolescence that could predict the onset of use and substance abuse by early adulthood or age 26. However, continuity of drug use in the later 30s basically depends on many factors that have little to do with chronological age and human development.

As reported by the national Survey on Drug Use and Health (Substance Abuse and Mental Health Services Administration [SAMHSA], 2003), individuals in the "emerging adulthood" stage of life also have the highest rate for most types of drug use and drug abuse. The younger adulthood population has many similarities as compared to the emerging adult in reference to the developmental characteristics and other related issues, including the tendency of substance abuse. According to the 2010 National Survey on Drug Use and Health, Substance Abuse and Mental Health Services Administration conducted by the U.S. Department of Health and Human Services, the rate of current illicit drug use among young adults ages 25 to 30 increased from 19.6 percent in 2008 to 21.2 percent in 2009 and 21.5 percent in 2010, driven largely by an increase in marijuana use (from 16.5 percent in 2008 to 18.1 percent in 2009 and 18.5 percent in 2010). Among emerging young adults, the rate of current nonmedical use of prescription-type drugs in 2010 was 5.9 percent, similar to the rate in the years from 2002 to 2009. In addition, current use of cocaine and methamphetamine among young adults decreased from 2002 to 2010. In 2010, the rate of current illicit drug use among adults aged 26 or older was 6.6 percent, with 4.8 percent current users of marijuana and 2.2 percent current nonmedical users of psychotherapeutic drugs. Less than 1 percent each used cocaine (0.5%), hallucinogens (0.2%), heroin (0.1%), and inhalants (0.1%). These rates were similar to those reported in 2009. However, the rate of current marijuana use in 2010 was significantly higher than the rates in 2002 through 2008.

With respect to gender difference, in 2010, the rate of current illicit drug use among persons aged 12 or older was higher for males (11.2%) than for females (6.8%). Males were more likely than females to be current users of several different illicit drugs, including marijuana, nonmedical use of psychotherapeutic drugs, cocaine, and hallucinogens. According to the study, among pregnant women aged 15 to 44, 4.4 percent were current illicit drug users based on data averaged across 2009 and 2010. Clearly the need for professional counseling related to substance abuse continues to increase in spite of efforts to raise awareness about potential health damages to this population.

According to Arnett (2000), one of the major issues that contribute to substance abuse among emerging adults is identity exploration. Many individuals in this group want to have a wide range of experiences before they settle into adult life, and many of them use substances as a way of relieving their identity confusion. In addition, this period is also a time of great instability for this population due to frequent changes in their lives in reference to love partnerships, educational experiences, and vocational choices and development. Other contributors in reference to substance abuse among young adults include genetic/physiological factors; parenting and family influence (socioeconomic disadvantage such as poverty and poor housing environment, low bonding to family; etc.); academic failure and low degree of commitment to school; peer pressure and rejection; alienation and rebelliousness; and so on.

Substance abuse during the transition period from emerging adulthood to young adulthood leads to devastating implications for the population that continues to abuse alcohol and drugs into adult life. Many research studies indicated that drug abuse contributes to lung cancer, coronary heart disease, acquired immune-deficiency syndrome (AIDS), violent crimes, child abuse, and unemployment. The negative consequences of substance abuse for developing young adults also include slow cognitive processes, lack of motivation, debilitating mood disorders, and accidental injury or death. This leads to high costs in health care, increased crime, and increased mental health services and substance abuse treatment costs for society (Center for Substance Abuse Treatment, 2004).

Treating substance abuse addiction in young adults requires a comprehensive treatment plan that is designed to address specific issues of the client. The counselor must first understand that the substance abuse addiction lifestyle influences decision-making and problem-solving skills, and this affects the individual's decision to seek professional help. The counselor should be aware that young adults who abuse substances may lack concrete thinking skills and have difficulty with understanding consequences. It is well documented that substance abuse by young adults often accompanies problems with coping skills and appropriate interpersonal relationships. However, they do respond well to treatment and thrive with guidance in the development of healthy relationships. The counselor should also understand young adults express anxiety in social situations, and they tend to use alcohol and drugs to suppress their feelings. In addition, depression, bipolar disorders, and other mood disorders are often diagnosed during treatment for substance abuse.

Violence

Another risk to healthy development during the early adulthood stage is violence. While death rates due to disease are low, the rate of violence-related deaths is high. During this stage of life, motor vehicle crashes, suicide, and homicide are the primary causes of death (Centers for Disease Control and Prevention, 2012). Globally more than nine people die every minute from injuries or violence. The CDC reports that of approximately 50,000 violent deaths in the United States each year, more than 56% of those deaths are suicides, and 30% are homicides. However, death is not the only result of violence. Many more survive violence and are left with permanent physical and emotional impairments. A disability inherited or acquired can significantly affect a person and many aspects of his or her life. Having a disability can affect many life domains, which include physical, social, psychological, economic, vocational, spiritual, and recreational pursuits. The social and psychological experiences of having a disability have been shown to be among the most damaging consequences to daily functioning (Livneh & Bishop, 2012).

The ages during early adulthood are seen as prime times in a person's life. With having a disability or acquiring a disability, many things can be affected. If injured severely, would the individual with the disability lose close relationships with a significant other, friends, or even family members? Would a person with a disability prefer to be at home or away from home during rehabilitation, education, work, and life? Would people respond differently to a male or female? Would the different type of disability affect the response of others? (Dell Orto & Power, 2007). These questions give a brief view of possible effects a disability could have in the life of an individual in early adulthood.

Additionally, one of the central goals of most individuals in early adulthood is to acquire employment and begin the possible growth of vocational ability. This includes salary and employment status. One fact that still remains, is that the difference between individuals with and without disabilities in their early adulthood stage has not changed with respect to gainful employment in the past three decades.

A comparison between the two peak economic years 1988 and 1999 shows that the prevalence of work limitations (i.e., the percentage of the population reporting work limitations) for 15- to 29-year-olds declined by 6.4%. There was a substantial decline for males in this age group by 15.9%, but the prevalence of work limitations actually increased for females by 5.9% (Kruse & Schur, 2000).

The work limitations that disability can create have been shown to decrease the ability to work. In a population survey, men with no limitations were 93.4% employed, and men with work limitations were only 28.0% employed. Women without limitations were 79.3% employed, and women with limitations were 25.9% percent employed (Mitra & Sambamoorthi, 2005).

With the strong goal of employment in this developmental stage, vocational abilities of the client with a disability may be an issue needing to be focused on. Education, prevention, and intervention strategies can be incorporated to assist in developing, selecting, gaining, and increasing the long-term career in a client's life. This can make life fuller and more rewarding (Burkhauser & Houtenville, 2010).

Guided Practice Exercise 10.1

Interview a person with a disability. Consider the following questions:

- What is his or her disability? Was it inherited or acquired?
- How has the disability affected his or her life and activities (e.g., physical, social, psychological, spiritual, and recreational)?
- How has the disability affected his or her pursuit of education and employment?
- What does he or she feel about his or her disability?
- Now, imagine that you have the same disability of the person you interviewed. What could be different in your past, present, and future life if you had the same disability as the person you interviewed?

Counseling Issues

Counseling issues during early adulthood often center on the struggle to find meaningful relationships with others through friendships, sexual relationships, the starting of a family, or colleagues in a work environment. If negotiating these struggles is successful, then an individual often experiences intimacy on a deep level; however, if these struggles are not successful, then isolation may occur.

Relationships With Others

Think back to Chapter 5 when we discussed attachment theory with infants and primary caregivers. Those early relationships form the foundation for the intimate relationships that we have as adults. That early attachment shaped your brain, profoundly influencing your self-esteem, your expectations of others, and your ability to attract and maintain successful adult relationships. The emotional attachment that grew between you and your caregiver has determined how you relate to other people throughout your life because it established the foundation for all verbal and nonverbal communication in your relationships. Table 10.2 Impact of Attachment on Adult Relationships demonstrates how early attachment impacts adult relationships.

Table 10.2   Impact of Attachment on Adult Relationships

Attachment Style	Parental Style	Adult Characteristics
Secure	In tune with the child's emotions	Able to create healthy, meaningful relationships; empathetic
Anxious-Resistant	Inconsistent parenting; sometimes intrusive	Anxious and insecure; clingy, emotionally needy; controlling; blaming
Avoidant	Unavailable or rejecting	Fear of closeness; critical; intolerant
Disorganized-Disoriented	Ignored child's needs; traumatizing parental behavior	Insensitive; explosive; abusive; untrusting

However, using knowledge from the infant-caregiver attachment theory, counselors can work with adults who are struggling with their intimate relationships. Adult relationships depend on nonverbal forms of communication for their success. Consider infants—they cannot talk or reason, yet they can communicate their needs. In secure relationships, their caregivers understand and meet their needs. The same is true for adult relationships. Nonverbal cues deeply impact intimate relationships. As counselors, we can help adults struggling with relationships to examine their understanding of **nonverbal cues** and recognize expectations and attitudes resulting from insecure attachment bonds.

According to Erikson, early adulthood is a time of being ready for intimacy. If identity formation from the adolescent years was successful, the individual now has the capacity to commit to partnerships. Robert Sternberg proposed that love consists of three components: **passion**, **commitment**, and **intimacy**. Passion includes physical and sexual attraction, while commitment refers to the intent and ability to maintain the relationship over an extended period of time and under adverse conditions. Intimacy is having a close, warm, caring relationship with another person. Intimacy can be expressed either physically, such as sexual activity; psychologically, such as sharing feelings and thoughts; and socially, such as enjoying the same friends or types of activities. Sternberg goes on to describe seven varieties of love that consist of varying degrees of passion, commitment, and intimacy, which can be seen in Figure 10.2 Sternberg's Theory of Love.

Lifestyle Options

Staying Single. While many assume that healthy adults eventually marry, today, many people are choosing to be single and are leading satisfying and rewarding lives. In fact, according to the 2012 State of Our Unions Report from the National Marriage Project, there has been a 50% decrease in marriage from 1970 to 2010. This may be due to cohabitation, but many are choosing lifelong singlehood. However, those living single may still struggle with the idea of never finding the right person. They may ask questions, such as what's wrong with me? Or they may be completely comfortable with being single and get annoyed when others continuously ask why they haven't found someone yet. As counselors, it is important to help clients explore their own feelings of self and become comfortable with their current position in life.

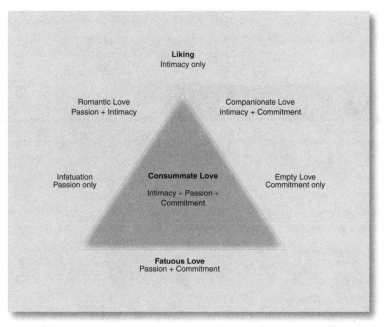

Figure 10.2   Sternberg's Theory of Love

Cohabitation. The number of unmarried couples has increased dramatically over the past several years. Most people now live together before they marry for the first time (National Marriage Project, The Center for Marriage and Families, and The Institute for American Values, 2012). Approximately 25% of unmarried women age 25 to 39 are currently living with a partner. More than 60% of first marriages are now preceded by living together compared with virtually none 50 years ago (Kennedy & Bumpass, 2008). Studies reveal that cohabitation is also popular in Denmark, Estonia, Finland, France, Luxembourg, and Norway and is also more frequent among adults ages 20 to 34 worldwide (Organization for the Economic Co-operation & Development, 2010). Cohabitation is more common among individuals who have been divorced or who have experienced parental divorce. Individuals who grew up without a father or who witnessed high levels of marital discord during childhood also seem to seek out cohabitation. This lifestyle is also more common among those of lower educational and income levels and those who are less religious than their peers (National Marriage Project, The Center for Marriage and Families, and The Institute for American Values, 2012). Research also reveals that 42% of children will experience a parental cohabitation by the age of 12, and 65% of children born into cohabitation families will see their parents separate by the age of 12 (Kennedy & Bumpass, 2008). It is important to note that studies indicate children reared in cohabitation households are more likely to suffer from a range of emotional and social struggles, such as depression, dropping out of school, and drug use, when compared to children in two-parent, married families.

Marriage. The percentage of adults who are currently married in the United States has declined by 16% since 1960. It has declined greatest among African Americans, with a 31% reduction. Studies reveal that individuals who do choose to marry are choosing to marry later in life with the current median age at first marriage increasing to age 26.5 for females and 28.7 for males (National Marriage Project, The Center for Marriage and Families, and The Institute for American Values, 2012). However, marriage remains the primary lifestyle choice for adults in the United States, Asia, and the Middle East (Social Trends Institute, 2012). Marriage can be beneficial. Research indicates that married people tend to lead healthier, happier lives when compared to those who have never been married, divorced, or widowed. Married males also live longer than single males. While marriages often seem happiest in the early years, marital satisfaction increases again after parental responsibilities end and finances stabilize. However, numerous concerns and conflicts can arise in any long-term relationship. Unrealistic expectations about marriage, sexual frequency, finances, household responsibilities, and parenting can lead to struggles within the relationship. Additionally as dual-career marriages become more common, stress within the home also increases. However, having multiple roles, such as spouse, parent, and worker, can be positive and rewarding. If balance is achieved, then a person can experience an increase in self-esteem levels, feelings of independence, and a greater sense of fulfillment.

CASE ILLUSTRATION 10.2 DUAL CAREER FAMILY

Brady and Marcie have been married for 6 years. Since marriage, they have had two children. Their elder will be starting kindergarten in the fall, and the younger will be going to day care. Recently, Brady and Marcie have been struggling with the balance of work and family. Marcie works 10-hour days and is off 3 days a week. Brady is supposed to work 10 hours per day and be off 3 days a week as well; however, he has been working more than that. Last week, Brady ended up working an average of 15 hours per day. Marcie was not happy about him working so much because he never has time to see his family. She wants him home for dinner some nights, and he claims that with his job, he cannot be there. She is worried that when their children become old enough to play sports that Brady will not be able to attend any of their events. She has tried her hardest to talk him into being home on time and spending time with their children, but he does not understand why she does not want him to succeed with his job. He says the more he works, the more likely he will be able to advance in his job, which will lead to more money. Marcie does not care about the money. All she wants is for her family to be together.

Practice Exercise:

Because career is important to Brady and family is important to Marcie, the counselor will want to make sure that both Brady and Marcie are participating in counseling. Both sides need to explore what they desire from their relationship and focus on the present. Is there a way to manage both career and family? What sacrifices will need to be made and what sacrifices are acceptable to both parties?

Family. The average size of the family has also decreased in recent years. In 2011, the American total fertility rate was 1.89 children per woman, due in part to the relatively high contributions of the Hispanic population. However, this rate is below the replacement level of 2.1, which is the level that would be required to replace the population through births alone. Most European and several Asian nations have levels that are even lower than those of the United States. Only 32% of households in the United States now include children (National Marriage Project, The Center for Marriage and Families, and The Institute for American Values, 2012). Of those families with children, motherhood appears to be particularly stressful due to the effort of balancing motherhood and career. However, while many struggle with finding this balance, researchers are finding that working mothers who obtain personal satisfaction from employment, who do not feel excessive guilt, and who have adequate household arrangements, are likely to perform as well as or better than the nonworking mother (Gani & Ara, 2010).

The percentage of children who are growing up in single parent homes has grown tremendously due to divorce, out-of-wedlock births, and unmarried cohabitation. Currently 26% of children are being reared by a single parent (National Marriage Project, The Center for Marriage and Families, and The Institute for American Values, 2012). Single parents are often faced with challenges, such as financial struggles, lack of free time, and balancing work and parental responsibilities. Nearly half of all single parents live below the poverty line. Unfortunately being reared in a single-parent home also negatively impacts the children. Research indicates that these children are two to three times more likely to experience negative life outcomes when compared to children in married, two-parent families. It is also important to note that approximately 9% of families are stepfamilies. Studies reveal that children in stepfamilies suffer the same risks as those in single-parent homes.

Separation and Divorce. According to the National Marriage Project, The Center for Marriage and Families and The Institute for American Values (2012), the average number of divorced individuals worldwide is currently 4%, while in the United States the average number of divorced individuals is 8%. In fact, approximately 25% of children born to married parents in the United States will see their own parents divorce or separate before the age of 12. Furthermore, Barker's (2012) research indicated that 50% of first marriages, 67% of second marriages, and 74% of third marriages end in divorce in the United States. Men are more likely to remarry and generally tend to remarry sooner than women. Those more at risk of divorcing include teenagers, nonreligious individuals, and those with less education (Barker, 2012). Both the process and aftermath of a divorce can place a great amount of stress on everyone in the family, including financial difficulties, anxiety, and depression.

Same-Sex Relationships. According to the 2010 United States Census Bureau data (Lofquist, Lugaila, O'Connell, & Feliz, 2012), 0.6% of households consist of same-sex partners. Lesbian and gay couples generally have the same relationship goals and face the same relationship challenges as heterosexual couples. However, studies reveal that these couples tend to be more upbeat in the face of conflict when compared with heterosexual couples. They tend to use more affection and humor when in a disagreement and demonstrate more fairness and power-sharing behaviors between partners. Lesbians tend to be more emotionally expressive than gay men, which is probably indicative of society's expectation that females in general are expressive. Gay men, however, need to be careful to avoid negativity during conflict because studies reflect that a gay partner may have a difficult time recovering from negative comments during an argument (Gottman & Levenson, 2013).

The myriad of lifestyle options described above provide numerous issues for counselors to explore with clients. From communication skills to parenting behaviors, counselors can work with couples to strengthen happiness and success in their relationships.

Guided Practice Exercise 10.2

Of the various lifestyle options discussed in this chapter, consider those that you have experienced in your life through your parents, your friends, and yourself. Discuss the impact that you believe these relationships have on your current intimate relationships. What are your underlying beliefs about relationship satisfaction? What characteristics do you believe are critical for a successful, long-term relationship?

Friendships

Friendships also play an important role in the lives of early adults. According to Sternberg, intimacy, without passion or commitment, characterizes friendship with feelings of closeness and warmth. In early adulthood, friends typically have similar backgrounds, interests, and simply enjoy each other's company. Adult friendships tend to be same-sex and involve respect, trust, understanding, and acceptance. Females tend to be more relational, often confiding their problems and feelings to their friends, and tend to have friends who have children the same age. Males, however, tend to seek out common-interest activities and friends from work. Friendships, however, can be difficult to maintain during this time period because of other pressures, such as working and starting a family.

Career Decisions

Besides family life, vocational life is a vital domain of social development in early adulthood. Emerging young adults must learn how to perform work tasks well, get along with coworkers, respond to authority, and protect their own interests. When work experiences go well, young adults develop new competencies, feel a sense of personal accomplishment, make new friends, and become financially independent and secure.

As mentioned earlier, finding personal relationships as well as work environments that are satisfying are both important during early adulthood. Work plays an important part in the lives of adults not only because of the income it brings but also because it is linked to the individual's self-identity. Career choice affects friendships, living location, child care, job stress, and other aspects of life. Some individuals may still be going through the process of defining their careers as discussed in the previous chapter, while others are getting settled into their careers. Realizing that achievement, recognition, satisfaction, security, challenge, and relationships with colleagues are all important to having a satisfying career, counselors can work with clients at both of these stages in career development to encourage a positive work environment.

Even for those who enter their chosen field, initial experiences can be discouraging. Adjusting to unanticipated disappointments in salary, supervisors, and coworkers is difficult. As new workers become aware of the gap between their expectations and reality, resignations are common. On average, people in their 20s move to a new job every 2 years (Peterson & Gonzalez, 1999). After a period of evaluation and adjustment, young adults generally settle into their work. In careers with opportunities for promotion, high aspirations must often be revised downward because the structure of most work settings resembles a pyramid, with few high-level executive

CASE ILLUSTRATION 10.3 CHILDBEARING DECISIONS

Genesis recently finished graduate school and was given a job at an accounting firm right outside her hometown. At first, she thought this job was going to be a great fit for her. However, now that she has worked there for a year and a half, she realizes that she wants to work for a corporation. When she starts to look for jobs that she believes would be a better fit for her, she discovers that it is harder than she thought because she has to think about her husband as well. Her husband cannot change jobs right away, and a lot of the jobs she started looking at are out of state. Furthermore, she has been talking with her husband about starting a family. He is really excited about the idea but knows Genesis does not want to have a baby until she settles down with her career. Genesis cannot decide if she wants to take a job out of state, move after her husband can relocate, and not have a baby right away or if she wants to find a job close by so they can go ahead a start a family.

Practice Exercise:

Decisions about when to have a child can be very difficult. In Genesis's case, she has a very supportive spouse who is excited about having a child, but she is struggling with her career options when timing her upcoming pregnancy. As a counselor, it will be important to help Genesis and her spouse explore their career options. Can her husband change jobs easily? Is one person's career more financially secure than the other person's? How would the timing of the baby impact the finances? Additionally, the counselor may want to explore life after the baby with the couple.

Guided Practice Exercise 10.3

Interview a person who is currently in early adulthood. What has been his or her primary goal during this phase of life? Did he or she struggle with intimacy versus isolation? What is his or her current relationship status? Where is he or she in regard to career? How is he or she similar or different from what you have read in this chapter?

and supervisory jobs. Besides opportunity, personal characteristics affect career progress. As we will see, a sense of self-efficacy is influential. Young people who are very anxious about on-the-job failure tend to set their career aspirations either too high or too low.

SUMMARY

- ➢ The journey from adolescence through early adulthood involves many changes and adjustments and entails considerable individual variation from one person to another.
- ➢ Biological function and physical performance peaks between the ages of 20 and 35
- ➢ Diseases such as testicular cancer, cervical cancer, and Hodgkin's lymphoma are a threat to this age group
- ➢ Postformal thought, occurring during early adulthood, acknowledges that the world sometimes lacks pure right and wrong solutions so adults must draw upon prior experiences to solve problems.

> The primary conflict for individuals ages 18 to 40 is intimacy versus isolation.
> Because the development of intimate relationships is critical to life happiness at this phase of life, the lack of these relationships can be a risk for healthy early adulthood development.
> Depression is a major concern for individuals in their 20s to mid-30s, with most people being diagnosed with major depression during this time of life.
> During this stage of life, motor vehicle crashes, suicide, and homicide are the primary causes of death.
> Having a disability can affect many life domains, which include physical, social, psychological, economic, vocational, spiritual, and recreational pursuits. The social and psychological experiences of having a disability have been shown to be among the most damaging consequences to daily functioning.
> Counseling issues during early adulthood often center on the struggle to find meaningful relationships with others through friendships, sexual relationships, the start of a family, or colleagues in a work environment. If negotiating these struggles is successful, then an individual often experiences intimacy on a deep level; however, if these struggles are not successful, then isolation may occur.

ADDITIONAL RESOURCES

Websites

American Foundation for Suicide Prevention. http://www.afsp.org/.
Centers for Disease Control and Prevention. http://www.cdc.gov/ViolencePrevention/index.html.
Center for Substance Abuse Treatment.http://www.samhsa.gov/data/nsduh/2k10nsduh/2k10results.htm#2.4.
Homicide Survivors—Dealing with Grief. http://crcvc.ca/docs/homsurv.pdf.
National Institute of Mental Health. www.ncbi.nlm.nih.gov/pubmedhealth/PMH0001941/.

Books

Figler, H. (2007). *The career counselor's handbook.* Berkeley, CA: Ten Speed Press.
Lowenstein, L. (2008). *Assessment and treatment activities for children, adolescents, and families: Practitioners share their most effective techniques.* Toronto, Canada: Champion Press.
O'Leary, K. D., Heyman, R. E., & Jongsm, Jr., A. E. (2011). *The couples psychotherapy treatment planner.* Hoboken, NJ: John Wiley.
Patterson, J., Williams, L., Edwards, T. M., Chamow, L., Grauf-Grounds, C., & Sprenkle, D. H. (2009). *Essential skills in family therapy.* (2nd ed.). New York, NY: Guildford Press.
Pichler, T. F., Veronneau, M. H.,& Dishion, T. J. (2012). Substance use progression from adolescence to early adulthood: Effortful control in the context of friendship influence and early-onset use. *Journal of Abnormal Child Psychology, 40,* 1045–1048. doi:10.1007/s10802–012–9626–7
Zichy, S. (2007). *Career match: Connecting who you are with what you'll love to do.* New York, NY: AMACOM.

REFERENCES

Arnett, J. J. (2000). Emerging adulthood: A theory of development from the late teens through the twenties. *American Psychologist, 55,* 469–480.
Arnett, J. J. (2004). *Emerging adulthood: The winding road from the late teens through the late twenties.* New York, NY: Oxford University Press.
Arnett, J. J. (2006). Emerging adulthood: Understanding the new way of coming of age. In J. J. Arnett, & J. L. Tanner (Eds.), *Emerging adults in America: Coming of age in the 21st century* (pp. 3–19). Washington, DC: APA Books.
Arnett, J. J. (2012). New horizons in emerging and young adulthood. Early adulthood in a family context. In A. Booth & N. Crouter (Eds.), *Early adulthood in a family context.* New York, NY: Springer.

Avolio, B. J. (1991). Levels of analysis. In K. W. Schaie (Ed.), *Annual review of gerontology and geriatrics* (Vol. 11, pp. 239–260). New York, NY: Springer.

Barker, J. (2012). *The divorce rate in America for first marriage, vs. second or third marriage.* Springfield, MO: Forest Institute.

Begley, S. (2000). Getting inside a teen brain: Hormones are not the only reason adolescents act crazy. Their gray matter differs from children's and adults'. *Newsweek,* 58–59.

Berk, L. E. (2010). *Exploring lifespan development* (2nd ed.). Boston, MA: Allyn & Bacon.

Burkhauser, R. V., & Houtenville, A. J. (2010). Employment among working-age people with disabilities: What the latest data can tell us. In E. M. Szymanski, & R. M. Parker (Eds.), *Work and disability: Contexts, issues, and strategies for enhancing employment outcomes for people with disabilities* (pp. 49–86). Austin, TX: PRO-ED.

Cash, T. F., Phillips, K. A., Santos, M. T., & Hrabosky, J. I. (2004). Measuring "negative body image": Validation of the body image disturbance questionnaire in a nonclinical population. *Body Image: An International Journal of Research 1,* 363–372.

Cash, T. F., Pruzinsky, T. (2002.). *Body image: A handbook of theory, research and practice.* New York, NY: Guildford Press.

Center for Substance Abuse Treatment. (2004). *What is substance abuse treatment? A booklet for families.* DHHS Publication No. (SMHSA) 04-3955. Rockville, MD: Substance Abuse and Mental Health Services Administration. Retrieved from http://www.samhsa.gov/data/nsduh/2k10nsduh/2k10results.htm#2.4.

Centers for Disease Control and Prevention. (2012). *Injuries and violence are leading causes of death: Key data & statistics.* Retrieved from http://www.cdc.gov/injury/overview/data.html.

Cote, J., & Bynner, J. M. (2008). Changes in the transition to adulthood in the UK and Canada: The role of structure and agency in emerging adulthood. *Journal of Youth Studies 11*(3):251–268.

Dell Orto, A. E., & Power, P. W. (2007). Perspective exercise 2: Prime of life. In A. E. Dell Orto & P. W. Power (Eds.), *The psychological and social impact of illness and disability (5th ed.,* pp. 269–270). New York, NY: Springer.

Dube S. R., Felitti, V. J., Dong, M., Chapman, D. P., Glies, W. H., & Anda, R. F. (2003). Childhood abuse, neglect, and household dysfunction and the risk of illicit drug use: The adverse childhood experiences study. *Pediatrics, 111,* 564–572.

Erikson, E. (1968). *Identity: Youth and crisis.* New York, NY: Norton.

Furstenberg, F., Rumbaut, R. G., & Settersten, R. A. (2005). On the frontier of adulthood: An introduction. In R. A. Settersten, F. Furstenberg, & R. G. Rumbaut (Eds.), *On the frontier of adulthood: Theory, research, and public policy* (pp. 3–28). Chicago, IL: University of Chicago Press.

Gani, B., & Ara, R. (2010). Conflicting worlds of working women: Findings of an exploratory study. *Indian Journal of Industrial Relations, 46*(1), 61–73.

Gottman, J., & Levenson, R. W. (2013). *The 12 year study.* Retrieved from http://www.gottman.com/49850/Gay—Lesbian-Research.html.

Heckhausen, J. (1999). *Developmental regulation in adulthood.* Cambridge: Cambridge University Press.

Johnson, J. G., Cohne, P., & Kasen, S. (2009). Minor depression during adolescence and mental health outcomes during adulthood. *British Journal of Psychiatry, 195,* 264–265. doi: 10.1192/bjp.bp.108.054239

Keating, D. P. (1990). Adolescent thinking. In S. S. Feldman & G. R. Elliot (Eds.), *At the threshold: The developing adolescent* (pp. 54–89). Cambridge, MA: Harvard University Press.

Kennedy, S., & Bumpass, L. (2008). Cohabitation and children's living arrangements: New estimates from the United States. *Demographic Research, 19,* 1663–1692.

Kins, E., & Beyers, W. (2010). Failure to launch, failure to achieve criteria for adulthood? *Journal of Adolescent Research, 25,* 743–777. doi: 10.1177 /0743558410371126

Kruse, D., & Schur, L. (2000). Employment of people with disabilities following the ADA. *Industrial Relations 42*(1), 31–66.

Levinson, D. (1978). *The seasons of a man's life.* New York: Knopf.

Livneh, H, & Bishop, M. L. (2012). The psychosocial impact of chronic illness and disability. In R. M. Parker, & J. B. Patterson (Eds.), *Rehabilitation counseling: Basics & beyond* (pp. 167–197). Austin, TX: PRO-ED.

Lofquist, D., Lugaila, T., O'Connell, M., & Feliz, S. (2012*). Households and families: 2010: 2010 census briefs.* Retrieved from http://www.census.gov/prod/cen2010/briefs/c2010br-14.pdf.

Mitra, S., & Samamoorthi, U. (2005). The employment of persons with disabilities: Evidence from the national sample survey. New York, NY: Fordham University.

National Marriage Project, The Center for Marriage and Families, and The Institute for American Values. (2012). The state of our unions marriage in America 2012: The President's marriage agenda. Charlotte: University of Virginia.

Organization for the Economic Co-operation & Development. (2010). *Sf3.3: Cohabitation rate and prevalence of other forms of partnership.* Retrieved from http://www.oecd.org/els/soc/41920080.pdf.

Peterson, N., & Gonzalez, R. C. (1999). Career counseling models for diverse populations: Hands-on applications for practitioners. Pacific Grove, CA: Brooks/Cole.

Social Trends Institute. (2012). *What do marriage and fertility have to do with the economy?* Charlottesville, VA: Author. Retrieved from http://sustaindemographicdividend.org/wp-content/uploads/2012/07/SDD-2011-Final.pdf.

Santrock, J. (2009). Life-Span development. Physical and cognitive development in early adulthood. (12th ed.). New York, NY: McGraw Hill.

Sartor C. E., Lynskey, M. T., Heath, A. C., Jocob, T., & True, W. (2006). The role of childhood risk factors in initiation of alcohol use and progression to alcohol dependence. *Addiction, 102*, 216–225.

Sarwer, D. Grossbart, T. Diddie, E. (2003). Beauty and society. *Semin Cutan Surg. 22*(2), 79–92. CrossRef.

Schaie, K.W., & Willis, S. L. (2000). A stage theory model of adult cognitive development revisited. In R. Rubinstein, M. Moss, & M. Kleban (Eds.), *The many dimensions of aging: Essays in honor of M. Powell Lawton* (pp. 175–193). New York, NY: Springer.

Smith, J., Staudinger, U. M., & Baltes, P. B. (1994). Occupational settings facilitating wisdom—related knowledge. *Journal of Consulting and Clinical Psychology, 62*, 989–999.

Weinshenker, N. (2002). Adolescence and body image. *School Nurse News, 19*(3), 12–16.

Whitbourne, S. K. (2001). Adult development and aging: Biopsychosocial Perspectives. New York, NY: John Wiley.

Williams, P. (2004). Body image. Past, present and future. *Body Image: An International Journal of Research*, 1:15

Middle Adulthood (Ages 36 to 60)

> Midlife is the time to let go of an over dominant ego and to contemplate the deeper significance of human existence.
>
> C. G. Jung

Middle adulthood is marked by many changes and events in a person's life. During middle adulthood, we find significant changes that have been reported across many areas of human life development. One of those life changing events is what is called *midlife crisis*.

When you hear the term *midlife crisis*, do you think of Carl G. Jung's description of an individual seeking deeper significance of human existence or a balding male dressed with inappropriate attire, driving a sports car, and attempting to reclaim some unidentified youthful glory days? Sadly, for those fitting such a categorization, the period of middle adulthood may be a period where true development has been mired in stagnation. For those who arrive at this period of development, having successfully navigated the previous challenges, and arriving in relatively good health, with a good sense of self and a valuing of their relationships, this life period is a midlife transition. Middle adulthood can be the period in which people "let go of an over dominant ego" and allows the opportunity to contemplate and to seek "deeper significance in human existence." Middle adulthood has been described by Erik Erikson as a period in which we establish our careers, settle down within a relationship, start a family, develop an optimistic sense of responsibility, and are full of plans for the future (Erikson, 1982). See Table 2.2, Erikson's Stages of Psychosocial Development, in Chapter 2. We give back to society through raising our children, being productive at work, and becoming involved in community activities and organizations. However, Erickson notes that failing to achieve these objectives places the person at risk of becoming stagnated and feeling unproductive.

This chapter will review both the opportunities and challenges presented during this period of development called middle adulthood. Specifically, after reading this chapter you will be able to

1. describe the significant events that take place during **middle adulthood**, such as balancing life, family, work, and midlife changes;

2. describe midlife crisis and other life changes, including renewal and counseling issues during middle adulthood;

3. explain the psychosocial turning point of **generativity versus stagnation** and central processes through which this defining life stage can be resolved;

4. explain the implications of person-environment and culture interaction, socioeconomic status, and coping with covert discrimination during middle adulthood; and

5. discuss how counselors can assist with specific techniques that are age- and time-appropriate for counseling intervention.

A Period of Recent Recognition

In the early 1900s, there were no major initiatives to study lifespan development, particularly as it relates to middle adulthood. Over the past 100 years the average **lifespan** and **life expectancy** has increased well over an additional 31 years, now standing at 78.7 years (CDC, 2011). As the average human lifespan and life expectancy increased, so did awareness of the changes that occurred during the extended period of adulthood and the opportunities to look at the human lifespan in multiple dimensions based on human development stages, individual needs, and the unavoidable transitions of individuals through their lifespan (Kinsella, 2011).

During middle adulthood, significant changes occur across the physical, cognitive, and social domains of development. And while these changes will be discussed in detail below, it is important to note that the significance of this period of development rests not so much in these domain changes but in the fact, as noted by the quote with which we opened this chapter, that it invites individuals begin to *reexamine* their lives, relationships, work and professional affiliations, and even to question the meaning of all that has taken place in their lives.

This process of reexamination has been referred to as the beginning of midlife crisis. As discussed below, the concept of the term *crisis* when used correctly is not meant to signal a form of disaster or upset but rather a critical time that brings about an opportunity to stop, reflect, and, if so desired, make changes and reinvent the self.

Photo 11.1   Is it midlife crisis? Joining a bikers club and riding a Harley over the weekends with friends may be a sign of doing new things or perhaps enjoying the still youthful years.

Source: iStockphoto.com/drjones.

Changes in Middle Adulthood

The Beginning of Middle Adulthood

While adolescence can be identified as a period of development starting with puberty and entry into early adulthood as marked by the gaining of psychological, physical, and financial independence, the beginning of middle adulthood is not so clear or concretely fixed. Research indicates that chronological age is an imperfect guide to human development (Moody & Sasser, 2012), and this is certainly true when applied to middle adulthood. A more useful way of noting the beginning of this period would be to focus on the values and functions of the individual, rather than age.

For those entering middle adulthood, there is a sense of bewilderment and disorientation that creates an urgency to reexamine the self as it relates to past and present experiences and possible opportunities for the future. This is reflected in the following statement related to the onset of midlife by Becker (2006): *"All of a sudden I am scared that the end will come and I will be all alone and I will have to decide what to do with myself. How come everything was fine up until now?"*

Midlife is a critical point in adulthood development when one can evaluate whether previous **social roles** and responsibilities may be going through significant change.

The Central Theme of Middle Adulthood

During this time of consolidation and refinement, individuals tend to reassess their life goals in comparison with accomplishments they have obtained. Actual skills, needs, values, and life situations are evaluated and restructured according to the individual's life experiences and assessment of future possibilities. Although midlife marks the beginning of decline in physical development, it is also true that significant intellectual, social, emotional, and spiritual growth is still developing and available to the individual. Having an opportunity to speak directly with someone in the late part of middle adulthood will provide insight about the person's changes and experience. Practice with the following Guided Practice Exercise 11.1.

Guided Practice Exercise 11.1 Central Theme of Middle Adulthood

Instructions: Conduct an interview of a person in late adulthood to explore issues related to the transition into this life stage. Prepare your interview based on the characteristics of middle adulthood of consolidation and refinement and reassessing one's life. Try to get insight into the person's changes and experiences related to issues that have been comfortable to adjust to and those that have been challenging for the person. After completing the interview, reflect on what you have learned and what the individual has told you. It is suggested that you reflect and discuss with other students and colleagues your findings and learning experience.

While most of life's day-to-day challenges are manageable on a personal level, some personal problems can become too large or too difficult to handle. Or for some, recognizing that we are moving through life becomes anxiety provoking. During middle adulthood, counseling can provide therapeutic assistance to support and facilitate the life journey to be taken.

Counselor-client interaction is an important part for the success of the intervention. It can open the door to deeper personal insight, which helps the client to grow and take control of possible anxieties. Counseling is a collaborative process in which a unique, confidential, helping relationship is developed between a counselor and a willing client, who work together to facilitate the desired change (ACA Code of Ethics, 2005) In this relationship, the professional counselor acts as a facilitator to help clients understand themselves and the wider environment around them more accurately. A middle-aged client conveys multiple issues and expectations, dreams, and accomplished and unaccomplished personal goals. Working together, the client and counselor can explore the client's feelings and behaviors, relationships with others, choices and decisions, as well as the client's current situation in a quest to find a means to a possible solution. Counseling at this stage of life allows the client to face fears and anxieties with the priority they deserve and move on to plan for the future.

Physical Changes

As life expectancy increases, this translates into an increased emphasis on the physical changes and cognitive and emotional needs of the growing numbers of middle-aged adults. Like every period in the lifespan, middle adulthood is associated with certain characteristics that make it distinctive. The most visible signs of physical changes in middle adulthood involve physical appearance. This can actually shape how the individual will perceive himself or herself (Stone, Schwartz, Broderick, & Deaton, 2010).

The programmed effects of specific genes and the random cellular events believed to underlie biological aging make physical declines more apparent in middle adulthood. For those in middle adulthood, aging signs are inevitable. There are many unfavorable myths about middle adulthood, such as the traditional beliefs concerning the physical and mental deterioration that are believed to accompany the cessation of the reproductive life and the emphasis on the importance of youth as compared with the reverence for old age found in many cultures. By age 40, visible aging signs are apparent, such as small localized areas of pigmentation in the skin that produce age spots, especially in areas that are exposed to sunlight, such as hands and face. Hair becomes thinner and gray, wrinkles become more apparent due to a decline in melanin production, finger and toenails develop ridges and become thicker and more brittle, diminished eyesight and some hearing loss may also occur. Internally, changes are taking place as well, with some slow decline in the major organs, including the lungs, heart and digestive system; additionally, women undergo menopause between the ages of 42 and 51, limiting the reproduction years along with other physical and psychological consequences. In menopause, production of estrogen by the ovaries declines dramatically, and this decline produces uncomfortable symptoms in some women such as "hot flashes," nausea, fatigue, and rapid heartbeat, and the possible onset of osteoporosis (Sievert & Obermeyer, 2012). Men also observe some hormonal changes. Testosterone production begins to decline about 1% per year during middle adulthood, and sperm count usually shows a slow decline, but men do not lose their fertility in middle age. What has been referred to as "male menopause," probably has less to do with hormonal change than with the psychological adjustment men must make when they are faced with declining physical energy and with family and work pressures. Developmentalists call these age-related changes primary aging, meaning that the changes are inevitable and happen to everyone regardless of race, ethnicity, culture, or socioeconomic status.

Primary aging, or inevitable changes in the body, occurs regardless of human behavior and also may include visible blood vessels on the skin and fat deposits on the chin or abdomen that affect those in this age group. But in most cases, primary aging alone will not cause organ failure. It is secondary aging—caused by unhealthy behaviors such as smoking, drug and alcohol abuse, unhealthy eating, obesity, and lack of exercise—in combination with primary aging that causes physical changes and illnesses that typically affect middle-aged adults. A healthy life can slow down negative physical changes related to this stage in life.

Since a youthful appearance is stressed by societies in many cultures, individuals strive to make themselves look younger. Middle-aged individuals have shown a strong interest in methods of rejuvenation such as cosmetic plastic surgery and the use of Botox, which may reflect their desire to slow down the aging process (Brun & Brock-Utne, 2012).

Cognitive Changes

A better understanding of midlife cognitive changes and related factors is increasingly important as middle-aged individuals reach old age and cognitive aging affects an increasingly large proportion of the overall population. For developmental growth, cognition is one of the key competencies needed in young and old age to meet the challenges of education, job demands, and everyday life (Baltes & Lang, 1997; Martin & Zimprich, 2003).

Studies of cognitive development in midlife can be characterized by two main approaches. On one hand, the decline of cognitive resources is a main concern for persons from middle age onward (Lawton et al., 1999). Thus, studies on midlife cognition have focused on the question of whether groups at risk for cognitive decline in middle adulthood could be identified. The timely identification of at-risk middle-aged individuals would permit preventive measures targeted at early stages of decline (Schaie & Hofer, 2001). On the other hand, midlife might be characterized by cognitively demanding activities and relatively high levels of cognitive performance. Thus, there is an interest in examining if and how demanding activities and a wide spectrum of interests in middle age may protect middle-aged adults from cognitive decline or at least provide compensatory potential for the later years of life. Schaie (1996) found that two intellectual abilities, numerical ability and perceptual speed, declined in middle age. Other intellectual abilities such as vocabulary, verbal memory, inductive reasoning, and adulthood orientation improved in middle adulthood. The focus on individual differences in different aspects of change in cognitive functioning across middle adulthood highlights that despite relatively high levels of performance, a large amount of cognitive developmental change occurs in midlife. More on the issue of emotional changes is addressed below with the explanation of Erikson's generativity vs. stagnation (see above mentioned Table 2.2 in Chapter 2).

Balancing Life, Family, and Work

The anxieties of middle adulthood result largely from difficulties in balancing multiple roles and striving to navigate through predictable and sudden role transitions (Elder, George, & Shanahan, 1996). The art of balancing life, family, and work has become a challenging task in recent years. Work and family are both central to modern life, and finding a balance between the two is important. Evaluating the psychosocial development of individuals in middle adulthood is fundamentally important for effective counseling. Significant social and emotional issues in the middle-age years center on the solidification of career path choices and on family relationships, especially parenting and the transition of children out of the family home. This is a time when individuals take stock of their

Photo 11.2   Balancing life, family, and work responsibilities can actually bring family members together.

Source: Jeff Randall/Digital Vision/Thinkstock.

life goals and make final commitments to family, career, and social paths. They reintegrate their life experiences into an evolving portrait of their meaning and purpose in life. Planning and managing numerous complex work and family roles is a source of stress for many families, particularly when assuming the various roles in balancing work and life. As noted by Newman and Newman (2012), in managing work and family life one must consider: **role overload**, **role conflict**, and **role spillover**.

Role overload occurs as result of too many demands and expectations to be handled in the time allowed. For example, a parent with three children ages 7, 10, and 14 may find that the demands of getting the children ready for school, attending functions at three different schools, picking up and dropping off the children at various places, managing the family home chores, and trying to be emotionally available are exhausting. Role overload can be experienced in one or more adult roles.

Role conflict occurs when the demands and expectations of various roles conflict with each other. For example, when a worker is expected to stay late at work to finish a project but that same night is a spouse's birthday or child's performance; role conflict may come into play.

Role spillover occurs when the demands of or pre-occupations with one's role interfere with the ability to carry out another role. For example, a person may be disrupted at work by worries about an ill child or elderly parent or distracted at home by a work assignment that is due the next day (Newman & Newman, 2012).

The combination of role conflict, role overload, and role spillover can set the stage for reduced satisfaction at work, in family life, and sometimes generally by causing a decline in the person's sense of well-being (Kinnumen, Feldt, Mauno, & Rantanen, 2010). While on first view it may be assumed simply that too much, or too many roles, are being asked of the individual in middle adulthood, evidence suggests that it is not the existence of multiple roles but rather the conflict, overload, and spillover that cause stress. In fact, there is evidence that, in contrast, multiple role involvement has been shown to contribute to health and well-being and increased spousal support. The partner's involvement in work can increase self-satisfaction and a sense of success, and pride in one's accomplishments at work can also contribute to marital satisfaction (Dreman, 1997). Case Illustration 11.1, highlights the delicate nature of this work-family balance.

CASE ILLUSTRATION 11.1 BALANCING LIFE, FAMILY, AND WORK

Instructions: Case Illustration 11.1 presents a picture of Bill and Jan, a couple confronted with the necessity to make drastic life and work changes. After reading the case illustration, it is suggested that you reflect upon and discuss with a student or colleague the questions posed at the end.

Bill and Jan

Bill and Jan like their jobs very much and have a relatively comfortable life full of social activities and interaction with friends. Without much planning, the couple's family expanded after the birth of their twin boys. The couple had to make drastic changes in their work schedules and lifestyles. They needed to keep their jobs and raise the twins and did not want the additional expense of paying for a babysitter. They reached out for help from one of the twins' grandmothers. Bill's mother, who was 72 years old, recently retired, and with some health issues, became the twins' babysitter 5 days per week, including some weekends as needed. She felt pressure to support her family and did not receive financial compensation for the working hours. Bill and Jan presented this scenario to her as a temporary period in their life until they got used to the new parenting experience and adjusted to a new schedule of family, work, and social life. A year later, the grandmother was still babysitting. While she loved the twins dearly and adjusted to the daily childcare, she also wanted out of this situation so she could have her "life back," take care of her husband, and continue her retirement years as she had planned. The stress caused by this situation created a friction among the family members involved.

Questions for Reflection and Discussion:

1. Where might there be evidence of role conflict? Role spillover? Role overload?

2. What specific steps might be instituted to regain a balance of work and family?

Counselors working with issues related to balancing life, family, and work need to implement a number of techniques to help bring the client into focus to clarify and find possible solutions for his or her dilemma. There are four processes that can help the counselor and client evaluate a situation or problem and make changes: (1) clarifying values, (2) setting realistic goals and expectations, 3) setting priorities and managing time, and (4) letting go and understanding control. Using these processes in a coordinated way can bring about the client's needed change (Kiger & Riley, 2000).

Career Changes

Besides family, the work domain is one of the most important goal domains from emerging middle adulthood through the age of retirement (Nurmi, 1991, 1992). It is not surprising that the importance of setting goals (selection), pursuing and achieving goals (optimization), and maintaining goals when faced with setbacks or a decline (compensation) have been extensively studied in the context of work (Baltes & Dickson 2001; Locke & Latham, 2002; Wiese & Freund, 2005; Young, Baltes, & Pratt 2007). When exploring changes in the work domain in light of the increased life expectancy, it is common to find many individuals who, during their middle adulthood, have the desire or need to make midlife career changes.

Managing a career does not necessarily mean remaining within the same occupational structure throughout adult life. It is well documented that the rate of job turnover slows down after age 35; however, people still need to remain flexible in their attachment to a specific job or career (Newman & Newman, 2012). Therefore, work activities or work-related goals may change for at least five reasons during middle adulthood:

1. Some careers end during middle adulthood. An example is the career of the professional athlete, whose strengths, reaction time, speed, and endurance decline to the point where he or she can no longer compete.

2. Adults resolve conflicts between job demands and personal goals. Some workers recognize that the kinds of contributions they thought they could make are not possible within their chosen work structure.

3. Some individuals realize that they have succeeded as much as possible in a given career. Individuals may realize that they cannot be promoted further, or that changing technology has made their expertise obsolete. In this case, they may decide to retrain for new kind of work or to further their education in order to move in new career directions.

4. Women may decide to withdraw from work due to parenting roles and family reasons and re-enter the workforce once their children are in high school or college. As they return to work, they have a midlife career change; their priorities shift, and they may be expected to combine responsibilities as homemakers with career goals. Other women, who have never worked before marriage, face the labor market as novices for multiple reasons. These women are sometimes referred to as displaced homemakers.

5. With the restructuring of the workforce, some workers are laid off and are unable to find work in the same field. They may have to retrain for a new line of work or similar work in a new industry. Consider the factors presented in Case Illustration 11.2.

CASE ILLUSTRATION 11.2 CAREER CHANGES

Instructions: Case Illustration 11.2 presents an example of career change during middle adulthood and the multiple concerns that need to be considered. After reading the illustration, it is suggested that you reflect upon and discuss with a student or colleague the questions posed at the end.

Liz's career change concerns

Liz attended the local community college where she took culinary courses and specialized as a pastry chef. She thought of this decision as something easy and new to learn. Encouraged by family, she got a job with a reputable bread and pastry company that was a big distributor in her town. She learned the trade of the job and some of the business management aspects of it. Soon her working hours became complicated, and she decided that she was ready to start her own business. With her savings and financial help from her family, she opened a bakery in her community and, a year later, added a bakery school for children and young adults in the back of the store. She said that "entering the competitive world of food service was difficult and demanding, but the reward was to be your own boss, teach others, and contribute to your community." By the third year in business, the stress of her new responsibilities was overwhelming, and she became concerned about her future. Her concerns were fear of business competition, inability to upgrade and expand, financial security, disappointing her family, possible business failure during her middle-age years, and most of all, her self-esteem and self-confidence. She was afraid, and she needed help to identify the problem and find solutions.

Questions for Reflection and Discussion:

1. How can Liz regain her entrepreneurship spirit during her middle-age years?

2. What skills does she need to develop to protect herself and her business?

3. What counseling techniques would best work in this situation?

While changing career paths, when desired and successful, may support healthy middle adulthood development, for those who have career changes imposed, the experience can be less than an opportunity for growth. For example, it is common for middle-age corporate executives to become disillusioned or displaced as a result of reorganization. In some cases, some individuals may be able to start their own business. Those who are successful with their new ventures are able to see the change as an opportunity to achieve new goals; those who do not succeed may see it as a personal failure and, as a result, need to rebuild their self-esteem and morale. In such cases, good counseling skills can make a change for the client.

Midlife Crisis or Midlife Transition

As noted in the introduction, the midlife crisis or midlife transition serves as a choice point, an opportunity to stop and reflect on what was, in light of what was hoped for, and implications for what is next. The common term of *midlife crisis* was never a formal diagnostic category. For most, it is a time of questioning priorities and adjusting lifestyles to fit better with emotional needs. Midlife crisis invites the individual to consider the deeper possibility to achieve his or her dreams. For others, midlife can bring about a true crisis, one that causes them to stray outside the usual way of life and question every choice made during the first half of their lives. Some signs of midlife crisis are

1. feelings of depression that affect the person's mood to the point that activities and relationships are negatively affected;

2. a loss of interest in things that used to be important and questioning values and beliefs;

3. feeling a need for adventure and change with a curious mind and change in behavior;

4. feelings of anger and blaming others due to lack of desire to continue as the same person he or she was and for caring for the same people (spouse, children, and friends);

5. an inability to make decisions about the future, even questioning who and what should be part of the future; and

6. a desire for new intimate relationships that challenge family and social norms.

Midlife crisis and possible midlife changes are components of growth and part of the midlife transition. Adult development theories trace back to Jung's (Adler, Jaffe, & Hull, 1973) clinical and theoretical work on the dynamic interplay of psychological opposites, particularly as they manifest themselves at the junction of youth and middle age. The critical problems of life are often solved during midlife through counseling by suggesting attainable goals, a considerable achievement. As Jung (Adler et. al,1973, p. 87) noted:

"Thoroughly unprepared we take the step into the afternoon of life; worse still we take this step with the false presumption that our truths and ideals will serve us as previously. But, we cannot live the afternoon of life according to the program of life's morning—for what was great in the morning will be little at evening, and what in the morning was true will at evening have become a lie."

Midlife, or the afternoon of life as Jung called it in his essay "The Stages of Life," has become a period of great interest to scholars of the lifespan, and today it is one of the most significant life stages for the counseling profession to take into consideration for practice. The midlife transition, a time which bridges two major eras of life, early adulthood and middle adulthood, is a crucial period that impacts a person's career, family, and self (Jung, 1971). This period in the lifespan is characterized by a complex interplay of multiple roles. There are salient issues of midlife, such as balancing work and family responsibilities in the midst of the physical and psychological changes associated with aging and the environment.

Counselors need to pay attention to multiple patterns of gains and losses and changes in midlife within the domains of personality and the self, cognitive functioning, the ability to deal with multiple roles and stress, emotions, social relationships, work and career, and physical and mental health as it applies to middle adulthood. For some individuals, midlife can become a **neurotic crisis** from within. Jung (Adler et al., 1973) describes the neurotic disturbances of adults as the common desire to prolong youth and restrain oneself from crossing the threshold into maturity. In these contexts, transition and crisis can no longer be viewed as deficiencies of character or spirit but rather the norm.

While many experience a crisis in midlife, it is not a must or an automatic event. Research has shown that often individuals continue to proceed along the life cycle without disruption or reexamination (Eichorn, Clausen, Haan, Honzik, & Mussen, 1981), whereas others have found that the salient issues and demands of midlife differ from earlier age periods and do require lifespan adjustment to negotiate new challenges.

Triggers to Midlife Crisis and Transition

There have been a number of speculations as to the trigger for such reflection and adjustment. Jacques (1965), for example, suggested the midlife crisis is driven by fear of impending death. Others have suggested that the typical sources of the crisis are not death related but reflect normative major life events, such as job loss, financial difficulties, illness or divorce, events that need not be confined to the midlife period (Lachman & Bertrand, 2001; Lachman, Lewkowicks, Marcus, & Peng, 1994; Wethington, Kessler, & Pixley, 2004). Finally, some have argued that those who have exhibited personalities prone to distress are more likely to experience midlife crisis when faced with the challenges presented in this phase of development (Costa & McCrane, 1980; Whitbourn & Connolly, 1999).

But regardless of the stressor or trigger that may have invited the midlife crisis, the way one responds is that which needs to be highlighted. One can certainly surrender to the changes encountered or approach midlife as an opportunity to reexamine and redefine, or one can sense a loss of control, which in turn can provide motivation to challenge impending declines on many domains, including mental health or cognitive functioning (Lachman & Firth 2004; Miller & Lachman, 2000).

Midlife Crisis: A Normal Transitional Stage in Life

The midlife transition is looked on, more and more, as a normal part of life. Daniel Levinson (Levinson, Darrow, Klein, & Levinson, 1978) proposed in his well-regarded theory of adult development, that all adults go through a series of stages. At the center of his theory is the life structure, which is described as the underlying pattern of a person's life at any particular time. For many people, the life structure involves mainly family and work, but it can also include religion and economic status, for instance. According to his theory, the midlife transition is simply another normal transition to another stage of life. During middle adulthood, individuals deal with their particular individuality and work toward cultivating their skills and assets. This is a good time to reflect on success and failures, develop a life structure, and enjoy the rest of life.

A Call for Renewal or Crisis

The need for self-renewal is a strong but elusive force. There are many reasons why an individual may have the need to renew during the middle adulthood stage. Beyond improving oneself and developing others, personal renewal is a focused field of practice in counseling and research, which includes personal development methods, learning programs, assessment systems, tools, and techniques. Any form of this need to renew and enhance quality of life, whether it is biological, health-related, organizational, or personal, requires a framework if one wishes to know whether change has actually occurred. In the case of personal renewal, an individual often acts as the primary judge of improvement, but objective validation of improvement requires assessment using standard criteria. Personal renewal frameworks may include goals or benchmarks that define the end points, strategies, or plans for reaching goals. They also measure and assess progress, defining levels, stages, or milestones along a development path, and include a feedback system to track changes (Newman and Newman, 2012).

Personal renewal may direct one to engage in counseling. In this circumstance, the counseling will be directed to assisting in specific areas of desired renewal or with the process of re-energizing prior to a significant life change or after an unplanned change.

The need to be renewed in an ever-changing family and society scene becomes a challenge. The following Case Illustration 11.3 presents a typical example of the need for individual growth and renewal within a marriage based on societal norms and takes place when a woman who has been primarily responsible for child care and household management decides to enter the competitive labor force. The case illustrates the challenge in engaging in such a renewal.

Generativity Versus Stagnation

Erik Erikson first introduced the concept of generativity in 1950 as part of his overall model of lifespan development and what he termed psychosocial crisis. The challenge as identified by Erikson (1964) was to decide where

CASE ILLUSTRATION 11.3 A CALL FOR RENEWAL OR CRISIS

Instructions: Case Illustration 11.3 provides a case example of Anne's need to renew and this decision can affect the family. After reading the case illustration, it is suggested that you reflect upon and discuss with a student or colleague the questions posed at the end.

Anne's renewal decision

Anne worked as a teacher before she married, and after raising her children, she decided that it was time to go back to work. Her two children were in school near her home, and her husband, Eric, had a full-time job; so Anne was alone most of the day not knowing what to do with herself. She began to feel depressed and envious of everyone's active lives, so she took a position at the local school working afternoons until 5 p.m. Her husband, Eric, did not want her to work and expressed that by reminding her that they did not need the extra money, and that he likes to know that she is home when the children and he get home every day. He also was not ready to take the children to their after-school activities while she was working. Anne insisted that working was good for her own mental health and happiness. The first months of work did not go well at all, and she wondered if she had made the right decision. However, the value of being able to work, her renewed personal identity, her increased self-confidence, and her ability to return home after a day's work with new energy and enthusiasm for the children and her husband was worth it. Eric got more involved in the children's activities, and they all looked forward to the weekends to spend time together. Eric and the children began to see Anne as a professional with multiple responsibilities. The family felt closer with shared responsibilities, independence, and new levels of involvement in each other's lives.

Questions for Reflection and Discussion:

1. How might child-rearing responsibilities prevent new growth and renewal for women or men in their middle adulthood?

2. How does Anne's decision lead to new opportunities for family growth?

3. What are some alternatives that Anne might have considered that could have satisfied her needs for continued need to renew?

4. How would you, as a counselor, have guided Anne in this situation?

to direct one's life energies, either toward self (stagnation) or toward improving life conditions for future generations (generativity; See previously cited Table 2.2, Chapter 2).

Generativity During Midlife

Based on Erikson's theory, generativity reveals a concern for establishing and guiding the next generation. Generativity is closely linked, but not limited, to parenting because it can also be expressed by teaching and mentoring or by taking productive roles in society through creativity and social responsibility. These kinds of activities not only provide guidance and inspiration for younger generations but also for all people and, in principle, for all

Photo 11.3   Sharing daily recreational activities strengthens family relationships across age groups.

Source: Jupiterimages/Bananastock/Thinkstock.

people living in the near or distant future. The central strength fostered by generativity is the desire to care for someone or something and to be sure not to do something harmful or destructive (Fiske & Chiriboga, 1990).

Stagnation During Midlife

Stagnation, the opposite pole of generativity, was less elaborated on in Erikson's writings, in particular in his earlier work. Stagnation represents a lethargic stance toward the world and is most commonly seen during middle adulthood. According to Hamacheck (1990), the stagnant individual is no longer participating in or contributing to society and ceases to be productive, preferring a stagnant type of life. Stagnant people are primarily interested in themselves and their own needs. They show no interest in others, nor do they want to make the world a better place to live for everyone. In counseling, stagnation has been referred to as "self-absorption," which can be considered as caring for no one except oneself. An extreme level of stagnation leads to **rejectivity**, which is defined as the "unwillingness to include specific individuals or groups in one's generative concern—one does not "*care to care*" for anyone" (Erikson, 1982, p. 68). In some extreme levels, "non-familiar others are excluded to the point of being dangerously different."

Stagnation is assumed to reflect the absence of involvement and inclusivity. In terms of involvement, stagnant individuals have low levels of "active concern for the growth of oneself and others in terms of behaviors." Neither do they show a "sense of responsibility for developing and sharing skills and knowledge, and the ability to follow through with commitments." Moreover, with respect to inclusivity, it has been asserted that the stagnant individual's caregiving activity is typically narrow in scope "in terms of who or what is to be included or excluded." These are important characteristics that a counselor needs to identify early on in the counseling relationship in order to help clients to assess and correct themselves. Stagnation is positively associated with the personality characteristic of neuroticism, indicating high levels of worry, and negatively associated with the personality characteristics of extraversion and openness to experience, indicating difficulties in social relationships, problems achieving a sense of social acceptance, and being highly controlled. Stagnation characteristics in middle adulthood identify the individual not only as closed off to experiences with others but also lacking in experiences that would promote self-development (Van Hiel, Mervielde, & DeFruyt, 2006).

A common source of stagnation in middle adulthood is the role stagnation associated with employment. An individual who has been in the same job for a long time may feel threatened by younger workers, stuck in a routine job, or passed over for promotion and leadership. Rather than taking up the challenge to continue to be engaged with coworkers, the person becomes resentful, avoidant, and withdrawn and may develop physical or emotional symptoms associated with stress and frustration (Clark & Arnold, 2008). Middle adulthood extends over many years with many complex challenges for which individuals may not be prepared. During moments of crisis in midlife, individuals may become entrapped in a process of self-protection and withdrawal that results in permanent stagnation. Counselors have the responsibility to help clients see life from a new perspective and find resources that will permit continued growth and the expansion of generativity.

Person-Environment, Culture Interaction, and Socioeconomic Status

The interaction between the demands of a person's immediate environment and one's own needs, skills, and interpersonal cultural-based style are important factors for the counseling process. Person-environment and culture interaction influences personality and growth as well as adaptation, coping skills, resilience, and ultimately quality of life through the lifespan. The **person-environment perspective**, consistent with the framework of the interaction of physiology, psychology, and social changes, suggests that the environment is not static but changes continually as the person in midlife transition takes from it what is needed and controls what can be modified. Adaptation to the environment during middle adulthood, in particular a new environment, implies a dual process in which the individual adjusts to some characteristics of the social and physical environment (Hooyman & Kiyak, 2011).

Considering the interaction of culture with the environment, society creates another dimension that is very important for counselors to understand for their own professional growth and for the counselor-client therapeutic relationship and intervention outcomes. It has been defined that culture is a system of shared beliefs, values, customs, behaviors, and artifacts that members of a culturally based society use to interact with their word and with one another (Zion, Kozleski, & Fulton, 2005). Understanding the complexity of culture is critical for counselors because our individual cultural orientations are present in every interaction. We tend to make assumptions about a person's beliefs or behaviors based on a single cultural indicator, particularly race in a political context or ethnicity, when in reality, our cultural identities are a complex weave of all the cultural groups we belong to that influence our values, beliefs, and behaviors. We are all members of cultural groups and develop cultural identities based on those memberships and influences. Culture is a very significant aspect in the life of middle-age individuals.

Cultural Identity

The development of **cultural identity** is an ongoing process, as we are exposed to more and different sets of beliefs and values and may choose to adopt ones that were not part of our original upbringing. Cultural identity is constructed within the individual but continually influenced by the interaction among and between people, the environment, and society. Culture is not static; it is dynamic and consists of a combination of thoughts, feelings, attitudes, beliefs, values, and behavior patterns that are shared by racial, ethnic, religious, or social groups of people. This combination of variables is very significant during middle adulthood.

After many years of research and knowledge translation of the meaning of culture and cultural identity, cultural competence and multiculturalism in the counseling profession strives to prepare counselors that reflect this knowledge and can apply it in the culturally diverse society that we live in, as in the case of the United States. The counseling profession makes a conscious effort to learn and understand the concept of culture and cultural influence on identity development through the lifespan. A well-trained and experienced counselor will reject the wrongful assumption of privileging his or her own cultural identity at the expense of those who have different beliefs or values. The objectives in counseling, as it relates to understanding cultural diversity to better serve clients, are to

1. define and understand the different factors that impact our cultural identity development;

2. gain a perspective on the way that others may differ or may be similar;

3. understand differences as something to celebrate and learn about rather than to reject, by becoming culturally responsive; and

4. understand culture as an ongoing evolution as we grow and develop over the course of our lifespan (Wong & Wong, 2010).

One of the major challenges that counselors encounter is how to appropriately respond to middle-age individuals who are greatly influenced by their cultural backgrounds, which may be different from the counselor's own culture. According to Locke (1992), counselors cannot explore only those factors relating to individuals' experiences in the present. Counselors must understand and have empathy for those events from the past or future that have an impact on the client's present. Although much of the evidence confirms that the history of culturally diverse groups in the United States often is unpleasant, counselors must be willing to explore this unpleasant material so that culturally diverse clients can better deal with events in the present. In most cases with culturally diverse individuals, a recollection of the past contributes to their willingness or unwillingness to interact with the dominant culture creating an opportunity for therapeutic intervention. We can best meet the challenges of responding to middle adulthood diversity within the context of our own cultural backgrounds and by making realistic and relevant plans in a culturally responsive way.

Cultural Responsiveness

Cultural responsiveness is an important factor to be considered when assessing the counseling needs of middle-aged individuals who might be deeply rooted in their cultural ways, which might be very different than the counselor's culture. Cultural responsiveness is not something that we can master and then forget; and it is not about changing others to be more like us. It is about cultivating an open attitude and acquiring new skills, and it involves exploring and honoring our own culture while learning about and honoring other people's cultures. In counseling, as in many other human service professions, developing the ability to be culturally responsive is a lifelong journey that is both enriching and rewarding and an important component of the ethical standards of the counseling profession (Algozzine, O'Shea, Obiakor, 2009; Wong & Wong, 2010). Cultural responsiveness in counseling and positive cultural identity can play major roles in effective counseling of clients in middle adulthood and achieving

Table 11.1   Benefits of Becoming Culturally Responsive

What Are the Benefits of Becoming Culturally Responsive?
These are varied and dependent upon the individual, but the following are common benefits: • Increased level of comfort with members of different cultures   • Increased knowledge of own culture   • Increased freedom to explore other ways of knowing and being   • Discovery of passions and interests that complement current interests   • Increased capacity to work with members of diverse cultures   • Increased resources and knowledge for professional identity

resilience to manage life events. Unfortunately, society challenges us to work with individuals from diverse backgrounds who are or have been discriminated against, and we may have found ourselves having been in the same situation. See Table 11.1 Benefits of Becoming Culturally Responsive.

Socioeconomic Status

Theories of social class and social stratification suggest a variety of bases for social hierarchies among middle-adulthood social groups. On an empirical basis, different indicators of socioeconomic status (SES) show similar graded relationships with health and well-being, despite the fact that they are only moderately interrelated. SES is a combination of education, occupation, and income and accumulated assets that an individual may possess. This is a complex concept and one that can create questions and concerns during the productive years of middle adulthood. Each of these components is related to specific adulthood developmental stages and has a direct impact on life events that could affect family life, health, and interrelationships. In addition, they locate individuals in relevant social hierarchies, where relative position itself may be a risk or protective factor. It is normal for individuals to sense their place on the **social ladder**, which takes into account their standing on multiple dimensions of SES and social position (Adler, Epel, Castellazzo, & Ickovics, 2000).

Counseling is not an isolated profession that looks only at the client's present issues. It requires a more holistic approach, as the structure of our society cannot be separated from the role of the counselor. Perhaps this is why paying attention to the individual's SES is of vital importance to better understand stressors and other related concerns that clients present during the counseling session. As indicated by Miech, Shanahan, & Elder (2000), the investigations into the mechanisms that link SES and depression have developed without support of the life-course perspective, which is the relationship between time and human behavior; therefore, we are limited in what we know about the ways in which socially structured experiences and processes influence or vary throughout the phases of life. Research indicates that the association between depression and SES indicators strengthens significantly through the phases of middle adulthood (Miech et al., 2000).

Counselors should also note that a life-course approach explicitly focuses on the aging process and thereby directs attention to how the overall association between SES and mental health issues, as well as the stress processes that account for it, may vary across life stages in middle adulthood. A major focus of life-course theory centers on the timing of lives and the extent to which events and social roles, as well as their consequences, are age-graded across the life course (Elder et al., 1996). When looking into the overall association between SES and depression over the life course and its implications for counseling, current theoretical and empirical research suggests that the association between SES and depression steadily increases over the years of middle-adulthood life.

Anger, in particular, during middle adulthood, is another theoretically important response pattern that has not received systematic empirical examination in the literature in reference to how individuals can benefit from counseling such as anger management techniques or holistic counseling (Grier & Cobbs, 1968). Discrimination based on SES and racial status causes deep anger and appears to be an important class of stressful life experiences neglected by traditional approaches to the measurement of stress and professional counseling interventions. Although these experiences are not limited to any segment of society, they appear to be more prevalent for racial minorities, individuals from diverse cultural and ethnic backgrounds, and other stigmatized groups than for the general population. Therefore, it seems important to include measures of discrimination in studies of racial/cultural/ethnic minorities and in analyses of racial differences in health and needs for counseling interventions. Discrimination and differential treatment are unlikely to be a mediator of the SES-health and counseling relationship, but it may highlight the association between SES and health. It may also make an incremental contribution to the health and well-being of racial/cultural/ethnic diversity over and above indicators of SES during middle adulthood (The John D. and Catherine T. MacArthur Foundation (MIDMAC, 2004).

A major psychosocial motivation for understanding the association between SES and mental health issues is to further the knowledge about the social arrangement of society and its consequences on the individual.

Counseling through the lifespan perspective contributes to this endeavor, offering insights that individuals experience in their social environment, as well as their reaction to it, and differs in systematic ways across early, middle, and late adulthood. Greater attention to lifespan-specific stressors and processes, as well as analytical strategies that are sensitive to the conditioning influence of life stages, leads to a fuller understanding of clients' social conditions and their impact on physical and mental health and well-being outcomes and the type of counseling intervention to be provided. There are many forms of social discrimination, and one that is common in our society and has negative consequences is covert discrimination, which is often experienced during middle adulthood.

Coping With Covert Discrimination

As previously mentioned, there are many types of discriminations in society, and counselors come across many cases of individuals who have been affected by these actions. Unlike overt discrimination, **covert discrimination** is a far more subtle kind of discrimination. It operates beneath the surface and involves deliberate acts of deception. Those who experience covert discrimination find it very difficult to deal with. However, despite its subtle nature, the emotional and psychological damage that it causes is not any different than the blatant, overt version. Covert discrimination requires more cunning and deception by the perpetrators. An example would be middle-aged workers who have not been employed or promoted in a position to which they are qualified and are of course not told that it is because of their age, sexual orientation, religious affiliation, nationality, disability, or gender. Instead, they are given more palatable and nondiscriminating reasons. Covert discrimination is also manifested by not acknowledging any positive contributions people make in their place of employment or membership associations. This is a common case situation that counselors face with their middle-age clients. By its nature, covert discrimination is a lot more difficult to prove by those experiencing it but equally damaging to the victims. Coping with these situations is very difficult and damaging not only for the individual's mental and physical health but for society at large. Perceived covert discrimination in the workplace has been associated with lower job satisfaction, reduced life satisfaction, multiple health problems, depression, and general anxiety (Feagin & McKinney, 2003). A typical common case that counselors deal with is when middle-age clients, as targets of covert discrimination, give up and have a higher risk of addictive behaviors such as drug and alcohol dependency and abusive behaviors against significant others.

Counselors are able to identify how covert or overt discrimination drains the victims of their confidence, dignity, and self-respect. It is a demeaning experience that forces people to look at themselves and consider their sense of place in the world as a fragile one. In looking at the nature of covert discrimination, in particular during middle adulthood, the attempt is to connect the practice to a new counseling dimension, creating new challenges and opportunities for counselors to learn and apply their therapeutic knowledge and advocacy skills to the practice of counseling for best outcomes for their clients. As indicated above, counselors must explore what the actual oppression of covert discrimination has done to the psychological adjustment of culturally diverse clients.

Guided Practice Exercise 11.2 Coping With Covert Discrimination

Instructions: While overt discrimination is easily identifiable, covert discrimination presents a far more difficult concept to unravel. Reflect on the possibility that covert discrimination could be all about interpretation and people being unnecessarily oversensitive and whether this area of discrimination can be resolved through therapeutic counseling?. It is suggested that you reflect and discuss with other students or colleagues the questions posed below.

Exercise Questions:

1. Is discrimination only in the minds of the victims? How can counseling help if it is?

2. What are the effects of covert discrimination on the people who experience it?

3. Who is most likely to use discriminatory practices against other people?

4. How can counseling best assist people who have suffered this or any type of discrimination to regain their confidence and self-esteem?

Guided Practice Exercise 11.3 Identifying Covert Discrimination

Instructions: According to scholars, covert discrimination is often disguised or rationalized with an explanation of an unintended reason that society is willing to accept. This clandestine bias causes a variety of social inequalities and empowers the oppressor while diminishing the rights and powers of the oppressed individual being discriminated against. While covert discrimination is easily identifiable, it presents a far more difficult concept to unravel.

It is suggested that you reflect and discuss with other students and colleagues if covert discrimination could be an issue of culturally based interpretation and people are being unnecessarily overly sensitive.

Explain whether the impact of this type of discrimination on the individual can be resolved through therapeutic counseling.

Cultural Competence Practice

Due to the American society's diversity, a cultural approach to counseling continue to evolve, and the implications for culturally based practice are still being developed and adapted. There is some agreement, however, that while maintaining the integrity of the distinctive new approach, multicultural counseling should strive to select and build on the best of current counseling practice. A conceptual framework for cross-cultural competencies can help with providing culturally competent counseling to diverse clients during their middle adulthood as they continue to develop through their lifespan. This framework consists of the three major points in which it is claimed most cross-cultural skills can either be organized or developed (Sue, Arredondo, & McDavis, 1992). This framework was further developed by Sue and Sue (2008), who identified the competencies required by the culturally skilled counselor when working with middle-age adults as being (1) awareness of own assumptions, values, and biases; (2) understanding the worldview of the culturally different client; and (3) developing appropriate intervention strategies and techniques.

Increasing Self-Awareness

Many authors in the area of multicultural counseling advocate the need for all practitioners to start on a continual process of multicultural self-awareness by following simple steps: (a) think about yourself; (b) identify the values of the dominant culture in which you practice counseling or communication; and (c) examine alternative value orientations. For example, in Guided Practice Exercise 11.4 regarding increasing self-awareness.

Guided Practice Exercise 11.4 Increasing Self-Awareness

Instructions: The transition of cultural heritage from one generation to the next contributes significantly to an individual's cultural identity through the lifespan. It is also more difficult to adjust to a new culture or reject one's own culture during middle adulthood. It is suggested that you reflect and discuss the values, beliefs, opinions, and attitudes that you believe identify your own culture and how these variables affected your decision to become a counselor.

Developing Culturally Based Skills

In addition to working toward a greater cultural self-awareness and developing counselors' knowledge and understanding of clients' differences, practitioners need to think about the way in which their skills should to be adapted or changed to accommodate the particular needs of clients during their life state of middle adulthood.

Ivey, Ivey, & Simek-Morgan, (1997) and Ivey (1994) suggested that culturally appropriate nonverbal behavior is crucial to successful counseling outcomes. Further, Ivy (1994) suggests that practicing counselors should begin a lifetime study of nonverbal communication patterns and their variations to better understand cultural differences. Various categories of nonverbal behavior can be identified, and some cultural implications for each category (e.g., eye contact, posture, touching, body to body proximity, vocal tracking) should be discussed (p. 29).

Multicultural counseling practice, when working with individuals in middle adulthood, should include an emphasis on social inclusion and access to human services, such as counseling services. This highlights the need for professional counseling practice that is responsive to and accommodates the important issues of middle-age clients in an effective manner. This understanding begins with the notion that culture is learned, not biologically inherited (Huff & Kline, 1999). Counselors, early on in their careers, will understand that to embark on the journey toward cultural proficiency and understanding another person's perspective, it is important to understand culture, its many components, and its influence on everyday life and middle-age life.

Counseling Issues

Middle adulthood is a time of stress and potential transitional crisis. Radical adjustments to changed roles and patterns of life, especially when accompanied by physical changes, always tend to disrupt the individual's physical and psychological homeostasis and lead to a period of stress when a number of major adjustments must be made in the family home, career, and social aspects of his or her life. According to Keyes & Ryff (1999), stress during midlife can manifest itself due to multiple reasons and in different categories.

Categories of stress in middle adulthood are

Somatic stress is due to physical evidences of aging.

Cultural stress stems from the high value placed on youth, vigor, and success by the cultural group.

Economic stress results from the financial burden of educating children and providing status symbols for all family members.

Psychological stress may be the result of the death of a spouse, the departure of children from the home, boredom with marriage, or a sense of lost youth and approaching death.

In the case of women, most experience a disruption in homeostasis during their 40s, when normally they go through physiological changes, and family situations may change such as children leaving home, thus forcing them to make radical readjustments in the pattern of their entire lives. For men, by contrast, the climactic event comes later—generally in the late 50s, as does the imminence of retirement with its necessary role changes.

The counseling issues that individuals in middle adulthood may have include personal growth as well as remediation of problems situations. Knowledge of normal aspects of middle adulthood and later-life development are essential if counselors are to effectively meet the needs of clients in both of these areas. To make further progress and enhance counseling competencies, researchers and counselors must recognize the multidisciplinary nature of middle adulthood and focus on the interaction of biopsychosocial and environmental factors (as indicated in Chapter 1) during this period of midlife. Middle adulthood can provide a window into later life while there is still time to grow, adjust, and engage in actions to influence some aspects of the course of life. Counselors need to become competent in understanding and attending to the common issues faced by individuals in midlife transition. Research indicates that among the most common issues in this lifespan period are changes in physical conditions, health, and mental functioning as part of the aging process. Other issues are related to career, finances, and family, including divorce, relocations, child rearing, and caring for elderly parents. Equally important, and heightened with age, are personal issues based on societal biases related to social class, race, culture, ethnicity, and SES. These issues affect the individual's well-being and, in particular, the ability to adjust and cope at a later stage of life. The new challenges in today's society emphasize the need for counselors to become competent in areas that cover the diversity of clients during their middle adulthood and the multiple and varied issues that affect their lives.

Psychological resources can be beneficial in adapting to life changes and physical and social losses that occur during midlife. When desirable outcomes are not attainable, it is possible to allow a process for adjustment (Heckhousen, 2001). Selective optimization processes can enable the resilient middle-age adult to draw on social and psychological resources to compensate for biological decline (Staudinger & Bluck, 2001). The well-being of middle-aged adults affects others with whom they interact or give care, advise, or influence. Therefore, a better understanding of this stage of life can have far-reaching consequences to persons of all age groups, impacting those who are younger or older in the family, those in the workplace, and those in the community and in society as a whole.

CASE ILLUSTRATION 11.4 COUNSELING ISSUES

Instructions: Case Illustration 11.4 presents a situation where Bob challenges himself with new life goals. After reading the illustration, it is suggested that you reflect upon and discuss with a student or colleague the questions posted at the end.

Setting goals during middle adulthood

Bob is a 46-year-old, married, recovering alcoholic who finds himself disturbed by feelings he does not know how to handle. He stopped drinking 2 years ago with the help of an Alcoholic Anonymous (AA) 12-Step Program and thought that after 2 years of not drinking he was "home free" from falling into drinking again. He lost his previous job after 6 years with the company, and he knows that his drinking and erratic behavior had something to do with losing his job. He is now employed but fears that the same thing will happen again. He sometimes feels out of control emotionally and reacts

(Continued)

(Continued)

with rage to minor irritation. Bob's goals are to return to the equilibrium he had without returning to drinking. His counselor recommended another goal: to develop a dynamic self-understanding to get a better handle on what is happening to him. The counselor explained that it is common for drinking to be used unconsciously or consciously to suppress feelings and assures him that the disturbing emotions he feels now are also common. As Bob develops an understanding of personal tendencies that led to his drinking, he will be able to better manage his emotions and fears. Bob also decides to set a goal of changing some of the places he goes to and people with whom he spends time by modifying his social networks. He understands that his increased sensitivity makes his job more difficult since he has to deal with customers all the time. It also puts a lot of stress on his marital relationship. The final step now is to develop an action plan for Bob to master strategies that will enable him to reach his goals.

Questions for Reflection and Discussion:

1. How would you guide Bob to develop his action plan?

2. Should Bob include AA meetings in his action plan?

3. What strategies should Bob use to eliminate the fear of losing his job?

4. How can Bob reframe his life and develop hope and optimism?

Gender issues in middle adulthood are also a significant factor for counseling practice. It is well known that middle-age women have gender-specific needs for counseling and also that women live longer than men. Middle-age women have unique situations in life such as marriage and divorce, motherhood and single motherhood, widowhood, childlessness, employment limitations, stereotyping from the medical profession (i.e., needy and **hypochondriasis**), and general devaluing in a society that emphasizes youth, beauty, and physical ability. The demographics suggest that middle-age women are likely to be at higher risk for physical and emotional maltreatment, loneliness and isolation, severe depression, and drug and alcohol abuse. In addition, middle-age women, in particular those from diverse cultures, races, or ethnic backgrounds or disability experiences, have the cumulative results of a lifetime of social discrimination, particularly in the job market. Identifying personal dilemmas and how they affect the individual during middle adulthood will avoid further deterioration of the person and future problems in later adulthood life.

Guided Practice Exercise 11.5. Counseling Issues

Instructions: Many unique challenges faced by individuals in their middle adulthood were discussed in this chapter, and one of them is the issue of middle-age crisis. It is suggested that you reflect and discuss with other students or colleagues some of the counseling considerations when working with this population, in particular related to the areas of family and job responsibility and how middle-age crisis could be a special factor.

SUMMARY

- ➤ Developmental maturation of middle adulthood leads to relatively minor changes, such as slowing down and the use of simpler language as age advances but also to greater emotional complexity and a wealth of life experience upon which to draw when providing counseling intervention to middle age adults.
- ➤ Erikson stated that the primary psychosocial task of middle adulthood is to develop generativity, or the desire to expand one's influence and commitment to family, society, and future generations. The middle-age adult who fails to develop generativity will fall into stagnation, or self-absorption, which is associated with self-indulgence and isolation.
- ➤ Middle adulthood is a critical period of the lifespan. How we develop in middle age, the central period of our lives, can influence how well we will cope in our later years.
- ➤ These counseling competencies are presented from a perspective of human development that takes into consideration and examines the developmental changes that individuals in their middle adulthood experience as they proceed through their lifespan.
- ➤ While middle adulthood may be characterized as a time of relative stability, the counseling implications for assisting individuals in their midlife are multiple and complex.
- ➤ Consideration of the possible crisis of generativity and stagnation are examined since they mark a significant transition in middle adulthood.
- ➤ The challenges of longevity also need to be considered in the counseling profession since never before has the population lived this long and had to deal with the multiple and diverse issues that affect society.
- ➤ Counselors are alerted to consider the issues of covert discrimination and cultural responsiveness when working with clients in our ever-changing and diverse society.
- ➤ Multicultural counseling is an integral part of counseling skills and practice.

ADDITIONAL RESOURCES

Providing information to students, counselors, and clients remains the most important current application of the Internet. Most professional organizations now offer websites with information such as ethical codes.

Websites

American Association for Marriage and Family Therapy. www.aamft.org
American Counseling Association (ACA). www.counseling.org
American Psychological Association. www.apa.org
American Rehabilitation Counseling Association (ARCA). www.arcaweb.org
National Board for Certified Counselors. www.nbcc.org

RECOMMENDED SUPPLEMENTAL READINGS

Comstock, D. (Ed.). (2005). *Diversity and development: Critical contexts that shape our lives and relationships.* Belmont, CA: Thomson Brooks/Cole.
Corey, G. (2008). *Theory and practice of counseling and psychotherapy* (8th ed.). Pacific Grove, CA: Brooks/Cole.
Corsini, R., & Wedding, D. (2007). *Current psychotherapies* (8th ed.). Pacific Grove, CA: Brooks/Cole.
Egan, G. (2009). *The skilled helper: A problem-management approach to helping* (9th ed.). Pacific Grove, CA: Brooks/Cole.

Ivey, A. E., Ivey, M. B., Myers, J. E., & Sweeney, T. J. (2004). *Developmental counseling and therapy: Promoting wellness over the lifespan*. Boston, MA: Houghton Mifflin/Lahaska.

Ponterotto, J. G., Casas, J. M., Suzuki, L. A., & Alexander, C. M., (Eds.). (2001). *Counseling across multicultural counseling*. Thousand Oaks, CA: Sage.

REFERENCES

Adler, G., Jaffe, A., & Hull, R.F.S. (1973). *C.G. Jung letters*. Princeton, NJ: Princeton University Press.

Adler, N. E., Epel, E. S., Castellazzo, G., & Ickovics, J. R. (2000). Relationship of subjective and objective social status with psychological and physiological functioning: Preliminary data in healthy white women. *Health Psychology, 19*(6), 586–592.

Algozzine, B, O'Shea, D. J., Obiakor, F. E. (2009). *Culturally responsive literacy instruction*. Thousand Oaks, CA: Corwin.

American Counseling Association (ACA). (2005). *Welfare of those served by counselors. Section A: Counseling Relationship. C. Counseling Plan,* ACA Code of Ethics, A.1.c. Alexandria, VA: Author. Retrieved from www.counseling.org.

Baltes, B. B., & Dickson, R. A. (2001). Using life-span models in industrial-organizational psychology: The theory of selective optimization with compensation. *Applied Developmental Science, 5,* 51–62.

Baltes, M. M., & Lang, F. R. (1997). Everyday functioning and successful aging: The impact of resources. *Psychology and Aging, 12,* 433–443

Becker, D. (2006). Therapy for the middle-aged: The relevance of existential issues. *American Journal of Psychotherapy, 60(1)*:87–99.

Brun, C., & Brock-Utne, J. (2012). Paralyzed by beauty. *Journal of Clinical Anesthesia, 24*(1), 77–78.

Centers for Disease Control and Prevention (CDC). (2011). *Health, U. S. 2012: Special feature on emergency care,* U. S. Department of Health and Human Services. *DHHS*/CDC Publication No. 2011–1232.

Clark, M., & Arnold, J. (2008). The nature, prevalence and correlates of generativity among men in middle career. *Journal of Vocational Behavior, 73,* 473–484.

Costa, P. D., & McCrane, R. R. (1980). Still stable after all these years: Personality as a key to some issues in adulthood and old age. In P. B. Baltes, & O. G. Brim (Eds.), *Life-span development and behavior* (pp. 65–102). New York, NY: Academic.

Dreman, S. (1997). *The family on the threshold of the 21st century: Trends and implications.* Mahwah, NJ: Erlbaum.

Eichorn, D. H., Clausen, J. A., Haan, N., Honzik, M. P., & Mussen, P. H. (Eds.). (1981). *Present and past on midlife.* New York, NY: Academic Press.

Elder, G. H., Jr., George, L. K., & Shanahan, M. J. (1996). Psychosocial stress over the life course. In H. B. Kaplan (Ed.), *Psychosocial stress: Perspective on structure, theory, life course, and methods* (pp. 247–291). Orlando, FL: Academic Press.

Erikson, E. H. (1964). *Insight and responsibility.* New York, NY: Norton.

Erikson, E. H. (1982). *The life cycle completed: A review.* New York, NY: Norton.

Feagin, J. R., & McKinney, K. D. (2003). *The many costs of racism.* Lanham, MD: Rowman & Littlefield.

Fiske, M., & Chiriboga, D. A. (1990). *Change and continuity in adult life.* San Francisco, CA: Jossey-Bass.

Grier, W. H., & Cobbs, P. M. (1968). *Black rage.* New York, NY: Harper Collins.

Hamachek, D. (1990). Evaluating self-concept and ego status in Erikson's last three psychosocial stages. *Journal of Counseling and Development. 68:*(6), 677–683.

Heckhousen, J. (2001). Adaptation and resilience in midlife. In M.E. Lachman (Ed.), *Handbook of midlife development* (pp. 345–391). New York, NY: Wiley.

Hooyman, N. R., & Kiyak, A. H. (2011). *Social gerontology: A multidisciplinary perspective* (9th ed.). Boston, MA: Allyn & Bacon.

Huff, R. M., & Kline, M. V. (1999). *Promoting health in multicultural populations: A handbook for practitioners.* Thousand Oaks, CA: Sage.

Ivey, A. E. (1994). Intentional interviewing and counseling: Facilitating client development in a multicultural society. Belmont, CA: Brooks/Cole.

Ivey, A. E., Ivey, M. B., & Simek-Morgan, L. (1997). Counseling and psychotherapy: A multicultural perspective (4th ed.). Boston, MA: Allyn & Bacon.

Jacques, E. (1965). Death and the mid-life crisis. *International Journal of Psychoanalysis, 46,* 502–514.

The John D. and Catherine T. MacArthur Foundation. (2004). *How healthy are we? A national study of well-being at midlife.* Research Network on Successful Midlife Development. MIDMAC. Chicago, IL: University of Chicago Press.

Jung, C. G. (1971). The stages of life. In J. Campbell, *The portable Jung* (p. 108). New York, NY: Viking Press.

Keyes, C. L. M., & Ryff, C. D. (1999). Psychological well-being in midlife. In S. L. Willis & J. D. Reid (Eds.), *Life in the middle: Psychological and social development in middleage* (pp. 161–178). San Diego, CA: Academic Press.

Kiger, G., & Riley, P. (2000). *Helping dual-earner couples balance work and family responsibilities*. Retrieved from www.cyfernet .org/parent/workandfamily/utah_findings.html.

Kinnumen, U., Feldt, T., Mauno, S., & Rantanen, J. (2010). Interference between work and family: A longitudinal individual and cross-over perspective. *Journal of Occupational and Organizational Psychology, 83,* 119–137.

Kinsella, K. (2011). Changes in life expectancy 1900–1990. Washington, D.C: Center for International Research, U.S. Bureau of the Census. Retrieved from www.ajcn.org.

Lachman, M. E., & Bertrand, R. M. (2001). Personality and the self in midlife. In M. E. Lachman, *Handbook of midlife development* (pp. 279–284). New York, NY: Wiley.

Lachman, M. E., & Firth, K. (2004). The adaptive value of feeling in control during midlife. In Brim et al., *How healthy are we? A national study of well-being in midlife* (pp. 320–349). Chicago, IL: University of Chicago Press.

Lachman, M. E., Lewkowicks, C., Marcus, A., & Peng, Y. (1994). Images of midlife development among young, middle-aged, and older adults. *Journal of Adult Development, 1,* 201–211.

Lawton, M. P., Moss, M., Hoffman, C., Grant, R., Ten Have, T., & Kleban, M. H. (1999). Health, valuation of life, and the wish to live. *The Gerontologist, 39*(4), 406–416.

Levinson, D. J., Darrow, C. N., Klein, E. B., & Levinson M. (1978). *Seasons of a Man's Life.* New York, NY: Random House.

Locke, D. C. (1992). Increasing multicultural understanding: A comprehensive model. Thousand Oaks, CA: Sage.

Locke, E. A., & Latham, G. P. (2002). Building practically useful theory of goal setting and task motivation: A 35-year odyssey. *The American Psychologist, 57,* 705–717.

Martin, M., & Zimprich, D. (2003). Are changes in cognitive functioning in older adults related to subjective complaints? *Experimental Aging Research, 29,* 335–352

Miech, R. A., Shanahan, M. L., & Elder, G. H., Jr. (2000). Socioeconomic status and depression in life course perspective. *Journal of Health and Social Behavior, 41*(2), 162–176.

Miller, L. S., & Lachman, M. E. (2000). Cognitive performance and the role of health and control beliefs in midlife. Aging, neuropsychology and cognition. *Journal on Normal Dysfunctional Development, 7,* 3–23.

Moody, H. R., & Sasser, J. R. (2012). *Aging: Concepts and controversies* (7th ed.). Thousand Oaks, CA: Sage.

Newman B. M., & Newman, P. R. (2012). *Development through life: A psychological approach* (11th ed.). Belmont, CA: Wadsworth/Thompson.

Nurmi, J. E. (1991). *The development offer-orientation in life-span context.* Helsinki, Finland: University of Helsinki.

Nurmi, J. E. (1992). Age differences in adult life goals, concerns and heir temporal extension: A life course approach to future-oriented motivation. *International Journal of Behavioral Development, 15,* 487–508.

Schaie, K. W., & Hofer, S. M. (2001). Longitudinal studies in aging research. In K. W. Schaie & J. E. Birren (Eds.), *Handbook of the psychology of aging* (pp. 53–77). San Diego, CA: Academic Press.

Schaie, K. W. (1996). *Intellectual development in adulthood. The Seattle Longitudinal Study.* Cambridge, UK: Cambridge University Press.

Sievert, L. L., & Obermeyer C. M. (2012). Menopause: Symptoms cluster at midlife a four-country comparison of checklist and qualitative responses. PUBMed. *U.S. National Library of Medicine, National Institute of Health 19*(2), 133–144. doi: 0b013e3182292af3

Staudinger, U. M., & Bluck, S. (2001). A view on midlife development from life-span theory. In M. E. Lachman (Ed.), *Handbook of midlife development* (pp. 3–39). New York, NY: Wiley.

Stone, A. A., Schwartz, J. E., Broderick, J. E., & Deaton, A. (2010). *A snapshot of the age distribution of psychological well-being in the United States.* Proceedings of the National Academy of Sciences, *107*(22), 9985–9990. Retrieved from http://dx.doi .org/10.1073/pnas.1003744107

Sue D., & Sue, D. (2008.). *Counseling the culturally diverse.* Hoboken, N.J: John Wiley.

Sue, D. W., Arredondo, P., & McDavis, R. J. (1992). Multicultural counseling competencies and standards: A call to reform the profession. *Journal of Counseling and Development, 70,* 477–486.

Van Hiel, A., Mervielde, I., & De Fruyt, F. (2006). Stagnation and generativity: Structure, validity, and differential relationships with adaptive and maladaptive personality. *Journal of Personality, 74*(2), 543–574.

Wethington, E., Kessler, R., & Pixley, J. (2004). Turning points in adulthood. In O. G. Brim, C. D. Ryff, & R. Kessler (Eds.), *How healthy are we? A national study of well-being in midlife* (pp. 586–61)1. Chicago, IL: University of Chicago Press.

Whitbourn, S. K., & Connolly, L. A. (1999). The developing self in middle. In S. L. Willis & J. D. Reid, *Life in the middle: Psychological and social development in middle age* (pp. 25–26). San Diego, CA: Academic Press.

Wiese, B. S., & Freund, A. M. (2005). Goal progress makes one happy, or does it? Longitudinal findings from the work domain. *Journal of Occupational and Organizational Psychology, 7,* 2–304.

Wong, W. D., & Wong, H. L. (2010). Chronic illness, disability, secondary conditions and the culturally diverse family. In J. D. Atwood, & C. Gallo, *Family therapy and chronic illness.* New Brunswick, NJ: Transaction.

Young, L. M., Baltes, B. B., & Pratt, A. K. (2007). Using selection, optimization, and compensation to reduce job-family stressors: Effective when it matters. *Journal of Business and Psychology, 21,* 511–539.

Zion, S., Kozleski, E., & Fulton, M. L. (2005). *Understanding culture.* Tempe, AZ: The National Institute for Urban School Improvement.

PART IV

Late Adulthood
(Ages 61 to 75)

12

Old age is like everything else. To make a success of it you have to start young.

F. Astaire

Late adulthood or "golden years" is not the period of dependency and deterioration that many people think it is. These are years to spend time with the family, grandchildren, and friends; putter in the garden; go fishing; or simply sip your coffee with no need to rush anywhere. These same late adulthood years can also be times of physical decline, mental challenge, and socioemotional loss. While the path experienced is clearly influenced by the conditions and context of one's life, it is also a reflection of the developmental path that one has taken to this point.

Although many people maintain that old age is a state of mind, there are several life events that signal the beginning of late adulthood. These are tied to chronology, just as other life events are in previous stages of the lifespan. This stage of the lifespan is a dynamic period with unique challenges and problems that deserve the attention of the counseling profession.

This chapter will review the uniqueness of this developmental period. After reading and discussing this chapter the reader will be able to

1. describe the natural transition into late adulthood and how aging may heighten the need for a more specific type of therapeutic counseling,

2. understand the application of age-appropriate gerontological skills that will enhance the counseling process with older adults,

3. describe older adults' lifespan events to be considered in their assessment and clinical counseling, and

4. explain the psychopathology and aging process in late adulthood.

Responding to the Counseling Needs of a Growing Aging Population

Photo 12.1   Intergenerational families have more support to offer to each other, and their quality of life is enhanced by their interaction.

Source: BananaStock/BananaStock/Thinkstock.

The drastic increase of the aging population in the United States has created a shift in society that will more than double the number of persons in late adulthood by 2020; approximately 16.5% of the population will be 65 years of age or older. This percentage is expected to increase to 20.8% by 2060 (U.S. Census Bureau, 2002).

This demographic change has been labeled the **"age wave,"** fueled by the **Baby Boomer** generation. The age wave is estimated to reach our communities and family structures in an unprecedented manner that will impact almost all aspects of our existence, including family structure, health care provision, economy, and sociopolitical system. Although improved human **longevity** is a great success, which offers exciting opportunities, it causes tremendous challenges as well. Among these challenges are the growing threats of mental health issues and chronic diseases associated with changing patterns of aging and the need for support systems, including gerontological counseling and elderly-care (Dychtward & Flower, 1990).

Longer lifespan has created an emergent need for trained professionals who provide services to older adults to enhance their quality of life and maximize their potentials. As indicated in Chapter 13, the social phenomenon recognized as the **"graying of America"** changes the fabric of every aspect of society and highlights the diversity of older adults and their specific needs (Himes, 2001).

The field of counseling, as it relates to gerontological counseling, will soon be responsible for a large number of older adults among over 40% of the U.S. population, which comprises a generation of Baby Boomers (Morgan, 1998). The number of adults 65 years old and older has raised awareness about this population's needs, challenging professionals in the **human services** and counseling fields to implement more effective therapeutic practices. These needs are evident within the counseling profession since the desire and growing demand for professional counseling services for older adults is experiencing a parallel increase. As indicated by Sinick (1976), unfortunately, the counseling profession has not been well-prepared to meet this demand because most counseling techniques, aids, and programs are designed for use with younger groups, covering a much shorter individual lifespan (pp.18–21). Taking into account this shift in demographics and human service needs, Myers (1981), concurs that currently there is a great need for the development of counseling services methods and aids specifically appropriate for use with older adults (p. 21).

Counseling older adults is not equivalent to counseling the general younger population. Specialized skills and knowledge, as well as sensitivity to the contexts in which older adults in late adulthood live and their lifespan experiences, are essential to working successfully with this population. For the counseling profession, it is important to acknowledge gerontological issues and what is referred to as the **normal aging** process in order to enhance counseling competencies. As indicated by the American Psychological Association (APA; 2009), as Baby Boomers continue their aging process over the next several years, one can expect both the needs and the demands for mental health services to increase. These needs may also be consequences of secondary chronic health conditions that are also likely to increase. Individuals in late adulthood have a higher prevalence of depression and other mental disorders when compare to other cohorts, like the **GI Generation** and **Great Depression** eras cohorts. In addition, clinical demands may change because this generation has typically been psychologically minded and relatively high consumers of mental health services, in spite of the notion of underutilization of these types of services by older adults.

The staggering increase of the late adulthood population presents a new challenge that generations before us have never experienced. This chapter provides an introduction to gerontological-based counseling, integrating the basic skills of working with older adults with counseling skills to address the multiple issues that are accumulated during this lifespan.

The Aging Process

Most theorists agree that there is no uniform aging process. In a broad sense, one might define that aging is "a total process that begins at conception," but aging is normally identified with changes that come after maturity (Meiner, 2011; Moody & Sasser, 2012). Aging can also be defined as the time-dependent series of cumulative, progressive, intrinsic, and harmful changes that begin to manifest themselves at reproductive maturity and eventually end with the end of life (Arking, 1998).

Accepting One's Life

One of the challenges in late adulthood is to accept life on its own terms. This challenge is also an accumulation of life events and the ability to resolve or accept issues affecting one's life, and, in many cases, the lives of others. Accepting one's life, particularly during late adulthood, is directly related to age and happiness. Some studies of adults have indicated that happiness increases with age (Rodgers, 1982); others demonstrate no differences in happiness for adults of different ages (Ingelhart, 2002); and yet others have found a *U*-shaped result with the lowest happiness occurring at 30 to 40 years of age (Mroczek & Kolarz, 1998). In addition, research findings suggest that, at least in the United States, adults ages 18 to 88 are happier as they age; therefore, accepting life throughout their lifespan can bring happiness in later life (Ehrlich & Isaacowitz, 2002; Reynolds, & Gatz, 2001; Yang, 2008).

Erik Erikson's theory of psychosocial development is highly regarded and a meaningful concept that is very useful in counseling assessment and application techniques. Erikson's (1950, 1982) final psychosocial development theory, as indicated in stage eight, **ego integrity versus despair**, ages 65 and older, involves a possible conflict of coming to terms with one's life, and it is related to accepting one's life (see Table 2.2, Chapter 2). As indicated in previous chapters, Erikson's theory explains eight developmental stages in which physical, cognitive, instinctual, and sexual changes combine to trigger an internal crisis, whose resolution results in either psychosocial regression or growth and the development of specific virtues or "inherent strength," which translates into wisdom.

CASE ILLUSTRATION 12.1 ERIKSON'S THEORY OF EGO INTEGRITY VERSUS DESPAIR

Instructions: According to Erikson's theory, personality development goes through a series of eight, hierarchically ordered stages. Associated with each stage is a psychosocial crisis that the individual either successfully resolves or fails to resolve. Failure results in incomplete development of the personality and inhibits further development of the personality. The final stage of Erikson's (1982) theory is matured adulthood (age 65 years and older). Below you will find a case illustration with Albert and Glenn. As your read the illustration, consider the various challenges as well as opportunities presented to both friends even at this later time in their lifespan development. Following the case there are a number of questions for your reflection and discussion. Discuss your observations with a classmate, colleague, or professor.

Albert and Glenn

Albert and Glenn have been friends since their high school days. Albert is 68, and Glenn is 69. Both had military and professional careers, married very young, and raised their families. Often, the two friends reminisce about the good old days to count their blessings and remember the difficult challenges of life. Albert is grateful for all that he has and looks forward to seeing his family grow and enjoy life. Glenn, on the other hand, while glad that he has a family, remembers more of the bad days and questions his contributions to his family and his future life. Glenn also complains about health issues and has removed himself from activities that he used to enjoy, instead spending more time by himself thinking about the end of life.

Practice Exercise:

1. How can you use Erikson's life stage to understand each of the friend's feelings?

2. What would you recommend to Glenn to do about his concerns about past and future life?

3. What is a significant difference between Albert and Glenn?

4. Is there a personal crisis that has not been resolved in one of the friends?

Life is a series of lessons and challenges which help us to grow, and Erikson's theory helps to explain this growth. Erikson believed if we see our lives as unproductive, feel guilt about our past actions, or feel that we have not accomplished our life goals, we become dissatisfied with life and develop feelings of hopelessness and despair, often leading to depression and extreme alienation. These feelings, while they could happen at any stage of the lifespan, are more evident in late adulthood when there are personal unresolved issues pending. See Table 12.1 Erikson's Psychosocial Development Theory, Stage 8 description of ego integrity versus despair.

Of interest to counseling is that older adults, who reach a sense of integrity, feel whole, complete, and satisfied with their achievements. This is an indication that they are resilient and have adapted to accomplishments and inevitable disappointments and realize the paths they have followed, abandoned, and never selected have been necessary for forming a meaningful life course. According to Erikson, Erikson, and Kivnick (1986), accepting one's life, based on the psychosocial model, involves specific steps and actions marked by different life stages that are more evident in late adulthood:

Table 12.1 E. Erikson's Psychosocial Development Theory

Stage 8: Integrity Versus Despair				
Life Stage	*Integrity*	*Despair*	*Virtue*	*Related Psychopathology*
Age 60 and older. Concern with life in late adulthood, quality of life, society, world events, meaning and purpose of life, personal life achievements, and acceptance by others.	Feeling at peace with oneself, others and the world. No regrets or recrimination.	Feeling regrets of wasted life and opportunities. Desiring the ability to turn back time to have a second chance in life, and fear of end of life.	Wisdom and renunciation. Calmness, tolerance, appropriate emotional detachment, non-projection, no regrets, non-judgment, peace of mind, spiritual and universal reconciliation, acceptance of inevitable departing life.	Extreme alienation and maladaptation. Feeling disdain, unfulfilled, blaming self and others, depression, mood changes, unsatisfied with past and present life. Disgusted with external world, and contemptuous of persons as well as institutions

Source: Adapted from information from Krauss, W. S. (2002). *The aging individual. Physical and psychological perspective* (2nd ed.).

1. Over the lifespan people confront the challenges of balancing and matching a variety of opportunities with fluctuations in resources.

2. Life satisfaction and a sense of well-being are linked to selecting specific goals as important areas of functioning and then effectively directing both internal and external resources in order to maximize their level of functioning.

3. Adaptation is needed and requires the integration of three processes:

    a. *Selection*—identifying opportunities or domains of activity that are of greatest value or importance

    b. *Optimization*—allocation and refining resources in order to achieve higher levels of functioning in the selected domains

    c. *Compensation*—under conditions of reduced resources, identifying strategies to counteract loss and minimize the negative impact on functioning in the selected domains (Erikson, Erikson, & Kivnick, 1986)

As in working with specific populations, there are some counseling implications to be considered and there are many theories and concepts that have been well researched and can have a beneficial application depending on the situation at hand. The following are some examples:

1. Application of Erikson's stages of psychosocial development helps in assessing client's symptomatic behavior in the context of painful and stressful past experiences and struggles with current developmental tasks.

2. The appropriate intervention and assistance from the counselor/therapist can provide an opportunity to rework early developmental stages, when clients' resolution to previous psychosocial stages has been so ineffective as to seriously compromise their late adulthood development (Sadock & Sadock, 2007, 63–69 & 75).

3. The objective of counseling is not only to help prevent future conflicts but to assist the client in finding solutions and emerging from each crisis with an increased sense of inner unity, good judgment, and the capacity to do well according to his or her own standards and to the standards of those who are significant to them (Erikson, 1968).

Late adulthood is the appropriate time to understand life events, why and how they happened, and accept life in a positive manner that will contribute to the well-being of the individual and others in later years. This is a stage of life where renewed and new life goals are set, and life satisfaction becomes a priority or concern.

Life Goals and Satisfaction

Individuals in late adulthood are no longer a portrait of the frail elderly of yesterday. Many live well into their 90s remaining robust older adults.

For many, the challenge is to embrace the degree to which their life goals have been met and to experience the satisfaction of a job well done. However, the opportunity to experience life satisfaction is influenced by an array of factors depending on the individual's life experience (Halisch & Geppert, 2001; Hooker & Siegler, 1993). There are external and personal influences, such as socioeconomic status and financial adequacy; psychological factors, like perceived heath status, vitality, sociability; or, as shown in a study by Harlow and Cantor (1996), participation in culturally valued tasks (e.g., community services and social life participation).

Large numbers of individuals in late adulthood are staying healthier longer and are functioning well at more advanced ages. Health and function are important lifespan issues, which require age-appropriate counseling and updated counseling skills. Life cycle and event-history have encountered new modifications as a result of the modernization of society.

As life expectancy increases, people plan their lives differently, set new goals, and, thus, change the timing, sequence, duration, and spacing of key events, including marriage and childbearing, education, work life, and retirement (Elder, 1985; Krecker, 1990), all of which have implications in late adulthood life satisfaction.

During late adulthood, individuals continue to aspire for new goals and attempt to achieve new levels of optimal functioning and autonomy. A person's life **goals** and needs may change over the course of late adulthood, depending on life circumstances, and contrary to facing a role-less future, older adults continue to formulate personal goals and assess their current life satisfaction in light of how well they are able to achieve those goals. The life journey through this stage of late adulthood development can also be the reason for individual confusion, higher expectations and demands, and a rush to do it all quickly. For counselors and clients, it is vital to understand the link between life goals and life satisfaction. It is important to consider the three aspects of life goals: **goal domains**, **goal orientation**, and **goal-related action** that are aligned with achieving valued goals to achieve life satisfaction. See Table 12.2. Aspects of Life Domains.

Some studies of goal domains include self-reliance or autonomy goals and leisure time and physical activity goals in their analyses of the link between life goals and life satisfaction (Straechan, Brawley, Spink, & Glazebrook, 2010; Wong & Lou,

Photo 12.2   Keeping active contributes to healthier lifestyles.

Source: Jupiterimages/Stockbye/Thinkstock.

Table 12.2 Aspects of Life Domains

Life Goal Domains	Life Goal Orientation	Goals-Related Actions
Social relationships and family	Agentic	Coping
Work and daily-living activities	Communal	Intentional self-development
Finances	Self-preservation	Cascading facilitation of related goals
Health and fitness	Well-being of others	Matching goals and activities
Leisure activities		
Self-reliance		

2010). For example, individuals in late adulthood show different patterns of investment in these goal domains and in the specific activities or achievements within domains. The combination of one's own culture and life experiences shapes an imagined self, moving into the future and how these life goals will be achieved. The counseling intervention will identify that as a person begins the process of accepting one's life in late adulthood, there is tendency to return to the personal goals that were envisioned at that earlier time in life in order to assess the extent to which they were realized, and perhaps to reevaluate their importance, given the 60 years or more of life that have transpired since the goals were formed (Cappeliz, 2008; Wong & Watt, 1991). In reference to goal orientation, in addition to the specific goals clients aspire to, the literature suggests that older adults differ in their goal orientation. Some individuals are more **agentic** in their goal striving, which is having the capacity to make choices. In cases of clients managing their anxiety to achieve new goals, the counselor may identify that client's important goals focus on achievement, power, and the expression of personal abilities. In other cases, clients are more **communal** in their goal striving, and their goals focus on intimacy, affiliation, and contributions to the moral community (Pohlmann, 2001). Some studies have contrasted goals that seem to emphasize self-preservation with those that focus on the interest in and well-being of others. One might look back, in Chapter 11, at the psychological crisis of middle adulthood, generativity versus stagnations, and consider that the profile of goals emerging from that period of life might differ for those who resolved the crisis in the direction of generativity compared with those who resolved it in the direction of stagnation with a different set of outcomes (Lapierr, Bouffard, & Basin, 1997).

In the process of older adults making progress on the developmental task of accepting their lives, they are able to integrate their goals and their goal-related activities in order to experience a sense of personal fulfillment. Goal-related actions, for those in late adulthood who have a strong sense of self-directed goals, strengthen life satisfaction and feed back into their life goals, reinforcing the individuals' sense of purpose and providing renewed energy. Individuals, during their late adulthood, find that their goals support one another, and that they can invest more energy in personal goal pursuits as their obligations to other competing roles and role demands decline (Riediger, Freund & Baltes 2005). When counselor and client are able to closely match the client's activities with valued goals, the client's life satisfaction most likely will improve. Case illustration 12.2 invites you to review the life of Tom Sullivan. As you do, look at evidence of the way Tom resolved his stagnation versus generativity crisis and is approaching his current state of late adulthood.

As evident in our case illustrations, one's life goals do not have to end at retirement. However, it is clear that with retirement one's occupational involvement needs to be replaced by other useful and satisfying activities (Havinghurst, 1960, 1972; Neugarten & Hagestad, 1976).

Well-Being and Personality

The well-being concept has been a topic of extensive research. Well-being represents a positive outcome that is meaningful to individuals and suggests that people perceive that their lives are going well. According to

CASE ILLUSTRATION 12.2 LIFE GOALS AND SATISFACTION

Instructions: Below you will find the case illustration of Tom Sullivan, a man well into his late adulthood. As your read the illustration, consider the various challenges as well as opportunities presented to Tom even at this later date in his lifespan development. Following the case there are a number of questions for your reflection and discussion. Share your observations with a classmate, colleague, or professor.

Tom Sullivan

Tom Sullivan grew up on farm in rural Kentucky, and he lived a life full of transitions and experiences until he was 99 years old. After receiving his bachelor's degree in education at the local state university, he taught school in a one-room schoolhouse for 2 years and then became principal of a high school in Indiana. He left the rural Midwest to attend Columbia University in New York, where he earned his PhD. He became a professor of history and taught at Ohio State University until he retired at age 65. Then, Tom and his wife, Sarah, bought an abandoned farm of several acres in Ohio, remodeled the farm house, and settled into farming. In the early years of retirement, he cleared and thinned the trees on the hills and mountains of his farm. After a while, he stopped working the hillsides, and with his wife, he planted a large vegetable and flower garden with a power tiller. When he was 80, he bought a riding tractor. When he could no longer manage the large garden, he focused on small border garden and four large window boxes that he and his wife planted with flowers. As his eyesight became more impaired, he shifted from reading to listening to talking books, and when he had to give up actually planting the window boxes, he enjoyed watering them and looking at the flowers. Sarah said that he never complained about any of his declining aging process changes. Tom approached each new challenge of physical decline by correctly assessing his abilities, investing in a new project, and taking pride in his achievements within that domain.

Practice Exercise:

1. Where might you see evidence of Tom transitioning from a position of generativity to one of ego integrity?

2. In this case, Tom drew on early life experiences growing up on a farm to guide his goals in later life. What are some other examples of how earlier life roles might be integrated into a satisfying lifestyle in late adulthood?

3. Based on the information provided, what do you think Tom's goals were in the later part of his life?

4. What are some of the resources Tom had that allowed him to achieve new goals for mastery?

Diener, Scollon, and Lucas (2009) and Frey and Stutzer (2002), well-being generally includes global judgments of life satisfaction and feelings ranging from depression to joy. While there is no consensus around a single definition of well-being, there is general agreement that at minimum, well-being includes the presence of positive emotions and moods (e.g., contentment and happiness), the absence of negative emotions (e.g., depression and anxiety), satisfaction with life, fulfillment, and positive functioning (Andrews & Witney, 1976; Ryff & Keyes, 1995). In simple terms, well-being can be described as judging life positively and feeling good about one's life. As such, well-being is highly subjective, and it is typically measured with self-reports (Larsen, Eid, & Diener, 2008).

While subjective reporting and personal experience is key to the identification of well-being, there have been some attempts to develop accurate scales and measures. For example, over the years, for public health surveillance purposes, the Centers for Disease Control and Prevention has measured well-being with different instruments, including some that are psychometrically based, utility-based, or with single items (CDC, 2012). The following Table 12.3 provides an overview of some the instruments that are frequently used by CDC for pubic surveillance purposes to measure well-being with different instruments including some that are psychometrically based, utility-based, or single items.

As there is no one measure or one clear definition of well-being, there is no single determinant of individual well-being. Rather, well-being is dependent upon good health, positive social relationships, and availability and access to basic resources (e.g., shelter, income, etc.). Consideration is given to some general findings on associations between well-being and its associations with other factors.

Tracking these conditions is important for counselors since the well-being of a client is of great importance for the counseling intervention. But because of the high degree of subjectivity connected to the experience of well-being, a counselor must not only assess the presence of supportive or challenging conditions but also assess the individual's experience with these conditions.

Well-Being and Health and Illness

While it may be obvious, it is important to note that health and the absence of illness are pivotal to an overall sense of one's well-being and life satisfaction. For the aged, concerns about health and illness center not only on

Table 12.3 Instruments for Surveillance of Well-Being

Survey	Questionnaires
National Health and Nutrition Examination Survey (NHANES)	General Well-Being Schedule (1971–1975)
National Health Interview Survey (NHIS)	Quality of Well-being Scale Global life satisfaction Satisfaction with emotional and social support Feeling Happy in the Past 30 Years
Behavioral Risk Factors Surveillance System (BRFSS)	Global life satisfaction Satisfaction with emotional and social support
Porter Novelli Health-Styles Survey	Satisfaction with life scale Meaning in life Autonomy, competence, and relatedness Overall and domain specific life satisfaction Overall happiness Positive and negative affect scale

Source: Adapted from CDC, 2012.

the inconvenience of illness but also on its social-psychological consequences, such as loss of personal autonomy and economic security. Poor health, more than other changes commonly associated with aging, can reduce a person's competence in mastering his or her environment and ultimately the person's quality of life (DeLozier & Gagnon, 1991).

Good health is more than merely the absence of disease or a chronic disabling condition. As defined by the World Health Organization (WHO, 2008), "good health is a state of complete physical, mental, and social well-being" The concept of health implies interaction and integration of body, mind, and spirit; a perspective that is reflected in the growth of health promotion programs and alternative medicine and one that is congruent with the concept of active aging (Hooyman & Kiyak, 2011). Within these areas, there is so much that counselors and an effective counseling intervention can do if requested by clients.

Among older adults, the most common complaints are cardiovascular disease, hypertension, arthritis, hearing impairment, cataracts, glaucoma, and lower back problems. Older adults also experience acute illnesses but less frequently than younger people. However, when they acquire an acute illness such as influenza, it tends to be more severe and of longer duration than it is among younger people. It is important for counselors to be familiar with the types of illnesses that are common among older adults in order to understand the symptoms and consequences and what other implications there might be that need to be addressed during the counseling process.

As in any damaging and long-term disabling condition, there are psychological implications such as feelings of helplessness, fear, and depression among many others. Counseling can have a significant impact on the way the affected client may react to the limitations posed by the condition and on developing coping skills and adapting to a new physical and mental condition.

Mental health issues among older adults continue to be a reason for clinical counseling and other related human services. One of the greatest fears people have about becoming old is that they will lose their mental capacities or become senile. **Senility**, in general terms, describes what many believe are the consequences of old age, such as loss of mental and emotional abilities, helplessness, and confusion and disorientation. Senility is technically referred to as **dementia** (Vinters, 2004).

Dementia is a global term for a variety of organic brain disorders related to brain cell impairment. The symptoms of these disorders can include disorientation of time, place, or people; memory loss; disturbances in thinking, especially in abstract thinking and reasoning; impairment of judgment; or inappropriate emotional responses (Saxon & Etten, 1978; Vinters, 2004).

It is important for counselors working with older adults to have knowledge of symptoms and psychological consequences of common health conditions that may affect individuals during their late adulthood, such as depression, anxiety, dementia, posttraumatic stress disorder (PTSD), and bipolar disorder, which are among the observed diagnoses of older adults. Dual diagnoses of alcohol, prescription drug addiction, or intoxication occur frequently, but sometimes they are not acknowledged as primary conditions or that they exist. Another serious issue with late adulthood clients is their medication management. Many elderly clients face a variety of medical problems (heart disease, blood circulation and hypertension, respiratory illness, infection, digestion, etc.).

Unfortunately, very frequently, other nonmedical professionals are consulted as a referral. However, it is the clinician counselor who becomes the client's advocate, as he or she sees the possible effects of the medications, noting that the client's functioning, thinking, acting, mobility, vision, hearing, or so on is impaired. Concerned counselors frequently become a conduit between the client and the physician with respect to medications' side effects and patient-doctor choices. The interdisciplinary team approach to provide services to older adults is very important, and counselors have an important role to play in this approach without overstepping professional boundaries.

Longevity Expectations

In biological terms, humans have a lifespan or potential longevity of nearly 120 to 125 years. Life expectancy depends on basic factors, such as having access to nutritional resources, being free of fatal diseases, avoiding environmental hazards, and eliminating extreme risks of poverty and civil unrest, just to mention a few. Among global communities, evaluations about life expectancy vary. As a result, people from different cultures have different concepts about longevity expectations. Some examples are life expectations when one is an older adult, or very old; how one ought to behave at a particular age; or what one may expect in terms of sociorewards at a given age based on sociocultural norms (Lehr, Seiler, & Thomae, 2000).

Improved health and increased longevity in societies may set in motion a self-perpetuating system of longevity extension (Carey & Judge, 2001). Based on the Centers for Disease Control and Prevention (CDC, 2012) data, the U. S. general average population life expectancy is 78.61 years, marking an increase of years of life expectancy to 77.1 years for men and 81.9 years for women. It is important to note that women over the age of 80 are the largest and oldest population within the late adulthood population. This fact emphasizes the urgent need for professionals specialized in gerontological counseling. In general, most people expect to reach a longevity that is desirable and trouble free from biological, psychological, social, and financial burdens.

Research conducted by Bloom and Canning (2000) on the health and wealth of nations suggests that with this increase in longevity, quality of life is a major concern. One strong reason is that nearly two thirds of older adults do not wish to live to the age of 100, because they do not think they could be that old and still enjoy a good quality of life. That consideration significantly influences the desired longevity. Top concerns about aging include poor health, inability to care for oneself, and losing mental acuity. Another major concern is the fear of being alone and isolated, which is linked to depression and other mental and physical health issues. Lack of financial security, ability to be mobile, and being a burden on others are also among the concerns. This is an area that counselors need to be aware of and competent to identify in order to help clients find solutions to alleviate these concerns from becoming a barrier to obtain the desired longevity and quality of life.

Photo 12.3   Developing friendships is vital for enhancing social networks among older women.

Source: Liz Gregg/Digital Vision/Thinkstock.

Aging: A Natural Transition and a Factor in Counseling

Developmental age maturation leads to relatively minor changes, such as slowing down, but also to greater emotional complexity and a wealth of life experiences upon which to draw (APA, 2009; McInnis-Dittrich 2009; Moody & Sasser, 2012). As a person ages, some unavoidable deterioration in physical, motor, and cognitive abilities takes place as a natural transition into aging. The rate and degree of deterioration appears to be individualized and commensurate with lifestyle, environment, culture, genetic factors, heredity, and other psychosocial issues. It is projected, that as the population, between the ages of 60 and 75, increases, the likelihood of reaching years of longevity to 90 and older will also increase. The need for comprehensive health care services, including mental health services, with concerns for appropriate and culturally based counseling, and psychotherapeutic approaches, to enhance well-being and quality of life, has become a significant challenge (Foos & Clark, 2008; McInnis-Dittrich, 2009 and; Moody & Sasser, 2012).

There are different concepts of age that are integral parts of understanding older adults. According to some lifespan experts, chronological age is not necessarily relevant to understanding a person's psychological development (Botwinick, 1978). We know, as is true for all developmental periods, there is a wide range of variability and individual differences that can be presented, and that a focus on chronological age can place more emphasis on limitations than on the continuum of human development (Baltes, 1987). However, considering the impact of the age as viewed from a wider perspective, one including chronological, biological, psychological, and social age, is essential for effective counseling with clients in this developmental period. And with this perspective, counseling modalities should be adapted to the client's situation depending on his or her lifespan experience, capabilities, and needs. This is very true when working with adults in late adulthood.

Expanding Our Perspective

One limitation of many developmental theories, as noted by Gatz, Popkin, Pino, and Vanden Bos (1985), is that they tend to focus on aging as only a time of loss. An alternative view of aging is that it is potentially a time of both positive and negative transitions and transformations. With this broader perspective, counselors can approach older adult clients differently, from a transformational rather than declining perspective as a foundation for understanding later life (Myers, 1990). This approach takes age into consideration as part of the lifespan but not as major factor that could turn into a negative outcome for both counselor and client. The focus instead can be on understanding the individual and his or hers needs.

Tailoring Counseling

The literature drawn from lifespan developmental psychology, social gerontology, gerontological counseling, and clinical counseling theories leads one to conclude that a **trans-theoretical framework** for understanding both the needs and challenges of an aging client and the types of approaches and interventions required is needed. As such, engagement of a multidisciplinary team is often most effective. Lichtenberg (1999), for example, noted that the high prevalence of medical disorders among individuals in late adulthood requires that more attention be given to physical causes of symptoms and **iatrogenic** effects of medications contributing to the problems being experienced. In addition, due to a higher prevalence of the dementias that occur in late life, some level of **neuropsychological screening** is essential, as well as comprehensive client assessment for counseling interventions (Myers & Sweeney, 2005).

When focusing on the specific engagement of counselor and counseling intervention, it is clear that counseling modalities and other types of psychotherapies need to be modified when working with individuals in late adulthood. These modifications should take into consideration the client's medical needs, social supports, level of cognitive functioning, and also the very rich lifespan experiences he or she brings to counseling. The major reasons for adapting counseling techniques and therapy modalities, when working with older clients, are not due to developmental differences but to context effects, cohort effects, and specific challenges common in late adulthood.

The ability to work with clients in late adulthood and to identify treatable aspects of their problems requires an understanding of the aging process, including the potential for decline and disability, as well as the possibilities for continued growth and change. Paul Baltes (1987, 1997) provides a number of key points regarding the dynamic interplay of growth and decline in later life.

1. *Aging as a multidimensional process.* Aging can best be viewed as the interaction of biological, psychological, and social processes. We typically think of aging as a biological process marked by outward signs such as gray hair and wrinkles, but aging also can occur in psychological and social realms. Psychologically, the ways people learn and process information change but not always for the worse. Likewise, people move through social roles and transitions such as having children and seeing them mature, leave home, and have children of their own. These types of psychological and social changes have a profound effect on what we think of as aging. Consistent with this multidimensional perspective, clinical work with older adults is carried out best by multidisciplinary teams that pay attention to the whole person and not just to one symptom or system (e.g., doctors, physical and occupational therapists, nurses, counselors, social workers, etc.).

2. *Age or disease?* It is important to distinguish aging from disease. The normal aging process, whether viewed at a biological, psychological, or social level, is relatively benign and does not lead to catastrophic changes. Rather, dramatic decline occurs as a result of disease. As an example, at one time, it was believed that aging eventually led to senility, and that everyone would become senile if they lived long enough. We now know that the syndrome of severe, progressive memory and intellectual decline that we call senility or senile dementia results from several different diseases, such as **Alzheimer's disease**, but it is not a universal part of growing older. The risk of Alzheimer's disease, like many other illnesses, increases with advancing age, but a majority of people at 80 or 100 years old do not suffer from this type of mental decline (Johansson & Zarit, 1997). Aging is associated with an increased risk of developing various diseases, but the aging process is not inherently pathological. For counseling interventions, this distinction between normal aging and disease has practical significance. There has been a tendency to view all older adults as experiencing negative changes (e. g., senility, rigidity, etc.), but that is not the case. The majority of older adults is relatively healthy and should not be construed as having diminished capacity in their ability to carry out everyday activities. In other words, counselors should not view all older adults as having changes typical of dementia or other diseases. Even in the face of some chronic diseases, older adults may retain the resiliency to make creative adaptations.

Guided Practice Exercise 12.1 Sharing the Experience of Aging

Instructions: Arrange to have conversation with a person older than 72. Explore the persons' experience of aging in relationship to aging as a life process and the concern, by some, that aging is a period of disease. Following are some examples of possible questions that you can use. Follow up by discussing your findings with your professor, students, or colleagues and compare the different opinions.

1. How does it feel to have reached your age?

2. Are you experiencing what you expected from this life period?

3. Did you make any plans to fit your expectations of old age?

4. With the success of longevity today, are you concerned with any potential diseases that might be due to the aging process?

5. What is your message to other younger people in reference to what to expect from aging?

3. *Development as an ongoing process.* As we have indicated throughout the text, the term *lifespan development* implies development and aging are a continuing process. Development does not stop at particular age but continues throughout life. Although there can be decline, there is also the possibility of continued growth. People do not lose the capacity to grow or change at a particular age, whether at 50 or even 90. There are certain considerable individual differences in the degree of openness to new ideas and change. Some people at 20 or 30 are rigid and fixed in their ways, whereas others can demonstrate creative potential despite their age.

4. *Continuity in development.* As we observe people over time, we find evidence for both continuity and change in psychological functioning. How people function in the present is usually consistent with how they performed in the past. People do not take in a different persona or different qualities when they become old. There is no single or universal pattern of mental decline, nor do people enter a stage of life in which their behavior can be explained by a single rule or formula. Rather, as a person growths older, there is continuity with their previous life. An older person who is demanding and angry is likely to have been so when younger. Likewise, someone old who is vitally involved in everyday life most likely was like that earlier in life. In fact, personality characteristics are "age blind"; that is, they remain relative stable throughout adulthood (Costa & McCrae, 1998). The findings of continuity have practical importance for counselors who work with older adults. Understanding an older person means knowing about that person's past, including experiences, preferences, values, beliefs, hopes, and fears. Even when working with someone with severe chronic conditions, such as Alzheimer's disease, finding out about the person's past is important to developing a good relationship and providing effective therapeutic counseling.

5. *Patterns of change with aging.* There is unavoidable change throughout the lifespan. The changes that occur with aging can be viewed in two ways: as *interindividual* differences and as *intraindividual* differences. Interindividual differences refer to the ways that people differ from one another. There are many sources of interindividual differences, including aging, cultural background or ethnicity, prior experience, or other factors. People may also differ from one another on some ability due to their education or other factors. The rate at which abilities change can also vary from one person to the next. Intraindividual changes refer to the changes an individual experiences over time. People experience age-related changes at different time rates for different abilities. As an example, someone may experience a decline in cardiovascular fitness, which leads to limited mobility, but still be able to perform well at intellectual tasks. In other words, changes in abilities are often specific rather than global.

6. *Compensation for decline.* One of the most important aspects of aging is the ability to compensate for decline. Baltes (1987) calls this process "selective optimization with compensation." One of the earliest and most predictable changes with aging is a decline in reaction time, which typically begins around age 30. Although there are considerable interindividual differences in the rate of change in reaction time, individuals in late adulthood consistently perform worse on speed tasks than younger people. Older adults are able to use their experiences to offset an age-related decline in reaction time, suggesting that selective optimization with compensation is a common process (Salthouse, 1990).

7. *Improving with age: plasticity and training.* One important consideration is that change does not always involve decline. People can improve their performance on particular abilities through experience and training. Training can be used to overcome decline due to inactivity or lack of practice. It can also be used to demonstrate plasticity, that is, the capacity for new growth (Staudinger, Marsiske, & Baltes, 1995). There is clear evidence of plasticity in cognitive abilities of older adults. Older adults trained in skills that would help their performance on either fluid intelligence tasks, which are generally affected more by aging, or crystallized intelligence tasks, which tend to be stable with age, can perform their activities of daily living with fewer limitations. The possibility for plasticity and its limits can be demonstrated by testing the limits by pushing the client to higher levels of performance (Li, Schmiedek, Huxhold, Röcke, Smith, & Lindenberger, 2008).

There are significant implications of clinical counseling treatment and several challenges in planning and implementing treatment for late adulthood. An important consideration is to identify treatable aspects of the problem. As previously stressed, older adults retain the capacity to change even in the face of significant illness

---

Guided Practice Exercise 12.2 Ability to Compensate Decline

One of the most important aspects of aging is the ability to compensate for decline. Baltes (1987) called this process "selective optimization with compensation." One of the earliest and most predictable changes with aging is a decline in reaction time. Older adults are able to use their experiences to offset an age-related decline in reaction time, suggesting that selective optimization with compensation is a common process (Salthouse, 1990).

1. Give a brief description and example of the process Baltes explains as "selective optimization with compensation."

2. In what ways can the normal aging process contribute to a better understanding of gerontological counseling in later life?

3. When working with clients in their late adulthood, there are several assessment issues that need to be taken into consideration. Describe two of these assessment issues.

---

or difficult situations. However, due to prevailing stereotypes about aging, older adults are often regarded as untreatable clients who cannot respond to counseling as a treatment. Sometimes the gains will be slow and limited but important. It may not be possible to restore someone to a prior level of functioning, but treatment can nonetheless make the situation significantly better. For individuals diagnosed with dementia, it is currently not possible to do much to reverse the underlying illness, but with clinical counseling it is possible to make changes in the psychosocial aspects of the problem. Family caregivers can also learn more effective strategies for managing behavior problems associated with dementia or identify support and assistance available so that the daily care demands resting on them become more manageable (Zarit & Zarit, 1998).

Counseling Clients in Late Adulthood

As the number of older adults increases, counselors are in a position to serve as a valuable resource to not only intervene and assist individuals in overcoming the challenges they encounter but also to serve as advocates for the aged, stimulating the creation of social support programs and networks. Counselors can contribute to enhance their clients' intellectual, social, and emotional well-being. Equipped with facts about the myths and realities of aging, knowledgeable about the challenges older adults face, aware of how to assess and treat older persons, and familiar with broader professional issues in aging, counselors can greatly impact and assist this significant and diverse segment of our society.

A review of the counseling and gerontological literature and the principles of geropsychology might lead one to conclude that the way to help individuals in late adulthood with personal challenges involves working on their behalf with formal and informal supporters, such as family and health care and social services providers.

It is valid to say that we can find a growing body of both statistical data and anecdotal material indicating that older adults who receive counseling help are willing and able to make good use of the therapeutic relationship, often making significant changes in behavior and attitudes (Brink, 1986; Butler & Lewis, 1982; Myers & Schwiebert, 1996). While there may be barriers to successful treatment, counseling older adults on an individual basis is appropriate and worthwhile, and it is provided by professionals who have a solid grounding in both gerontological counseling knowledge and clinical training.

The counselor of today's aging society must understand normal aging and common problems of aging, including normal and pathological biological losses, many of which can have a significant impact on behavior, mood, and physical capabilities. Special consideration must be given to the fear of, and the actuality of, loss of power, role change, prestige, and independence. Reviewing past accomplishments and pointing out what the older adult client is to some extent successfully coping with often enables the client to mobilize strengths and capabilities. At the same time, understanding the importance of what Lowy (1989) calls the "continuum of dependence and independence" and recognizing ways in which necessary dependence can be used constructively cannot be overlooked. Clients often must be guided to admit to themselves that accepting some help is a sign of strength rather than weakness. For example, having an emergency response system may make it possible to remain in one's own home, while denial of need for this assistance can lead to unsafe situations that result in otherwise unnecessary institutionalizations.

In order to work well with older adults, the counselor should have certain personal qualities. The primary characteristic, of course, is that the counselor must have a capacity for fondness toward older adults and must be able to see them as having capabilities and strengths, while still being able to see each individual objectively. Counselors need to come to terms with their own feelings and to take constructive action on their own personal issues of aging if they are committed to helping elderly clients. Younger upcoming counselors, who lack this advantage, can learn a great deal by listening to and observing older clients and practitioners, by looking critically at their own biases and stereotypes, and, when necessary, by seeking professional consultation. This could be called *age responsiveness*.

Counselors who choose to work in this field understand that the knowledge base and the actual practice of gerontological counseling is constantly expanding and changing. Learning more about life review, the continuity theory of normal aging (Atchley, 1989), behavior modification, and group therapy, for instance, can help to modify and expand the counseling approach to fit the needs of each client. As we learn more about medical advances, nutrition, or physical activity and the impact on aging, we can be more helpful as well. Emphasizing what kind of person the counselor should be and what kind of basic knowledge is needed is in the long run more significant than applying any one theoretical treatment approach to day-by-day practice. This will also contribute positively to the counselor's own identity in a profession that cares for all populations.

Principles Guiding Practice

What does the increase in the number of the population in late adulthood mean to the counseling profession? It means that due to the demand for counseling services, more and more counselors will be working with the aging population. According to Myers and Schwiebert (1996), most counselors have had very little training and experience in this area. Examining the typical profile of clients in their late adulthood can help us to interact with and understand this population. Seligman and Csikszentmihaly (2000) suggested the following steps based on case-by-case priority:

1. Counselors need to examine the demands for counseling by older adults. As stated previously, being an older adult has a unique set of issues associated with lifespan and life events. Furthermore, the life events and experiences of someone during early developmental stages can certainly influence the person's attitude, perception, and worldview for the long term. Counselors use knowledge acquired and empathy much of the time in their daily work, for example, when adults counsel children and teenagers, when women counsel men, when nondisabled counselors counsel persons with disabilities, or when White counselors work with clients of different races and ethnicities. Knowledge, the desire to help, and empathy can go a long way in the work that counselors do for older adult clients.

2. Counselors can look at the effects of and frequency of losses that elderly clients experience and the associated grief over those losses including negative physical and mental consequences. One of the counseling

skills is to be aware of the grief cycle and how to help clients work through this situation. The difference with this situation is the frequency and magnitude of losses the elderly client is experiencing. While processing one loss, the client often experiences another loss. In order to help the client who is in an almost continuous state of grief or depression, the counselor must try to help the client to open up those feelings and move past the pain and toward acceptance. Another important consideration is that older adult clients might be resistant to accept counseling. They know little about how the therapeutic process works, and they may have little confidence in the outcome of counseling. Common statements heard are *At my age, why would I need counseling?* or *What can the counselor do for me?* In addition to trying to help the client to make the transition through grief, the counselor is also teaching the client about the counseling process and helping to gain confidence in the process at the same time.

3. Counselors should provide effective and clear communication. Age-sensitive communication skills must be developed to achieve greater effectiveness in assisting older adults. These skills should be guided by research findings on the development changes related to normal aging. Communicating with older clients is an important component of the counselor-client relationship and the therapeutic intervention. Frequently, individuals during their late adulthood experience some form of hearing loss, sometimes moderate, but often severe. This hearing loss sometimes is denied and often makes normal verbal communication a real challenge.

In approaching one's work with an aged client, the following set of principles can serve as a useful guide (Giordano, 2000). These principles are governed by the intention to preserve self-esteem and to clarify the needs of elderly clients. By using this approach with the older adult, the practitioner will achieve an effective communication process that generates accurate information, supports self-determination, and achieves a therapeutic process:

1. Physical aging-related changes can affect communication and understanding. Continue the dialogue on a topic for a while rather than shifting topics.

2. Listen to more than words since all behaviors are a form of communication. Pay attention to nonverbal clues including tone of voice, eye contact, body language, and personal care.

3. Be aware of your own nonverbal messages. Hearing loss makes voice sound and message difficult to understand; patience and speaking clearly is necessary.

4. Allow time for conversation as well as other information gathering. It is important to face the person when talking and to not leap in if there is a pause.

5. Encourage the use of an assistive listening device (hearing aids or phone voice amplifiers). This can improve communication in person and by phone.

6. Do not down-talk the client by using children's talk or child-like vocabulary. Always use age-appropriate language.

In addition to the above, it is also helpful to remain flexible, especially in terms of scheduling. Counseling appointments with older adults may be a challenge as well. Clients may have problems remembering or keeping appointments, making regular sessions a hit-or-miss affair. It is not unusual for elderly clients to have transportation problems, such as needing assistance to get to the counseling office or clinic, getting lost on the way even after a prior visit, or just not being mobile. Often, when working with elderly clients with some of these issues, you may find that the additional problems seem to negate any progress you and the clients are making. Carrying out the therapy sessions at their residences may diminish some of these losses; however, counselor and client may feel some of the professionalism may be compromised by not holding the sessions in the counselor's office.

Culturally Based Concepts of Aging

The cultural diversity of older adult clients adds an exciting and challenging element to the practice of counseling. Each client comes from a cultural context with a unique blend of values and beliefs. This uniqueness affects all aspects of the client's life, including the person-environment dimension. The ways in which a person interacts with family members, communicates, and views the future are in many ways the result of past experiences and the expectations of the people with whom that person comes in contact. Culture is learned or acquired through socialization. Culture is not carried in a person's genetic makeup; rather, it is learned over the course of a lifetime. Obviously, then, the context and environment in which each person lives are central to his or her culture. A person's environment may demand or offer opportunities for some types of behaviors and restrict opportunities for other types. Cultural influences shape how we perceive aging in humans and so do social factors, such as the ability to perform certain jobs and duties, family and community roles, social policies, and support programs among others.

Older adults from diverse cultural and ethnic backgrounds constitute the faster-growing segment of age 60 and over in the United States. The number of elderly minority groups currently represents over 10% of all older adults, and they will account for more than 15% of older adults by 2030 (CDC, 2012). Although the White elderly population will represent the majority of the aged population, minority elderly will become "an even larger and more important component of the aging in America" (Angel & Hogan, 1991)

As effective and ethical counselors, we need to be culturally responsive and competent when working with diverse groups, regardless of age and background. It is significant for counselors to understand that the cohort of culturally diverse individuals in their late adulthood has experienced a unique history, typically including substantial family and social involvement, problems associated with immigrant status, as well as great perseverance in the face of racism and institutionalized prejudice (Hooyman & Kiyak, 2011). The unique assets and problems of minority elders have, to a large extent, been ignored by mainstream social scientists, policy makers, and service providers. There is a need for accurate, relevant knowledge regarding culturally diverse elders, in order to assure that the needs of all older adults are adequately met and understood (AoA, 2008). This emphasizes the argument that counselors of today and tomorrow must acquire the competencies and skills needed to understand the complexity of the aging population and its diverse nature in culture, ethnicity, lifestyle, and life experience through the lifespan. Before attempting to provide counseling, as a therapeutic intervention, to individuals in their late adulthood from diverse backgrounds, one must become aware of and analyze one's own prejudices and biases about the dimensions of life that create diversity. See below Guided Practice Exercise 12.3 Attitude Self-Analysis. Reflect and practice answering these questions about yourself and practice as a counselor.

Guided Practice Exercise 12.3 Attitude Self-Analysis

Self-Analysis	Yes	No	Need Improvement	Need Training and Information
1. Do I believe it is important to consider culture when counseling clients in their late adulthood?				
2. Am I willing to lower my defenses and take risks to help older adult clients?				

Self-Analysis	Yes	No	Need Improvement	Need Training and Information
3. Am I willing to practice behaviors that may feel unfamiliar and uncomfortable to benefit the older adult client with whom I am working?				
4. Am I willing to set aside some of my own cultural and valued beliefs to make room for others whose values are unknown to me?				
5. Am I willing to change the ways I think and behave when working with culturally different older adult clients?				
6. Am I sufficiently familiar with my own heritage, including place of family origin, language(s) or dialect spoken, time of and reasons for immigration to the USA.?				
7. What values, beliefs, and customs are identified with my own cultural heritage?				
8. In what ways do my beliefs, values, and customs interfere with my ability to understand those of other people?				
9. Do I view adults in late adulthood as a resource in understanding their cultural beliefs, family dynamics, and views of counseling?				
10. Do I encourage elder adults to use resources from their cultures that they see as important?				

CASE ILLUSTRATION 12.3 CULTURALLY BASED CONCEPTS OF AGING

Instructions: Below you will find the case illustration of Living in the New Culture, related to a couple, Olga and Antonio, well into their late adulthood. As your read the illustration, consider the various challenges as well as opportunities presented to both at this late cycle of their lifespan and individual

(Continued)

(Continued)

development. Following the case, there are a number of questions for your reflection and discussion. Share your understanding and observations with a classmate, colleague, or professor.

Living in the New Culture

Tony emigrated from Peru 12 years ago. It was expected that he would quickly settle in the new country and sponsor his parents, Olga and Antonio, to come to the United States. It took 9 years to reunite this family, during which time Tony married his college American girlfriend and had two children. Tony sponsored his parents to immigrate to the United States but could not sponsor his younger sister and brother. Antonio, now 66 years old, was a tailor and expected to find work and be able to continue to support his wife as well as to contribute to the overall family expenses. After some searching, he found work at the neighborhood cleaners. As expected by the Hispanic culture, Olga looked forward to contributing to the care of the new family home by helping her daughter-in-law with the grandchildren and household chores, but her daughter-in-law felt that Olga's assistance was not needed because that was her responsibility. Olga felt that maybe she had done something that offended her daughter-in-law, but she continued to be agreeable and helpful. Just as life was beginning to settle down, Tony announced to his parents that he had found them an apartment in a senior housing building several blocks away.

Olga and Antonio could not understand why they were being sent away. Tony, his wife, and their older grandson called frequently and visited them often. On weekends, they were invited to Tony's house to visit or for lunch. Other than for birthdays and holidays, these were the only times they spent together as a family. Definitely, that was not the way that it was in Peru with the family. There were social activities in the senior housing building, but Olga and Antonio did not become involved because of their language limitations. Olga was very uncomfortable with her limited English. She did not want to meet anyone in the building and got nervous when anyone knocked at the door. She never went out unless Antonio could go with her. Antonio began to make friends at work, and his English quickly improved. He tried to convince Olga that she needed to meet people and make friends. Olga became quite irritable and unfriendly. Her isolation increased, and she constantly expressed how much she missed her other children in Peru and her family home. She began to withdraw from her husband and Tony and his family. Her daughter-in-law mentioned counseling for Olga, but Tony and Antonio did not think Olga would agree to see a counselor.

Practice Exercise:

1. If Olga goes for counseling, what should the counselor know about Olga's background and expectations?

2. How can Olga be helped to understand her new life situation?

3. What should the family do to help Olga? Is it a conflict of cultures? Explain.

4. How would you, as a counselor, guide Olga to prevent her from serious mental health issues?

SUMMARY

- The developmental tasks of late adulthood focus on adjusting to the aging process and to role changes occurring at this stage of life.
- The challenges faced by this population become a concern for the counseling profession.
- There is an increasing need for counselors to become knowledgeable about aging and how this life transition can affect the counseling process.
- The lifespan and longevity changes pose both positive and negative influences on counseling therapy with older adults.
- The final psychological conflict of Erikson's theory, ego integrity versus despair, involves coming to terms with one's life.
- Adults who arrive at a sense of integrity feel whole and satisfied with their achievements.
- Despair occurs when elders feel time is too short to find an alternate way to reach integrity.
- Counselors working with older adults should learn about issues in aging, including chronic illnesses and their psychological impact, adherence to medical treatment, and assessing behavioral signs of side effects of medical reactions.
- Working with older adults involves specialized knowledge and specialized skills compared with other areas of psychotherapeutic and counseling practices where physical problems and the physical dimension of the person can be ignored.
- Some modalities of counseling argue that psychotherapy with older adults may be quite different from psychotherapy with younger adults, but that the source of most of these differences is not the developmental stage of the client.
- Greater influences on working with older adults are likely to arise from the contextual factors and from the specific challenges of later life. These contexts exert considerable influence over the lives, and the presenting problems, of clients in late adulthood.
- The specific challenges of late adulthood life include chronic illness, disability, quality of life, the higher prevalence of grief among the elderly, and the frequency with which older adults function as caregivers for other older adults.
- Some aging challenges require specialized responses such as neuropsychological assessment for dementia, assessment of remaining cognitive functioning, rehabilitation counseling, comfort with doing grief work, and familiarity with the dynamics of the caregiving family.
- During the counseling practice, the pace of counselor-client conversation with some clients may need to somewhat simple and slower.
- Counselors should express interest and openness about the culture and ethnic heritage of older adult clients and assess the level of comfort clients have in speaking about it.
- It is important to ask older adult clients to help you to understand their cultural heritage.
- Contextual differences refer to the ways in which age-specific social settings affect older adults in therapy.

ADDITIONAL RESOURCES

Websites

AARP Internet Resources on Aging—A link to the 1,200+ best sites for people age 50+. http://www.aarp.org/research/internet_resources/.

For an overview of resources and ideas about Erikson's stages of lifespan development, visit http://webspace.ship.edu/cgboer/erikson.html.

Recent report on healthy aging in America, see http://www.cdc.gov/chronicdisease/resources/publications/aag/aging.htm.

"The State of Aging and Health in America" (2007) at http://www.globalaging.org/health/us/2007/saha2007.pdf.

The Brookings Institute provides a timely article, "Mapping the Growth of Older America: Seniors and Boomers in the Early 21st Century" available at http://www.brookings.edu/research/papers/2007/06/12demographics-frey.

RECOMMENDED SUPPLEMENTAL READINGS

The following texts provide overviews of the aging populations in the United States, including various counseling approaches when working with older adults using basic counseling skills:

Depp, C., & Jeste, D. V. (2006). Definitions and predictors of successful aging: A comprehensive review of the literature. *American Journal of Geriatric Psychiatry, 14,* 6–20.

Feldman, D. B., & Periyakoil, V. S. (2006). Posttraumatic stress disorder at end of life. *Journal of Palliative Medicine, 9*(1), 213–218.

Hooyman, N. R., & Kiyak, H. A. (2011). Social gerontology: A multidisciplinary perspective (9th ed.). Boston, MA: Allyn & Bacon.

Lichtenberg, P.A. (2010). *Handbook of assessment in clinical gerontology* (2nd ed.). Cambridge, MA: Elsevier Press.

Worden, J.W. (2008). *Grief counseling and grief therapy: A handbook for the mental health practitioner* (4th Ed.). New York: Springer.

REFERENCES

Administration on Aging (AoA). (2008). *A profile of older Americans.* Washington, DC: U.S. Department of Health and Human Services. Retrieved from www. AoA.gov.

American Psychological Association (APA). (2009). *Psychotherapy and older adults guide.* Retrieved from http://www.apa.org.

Andrews, F. M., & Withey S. B. (1976). *Social indicators of well-being* (pp. 63–106). New York, NY: Plenum Press.

Angel, J. L., & Hogan, D. P. (1991). The demography of minority populations. In *Minority elders: Longevity, economic and health, building a public policy base* (pp. 1–13). Washington, DC: Gerontological Society of America.

Arking, R. (1998). *Biology of aging: Observations and principles* (2nd ed.). Sunderland, MA: Sinauer.

Atchley, R. C. (1989). Continuity theory of normal aging. *The Gerontologist, 29*(2), 183–190.

Baltes, P. B. (1987). Theoretical propositions of life-span developmental psychology: On the dynamics between growth and decline. *Developmental Psychology, 23,* 611–626.

Baltes, P. B. (1997). On the incomplete architecture of human ontogeny: Selection, optimization, and compensation as foundations of developmental theory. *American Psychologist, 52,* 366–380.

Bloom, D. E., & Canning, D. (2000). The health and wealth of nations. *Science* 287: 1207–1209.

Botwinick, J. (1978). *Aging and behavior* (2nd ed.; pp. 15–27). New York, NY: Springer.

Brink, T. L. (1986). *Clinical gerontology: A guide to assessment and intervention.* New York: Haworth Press.

Butler, R. N., & Lewis, M. (1982). *Aging and mental health.* (3rd ed.). St. Louis, MO: C. V. Mosby.

Cappeliz, P. M. (2008). Functions of reminiscence and emotional regulation among older adults. *Journal of Aging Science 22*(3), 266–272.

Carey, J. R., & Judge, D. S. (2001). Lifespan extension in humans is self-reinforcing: A general theory of longevity. *Population and Development* Review, *27,* 411–436.

Centers for Disease Control and Prevention (CDC). (2012). *National Center for Health Statistics fastStats.* Retrieved from: http://www.cdc.gov/nchs/fastats/lifexpec.htm.

Costa, P. T., Jr., & McCrae, R. R. (1998). Personality in adulthood: As six-year longitudinal study of self-reports and spouse rating on the NEO personality inventory. *Journal of Personality and Social Psychology, 54,* 853–863.

DeLozier, J. E., & Gagnon, R. O. (1991). *Utilization of ambulatory care in the United States.* Atlanta, GA: U.S. Department of Health and Human Services.

Diener E, Scollon C. N., & Lucas R. E. (2009). The evolving concept of subjective well-being: The multifaceted nature of happiness. In E. Diener (Ed.), *Assessing well-being: The collected works of Ed Diener* (pp. 67–100). New York, NY: Springer.

Dychtward, K., & Flower, J. (1990). *The age wave: How the most important trend of our time can change your future.* New York, NY: Doubleday Dell.

Ehrlich, B. S., & Isaacowitz, D. M. (2002). Does subjective well-being increase with age? *Perspectives in Psychology 5,* 20–26. Retrieved from http://dolphin.upenn.edu/upsych/journal.html.

Elder, G. H. J. (1985). Perspectives on the life course. In G. H. F Elder (Ed.), *Life course dynamics* (pp. 23–49). Ithaca, NY: Cornell University Press.

Erikson. E. (1950). Childhood and society. New York, NY: Norton.

Erikson, E. (1968). *Identity: Youth and crisis.* New York, NY: Norton.

Erikson, E., Erikson, J., & Kivnick, H. (1986). *Vital involvement in old age.* New York, NY: Norton.

Erikson, E. H. (1982). *The life cycle completed: A review.* New York, NY: Norton.

Foos, P. W., & Clark, M. C. (2008). *Human aging* (2nd ed.). Boston, MA: Allyn & Bacon.

Frey B. S., & Stutzer A. (2002). *Happiness and economics.* Princeton, NJ: Princeton University Press.

Gatz. M., Popkin, S. J., Pino, C. D., & Vanden Bos, G. R. (1985), Psychological interventions with older adults. In J. E. Birren & K. W. Schaie (Eds.), *Handbook of the psychology of aging.* New York, NY: Van Nostrand Reinhold.

Giordano, J. A. (2000). Effective communication and counseling with older adults. *International Journal of Aging and Human Development, 51*(4):315–324.

Halisch, F., & Geppert, U. (2001). Motives, personal goals and life satisfaction in old age. In A. Efklides, J. Kuhl, & R. Sorrentino (Eds.), *Trends and prospectus in motivation research* (pp. 389–409). *Max Planck Institute for Psychological Research.* Dordrecht, Netherland: Kluwer.

Harlow, R. C., & Cantor, N. (1996). Still participating after all these years: A study of life task participation in later life. *Journal of Personality and Social Psychology, 71*(6), 235–1249.

Havinghurst, J. R. (1960). Life beyond family and work. In E.W. Burger *Aging in Western societies* (3rd ed.; pp. 299–353). Chicago, IL: Chicago University Press.

Havinghurst, J. R. (1972). *Developmental tasks and education* (3rd ed.). New York, NY: David McKay.

Himes, C. L. (2001). Elderly Americans. *Population Bulletin, 56* (4), 4.

Hooker, K., & Siegler, I. C. (1993). Life goals, satisfaction and self-rated health: Preliminary findings. *Experimental Aging Research, 19,* 97–110.

Hooyman, N. R., & Kiyak, H. A. (2011). Social gerontology: A multidisciplinary perspective (9th ed). Boston, MA: Allyn & Bacon.

Ingelhart R. (2002). Gender, aging, and subjective well-being. *International Journal of Comparative Sociology; 43*(3–5):391–408. Retrieved from http://www.sagepub.com/home.nav.

Johansson, B., & Zarit, S.H. (1997). Early cognitive markers of the incidence of dementia and mortality: A longitudinal population-based study of the oldest old. *International Journal of Geriatric Psychiatry, 12,* 53–59.

Krauss, W. S. (2002). The aging individual. Physical and psychological perspective (2nd ed.). New York, NY: Springer.

Krecker, M. L., & Orand, A. M. (1990). Concepts of the life-cycle: Their history, meaning and uses in the social sciences. *Annual Review of Sociology, 16,* 241–262

Larsen, R. J., Eid, M., & Diener, E. (2008). The science of subjective well-being. In R. J. Larsen & M. Eid (Eds.), *The science of subjective well-being* (pp. 1–12). New York, NY: Guildford Press.

Lapierr, S., Bouffard, L., & Basin, E. (1997). Personal goals and subjective well-being in later life. *The International Journal of Aging and Human Development, 45,* 287–303.

Lehr, U., Seiler, E., & Thomae, H. (2000). Aging in a cross-cultural perspective. In A. L. Comunian & U. P. Gielen (Eds.), International perspective of human development (pp. 571–589). Lengerich, Germany: Pabst Science.

Li, S. C., Schmiedek, F., Huxhold, O., Röcke, C., Smith, J., Lindenberger, U. (2008). Working memory plasticity in old age: Practice gain, transfer, and maintenance. *Psychology and Aging, 23*(4), Dec 2008, 731–742. Doi: 10.1037/a0014343

Lichtenberg, P. A. (1999). *Handbook of assessment in clinical gerontology.* Hoboken, NJ: Wiley.

Lowy, L. (1989). Independence and dependence in aging: A new balance. *Journal of Gerontological Social Work, 13*(3/4).

McInnis-Dittrich, K. (2009). Social work with older adults: A biophysical approach to assessment and intervention (3rd ed.). Boston, MA: Allyn & Bacon.

Meiner, S. E. (2011). *Gerontologic nursing* (4th ed.). St. Louis, MO: Elsevier.

Moody, H. R., & Sasser, J. R. (2012). *Aging: Concepts and controversies.* (7th ed) Thousand Oaks, CA: SAGE.

Morgan, D. (1998). Facts and figures about the baby boom. *Generations, 22*(1), 10–15.

Mroczek, D. K., & Kolarz, C. M. (1998). The effect of age on positive and negative affect: A developmental perspective on happiness. *Journal of Personality and Social Psychology, 75,* 1333–1349.

Myers, J. E. (1990). Aging: An overview for mental health counselors. *Journal of Mental Health Counseling, 12*(3), 245–259. Retrieved from http://www.sagepub.com/home.nav.

Myers, J. E., & Loesch, L. C. (1981). *Counseling needs of older persons.* Alexandria, VA: American Counseling Association.

Myers, J. E., & Schwiebert, V. L. (1996). *Competencies for gerontological counseling. Social and Cultural Foundations of Aging.* Alexandria, VA: The American Counseling Association.

Myers, J. E., & Sweeny, T. J. (2005). *Counseling for wellness: Theory, research, and practice.* Alexandria, VA: American Counseling Association.

Neugarten, B. L., & Hagestad, G. O. (1976). Age and the life course. In R. H. Binstcok & E. Shanas (Eds.), *Handbook of aging and the social sciences* (pp. 35–55). New York, NY: Van Nostrand.

Pohlmann, K. (2001). Agency and communication orientation in life goals: Impacts on goal pursuit strategies and psychological well-being. In P. Schmuck & K. M. Sheldon (Eds.), *Life goals and well-being: Towards a positive psychology of human striving* (pp. 68–84). Ashland, Ohio: Hogrefe and Huber.

Reynolds, C., & Gatz, M. (2001). Age-related differences and change in positive and negative affect over 23 years. *Journal of Personality and Social Psychology, 80*(1), 136–151.

Riediger, M., Freund, A. M., & Baltes, M. (2005). Managing life through personal goals: Inter-goal facilitation and intensity of goal pursuit in younger and older adulthoods. *The Journal of Gerontology. Series B: Psychological Sciences and Social Services, 60B,* 84–91.

Rodgers, W. (1982). Trends in reported happiness within demographically defined subgroups, 19. 57–78. *Social Forces 60,* 826–42.

Ryff, C. D., & Keyes C. L. M. (1995). The structure of psychological well-being revisited. *Journal of Personality and Social Psychology, 69*(4):719–727.

Sadock, B. J., & Sadock, V. A. (2007). *Kaplan & Sadock's synopsis of psychiatry: Behavioral sciences/clinical psychiatry,* (10th ed). New York, NY: Lippincott, Williams, & Wilkins.

Salthouse, T. A. (1990). Cognitive competence and expertise in aging. In J. E. Birren & K.W. Schaie (Eds.), *Handbook of the psychology of aging.* (3rd ed.; pp. 310–391). New York, NY: Academic Press.

Saxon, S. V., & Etten, M. J. (1978*). Physical change and aging: A guide for the helping profession.* New York, NY: Tiresias Press.

Seligman, M. E. P., & Csikszentmihaly, M. (2000). Positive psychology: An introduction. *American Psychologist, 55*(1), 5–14. doi:10.1037//003-066X.55.1.5

Sinick, D. (1976). Counseling older persons: Career change and retirement. *Vocational and Guidance Quarterly, 25,* 18–25.

Straechan, S. M., Brawley, L. R., Spink, K., & Glazebrook, K. (2010). Older adults' physically-active identity: Relationships between social cognitions, physical activity, and satisfaction with life. *Psychology of Sport and Exercise, 11,* 114–121.

Staudinger, U. M., Marsiske, M., & Baltes, P. B. (1995). Resilience and severe capacity in later adulthood: Potential and limits of development across the lifespan. In D. Cicchetti & D. J. Cohen (Eds.), *Developmental psychology: Vol. 2. Risk, disorder, and adaptation* (pp. 801–847). New York, NY: Wiley.

U.S. Census Bureau. (2002). Population projections of the United States by age, sex, race, Hispanic origin, and nativity: 1999 to 2100. Retrieved from www.census.gov/population/projections/nation/summary/np-t3-a.txt.

Vinters, H. V. (2004). Pathologic issues and new methodologies in the evaluation of non-Alzheimer dementias. *Neuroscience Research 3,* 413–426.

World Health Organization (WHO). (2008). *The world health report.* The world health report archives. WHO reports (1995–2008). Retrieved from www.who.int/entity/whr/en/.

Wong, C. K., & Lou, V. W. Q. (2010). "I wish to be self-reliant.": Aspiration for self-reliance, need and life satisfaction, and exit dilemma of welfare recipients in Hong Kong. *Social Indicators Research, 95,* 519–534.

Wong, P. T. P., & Watt, L. M. (1991). What types of reminiscence are associated with successful aging? *Psychology and Aging, 6,* 272–279.

Yang. Y. (2008). Social inequalities in happiness in the United States, 1972 to 2004: An age-period-cohort analysis. *Journal American Sociological Review, 73*(2), 5–26.

Zarit, A. M., & Zarit, J. M. (1998). *Mental disorder in older adults: Fundamentals of assessment and treatment.* New York, NY: Guilford Press.

Oldest-Old Elderhood (Ages 75 and Over)

Age is an issue of mind over matter. If you don't mind, it doesn't matter.

Mark Twain

Aging takes place in sequential, environmental, and societal contexts, and it is shaped by these contexts (Wahl & Oswald, 2010). One of the best known examples for contextual influences on aging is the increase in longevity, which began to rise in Western countries and parts of Asia around the turn of the 20th century. Over time, rapid increases in life expectancy have made it possible to live up to 100 years old, currently a reality for more people worldwide. Today, we identify this diverse population of the oldest-old (often referred to as the very old) as individuals from age 75 to 100 and over. The counseling field has been awakened by the rapid growth of this sector of the aging population, and it considers this as a serious issue to improve counseling services for this population. Early on, Blake and Kaplan (1975) referred to older persons as "the forgotten and ignored" of the counseling profession (p. 136). Myers and Blake (1986; Myers 1995) have argued for the need to train counseling professionals to meet the needs of older adult clients. A strong point of this awareness has been that if counselors are to prepare with training to meet the needs of older adult clients, an infusion of gerontological issues into counselor preparation courses and curricula is and will be necessary for years to come (Blake & Kaplan, 1975; Myers, 1995).

This chapter highlights the importance of acquiring gerontological-based counseling knowledge in order to work with individuals through their advanced lifespan and the type of information and skills that are valuable for this endeavor. After reading and discussing this chapter the reader will be able to

1. understand the challenges and implications of quality of life and life satisfaction during the adjustment to advanced age,

2. apply gerontological-based counseling skills to effectively work with advanced aged clients and their family members,

3. understand the counseling skills needed to manage the psychosocial crises and challenges faced by the oldest-old population, and

4. analyze major issues and contextual influences such as culture related to aging.

Understanding Quality of Life and Life Satisfaction in Old Age

In previous chapters, we have discussed that aging is commonly understood as the process of maturing or becoming older; in fact, aging is a broad term that includes several processes: (a) those changes happening along the lifespan, (b) individual differences attributed to age and environmental issues, and (c) the aging process of the older to oldest adults in comparison with younger adults (Birren, 1996). As researchers have pointed out, across one's lifespan there is a continuous balance among stability, gains, and declines, especially after the individual reaches the third decade of life (Baltes, 1987). It is important to distinguish between biophysical and psychosocial changes that are part of this continuous balance of the aging process across a lifespan. According to Briggs (1990), biophysical systems are those that lose efficiency, psychological characteristics maintain stability, and show gains and declines depending not only on the biological organism but also on the sociocultural context, and on the control individuals exert through their behaviors; in other words, as Bandura (1997) pointed out, the organism, the person and his or her behavior, and the sociocultural context interact continuously.

Conceptions of quality of life and **life satisfaction** are diverse and unique to each situation. Currently, the term *quality of life* denotes two meanings: (a) the presence of conditions deemed necessary for a good life and (b) the practice of good living as such. Life satisfaction is based on the individual's interpretation of his or her life. When used at the societal level, only the former meaning applies (Myers & Diener, 1996). For the use of clinical counseling interventions, both meanings may be applied. In counseling practice, it is important to be aware of what definition will be used or attached to the uniqueness of the client.

The contents and specific measures of quality of life, however, vary between and within disciplines (Farquhar, 1995). The emphasis ranges from standards of living in the discipline of economy to perceived health status in the discipline of medicine. There have been more than 1,000 identified indicators that measure various aspects of quality of life (Hughes & Hwang, 1996) and more than 100 definitions of quality of life have been proposed (Cummins, 1997). Despite the lack of a widely accepted definition, most definitions of quality of life include a multidimensional functional status aspect and a **subjectivity** aspect (Muldoon, Barger, Flory, & Manuck, 1998; Pukrop, 2003). Multidimensional functional status incorporates physical well-being, functional ability, emotional well-being, and social well-being, while subjectivity refers to the individual's own perception of his or her quality of life (Muldoon et al., 1998). Therefore, while the subjectivity aspect of quality of life resembles life satisfaction, there is a multidimensional functional status dimension of the quality of life concept that life satisfaction clearly excludes.

There are indications of concepts and concerns related to quality of life expressed by cohorts of the oldest-old population that are different from the general population. Important to counselors is to understand that quality of life is described often with both **objective** and **subjective** dimensions based on individuals' life experiences during their lifespan.

Most people have an opinion about what is quality of life; however, there is disagreement on precisely what it means in general terms that can be applied to all individuals. Quality of life is highly individualistic and might even be an **idiosyncratic** mystery due to the high levels of variability between individuals, making it unsuitable for decision making. According to Brown, Bowling, and Flynn (2004), older adults, in particular the oldest-old population, have unique characteristics accumulated through a lifespan of experiences. Perhaps the perception that the oldest-old are particularly vulnerable is due to circumstances related to (a) the aging process, including declining physical and mental capabilities; (b) disengagement from active life; (c) greater dependence on others for financial and social supports; (d) decrease of extended family members and social networks; and (e) isolation due to death of loved ones, especially that of a spouse or partner and acquaintances of the same age group.

Life Satisfaction

The term *satisfaction* is perceived as a state of mind. It is also understood as an evaluative appraisal of something. The term refers to both contentment and enjoyment, and it covers cognitive, as well as affective, appraisals. Life satisfaction is a major issue for counseling needs during the oldest-old life stage. Satisfaction can be both temporary and stable through time and lifespan (Karatafl, 2005). A review of the literature indicates a consensus on the definition stating that life satisfaction is the degree to which a person positively evaluates the overall quality of his or her life as a whole. In other words, how much the person likes the life he or she leads (Myers & Diener, 1996).

Life satisfaction of an individual during the oldest-old lifespan is very much influenced by various factors, such as the ability to function independently, taking pleasure in participating in daily activities, meaningfulness in life, acceptance of desired and achieved goals, perceived health, financial security, and social contact. Because the oldest-old are especially susceptible to numerous potential threats to life satisfaction, such as the loss of a spouse, changes in social network, changes in housing/living arrangements, and age-related diseases and comorbidity, the consideration of life satisfaction is particularly important for working with this group. In addition, other factors that took place during earlier developmental stages of an individual's lifespan, such as the type of family he or she had, his or her relationships maintained with family members, availability of resources in the family, and the extent of participation in social and religious activities, might also affect life satisfaction in very old age. Individuals in advanced oldest-old age often have a decline in their daily routines, assuming that they are deprived of power by internal and external forces. In some cases, oldest-old individuals may feel worthless and powerless, and consider aging as a significant obstacle in obtaining satisfaction from life. All of the above aging issues are important variables that need to be taken into consideration not only to understand the oldest-old client but also to be able to provide counseling in the most effective manner. Most helping professionals subscribe to the notion that health is more than the absence of illness, and if there is health, there should also be quality of life. The presence or absence of disease, therefore, may not be a source of great concern to the oldest-old adult. The inability to perform activities of daily living is the greatest concern, which also interferes with quality of life (Haber, 2013).

In summary, in facing the challenges and rewards of working with an aging population, life satisfaction is an important factor that must be considered by counselors at all times. In spite of this fact, two main problematic issues have emerged: from a biomedical perspective, quality of life and life satisfaction are mainly reduced to health, and several health measures have been taken as quality-of-life measures. When several domains are considered, quality of life and life satisfaction are reduced to the individual's subjective appraisal of those domains (Fernández-Ballesteros & Santacreu,2010). This view determines the existence of a variety of self-report methods assessing quality of life combined with a minority of rating-by-other scales from different disciplines. With some exceptions, quality-of-life measures as they relate to aging can be placed in an undeveloped state. The focus here is to emphasize the multidimensionality of quality of life and the strong need to use both subjective and objective components of those dimensions during counseling assessments and counseling interventions.

Adjustment to Advanced Aging

Adjustment to advanced aging is how the individual perceives himself or herself in reference to health concerns in later life such as chronic conditions, disability, and dependency. Believing that advanced age is equal to lost vigor and decreasing strength, followed by a gradual decline in health, generally frightens everyone. The **epidemiology** of aging is concerned with diseases that cause morbidity and mortality and also with the causes of disability and the effect on functional independence. This often means marked revisions in the roles the oldest-old individual plays in the home and in the open environment. But the changes that accompany advanced aging are more than just changes in health. As people age, they are often faced with events that can dramatically alter their lives. For example, they may lose decision-making power on individual and family affairs or on their living arrangements (Ailshire & Crimmins, 2011). These changes may become an impediment to a progressive adjustment to advanced aging and have the potential of affecting the well-being of the individual.

A number of inevitable physiological changes occur as we grow older that can also affect how an older individual adjusts to the continuing process of aging. Some of the common changes that appear to be related to aging can be the result of long-term diseases or, perhaps, lifestyles and exposure to hazardous environmental elements. Most of the normal changes of the aging process have no impact on normal functioning, although they become apparent when the body is placed under stress (e.g., acute illness, physical exertion, etc.). It is important to be able to recognize the changes of normal aging versus the effects of disease or mental health issues, so the counseling process can be effective. An untreated disease can result in chronic disability and reduce the quality of life of individuals, making it very challenging to adjust to aging. In the counseling profession, like in other human service professions, it is essential to identify and understand the most important changes in the body that occur with aging. This approach will provide the counselor with details to better understand the aging individual and relate this information to the present situation in need of therapeutic counseling. Healthy aging (body and mind) has a positive impact on the adjustment to aging. Poor health in later life is not inevitable, and it can be managed. Many of the illnesses and disabilities associated with advanced aging are related to modifiable lifestyle factors that are present in previous developmental stages of the person (Baltes, 2004). How an individual adjusts to the aging process during advanced aging stages can be modified.

Some researchers have acknowledged the important role of preventive activities and reacting effectively toward stressful changes for adjustment to advanced aging, which translates positively into *successful aging*. Early in the history of gerontology, Paulus (1951) suggested that "successful aging must be prepared long in advance; a happy old age is the criterion and reward of a well conducted life" (p. 401). More recently, Kahana and Kahana (1996, 2001), in their model of preventive and corrective proactivity, described strategies to effectively deal with the unique stressors associated with aging in order to avoid negative outcomes. These strategies include not only corrective actions to cope with stressors once they have occurred but also several preventive actions made prior to the stressors' occurrence, in order to delay them or minimize them. These preventive behaviors include (a) health promotion to reduce the risk of declining health, (b) planning for the future, and (c) helping others in order to enhance the range of social resources that may be drawn upon in difficult times.

Interpersonal Relationships

The concept that old age is characterized by social isolation has been a topic of study by scholars from different disciplines. While counseling older adults, this concept plays an important role in assessing and providing effective therapeutic intervention when isolation and depression are suspected. It is well known that social connectedness and the avoidance of loneliness are important aspects of healthy aging. The psychological experience of loneliness is distinct from the objective lack of social connections. Researchers are beginning to explore how the feeling of loneliness may be a separate risk factor for poor health, different from the risks of objective social isolation or other feelings of psychological distress such as depression (Gironda & Lubben, 2002).

Among older adults, in particular the oldest-old, age is negatively related to interpersonal relationships, social network size, closeness to network members, and number of nonprimary-group ties (Crooks, Lubben, Petitti, Little, & Chiu, 2008). On the other hand, other studies by Hall and Havens (2002) suggest that age is positively related to frequency of socializing

Photo 13.1   As a reflection of younger years, couples continue to demonstrate love and affection toward each other during their elderly years.

Source: Dynamic Graphics/Creatas/Thinkstock.

with neighbors, religious participation, and volunteering. Interpersonal relationships are affected by later-life transitions, like retirement, limited financial resources, health conditions, and bereavement. However, they may also prompt greater connectedness with personal social networks, questioning the idea that aging is followed by isolation due to lack of interpersonal relationships.

People's interpersonal relationships and communication skills have been shown to influence physical and mental health, the magnitude of some illnesses, the likelihood of healing, whether a person will become institutionalized (nursing home) or not, and, to some degree, the amount of satisfaction they derive form their lives, (Neugarten, Havighurst, Tobin, & Sheldon, 1968). The aging experience demands continuous adaptation to changing social, physical, and psychological capacities. Counseling practice has focused primarily on the personal and family relationships that are vital during the time of elderhood. Offering an important new perspective is appropriate to emphasize a set of factors often ignored in literature and practice; these factors are personality characteristics, interpersonal skills, and ways of connecting with others that can enable the person to become an active agent in shaping his or her own life.

Valliant (2002) added an important concept to the understanding of the importance of social support in older adults' generativity. As previously indicated (Chapters 11 & 12), generativity is defined as feeling a sense of responsibility for the well-being of the next generation through physically and emotionally caring for younger people. Individuals during their oldest-old lifespan who nurture their relationships with family members at an intergenerational level had more motivation to do things, just by knowing that someone cared about them. These older adults are able to identify what is important to them in their lives, who cares about them, and what activities help them to maintain a positive self-image. Social isolation has been found to be a powerful risk factor not only for the development of cognitive and intellectual decline but also for physical illness (Rowe & Kahn, 1998).

Counselors can use their skills as active listeners and compassionate analytical thinkers to turn clients' feelings of isolation into actions that create opportunities for building interpersonal relations or to strengthen existing ones. The aging process presents a decline in physical and cognitive abilities that also limits older adults from being socially active; however, age should not be an obstacle for social interaction.

Decrease of Participation in Social Activities

Human behavior involves complex interrelationships among physical, psychological, and social factors. Both the nature and significance of biopsychosocial interrelationships change as aging occurs. Each individual during the later years of life remains a unique and complex being and can only be properly understood from a holistic perspective.

In order to be engaged in social activities, the oldest-old individual needs to have social and interpersonal relationships. In the social domain, there is considerable continuity across adulthood. Kahn and Antonucci (1980) described a social pattern common across cultures in which people form what are called **social convoys** or bands of people who accompany individuals through life. They further indicated that although these social convoys expand and diminish across adulthood, they involve a core set of people, who remain present for decades and whose presence predicts their functioning levels. In this regard, there is considerable stability in social network composition across older adults' lifespan. Some researchers argue that this social stability contributes to the continuity of personality and lifestyle and creates a safety network of aging individuals.

Although stable in their core, social networks decrease with time and age. For many years, this decreasing was presumed to be due primarily to morbidity (illness) and mortality (death) and decrease of social activities that placed older people at risk. A different process has been revealed through research. Long-term studies that have included participants ages 18 to over 100 suggest that adults engage in a sort of "pruning process," beginning long before oldest-old age, in which emotionally close social relationships are retained, while more peripheral relationships are increasingly excluded (Carstensen, 1992; Lang, 2000). During advanced old age, social networks comprise a relatively larger proportion of emotionally close social partners, a change that appears to have positive consequences for well-being in individuals among the oldest-old group (Lansford, Sherman, & Antonucci, 1998). The types and frequency of social activities may decrease in advanced age, and this could be a consequence of physical and mental health issues, living in an unfriendly environment that is not conducive for outdoor activities, mobility, socioeconomic status, and access to transportation. Another contributing factor is the fact that over time individuals in the oldest-old group may have fewer friends and even fewer family members to interact with at social activities.

It is also important for counselors to keep in mind that even in the strongest relationships, special strains occur in later life, and that these strains are different for women and men and are experienced quite differently across cultures and ethnic groups. These are situations in which the counselor will work with elderly clients as well as their family member caretakers to enable them to find possible solutions and support that will diminish the potential harm this difficult situation can create. In addition, aging-related needs and caregiving responsibilities often place restrictions on involvement in social activities, ranging from work to social engagement. Otherwise, pleasurable activities may be forgone so that other related daily routine issues can be attended to. Interestingly, social activity restriction appears to affect the relationship between the older adult and others more than the direct physical demands of caregiving that the aging process may require (Williamson, Shaffer, & Schulz, 1998).

One important point for counselors to consider about social activity networks and advanced aging is that, although research suggests that the overall size of social activity networks is relatively unimportant for well-being and that oldest-old people are not particularly vulnerable to isolation and loneliness, when they do occur, isolation and loneliness have notably damaging consequences for well-being, including an increase in morbidity and mortality (Berkman & Breslow, 1983; Hawkley & Cacioppo, 2003).

Strategies to Address Isolation and Loneliness

Many studies have developed recommendations to address the isolation and loneliness issues among older adults, and to do so, they have focused on three groups: older individuals, community groups and agencies, and program planners and policy makers. Local communities and agencies are advised to increase the availability of programs

Photo 13.2   Counseling and caring for older adults are unique skills that have become an urgent demand from society.

Source: Goodshoot/Goodshoot/Thinkstock.

and services for older adults, establish or enhance transportation programs and low-cost leisure and education activities, and involve seniors at all levels of planning. For their part, policy makers have been advised to increase barrier-free access and housing options that foster socialization. For the advocacy-type services providers, including clinical counselors, it is recommended to enhance communication between all levels of community and government to improve links among social services and health and education to reduce isolation and loneliness among all groups of older adults (Adams, Sanders, & Auth, 2004). From the counseling profession perspective, some of the common recommendations suggest that oldest-old individuals should keep regular contact with family members, friends, and neighbors in order to ensure that they feel needed and valued. Also suggested is the need to train counselors to work with the oldest-old population.

Emotional Impact of Chronic Illness and Disability

The emotional impact of a chronic illness and disability revolves around the person's ability to adjust. Adjustment is not just for the beginning stages of an illness or disability. The adjustment process may be a long-term change regarding many aspects of the person and the person's lifestyle and expectations. It includes decreased activities and capabilities, changes in priorities, financial status, self-image, and relationships that can all surface at the same time. The emotional impact could be devastating to the person. There is a continued need for emotional support as mental and physical changes become more evident and the person feels that he or she is not in control due to the complications of illness and disability.

A counselor has to be prepared to deal with oldest-old clients' issues of chronic illness, which often lead to feelings of helplessness, frustration, hopelessness, and great sadness. It is common for this type of client to express resentment at being ill or incapacitated and grief at the multiple aspects of functional loss. Regardless of the situation, there is a powerful emotional component that contributes to a need for physical and emotional support and care. The emotional wellness of an aging person has a major and marked impact on the physical symptoms under stress. Exactly how emotions, the mind, and the physical body relate is a complex issue that has not been well defined in reference to this advanced age group (Smyer & Qualls, 1999).

Improvement of emotional wellness may help control certain physical symptoms in some types of chronic or serious illnesses of the elderly. The counselor needs to address the emotional, as well as the physical needs of the client by taking proper actions and providing holistic care and support. Oldest-old clients react well when they feel that their circumstances and feelings are appreciated and understood without any judgment by the counselor. If the clients feel the attention and treatment they receive is genuine care and adapted to their needs, it is far more likely that they will develop trust and confidence in the counselor. This interaction is very important to maintain a positive counselor-client connection at all times.

The combination of aging progression and disability, combined with poor psychological and emotional health, damages physical and mental health outcomes, regardless of how advanced in age the person might be. For example, depression, stress, anger, and negative emotions, in general are strongly associated with increased physical problems. It is important for the counselor to have a holistic view of the client and to try to meet his or her emotional, physical, and spiritual needs when providing a therapeutic intervention (Siegel, 1990). Another example is that it is not just listening to the client but also understanding that the client may feel embarrassed or ashamed to talk about private feelings and problems. The counselor must show caring in a nonjudgmental approach to meet the physical, as well as the emotional, needs of the client.

Emotional Impact of Aging

Previous chapters have discussed the fact that as the body ages, there are a number of changes that occur. How older adults manage those changes can affect their entire outlook of life in their golden years of advanced aging.

Various studies about young-old perception indicate that younger people perceived older adults as lonely, hopeless, and sad. Even older adults who report high levels of satisfaction frequently express beliefs that most other older people are not faring well (Rocke & Lachman, 2008). The latest research, however, has shown that such negative views are unwarranted. Although many people are, indeed, facing mounting physical ailments, psychological stress, social losses, and increased dependency at the very end of life, older adults are well adjusted emotionally for the bulk of their later years (Carstensen, Pasupathi, Mayrs, & Nesselroade, 2000). Obviously, individual differences are apparent, and improvements to well-being are general trends, not guarantees. Dispositional tendencies, life events, and individuals' management of such events can all influence whether well-being improves or deteriorates with age. Nevertheless, research suggests that reasonably high levels of affective well-being and emotional stability are the norm, rather than the exception, at least until after adults reach 70 or 80 years of age (Teachman, 2006).

As people age and depend more on family, significant others, and the outside world to respond to their needs, feelings of guilt, shame, regret, and even anger can emerge. The prevalence of dependency increases with age and is related to the presence of prior disease and fragility. It presents challenges for the older person, family, caretaker, and help professionals. If relationships and the human dynamics of needs have been a lifetime source of struggle for an individual, the chances are high that the challenges of dependency will be experienced in an amplified and painful manner (Schulz & Beach, 1999). Dealing with the emotions that emerge from dependency and being clear and honest about what the person is (or is not) able to do for himself or herself will avoid affecting the relationship with family, friends, and caregivers. Table 13.1 is an illustration of this process.

Table 13.1 Physical and Emotional Impact of Aging

Physical and Emotional Impact of Aging	
Physical Impact	Energy level slows, less active, may gain weight
	Body systems deteriorate
	Sensory loss (hearing & vision) decreases safe movement, mobility, and communication
	External changes; skin wrinkles, sun spots, hair turns gray and becomes fragile
	Changes in bone mass (osteoporosis) and muscle strength; falls often result in serious injury
	Sensitivity to scents, light changes, and medication caused by changing body systems
Emotional Impact	Physical effects of aging may have high mental impact, and individuals may seek to change appearance with plastic surgery, improved nutrition, and anti-aging alternative methods. Embarrassment and shame at unexpected aging conditions (loss of hair, loss of vision, incontinence, dependence on others, and illness perceived as weakness, etc.)
	Interest in hobbies, social activities, and public events may lessen
	Social interaction and social engagements may be refused; isolation leads to loneliness
	Vulnerability may affect comfort level, anxiety, or trust of strangers
	Fear of disability and death; religious needs increase

Dependency due to increasing needs should not crumble an individual's sense of dignity. However, it requires a deliberate and ideally lifelong examination of relationships and skills of communication. The experience of dependency is a two-way street. Older people fear dependency because they see themselves as being unproductive, incapacitated, and treated as a burden. They fear losing relationships and respect because of their situation. If caregivers (family and professionals) are open to accept the dependent person who attempts to function at the highest level possible, while at the same time experiencing the grief of loss of functions, a more authentic and less fragile relationship could be established. When accepting the increased dependency that often comes with physical debilitating age, shared feelings can establish a stronger bonding. The adjustment to advanced aging is illustrated as a typical case in Case Illustration 13.1.

CASE ILLUSTRATION 13.1 ADJUSTMENT TO ADVANCED AGING

Instructions: Case Illustration 13.1 presents an example of a couple adjusting to aging and disability. After reading the illustration, it is suggested that you that reflect upon and discuss with students and colleagues the questions posed at the end.

Aging and Disability

John is 75 years old, White, and married, living with his wife, Ella, who is 65. They live in the home they bought 40 years ago in the same town where they grew up and worked. John has been ill many times with multiple health issues that he blames on aging. Lately, he refuses to go to the doctor and to take his prescription medications, which aggravate the situation. He is usually in a very bad mood, cannot control his temper, and complains about everything. He insists on doing physical chores that he should not do due to his health issues. He talks about the effects of aging and how limited he is and about how strong and agile he used to be, never needing his wife or anybody else to do things for him. Ella worries that John is harming himself and is having difficulty coping with aging, his chronic health condition, and his state of mind. They have agreed to seek counseling and find a solution for John's adjustment to aging.

Questions for Reflection and Discussion:

1. Given John's case, what would be an effective method to work with him?

2. Is the adjustment to aging the problem, or is there something else going on?

3. What can the counselor advise Ella to do to manage the situation?

4. Is this a case of dependency or fear of aging?

5. Are the effects of aging a reminder of something else?

Psychosocial Crisis

The oldest-old population is faced with multiple challenges, but none are more conflictive than the struggle between the acceptance of aging or end of life and the intensifying hope for more years of life. Having lived longer than their cohort of family members, and in some cases, their friends, the oldest-old struggle to find meaning of their survival (Zimbardo & Boyd, 2008). A psychosocial crisis in later life may be obvious by the expression and behavior of the elderly person, or it may be internalized and difficult to assess but remain with some signs that indicate confusion and anxiety. The psychosocial development stages (or crisis) theorized by Erikson include, as a last stage of life, ego integrity versus despair. Almost all older adults will experience recurring problems with this last stage. As indicated by Myers and Blake (1986), the central psychosocial crisis of later life is the search for ego integrity. The process of life review, as a therapeutic process for helping oldest-old individuals, is an essential means of achieving integrity or the sense that the life one lived is the best one could have lived.

Ego Integrity Versus Despair in Later Days

The ego integrity versus. despair phase of later life indicates the stage or maturity level that begins during late adulthood from age 65 to the end of life. With the basic conflict being ego integrity versus despair, the important event taking place will be a reflection on life, and the preferred outcome would be for older adults to look back on their lives and feel a sense of life fulfillment. Success at this stage leads to feelings of wisdom and satisfaction, while failure results in regret, bitterness, and old-age despair.

It is during this stage it is important that the individual evaluates his or her life, fears, and accomplishments. Individuals who fear their own death, feel abandoned or lost due to the loss of loved ones, experience chronic or terminal illness, or feel they have lost the ability to be self-sufficient can find themselves engulfed in a state of despair or regret over a life misspent. For situations with the oldest-old individuals, it is helpful to complete a life review as a therapeutic intervention. As Lewis (2001) indicated, "The life review is one counseling intervention which has been empirically shown to be useful with older adults" (p.234). There are many facets to the life review, each of which could provide positive results to the individual, especially when the life review is focused on the relationship to spirituality. During the life review process, individuals recall, evaluate, and then reintegrate their

Photo 13.3   The diversity and richness of older adults and their families requires specialization in culturally competent counseling skills.

Source: Jack Hollingsworth/Photodisk/Thinkstock.

memories, developing a holistic view of their self-concept. The life review has the primary purpose of helping the older adult client find integrity with the life lived (Lewis, 2001).

The most important event at this developmental stage is accepting one's entire life and reflecting on that life experience in a positive manner. According to Erikson and Erikson (1997), achieving a sense of integrity means accepting oneself fully and coming to terms with the reality of the end of life. Accepting responsibility for one's life, including past experiences, and achieving satisfaction with oneself is essential. The inability to take that important step results in feelings of sadness, depression, and despair (Krebs-Carter, 2007).

Pervin, Cervone, and Oliver (2005) suggest that through the progression of Erikson's stages, some individuals are capable of developing a "sense of intimacy, an acceptance of life's successes and disappointments, and a sense of continuity throughout the life cycle." However, "other people remain isolated from family and friends, appear to survive on a fixed daily routine, and focus on both past experiences of disappointments and future death," and are likely to find themselves rooted in despair (p. 111).

In counseling, we recognize that life is full of choices, and there are always many choices that were not the right ones to make. Everyone makes mistakes, including some major or even tragic ones. To be fulfilled does not mean that one has led a perfect life. But, if one has managed life reasonably well and has come to grips with one's shortcomings, practiced meaningful self-forgiveness when needed, and taken into account both positive and negative factors from one's past, then a positive sense of integrity follows. Despair, however, implies a lack of further hope and can result from unfulfilled potential or a feeling that one has wasted one's life, without hope for personal redemption. Despair is often disguised by an obvious attitude of contempt toward others. Such contempt, according to Erikson, really reflects contempt for the self, projected outward. After a lifetime of living and learning, Erikson stated that "wisdomism" is the basic strength and resilience associated with later years, based on the well-lived life. Disdain is the core pathology of this stage (Erikson, 1963).

CASE ILLUSTRATION 13.2 EGO INTEGRITY VERSUS DESPAIR

Instructions: Case Illustration 13.2 presents an example of where it is possible to identify ego integrity versus despair in old age. After reading the illustration, it is suggested that you reflect upon and discuss with students and colleagues the questions posed at the end.

Karl's case

Karl is a 78-year-old widower who lives in a senior citizen apartment complex. Though he is reasonably healthy, both physically and mentally, Karl rarely goes out and typically does not take part in activities offered through the local senior center. Rather, he mostly sits at home and complains about his life. He rarely interacts with his neighbors, and even his children and grandchildren avoid visiting him because all he does is complain how bad his life has been.

Questions for Reflection and Discussion:

Psychosocial crises can be successfully resolved, and mature adults can develop a sense of integrity. They see their lives as successful and worthwhile. They are proud of their work and their families, and they reap the benefits of a fulfilling life. The unsuccessful resolution is despair: a negative appraisal of one's life and the realization that it is too late to start over.

(Continued)

(Continued)

1. What can Karl do to feel better about himself?

2. What would be an appropriate counseling therapeutic intervention to help Karl?

3. Does the family play a role in Karl's situation?

4. How can the family help?

Older adults may develop a deep concern with the process of dying even though they may express that they see it as part of life. People can experience the proximity of death in many different ways. The psychological coping strategies may be different depending on the conditions of the experience. In previous chapters, it was mentioned that the Kübler-Ross model, commonly referred to as the "five stages of grief," describes the process of coming to terms with one's end of life. These stages include denial, anger, bargaining, depression, and acceptance (Kübler-Ross, 1969). These stages are further explained below in this chapter.

These emotional reactions, in particular among the oldest-old, are all important aspects of understanding how people may cope with the reality of their death. Counselors will learn that the differences in the conditions of death mean that this process is not likely to be experienced universally. Planning for the unavoidable end of life becomes an essential component of counseling interventions for the elderly individual and for their families.

End-of-Life Planning

In societies where the life expectancies have extended well into advanced oldest-old age, the largest proportion of deaths occurs among older adults. For example, the most recent published U.S. Mortality Statistics (U.S. Bureau of Population Statistics, 2007) clearly indicate that with age, the number of deaths increase. The CDC (2012) reports an increase of death of over 700,000 deaths for those 85 years and over (Murphy, Xu, & Kochanek, 2012). Coupled with society's glorification of youth, this close association between death and advanced age fosters a sense of devaluing older adults in many Westernized countries, as well as an attitude that many fear leads to less than optimal care for dying older adults. This attitude may even be assumed by older adults themselves and their level of expectation of quality of treatment from others during their last days may be low.

End-of-life planning has been receiving a significant and growing amount of attention from a variety of sources; however, much of the emphasis has been on the medical aspects of caring for the terminally ill, with significantly less attention on the relevant psychosocial issues (Chochinov, 2006). This is unfortunate because the important role that psychological and interpersonal factors play during the dying process has indicated that "control of pain, of other symptoms, and of psychological, social, and spiritual problems, is paramount" in planning end-of-life and **palliative care** (Chochinov, 2006). Consequently, although physical problems are important and should often take first priority, truly comprehensive end-of-life planning requires that psychosocial matters be assessed and addressed as well.

Although death is a universal human experience, planning for it is not, and the societal response to death varies according to prevailing attitudes and beliefs. There is enormous variation across cultures in how death is perceived and how grief is expressed. Many counselors are not professionally prepared to provide therapy to persons who are near the end of life. Although it can be difficult work, it is also very rewarding, and the hope is that counselors will be willing to take the time to learn more about providing this type of counseling. Multiple components of the death system (i.e., people, places, symbols, rituals, etc.) are involved in the important function of

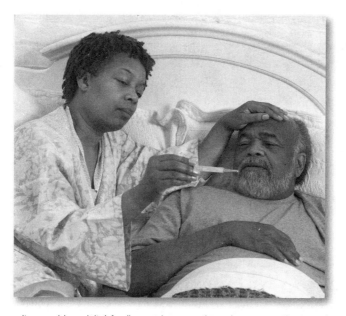

Photo 13.4 For some cultures, older adults' family members are the only resource they may have for assistance and caregiving during their elderly years.

Source: Tom Le Goff/Digital Vision/Thinkstock.

attending to the dying, but a culturally supported aversion to those who are old can result in their **social isolation** and neglect at a time when dying older adults are more likely to be frail and dependent upon others for their basic care (Lunney, Lynn, Foley, Lipson, & Guralnik, 2003)

The task of planning the end of life is complicated for those involved. Regardless of the health status, meeting the biological, psychological, social, and spiritual needs of older adults can take significant energy. Maintaining a sense of integrity while facing death in one's last years or days of life becomes challenging when there is also a functional decline. In addition to pain management, meeting physical needs may involve basic routine care including sensitive communication and taking care of pending personal issues, such as belongings and financial affairs. Counselors can be active in at least six roles that including being an advocate, counselor, educator, evaluator, multidisciplinary team member, and researcher. Because psychosocial issues are pervasive and can have enormous impact near the end of life, properly trained mental health professionals can play vital roles in alleviating suffering and improving the quality of life of people who are dying. Other areas that counselors need to explore during end-of-life planning are the client's religious, spiritual, and existential beliefs, expectations, experiences, and values; sense of personal meaning and fulfillment in life; philosophy of life; and worldview components.

Professional counselors are cautioned against taking a cookie-cutter approach with their dying clients and loved ones. As Erikson (1963) noted, the development tasks of each age period are anticipatory and reflective of both past and future developmental needs, and therefore there is considerable overlap with the issues and needs outlined in previous chapters. Regardless of what the age or developmental period, preserving dignity and fostering a sense of personal integrity in the face of dying and when planning for the end of life should be a fundamental right and an ethical issue for the counseling practice across the globe (Werth, 2013).

An emerging consensus among service providers and caregivers regarding end-of-life care is reflected in the development of a set of core principles for providers. See Table 13.2 Core Principles for End-of-Life Care. These 11 humanistic principles list the responsibilities of end-of-life caregivers to clients/patients and their families or support systems.

Table 13.2 The Core Principles for End-of-Life Care

The Core Principles for End-of-Life Care
Respecting the dignity of both the patient and caregivers
Being sensitive and respectful of the patient's and family wishes
Using the most appropriate measures that are consistent with patient choices
Encompassing alleviation of pain and other physical symptoms
Assessing and managing psychological, social, and spiritual/religious problems
Offering continuity (the patient should be able to continue to be cared for, if so desired, by his or her primary care and specialist providers)
Providing access to any therapy that may realistically be expected to improve the patient's quality of life, including alternative and nontraditional treatments
Providing access to palliative care and hospice care
Respecting the right to refuse treatment
Respecting the physician's professional right to discontinue some treatments when appropriate, with consideration for both patient and family preferences
Promoting clinical evidence-based research on providing care at end of life
Educate physicians, caregivers, and the public about good end-of-life care

Source: Adapted from APA, 2001 Position Statement on The Core Principles for End-of-Life Care.

CASE ILLUSTRATION 13.3 END-OF-LIFE PLANNING

Instructions: Case Illustration 13.3 presents an example of planning, including end-of-life decisions. After reading the illustration, it is suggested that you reflect upon and discuss with students and colleagues the questions posed at the end.

Nelly's Plans

Nelly is a 75-year-old Black woman who was born in rural Mississippi. At the young age of 16, Nelly was sent to a larger city in the northern part of the state to live with her grandmother, to attend school, and to get to know her family members who had moved away years ago in the pursuit of a better life. Nelly graduated from high school and soon got married, never returning to her hometown and family for many years. She regretted not having been in touch more often with her parents, now deceased, and her two younger brothers. She always planned, after raising her two daughters and after they had married, that she would go back home and live her last years there. She thinks that she owes that to her dead parents and to her family roots. Her daughters advised Nelly not to move back because of her health issues and the lack of support and health care that she will have to endure in that rural area, where she barely knows anyone. Nelly expressed feelings of guilt and regret and wants her last days to be where she was born. In the bigger city where her family lives, she has been alone in her house since she retired. Her activities include attending church once a week, doing some light shopping with a friend, and getting together with her family occasionally and on holidays.

Questions for Reflection and Discussion:

1. Why does Nelly want to go back to the place where she was born?

2. Is this a psychosocial crisis affected by cultural issues in Nelly's life?

3. Are there personal unresolved issues that Nelly needs to take care of?

4. Would Nelly's decision change if her life experience after retirement had been different?

5. What should the family do to support Nelly or perhaps make her change her plans?

6. How would you counsel Nelly? What are the options for this case?

It is a normal reaction to think about the possibility of our own mortality especially after experiencing the death of a loved one or watching the struggle for survival when dealing with near death experiences. At some point, during the later stages of life, we begin to think of time not as unlimited time to live but as time left to live. In old age, the reality of death and loss is inescapable and everyone faces the certainty of death (Broderick & Blewitt, 2014).

Counseling professionals will face the challenge of the emotionally difficult issues of death and dying with clients and their family members. When working with oldest-old clients, we can assume the prospect of death is constantly present, since death in later life is a reality that could arrive any day. The experience of death can be traumatic for anyone at any age. In general, most people think about it and even prepare of it, but the reality is that we are never fully ready to welcome the end of life; It is most common to discuss the issues of death and dying in the context of later life, however, many of the issues involved in death and dying are similar across the lifespan.

The experience of facing death is accompanied by multiple factors internal and external to the person and among them are (a) reluctance to talk about the topic of death openly, (b) anxiety about death that complicates this reluctance, (c) guilt that emanates from the lack of openness, and (d) the loneliness and isolation of the dying person. Early on in life, we learn that death is part of human life and its possibility is forever present. Why do we avoid talking about it? Counselors need to prepare themselves to walk clients going through the experience of death and dying through the process of understanding death and to answer this question. Obviously, death and dying represent unknown territory, and it is difficult to comprehend a more painful or stressful life event than the proximity of dying or of losing a loved one. According to May (1979), some existential therapists (philosophical method of therapy that operates on the belief that inner conflict within a person is due to that individual's confrontation with the givens of existence) believe that fear of death is the ultimate source of anxiety and the foundation of most depression and alienation. This notion can still be applied to today's more modernized and popular culture.

In more recent times, progress has been made in understanding death and dying. Palliative care, or comfort care, involves services provided by caregivers from several disciplines, including counseling for the client/patient and his or her family members as a strong component. It includes a comprehensive approach to care that addresses pain management, emotional and spiritual care, and psychological support for caregivers and survivors (Billings, 1998; Christakis, 2000). The **hospice movement**, which serves people suffering from terminal illness, is a good example of a palliative patient-centered approach.

Modern American culture is moving away from a perspective that denies and fears death to one that supports death with dignity. Pioneers, such as Elizabeth Kübler-Ross (1969), have emphasized attention to the issues facing the dying and the bereaved and, in doing so, have shed much-needed light on their needs and concerns. Our society is faced with a growing population of older adults, most significantly the oldest-old, and advances in research medicine and the field of counseling have taken steps toward more compassionate care of the dying. The five stages of grief developed by Kübler-Ross (1969), introduced in her book *On Death and Dying,* also considered as coping mechanisms, have contributed a great deal to how we approach death and dying. These stages are not intended to be a rigid series of sequential or uniformly timed steps, and they are not a process as such, they are a model or a framework to be considered when working with near death or dying clients and their family members:

1. *Denial* may follow the initial shock that is associated with news of a terminal illness. This stage temporarily protects the person from the reality of a frightening situation. Denial is associated with feelings of numbness or disbelief and buffers the person from the full weight of the treatment. Some measure of denial can be adaptive and allows the person to temper the emotional impact, thus rendering it more manageable (Janoff-Bulman, 1993).

2. *Anger* is a normal reaction to separation and loss. Anger may be directed toward God (Why me?), toward others (Why didn't you do something to help me?), or toward the disease itself, which is viewed as an enemy to be attacked. Often this is a very difficult response for family members to tolerate from loved ones who are dying. Resentment or hostility toward family members or caregivers who are healthy may reflect the depth of the dying person's pain and cries out for caregivers' compassion. Anger can flow throughout the course of illness, depending upon the individual and the specific circumstances (Rosenblatt, Walsh, & Jackson, 1972).

3. *Bargaining* is an attempt to try to postpone the inevitable by making promises, usually to a higher power. Sometimes individuals will try to delay death until some memorable event, such as an anniversary or child's marriage, takes place. The individual may offer some prize, such as "a life dedicated to God or helping the poor" if the chance to live longer is granted (Kübler-Ross, 1969).

4. *Depression* as a reaction to impending death is characterized by sadness and feelings of hopelessness. Kübler-Ross distinguished between reactive depression, or depression that results from loss of functioning or other problems associated with the disease process, and preparatory depression, which is related to prospective loss and separation.

5. *Acceptance* is characterized by a sense of peace and relative tranquility, which suggests that the person has come to terms with his or her impending death or the death of a loved one. This peace is only relative and clients/patients should not be evaluated on how quickly or completely they accept death (Kübler-Ross, 1969).

These reactions, although important, do not reflect all possible ways of managing the death and dying process. It is helpful for counseling professionals to understand that the dying process may also be distinguished by the nature of the illness (cancer, heart disease, dementia, etc.). Awareness of the transition individuals may encounter when facing the inevitable can enhance provision of counseling and palliative care.

Gerontological Counseling Expertise

The major issues related to aging have to do with the fact that societies worldwide are not prepared to face the rapid increase of this population, the longevity of the oldest-old, and the issues affecting this elderly generation. Also, helping professionals are not sufficiently trained to manage the multiplicity of challenges and opportunities this aging population has to offer.

Counselors, as the first professional in line to care for possible psychosocial issues affecting older adults, now understand that there are many myths regarding aging. Highlighting successful older adults may aid in dispelling myths and simultaneously encourage other older adults to increase social interaction, expand their social networks, reach out to the counseling profession for services if needed, and continue to contribute to society through successful or active aging.

Research suggests that mental health counselors are less likely to diagnose and recommend treatment for older adults in advanced age, possibly in part due to a clinician's lack of experience in working with this population and indifferent attitudes toward aging groups. For example, some studies have found that an identical set of symptoms is likely to be judged as less severe when experienced by a very old client, therefore creating a misdiagnosis and inappropriate treatment. Further studies have found that some physicians even believed that older adults at risk for suicide were less likely to benefit from counseling interventions, despite evidence to the contrary. The reality is that there are many more similarities in counseling with older persons and younger persons than there are differences. The entire collection of a mental health counselor's knowledge and skills will be required, including facilitative listening and responding, caring confrontation, questioning, and so forth, when working with older adults. Older persons are similar to younger persons in their need for support and challenge, respect, expectation for growth, self-understanding and acceptance, decision making, and action (Waters, 1984).

Capuzzi and Gross (2002) offered several group theories and approaches applicable to the aging population, such as reality orientation, milieu therapy, reminiscence groups, and remotivation therapy. There is a variety of theoretical applications included in the training of counselors. The need for specialized counseling of older adults is reinforced by the reality that current generations can expect to live well into their 80s and will benefit from counseling. The Council for Accreditation of Counseling and Related Educational Programs (CACREP) Standards Manual (2001) stresses the need for skills, techniques, and practices beyond the scope of the generalist counselor. New counseling students need to be made aware of the need for gerontological specializations, and current practitioners with an interest in working with the older adults must find training that will increase their competence in counseling aging Baby Boomers. Altekruse and Ray (1998) identified several principles and recommendations to apply to counseling mature adults:

1. Counselors need to demonstrate their competence in counseling the oldest-old population and should be cautious in the use of psychological testing with this population.

2. Counselors must respect and enhance the dignity and worth of older persons and be appreciative of their intelligence as well as their age differences.

3. Counselors, in order to accommodate the oldest-old clients, must attend to the physical environment of the counseling setting more than when counseling younger clients.

4. Counselors must serve more actively in the role of client-advocate and attend to the dependence and independence issue while working with older adults.

5. Counselors might help older clients to focus on short-term goals, emphasizing the present life of the client.

6. Counselors need to be especially aware of and sensitive to the cultural, environmental, and value differences between themselves and their clients and to possess some perspective on the clients' place in history, particularly if there is a so-called generation gap between them.

Development in later life can be viewed from at least two perspectives: developmental sequences and life transitions. The developmental perspective assumes a unidirectional, stepwise progression of events. Certain tasks must be mastered for successful development. The positive argument here is that development occurs and can be fostered throughout the lifespan. Older persons are not viewed as static, rigid, or poor prospects for therapeutic change. However, existing developmental theories seem insufficient to explain the complexities of later life. As indicated in previous chapters, some examples of developmental theories may serve to illustrate this point. Guided by theories and principles, gerontological-based counseling must include competencies necessary for working effectively with aging adults including the oldest-old. Myers (1996) recommended a number of essential competencies for a gerontological counseling specialist and an approach to counseling based on a wellness philosophy. Traditional work with older adults has focused on reactive and curative attitudes. Another perspective is Myers's (2003) work entitled "Wellness in Later Life," which brought attention to the unique nature of the new older adult or Baby Boomers and highlighted hope for the future, complementing theories of aging such as healthy aging and active aging.

According to Myers (1996), gerontological counselors who are trained according to CACREP Standards (2001) will demonstrate and actively advocate for positive, respectful, wellness-enhancing attitudes toward older adults and a concern for empowerment of older adults throughout their lifespan. A well-trained gerontological counselor will also demonstrate skills in

1. applying extensive knowledge of development for older persons including major theories of aging, the relationship between mental health and aging, the difference between normal and pathological aging processes, gender-related developmental differences, and coping skills for life's transitions and losses;

2. applying extensive knowledge of social and cultural foundations for older persons, including characteristics and needs of older minority subgroups, factors affecting substance and medication misuse and abuse, recognition and treatment of elder abuse, and knowledge of specific social service programs designed for this group;

3. recruiting, selecting, planning, and implementing groups with older persons;

4. applying extensive knowledge of career and lifestyle options for older persons;

5. applying current research related to the aging population;

6. applying extensive knowledge of the intellectual, physical, social, emotional, vocational, and spiritual needs of older adults;

7. applying appropriate intervention techniques, in collaboration with the medical community, for psychological impairments such as depression, suicide ideation, and organic brain syndrome;

8. use and application of a wide variety of therapies such as art, pet therapies, and peer counseling for use in coping with developmental and nonnormative issues; and

9. applying knowledge of ethical issue consideration in counseling older adults.

These are a few of the wellness-oriented competencies necessary for effective counseling that will address the unique needs and concerns that will confront approximately 76 million Americans in the next 20 years (U.S. Bureau of Population Statistics, 2007). Keys to effectiveness and achievement in empowering older adults are creativity, attitude, positivism, and wellness. There is no doubt that the professional identity of future counselors will be enhanced by the type of services they will provide to older adults. A highly skilled counselor will be needed to address the mental, physical, emotional, social, and spiritual issues of this challenging aging population.

Smyer and Intrieri (1990) suggested that mental health counseling with a broad spectrum of older persons requires an understanding of aging, counseling, and evaluation. They encouraged practitioners to include a focus on evaluation in all of their efforts, placing the responsibility for accountability in the hands of mental health counselors. It is up to each practitioner to use his or her skills and techniques with older clients with full consideration of whether the treatment program works and, if so, under what circumstances and conditions and with what types of clients. The challenge is to find what fits the counselor's knowledge and style as well as each of the older clients that are being served.

Counseling Issues

The inclusion of gerontological issues in counselor training and practice should always be a priority for counseling professionals. Contrary to the myth that counseling does not work with old people, studies of counseling service use and general outcome studies reveal that persons in the oldest-old age category respond well, and in some cases, better than younger persons to a variety of counseling techniques. Lack of knowledge about oldest-old clients' characteristics and needs may be a disincentive to counselor practitioners to offer services to this population (Hooker & Kiyak, 2011).

A stigma attached to receiving counseling or mental health services is common within the older population. This stigma is slowly declining as the general public becomes more aware of the benefits of therapeutic and supportive counseling services. As counselors, we must dispel myths associated with aging, advocate for the needs of older adults, and help this population adapt, thrive, and maintain a sense of life satisfaction and achievement as they go through the multiple changes associated with reaching the last stages of elderhood (Lyyra, Törmäkangas, Read, Rantanen, & Berg, 2006). Counselors who chose to work with the elderly population will likely be presented with a plethora of issues outside of that which brought the client initially into treatment. Due to the age of the client, the counselor will need to be aware not only of mental and emotional conditions but also those which may be of physical concern. Additionally, issues related to cognition may make the therapeutic process more difficult.

Older adults and their family members and caregivers often encounter new and challenging psychosocial issues that accompany aging. As with any stage in the life cycle, there are adjustments to make and social and emotional responses that need to be handled. As indicated above, older adults may face many changes in the social context of their lives. Retirement is often the major change as it relates to role change, which may have psychosocial consequences. It brings into question, what next? This may be frightening and confusing to older adults (Markson & Hollis-Sawyer, 2000). Loss of friends through relocation and death also occurs, leaving an empty feeling difficult to handle. Feelings of abandonment and loneliness are common. At times, oldest-old individuals feel adrift with little sense of purpose to their lives (Langlois, Vu, & Chassé, 2012). They may also face increasingly poor health that renders them less functional and independent. Feelings of dependency are usually unwelcome and may create a sense of shame and embarrassment. Emotional responses vary for each individual. Many, however, experience some type of depression due to the changes of aging. There are feelings of sadness, anger, and fear. Mood swings are often common and distressing to the person experiencing them, as well as to family members.

Family members also react to the aging changes of an oldest-old and close relative. Often, the dynamics and previous balance in the family are altered. This can be a difficult adjustment for all concerned, particularly if roles shift and if some family members (particularly adult children) take on caregiving responsibilities. There is evidence in counseling situations that, in some cases, the aging adult may refuse the care and attention given by family members or even a spouse. Feelings of resentment and anger may surface toward everyone involved and a sense of self-centeredness may be observed. The older adult may feel like a burden, and the caregiver may feel overwhelmed and burdened. Counseling can be very effective when communication among family members may be compromised. Painful feelings and responses are difficult to verbalize and may become internalized, creating more difficulties and barriers to open discussion and positive interpersonal relationships (Connell, Janevic, & Gallant, 2001).

For all of the above reasons, counseling and support services are extremely beneficial in managing these family-client gerontological issues. They can promote open communication as well as help to examine alternative solutions to various aging-related problems. Various therapeutic counseling options are available and should be explored to enhance the well-being of those involved.

Cultural Competence

It has been said that "it is not our differences that divide us. It is our inability to recognize, accept, and celebrate those differences." Providing culturally competent counseling means that a practitioner is sensitive to the cultural differences among clients, understands the influence of these differences on their clients' physical and mental health status, and can modify therapeutic interventions from a practical standpoint to meet the specific needs of diverse clients. Culturally competent counseling is necessary because years of studies consistently indicate that culture is a significant, common barrier to effective care for minority and immigrant clients. Cultural barriers may be quite obvious or more subtle. For instance, an elderly Hispanic immigrant client, who does not speak English, may be less likely to visit a local counseling center if he knows that the counselors do not speak Spanish, and there are no translation services. Counseling providers and their agencies, therefore, must be sensitive to the cultural implications that affect their elderly, culturally diverse clients.

The need for culturally competent mental health counselors in the United States is ongoing. Older adults from cultural, ethnic, and racial minorities are burdened with higher rates of disease, disability, and death and tend to receive a lower quality of services than nonminorities, even when access-related factors, such as insurance coverage status and income, are taken into account. Never before has society encountered such diversity among the rapidly growing aging population.

The challenge of developing multicultural counseling skills has occupied a prominent place in the counseling literature over the past 30 years. In spite of the complexity of opinion on the topic, many now argue that this is not an optional endeavor but a foundation for effective and ethical professional practice (Arredondo & Toporek, 2004; Marsella & Pedersen, 2004). Each person faces the challenge of identifying his or her current level of cultural competence and identifying the attitudes and beliefs, knowledge, and skills that are required when working with clients who are culturally different. To infuse culture effectiveness into counseling practice, counselors require a starting point from which to review their current perception of human diversity and professional practices. Codes of ethics provide an overarching view of counseling practices with culturally diverse clients (Pettifor, 2005). However, the details of how to improve standards of practice are not covered in most professional codes of ethics. What has emerged from the counseling literature are collections of competencies for multicultural counseling practice, organized according to various conceptual models (Sue, Arredondo, & McDavis, 1992; Sue Carter, Fouad, Ivey, & Jensen, 1998). These models assist counselors to move forward in their journey of developing multicultural competence and to incorporate new learning into professional practice as they acquire more experience working with their clients.

There is a need to address the counseling needs of older people from different cultural, racial, and ethnic backgrounds. Research indicates that members of ethnic minority groups are less inclined than Whites to seek treatment and to use outpatient treatment services. There is also an insufficient number of mental health professionals from ethnic minority groups. Furthermore, language barriers exist in the profession, possibly leading to inadequate services. One possible solution is the use of language interpreters in an ethical manner. Asking family members or other acquaintances to act as interpreters increases the older person's vulnerability, compromises their confidentiality, and can hinder a full and open discussion of the individual's mental health and counseling needs. More importantly, there is a need for counseling approaches that are effective for older adults from diverse backgrounds. Some strategies that counselors can implement include tailoring approaches to diverse populations of older adults by

1. recruiting, training, and employing counseling practitioners knowledgeable about the older adult population;

2. developing specialized diversity-oriented programs that include aggressive outreach efforts and encourage styles of practice best suited to the challenges of these populations;

3. training all mental health practitioners to be culturally competent by recognizing and responding to the concerns of diverse ethnic aging minorities and other special populations, including their histories, traditions, beliefs, and value systems;

4. encouraging all professional programs to include content pertaining to ethnic and cultural diversity, socioeconomic status, gender, sexual orientation, physical disability, and rural settings in their curriculum;

5. building systems that recognize, incorporate, practice, and value cultural diversity;

6. encouraging sensitivity to language assistance needs and assuring language assistance in the provision of mental health counseling services for older persons with limited English proficiency; and

7. recruiting and training an ethnically and racially diverse counselor workforce.

In conclusion, addressing these challenges will require the concerted efforts of all those working for better mental health and the well-being of older adults, including the oldest-old, in both the public and private sectors, including policy makers, practitioners and service providers, researchers, consumers and family members, and other advocates. We can take advantage of the numerous efforts in the mental health and counseling field that have been implemented and can use them as a foundation for research and practice that will enhance the well-being of all older persons and their families. The emerging crisis in gerontological counseling also provides the opportunity to work in partnership across service systems and disciplines to address the mental health needs of older adults (Dawson & Santos, 2000).

SUMMARY

- We have entered a period in history with increasing numbers of people living into the very oldest-old age.
- The need for interventions that influence the life expectancy and well-being at age 75 and older will continue to increase, as will the diversity and needs of the aging population.
- Life satisfaction and the prospect of aging well are very important to the future of the counseling profession.
- In the last decades, extensive empirical research efforts have been directed at the perception of life satisfaction in old age.
- The main finding is that life satisfaction is relatively stable across life, and both young and old adults have similar levels of life satisfaction.
- The identification of life satisfaction as a predictor of survival among the oldest-old further motivates the exploration of satisfaction in old age.
- The oldest-old population constitutes an increasing proportion of the population in Western societies and will require considerable societal support and resources.
- For counselors to prepare to meet the demands of our aging population, it is imperative to acquire knowledge of the needs of this population and the skills to provide effective helping interventions to meet those needs.
- There is a greater need for counselors specially trained in gerontological counseling to work with a variety of oldest-old clients.
- The specialty competencies were developed to help define more clearly the emerging specialty of gerontological-based counseling.
- It is assumed that a counselor will first meet all of the generic requirements for counselor preparation as defined in the CACREP standards. These competencies define an advanced level of preparation.
- Counselors are expected to understand the counseling skills needed to manage the psychosocial crises and challenges faced by the oldest-old population.
- The counselor can demonstrate positive, wellness-enhancing attitudes toward the human development needs of older persons.

ADDITIONAL RESOURCES

Organizations

AARP: www.aarp.org
Association for Gerontology in Higher Education Careers in Aging: http://www.aghe.org
Association for Adult Development and Aging: http://www. aadaweb.org
The Gerontological Society of America Careers in Gerontology: www.careersinaging.com/careersinaging
The American Counseling Association: http://www.counseling.org

RECOMMENDED SUPPLEMENTAL READINGS

Gillick, M. R. (2001). *Lifelines: Living longer, growing frail, talking heart.* New York, NY: W.W. Norton.

Honn Qualls, S., & Norman, A. (Eds.). (2000). *Psychology and the aging revolution: How we adapt to longer life.* Washington, DC: American Psychological Association.

Powell, D. H. (1988). *The nine myths of aging: Maximizing the quality of later life.* Thorndike, ME: Thorndike Press.

Wei, J. Y., & Sue L.. (2000). *Aging well: The complete guide to physical and emotional health.* New York, NY: Wiley.

REFERENCES

Adams, K. B., & Sanders, S., & Auth, E. A. (2004). Loneliness and depression in independent living retirement communities: Risk and resilience factors. *Aging & Mental Health, 8*(6), 475–485.

Ailshire, J. A., & Crimmins, E. M. (2011). Psychosocial factors associated with longevity in the United States: Age differences between the old and oldest-old in the health and retirement study. *Journal of Aging Research,* 2011, 10–20. Article ID 53053. doi:10.4061/2011/530534

Altekruse, M., & Ray, D. (1998). Counseling older adults: A special issue. *Educational Gerontology, 24,* 303–307.

American Psychiatric Association (2001). The core principles for end-of-life care. Position statement on the core principles for end-of-Life care. Retrieved from: www. psychiatric.org.

Arredondo, P., & Toporek, R. (2004). Multicultural competencies and ethical practice. *Journal of Mental Health Counseling, 26*(1), 44–45.

Baltes, P. B. (1987). Theoretical propositions of life-span developmental psychology: On the dynamic between growth and decline. *Developmental Psychology 23,* 611–626.

Baltes, P. B. (2004). *A general model of successful (proactive) aging: Selective optimization with compensation.* Paper presented at the 57th Annual Scientific Meeting of the Gerontological Society of America, Washington, DC.

Bandura, A. (1997). *Self-efficacy. The exercise of control.* New York, NY: Freeman.

Berkman, L.F., & Breslow, L. (1983). *Health and ways of living: The Alameda County study.* New York, NY: Oxford University Press.

Billings, J. A. (1998). What is palliative care? *Journal of Applied Medicine, 1,* 73–81.

Birren J. (1996). Introduction. In J. Birren (Ed.), *Encyclopedia of gerontology.* Aging, age, and the aged. New York, NY: Pergamon Press.

Blake, R., & Kaplan, L. S. (1975). Counseling the elderly: An emerging area for counselor education and supervision. *Counselor Education and Supervision, 13,* 136–137.

Briggs, R. (1990). Biological aging. In J. Bond & P. Coleman (Eds.), *Aging in society* (pp. 48–61). Thousand Oaks, CA: Sage.

Broderick, P., & Blewitt, P. (2014). *The Life span: Human development for the helping professionals* (4th ed.).Saddle River, NJ: Pearson Education.

Brown, J., Bowling, A., & Flynn, T. N. (2004). Models of quality of life. A taxonomy and systematic review of the literature. European Forum on Population Aging Research. Retrieved from http://www.shef.ac.uk/ageingresearch/pdf/qol.pdf.

Capuzzi, D., & Gross, D. (2002). *Counseling the older adult. Introduction to the counseling profession* (3rd ed.). Boston, MA: Allyn & Bacon.

Carstensen, L. L. (1992). Social and emotional patterns in adulthood: Support for socioemotional selectivity theory. *Psychology and Aging, 7*(3), 331–338.

Carstensen, L. L. Pasupathi, M., Mayr, U., & Nesselroade, J. R. (2000). Emotional experience in everyday life across the adult lifespan. *Journal of Personality and Social Psychology, 79,* 644–655.

Centers for Disease Control and Prevention (CDC). (2012). *The state of mental health and aging in America.* Report on Mental Health and Aging. Atlanta, GA: Department of Health and Human Services.

Chochinov, H. M. (2006). Dying, dignity, and new horizons in palliative end-of-life care. *A Cancer Journal for Clinicians, 56,* 84–103.

Christakis, N. (2000). *Death foretold: Prophecy and prognosis in medical care.* Chicago, IL: University of Chicago Press.

Connell, C. M., Janevic, M. R., & Gallant, M. P. (2001). The costs of caregiving: Impact of dementia on family caregivers. *Journal of Geriatric Psychiatry and Neurology, 14,* 79–187.

Council for Accreditation of Counseling and Related Educational Programs (CACREP). (2001). Standards manual. Alexandria, VA: American Counseling Association.

Crooks, V. C., Lubben, J., Petitti, D. B., Little, D., & Chiu, V. (2008). Social network, cognitive function, and dementia incidence among elderly women. *American Journal of Public Health, 98*(7), 1221–1227.

Cummins, R. A. (1997). Assessing quality of life for people with disabilities. In R. Brown (Ed.), *Quality of life for people with disabilities: Models, research and practice* (2nd ed., pp. 116–130). Cheltenham, UK: Stanley Thornes.

Dawson, G. D., & Santos, J. (2000). *Combating failure: An investigation of funding for the education and training of geriatric-care personnel.* Notre Dame, IN: University of Notre Dame

Erikson, E., & Erikson, J. (1997). *The life cycle completed: Extended version.* New York, NY: W. W. Norton.

Erikson, Erik. (1963). *Childhood and Society* (2nd ed.). New York, NY: W.W. Norton.

Farquhar, M. (1995). Definitions of quality of life: A taxonomy. *Journal of Advanced Nursing, 22*(3), 502–508.

Fernández-Ballesteros, R., & Santacreu, I. M. (2010). Aging and quality of life. In J. H. Stone & M. Blouin (Ed.), *International encyclopedia of rehabilitation.* Retrieved from http://cirrie.buffalo.edu/encyclopedia/en/article/296/.

Gironda, M., & Lubben, J. (2002). Preventing loneliness and isolation in older adulthood. In T. Gullotta & M. Bloom (Eds.), *Encyclopedia of primary prevention and health promotion* (pp. 666–671). New York, NY: Kluwer Academic /Plenum.

Haber, D. (2013). Health promotion and health. Practical applications for health professionals (6th ed.). New York, NY: Springer.

Hall, M., & Havens. B. (2002). *Social isolation and social loneliness. Writings in Gerontology.* National Council on Aging: Mental health and aging. Canadian Mental Health Association. Retrieved from www.cmhanl.ca.

Hooker, K., & Kiyak, H. A. (2011). *Social gerontology: A multidisciplinary perspective* (9th ed.). Boston, MA: Allyn & Bacon.

Hawkley, L. C., & Cacioppo, J. T. (2003). Loneliness and pathways to disease. *Brain, Behavior, and Immunity, 17* (Supplement 1), S98–S105.

Hughes, C., & Hwang, B. (1996). Attempts to conceptualize and measure quality of life (Vol.1). Washington, DC: American Association on Mental Retardation.

Janoff-Bulman, R. (1993). *Shattered assumptions: Toward a new psychology of trauma.* New York, NY: Free Press.

Kahana, E., & Kahana, B. (1996). Conceptual and empirical advances in understanding aging well through proactive adaptation. In V. L. Bengtson (Ed.), *Adulthood and aging. Research on continuities and discontinuities* (pp. 18 – 40). New York, NY: Springer.

Kahana, E., & Kahana, B. (2001). Successful aging among people with HIV/AIDS. *Journal of Clinical Epidemiology, 54,* S53 – S56.

Kahn, R. L., & Antonucci, T. C. (1980). Convoys over the life course: Attachment, roles and social support. In P.B. Baltes & O. Brim (Eds.), *Life-span development and behavior* (Vol. 3, pp. 253–286). New York, NY: Academic Press.

Karatafl, S. (2005). Elderly People Factors Affecting Life Satisfaction. In R. Binstock, L. George, S. Cutter, J. Hendricks, & James Schultz (Ed.), *Handbook of Aging and the Social Sciences* (6th ed, pp.245–269). New York: Academic Press.

Krebs-Carter, M. (2007). Ages in stages: An exploration of the life cycle based on Erik Erikson's eight stages of human development. Yale-New Haven Teachers Institute. Retrieved from http://www.yale.edu/ynhti/curriculum/units/1980/1/80.01.04.x.html#d

Kübler-Ross, E. (1969). *On Death and Dying.* London, UK: Routledge.

Lang, F. R. (2000). Endings and continuity of social relationships: Maximizing intrinsic benefits within personal networks when feeling near to death. *Journal of Social and Personal Relationships, 17*(2), 135–182.

Langlois, F., Vu T. M., & Chassé, K. (2012). Benefits of physical exercise training on cognition and quality of life in frail older adults. *Journals of Gerontology B: Psychological Sciences and Social Sciences.* doi:10.1093/geronb/gbs069

Lansford, J. E., Sherman, A. M., & Antonucci, T.C. (1998). Satisfaction with social networks: An examination of socio-emotional selectivity theory across cohorts. *Psychology and Aging, 13*(4), 544–552.

Lewis, M. (2001). Spirituality, counseling, and elderly: An introduction to the spiritual life review. *Journal of Adult Development, 8*(4). 231–240.

Lunney, J. R., Lynn, J., Foley, D. J., Lipson, S., & Guralnik, J. M. (2003). Patterns of functional decline at the end of life. *Journal of the American Medical Association, 289,* 2387–2392.

Lyyra, T-M., Törmäkangas, T. M. Read, S., Rantanen, T., & Berg, S. (2006). Satisfaction with present life predicts survival in octogenarians. *The Journals of Gerontology: Series B: Psychological Science and Social Science, 61,* 319–326.

Markson, E. W., & Hollis-Sawyer, L. A. (Eds.). (2000). *Intersection of aging: Readings in social gerontology.* Los Angeles, CA: Roxbury.

Marsella, A. J., & Pedersen, P. B. (2004). Internationalizing the counseling psychology curriculum: Toward new values, competencies, and directions. *Counseling Psychology Quarterly, 17,* 413–423.

May, R. (1979). *Psychology of the human dilemma.* New York, NY: Norton.

Myers, J. E. (1995). From 'forgotten and ignored' to standards and certification: Gerontological counseling comes of age. *Journal of Counseling and Development, 74(2)*, 143–149.

Myers, J. E. (2003). *Wellness in later life.* Paper presented at the annual meeting of American Counseling Association, Anaheim, CA.

Myers, J. E., & Blake, R. (1986). Professional preparation of gerontological counselors: Issues and guidelines. *Counselor Education and Supervision, 26,* 137–145.

Myers, D. C., & Diener, E. (1996). The pursuit of happiness. *Scientific American,* 54–56.

Muldoon, M. F., Barger, S. D., Flory, J. D., & Manuck, S. B. (1998). What are quality of life measurements measuring? *British Medical Journal, 316*(7130), 542–545.

Murphy, S. L., Xu, J. Q., & Kochanek, K. D. (2012). *Preliminary data for 2010. National vital statistics report, 60*(4). Hyattsville, MD: National Center for Health Statistics. Retrieved from http://www.cdc.gov/.

Neugarten, B. L., Havighurst R. J., Tobin, S.S., & Sheldon, S. (1968). Personality and patterns of aging. In B. Neugarten (Ed.), *Middle age and aging* (pp. 173–177). Chicago, IL: University of Chicago Press.

Paulus, J. (1951). Philosophy of human life, some of the conditions of a happy maturity and old age. *Dialectica, 5,* 393 – 401.

Pervin, L., Cervone, D., & Oliver, J. (2005). *Theories of personality* (9th ed.). Hoboken, New Jersey: John Wiley.

Pettifor, J. (2005). Ethics and multicultural counseling. In N. Arthurs & S. Collins (Eds.), *Culture-infused counseling: Celebrating the Canadian mosaic* (pp. 123–238). Calgary, AB: Counseling Concepts.

Pukrop, R. (2003). Subjective quality of life. Critical look at a modern construct. In G. Low & A. E. Molzahn (2003). Predictors of quality of life in old age: A cross-validation study. *Research in Nursing & Health, 30,* 141–130.

Rocke, C.,& Lachman, E. (2008). Perceived trajectories of life satisfaction across past, present, and future: Profile and correlates of subjective change in young, middle-age, and older adults. *Psychology and Aging, 23,* 833–847

Rosenblatt, P. C., Walch, R., & Jackson, D. A. (1972). Coping with aggression in mourning. *Omega, 3,* 271–284

Rowe, J. K., & Kahn, R. L. (1998). *Successful aging.* New York, NY : Pantheon.

Schulz, R., & Beach, S. (1999). Caregiving as a risk factor for mortality. The caregiver health effects study. *Journal of the American Medical Association, 282*(23), 2213–2219.

Siegel, J.M. (1990). Stressful life events and use of physician services among the elderly: The moderating role of pet ownership. *Journal of Personality and Social Psychology, 58*(6), 1081–1086.

Smyer, M. A., & Qualls, S. H. (1999). *Aging and mental health.* Malden, MA: Blackwell.

Smyer, M. A., & Intrieri, R. C. (1990). Evaluating counseling outcomes. *Generations, 14*(1), 11–14.

Sue, D. W., Arredondo, P., & McDavis, R. J. (1992). Multicultural counseling competencies and standards: A call to the profession. *Journal of Counseling and Development, 70,* 477–483.

Sue, D. W., Carter, R. T., Fouad, N. A., Ivey, A. E., & Jensen, M. (1998*). Multicultural counseling competencies: Individual and organizational development.* Thousand Oaks, CA: Sage.

Teachman, B. A. (2006). Aging and negative affect: The rise and fall and rise of anxiety and depression symptoms. *Psychology and Aging, 21,* 201–207

U.S. Bureau of Population Statistics. (2007). *Mortality Statistics. Extrapolation.* Retrieved from http://www.uspopstat.gov.

Valliant, G. E. (2002). *Aging well.* New York, NY: Little Brown.

Wahl, H. W., & Oswald, F. (2010). Environmental perspectives on aging. In D. Dannefer & C. Phillipson (Eds.), *The SAGE handbook of social gerontology* (pp. 111–124). Thousand Oaks, CA: Sage.

Waters, E. (1984). Building on what you know: Individual and group counseling with older persons. *Counseling Psychologist, 12*(2), 52–64.

Werth, J., Jr. (Ed.). (2013). *Counseling clients near the end of life. A practical guide for the mental health professional.* New York, NY: Springer

Williamson, G. M., Shaffer, D. R., & Schulz, R. (1998). Activity restriction and prior relationship history as contributors to mental health outcomes among middle-aged and older spousal caregivers. *Health Psychology, 17*(2), 132–162.

Zimbardo, P. G., & Boyd, J. (2008). *The time paradox: The new psychology of time that will change your life.* New York, NY: Free Press.

Epilogue: From the Author's Chair

Writing a text book is part research—part experience—but mostly the articulation of the author's unique perspective on practice and profession. Each author has made personal decisions on how to organize the book and what, from the mass of information available, should be included. These decisions reflect the author's bias—personal interest—values and professional identity. We, as editors of the series, have invited each author to respond to the following questions as a way of providing the reader a glimpse into the person and not just the product of the author.

It is our hope that these brief reflections will provide a little more insight into our view of our profession and ourselves as professionals.

RP/NZ

Interview With Daniel W. Wong

Question: There is certainly an abundance of insightful points found within this text. But, if you were asked to identify a single point or theme from all that is presented that you would hope would stand out and stick with the reader, what would that point or theme be?

Answer: One of the points that stands out is the cultural implications in combination with the contributions of biopsychosocial factors as they relate to human development across the lifespan. In studying human development, the contributions of cultural and biopsychosocial factors are interdependent of each other and they all play an important role of shaping a person's life.

Question: In the text there are many research-cited theories presented. Could you share from your own experience how the information presented within the text may actually look or take form in practice?

Answer: Theories developed by Erikson and Piaget have been ground-breaking and have provided the foundation for studying human development and its transition through developmental stages. However, in practice we should consider expanding beyond the cited research and theories, because the world and society continue to rapidly evolve, and the multidimensional and multicultural views of human development should be included for a more appropriate study of human development and counseling through the lifespan. A global and an all-inclusive society will be the future, and this will be a major contribution to how we are going to understand human development and how we, as professional counselors, can best to provide service to a complex and diverse population.

Question: As author(s) of this text, what might this book reveal about your own professional identity?

Answer: I am an individual with multiple cultural identities and cultural affiliations, and these cultural experiences have impacted my world view and professional identity tremendously. In writing this book, I realized that my professional identity is definitely influenced by my cultural affiliations, and it has also strengthened my resolve and my professional practice to continue to be a dedicated and effective counselor educator.

Question: What final prescription—direction—might you offer your readers as they continue in their journey toward becoming professional counselors?

Answer: To become a competent, sensitive, and compassionate counselor, one must have an open mind to learn how psychological, social, familial, economical, and environmental factors contribute to human development and counseling. By understanding these factors and understanding specific counseling skills to be applied to individuals from various age groups and from diverse cultural, ethnic, and socioeconomic backgrounds, one can become an ethical and effective counselor.

Interview With Kimberly R. Hall

Question: There is certainly an abundance of insightful points found within this text. But, if you were asked to identify a single point or theme from all that is presented that you would hope would stand out and stick with the reader, what would that point or theme be?

Answer: All counselors will work with clients, whether directly or indirectly, that encompass the entire span of life. One of the issues that stands out is that it is critical for counselors to realize that just because their clients are in a particular stage of development, they are always responding and reacting to individuals at different developmental levels. For example, through my own work with children and adolescents, I must keep in mind that these children have parents or caregivers at a different developmental level that may be going through their own developmental concerns while trying to effectively be parents. Siblings are also going through developmental stages as well as friends, teachers, etc. Everything is connected and has an impact—everything.

Question: In the text, there are many research-cited theories presented. Could you share from your own experience how the information presented within the text may actually look or take form in practice?

Answer: In my work with children and adolescents, developmental issues seem to always be present. However, these issues are also present in adults, though we tend not to label it as such. The truth is that we are always in a stage of development—constantly growing and changing—until the end of life. In practice, developmental knowledge should always be present. Developmental level determines the theory I choose, the interventions I implement, even discovering the root of the problem. I always consider the level of development that my client is in, how they got to this point, and what events have shaped their development thus far.

Question: As author(s) of this text, what might this book reveal about your own professional identity?

Answer: This book truly reveals my passion for understanding life as a whole—how each parent influences a child and how we each can positively or negatively impact the development of others including our students. Throughout life, we all have struggles, and we learn from those experiences. None of us are ever alone in this aspect—we all fail, we all succeed, we all strive to live the best way we know how.

Question: What final prescription—direction—might you offer your readers as they continue in their journey toward becoming professional counselors?

Answer: The journey toward becoming a professional counselor is so much more than textbooks, lectures, classes, and grades. It is about you delving into your own personal development, your own personal biases, and your own successes. It is discovering who you are, not what others perceive as you. It is critically examining why you believe what you do and making a conscious effort to continue with those beliefs or changing them if needed. Once you are comfortable with you, then you can truly enlighten others on their own journey of self-discovery.

Interview With Cheryl A. Justice

Question: There is certainly an abundance of insightful points found within this text. But, if you were asked to identify a single point or theme from all that is presented that you would hope would stand out and stick with the reader, what would that point or theme be?

Answer: The book is not just a textbook containing human development, but it has the additional counseling component.

Question: In the text there are many research-cited theories presented. Could you share from your own experience how the information presented within the text may actually look or take form in practice?

Answer: From my experience, I see counselors in training using information from the book academically and experientially.

Question: As author(s) of this text, what might this book reveal about your own professional identity?

Answer: I want my students to gain as much knowledge and real-world experience as possible during their educational journey.

Question: What final prescription—direction—might you offer your readers as they continue in their journey toward becoming professional counselors?

Answer: To keep their minds open to new ideas and become lifelong learners.

Interview With Lucy Wong Hernandez

Question: There is certainly an abundance of insightful points found within this text. But, if you were asked to identify a single point or theme from all that is presented that you would hope would stand out and stick with the reader, what would that point or theme be?

Answer: What stands out about this book from the beginning to the end is a greater appreciation for human development and its significant connection to the counseling process throughout the lifespan. The reader will learn the importance of being an ethical and effective counselor, and that one must understand that human development is an essential topic that needs to be fully understood and embraced by a competent counselor. The reader will also learn how to appreciate the relationship between human development and counseling, while obtaining knowledge from physical, cognitive, and emotional development from early childhood to the multiple challenges in later life.

Question: In the text there are a many research-cited theories presented. Could you share from your own experience how the information presented within the text may actually look or take form in practice?

Answer: Theories have helped me by serving as a road map to guide my understanding, such as the works of Erikson and Levinson that have given me the foundation to understand lifespan stages. Theories have enhanced my counseling skills and knowledge by facilitating my integration of self and external knowledge. I believe that by studying formative and contemporary theories related to counseling and human development, I will continue to improve my competency as a counselor educator and use this knowledge to enhance my professional practice.

Question: As author(s) of this text, what might this book reveal about your own professional identity?

Answer: My work on this book reveals that my professional identity is part of who I am. Understanding the relationship between human development and counseling, and how cultural factors have impacted all people, and relating this knowledge to my own cultural background and professional experience has enabled me to understand myself and my professional practice at a deeper level. This experience has strengthened my professional commitment and identity, and it has enhanced my professional knowledge to be able serve diverse individuals from an equally diverse society.

Question: What final prescription—direction—might you offer your readers as they continue in their journey toward becoming professional counselors?

Answer: In order to continue this professional journey and to make it a successful one, I would suggest a direction that begins with self-exploration—know and understand who you are first—in order to get to know and understand others. Become sensitized to the diversity, experience, and worldview of clients while maintaining focus on the purpose of the counseling intervention. Always offer the best possible assistance with respect, and expect the same from your clients. Entering the world of the stressful challenges of your clients requires knowledge, skills, sensitivity, and strength as a person and as a counselor.

Matrix Of Core Curricular Experiences

Core Requirements	Chapter 1	Chapter 2	Chapter 3	Chapter 4	Chapter 5	Chapter 6	Chapter 7	Chapter 8	Chapter 9	Chapter 10	Chapter 11	Chapter 12	Chapter 13	Chapter 14	Chapter 15
i. Professional orientation and ethical practice	X	X													
a. History and philosophy of the counseling profession	X		X												
b. Professional roles, functions, and relationships with other human service providers, including strategies for interagency/interorganization collaboration and communications	X		X		X	X	X	X							
c. Counselors' roles and responsibilities as members of an interdisciplinary emergency management response team during a local, regional, or national crisis, disaster, or other trauma-causing event	X		X												
d. Self-care strategies appropriate to the counselor role			X												
e. Counseling supervision models, practices, and processes															
f. Professional organizations, including membership benefits, activities, services to members, and current issues															
g. Professional credentialing, including certification, licensure, and accreditation practices and standards, and the effects of public policy on these issues															
h. The role and process of the professional counselor advocating on behalf of the profession															
i. Advocacy addressing institutional and social barriers					X	X	X	X							
j. Ethical standards of professional organizations and credentialing bodies and applications of ethical and legal considerations in professional counseling.															

Core Requirements

	Chapter 1	Chapter 2	Chapter 3	Chapter 4	Chapter 5	Chapter 6	Chapter 7	Chapter 8	Chapter 9	Chapter 10	Chapter 11	Chapter 12	Chapter 13	Chapter 14	Chapter 15
2. Social and cultural diversity															
a. Multicultural and pluralistic trends, including characteristics and concerns within and among diverse groups nationally and internationally	X	X	X	X	X	X	X	X	X	X	X	X	X	X	X
b. Attitudes, beliefs, understandings, and acculturative experiences, including specific experiential learning activities designed to foster students' understanding of self and culturally diverse clients.	X	X	X	X	X	X	X	X	X	X	X	X	X	X	X
c. Theories of multicultural counseling, identity development, and social justice	X		X												
d. Individual, couple, family, group, and community strategies for working with and advocating for diverse populations, including multicultural competencies					X	X	X	X				X			X
e. Counselors' roles in developing cultural self-awareness, promoting cultural social justice, advocacy and conflict resolution, and other culturally supported behaviors that promote optimal wellness and growth of the human spirit, mind, or body	X	X	X	X	X	X	X	X	X	X	X	X	X	X	X
f. Counselors' roles in eliminating biases, prejudices, and processes of intentional and unintentional oppression and discrimination			X												

Core Requirements

	Chapter 1	Chapter 2	Chapter 3	Chapter 4	Chapter 5	Chapter 6	Chapter 7	Chapter 8	Chapter 9	Chapter 10	Chapter 11	Chapter 12	Chapter 13	Chapter 14	Chapter 15
3. Human growth and development															
a. Theories of individual and family development and transitions across the lifespan	X	X	X	X	X	X	X	X	X	X	X	X	X	X	X
b. Theories of learning and personality development, including current understandings about neurobiological behavior						X	X	X	X	X	X	X			
c. Effects of crises, disasters, and other trauma-causing events on persons of all ages					X	X		X	X	X	X	X	X	X	X
d. Theories and models of individual, cultural, couple, family, and community resilience			X			X	X	X	X	X	X	X	X	X	X
e. A general framework for understanding exceptional abilities and strategies for differentiated interventions					X	X	X	X	X	X	X	X	X	X	X
f. Human behavior, including an understanding of developmental crises, disability, psychopathology, and situational and environmental factors that affect both normal and abnormal behavior	X	X	X	X											
g. Theories and etiology of addictions and addictive behaviors, including strategies for prevention, intervention, and treatment	X	X	X	X	X	X	X	X	X	X	X	X	X	X	X
h. Theories for facilitating optimal development and wellness over the lifespan	X	X	X	X	X	X	X	X	X	X	X	X	X	X	X

(Continued)

(Continued)

Core Requirements	Chapter 1	Chapter 2	Chapter 3	Chapter 4	Chapter 5	Chapter 6	Chapter 7	Chapter 8	Chapter 9	Chapter 10	Chapter 11	Chapter 12	Chapter 13	Chapter 14	Chapter 15
4. Career development															
a. Career development theories and decision-making models										X	X	X	X		
b. Career, avocational, educational, occupational, and labor market information resources, and career information systems										X	X	X	X		
c. Career development program planning, organization, implementation, administration, and evaluation										X	X	X	X		
d. Interrelationships among and between work, family, and other life roles and factors, including the role of multicultural issues in career development											X	X	X		
e. Career and educational planning, placement, follow-up, and evaluation															
f. Assessment instruments and techniques relevant to career planning and decision making															
g. Career counseling processes, techniques, and resources, including those applicable to specific populations in a global economy										X	X	X			

	Chapter 1	Chapter 2	Chapter 3	Chapter 4	Chapter 5	Chapter 6	Chapter 7	Chapter 8	Chapter 9	Chapter 10	Chapter 11	Chapter 12	Chapter 13	Chapter 14	Chapter 15
5. Helping relationships															
a. An orientation to wellness and prevention as desired counseling goals					X	X	X	X	X	X	X	X	X	X	X
b. Counselor characteristics and behaviors that influence helping processes			X		X	X	X	X	X	X	X	X	X	X	X
c. Essential interviewing and counseling skills															
d. Counseling theories that provide the student with models to conceptualize client presentation and that help the student select appropriate counseling interventions. Students will be exposed to models of counseling that are consistent with current professional research and practice in the field so they begin to develop a personal model of counseling			X												
e. A systems perspective that provides an understanding of family and other systems theories and major models of family and related interventions															
f. A general framework for understanding and practicing consultation															
g. Crisis intervention and suicide prevention models, including the use of psychological first aid strategies															

(Continued)

(Continued)

Core Requirements	Chapter 1	Chapter 2	Chapter 3	Chapter 4	Chapter 5	Chapter 6	Chapter 7	Chapter 8	Chapter 9	Chapter 10	Chapter 11	Chapter 12	Chapter 13	Chapter 14	Chapter 15
6. Group work															
a. Principles of group dynamics, including group process components, developmental stage theories, group members' roles and behaviors, and therapeutic factors of group work															
b. Group leadership or facilitation styles and approaches, including characteristics of various types of group leaders and leadership styles															
c. Theories of group counseling, including commonalities, distinguishing characteristics, and pertinent research and literature															
d. Group counseling methods, including group counselor orientations and behaviors, appropriate selection criteria and methods, and methods of evaluation of effectiveness															
e. Direct experiences in which students participate as group members in a small group activity, approved by the program, for a minimum of 10 clock hours over the course of one academic term															

Core Requirements	Chapter 1	Chapter 2	Chapter 3	Chapter 4	Chapter 5	Chapter 6	Chapter 7	Chapter 8	Chapter 9	Chapter 10	Chapter 11	Chapter 12	Chapter 13	Chapter 14	Chapter 15
7. Assessment															
a. Historical perspectives concerning the nature and meaning of assessment															
b. Basic concepts of standardized and nonstandardized testing and other assessment techniques, including norm-referenced and criterion-referenced assessment, environmental assessment, performance assessment, individual and group test and inventory methods, psychological testing, and behavioral observations															
c. Statistical concepts, including scales of measurement, measures of central tendency, indices of variability, shapes and types of distributions, and correlations															
d. Reliability (i.e., theory of measurement error, models of reliability, and the use of reliability information)															
e. Validity (i.e., evidence of validity, types of validity, and the relationship between reliability and validity)															
f. Social and cultural factors related to the assessment and evaluation of individuals, groups, and specific populations															
g. Ethical strategies for selecting, administering, and interpreting assessment and evaluation instruments and techniques in counseling															

(Continued)

(Continued)

	Chapter 1	Chapter 2	Chapter 3	Chapter 4	Chapter 5	Chapter 6	Chapter 7	Chapter 8	Chapter 9	Chapter 10	Chapter 11	Chapter 12	Chapter 13	Chapter 14	Chapter 15
	Core Requirements														
8. Research and program evaluation															
a. The importance of research in advancing the counseling profession		X													
b. Research methods such as qualitative, quantitative, single-case designs, action research, and outcome-based research		X													
c. Statistical methods used in conducting research and program evaluation		X													
d. Principles, models, and applications of needs assessment, program evaluation, and the use of findings to effect program modifications		X													
e. The use of research to inform evidence-based practice		X													
f. Ethical and culturally relevant strategies for interpreting and reporting the results of research and/or program evaluation studies.		X													

Source: Adapted from the Council for Accreditation of Counseling and Related Educational Programs (CACREP), 2009. Information retrieved from: www.cacrep.org/?s = standards + for = accreditation&btm = Search

Glossary

ACA Code of Ethics: A.1.c.: Counseling Plans—Counselors and their clients work jointly in devising integrated counseling plans that offer reasonable promise of success and are consistent with abilities and circumstances of clients. Counselors and clients regularly review counseling plans to assess their continued viability and effectiveness, respecting the freedom of choice of clients (See A.2.a., A.2.d., A.12.g.).

Adrenal gland: Endocrine glands are responsible for releasing hormones in response to stress and arousal and affect kidney function through the secretion of aldosterone, a hormone involved in regulating the osmolality of blood plasma.

Age clock: It is a biological age predictor that can be used to measure the age of most human tissues, cell types, or organs. Also known as epigenetic clock, Horvath's clock, or DNA methylation age.

Age wave: Concept that refers specifically to a massive population and cultural shift caused by the converging global demographic forces of the baby boom of the middle 20th century, increasing life expectancy, and the declining fertility rates of the later 20th and early 21st centuries.

Agentic: The means by which an effect or result is produced.

Alzheimer's disease: A degenerative brain disorder occurring commonly in late adulthood. It is characterized initially by forgetfulness, later by serious cognitive dysfunction, and eventually by complete loss of mental functioning and death.

American Academy of Pediatrics: Founded in 1930; a group that advocates for children and youth, public education, research, professional education, membership service, and advocacy for pediatricians.

American Psychological Association (APA): It is the largest scientific and professional organization of psychologists and the world's largest association of psychologists with scientists, educators, clinicians, consultants, and students.

Amnesia: The loss of memory. It is a deficit in memory caused by brain damage, disease, or psychological trauma.

Ancestors: A person from whom one is descended.

Anesthesia: Total or partial loss of sensation or ability to feel pain, especially tactile sensibility, induced by disease; injury; acupuncture; or an anesthetic, such as chloroform or nitrous oxide. There are different types of anesthia: (1) local or general insensibility to pain with or without the loss of consciousness, induced by an anesthetic. (2) a drug, administered for medical or surgical purposes that induces partial or total loss of sensation and may be topical, local, regional, or general, depending on the method of administration and area of the body affected.

Anterior cingulate cortex (ACC): It is the frontal part of the cingulate cortex, resembling a "collar" surrounding the frontal part of the corpus callosum. It appears to play a role in the automatic functions such as regulating the blood pressure and heart rate as well as cognitive functions such as decision-making impulse and empathy.

Anxious-resistant: A type of childhood insecure attachment style that consists of being anxious about exploring surroundings, even when the mother is present.

Applied behavior analysis: The science of controlling and predicting human behavior. Behavior analysis focuses on the observable relationship of behavior to the environment to the exclusion of what is called "hypothetical construct."

Attachment: An affectional bond that an infant forms with a caregiver; a tie that binds them together in space and endures over time.

Attachment parenting: An approach to raising infants that aims to promote a close relationship between the baby and his or her parents by methods such as feeding on demand and letting the baby sleep with his or her parents.

Attention deficit hyperactivity disorder (ADHD): Is one of the most common childhood brain disorders and can continue through adolescence and adulthood. Symptoms include difficulty staying focused and paying attention, difficulty controlling behavior, and hyperactivity (over-activity). These symptoms can make it difficult for a child with ADHD to succeed in school, get along with other children or adults, or finish tasks at home.

Authoritarian parent: An approach to child rearing in which the parents set limits and enforce rules but are flexible and listen to their child.

Authoritative parenting: It is characterized by a child-centered approach that holds high expectations of maturity. Authoritative parents can understand how their children are feeling and teach them how to regulate feelings. They often help their children to find appropriate outlets to solve problems. Authoritative parents encourage children to be independent but still place controls and limits on their actions.

Autism spectrum disorder: Is a complex neurobehavioral developmental disability that includes impairments in social interaction and developmental language and communication skills combined with rigid, repetitive behaviors. The disorder covers a large spectrum of symptoms, skills, and levels of impairment. It ranges in severity from a handicap that somewhat limits an otherwise normal life to a devastating disability that may require institutional care.

Autonomy: (1) Refers to functions over which we have no control, such as respiration, digestion, and circulation; (2) During toddlerhood, autonomy refers to a persistent, and often insistent, push toward independence. Autonomy is built on trust. Its result is competence, the ability to make productive and positive decisions.

Avoidant-attached: A pattern of attachment in which an infant rarely cries when separated from the primary caregiver and avoids contact upon his or her return.

Babbling: The extended repetition of certain syllables that begins when babies are between 6 and 9 months old.

Baby Boomers: Persons born during the demographic post–World War II, between the years 1946 and 1964, according to the U. S. Census Bureau. The term *baby boomer* is sometimes used in a cultural context.

Behavior management: Actions to enhance the probability that people choose behaviors that are personally fulfilling, productive, and socially acceptable.

Behavior modification: A treatment approach, based on the principles of operant conditioning, that replaces undesirable behaviors with more desirable ones through positive or negative reinforcement.

Biting: An act that occurs when an animal uses its teeth to pierce another object.

Body image: The mental representation we create of what we think we look like; it may or may not bear close relation to how others see us. It is subject to all kinds of distortion from internal elements like our emotions, attitudes of our parents, and much more, and it strongly influences behavior.

CACREP: Counseling for Accreditation of Counseling and Related Educational Programs (CACREP) is an independent agency recognized by the Council for Higher Education Accreditation to accredit master's degree programs in addiction counseling; career counseling; clinical mental health counseling; marriage, couple, and family counseling; school counseling; student affairs; and college counseling.

Cardiovascular system: The organs and tissues involved in circulating blood and lymph through the body.

Child Abuse Prevention and Treatment Act (CAPTA): Public Law 93-247 provides federal funding to states in support of prevention, assessment, investigation, prosecution, and treatment activities and also provides grants to public agencies and nonprofit organizations for demonstration programs and projects.

Child maltreatment: Also known as child abuse. It is intentional physical, sexual, or emotional harm or avoidable endangerment or neglect of anyone under 18 years of age.

Cognitive development: A field of study in neuroscience and psychology, focusing on a child's development in terms of information processing, conceptual resources, perceptual skill, language learning, and other aspects of brain development and cognitive psychology, as compared to an adult's point of view.

Cognitive-social learning counseling model: Learning that occurs as a function of observing, retaining, and replicating behavior observed in one's environment or other people.

Commitment: It is a promise to do or give something, a promise to be loyal to someone or something, or an attitude to support something.

Communal: Relating to different social groups or involving different groups within a society.

Conduct disorder: A range of antisocial types of behavior displayed in childhood and adolescence.

Conventional thought: Related to the conventional level of moral reasoning that is typical of adolescents and adults. To reason in a conventional way is to judge the morality of actions by comparing them to society's views and expectations. The conventional level consists of the third and fourth stages of moral development. Conventional morality is characterized by an acceptance of society's conventions concerning right and wrong. At this level an individual obeys rules and follows society's norms even when there are no consequences for obedience or disobedience.

Council on Social Work Education (CSWE): A nonprofit national association representing more than 2,500 individual members, as well as graduate and undergraduate programs of professional social work education.

Covert discrimination: A subtle type of discrimination equally as damaging as overt discrimination.

Cultural identity: Is the identity constructed by an individual, group, or culture as far as one is influenced by belonging to a group or culture.

Cultural responsiveness: The recognition and acknowledgment that society is pluralistic. In addition to the dominant culture, there exist many other cultures based on ethnicity, sexual orientation, geography, religion, gender, and class.

Culture: An integrated pattern of human knowledge, belief, and behavior that depends upon the capacity for symbolic thought and social learning and a set of shared attitudes, values, goals, and practices that characterize an institution, organization, or group.

Day care: The care of a child during the day by a person other than the child's legal guardian, typically performed by someone outside the child's immediate family.

Dementia: A serious loss of global cognitive ability in a previously unimpaired person beyond what might be expected from normal aging. It may be static as a result of global brain injury or the type of organic brain syndrome that is a neuropsychiatric disorder related to brain cell impairment.

Depression: Severe despondency and dejection, accompanied by feelings of hopelessness and inadequacy. It is a serious medical illness that affects one's thoughts, feelings, behavior, mood, and physical health. Depression is life long condition in which periods of wellness alternate with recurrences of illness.

Development: The pattern of change that begins at conception and continues through the lifespan. Most development involves growth, although it also includes decline brought on by aging and dying.

Developmental Theory: A group of ideas, assumptions, and generalizations that interpret and illuminate the thousands of observations that have been made about human growth. A developmental theory provides a framework for explaining the patterns and problems of development.

Difficult temperaments: Overactive and fussy children that often have irregular feeding and sleeping habits. They are often fearful of new people and situations and easily get upset by noise and commotion. They tend to be high strung and intense in their reactions.

Discipline: Training expected to produce a specific characteristic or pattern of behavior, especially training that produces moral or mental improvement.

Disorganized-disoriented: A child who shows extreme behaviors such as crying during separation, falling to the floor when around Mom, and even rocking or hitting himself or herself.

Domestic abuse: Violence toward one's spouse or domestic partner.

Dualistic thinking: The line of thought that believes in two mutually exclusive minds, like good and evil or Yin and Yang. These minds are direct opposites of each other but cannot exist on their own, only in relativity.

Early adolescent: The period of adolescence between the ages of 11 to 15, marked by the onset of puberty, changing gender roles, more autonomous relationships with parents, and more mature relationships with peers.

Early Screening Project: Studies the effectiveness of a functional screening and identification system for behavior problems among preschool children ages 3 to 5 years old.

Egocentrism: Piaget's term for young children's tendency to think about the world entirely from their own personal perceptive.

Ego integrity versus despair: Erikson's eighth psychosocial development stage. This final developmental task is about retrospection. People look back on their lives and accomplishments. They develop feelings of contentment and integrity if they believe that they have led a happy, productive life. If not, they may instead develop a sense of despair if they look back on a life of disappointments and unachieved goals. This stage can occur out of the sequence when individuals feel they are near the end of their lives.

Emerging adulthood: Is a phase of the lifespan between adolescence and full-fledged adulthood, proposed by Dr. J. Arnett in 2000. Emerging adulthood also encompasses late adolescence and early adulthood.

Emotional abuse: The debasement of a person's feelings that causes the individual to perceive himself or herself as inept, not cared for, and worthless.

Emotional development: Begins early in life and is closely connected with the emergence of cognitive, language, and social skills; the development of a full range of emotions.

Emotional intelligence: The ability to identify, asses, and control the emotions of oneself, of others, and of groups.

Epidemiology: The study of the distribution and determinants of health-related states or events (including disease) and the application of this study to the control of diseases and other health problems.

Erik Erikson: A German-born American (June 1902–May 1994) psychoanalyst heavily influenced by Sigmund Freud who explored three aspects of identity: the ego identity (self), personal identity (the personal idiosyncrasies that distinguish one person from another), and social/cultural identity (the collection of social roles a person might play). Erikson's model of psychosocial development explains the eight stages through which human development should pass from infancy to late adulthood.

Erik Erikson's Psychosocial Stages of Development: Erik Erikson's theory of psychosocial development is one of the best-known theories of personality in psychology. Like Sigmund Freud, Erikson believed that personality develops in a series of stages. Erikson's theory describes the impact of social experience across the whole lifespan.

Ethno culturally: Relating to or denoting a particular ethnic group.

Excessive distress: An unpleasant feeling or emotion that may cause problems when exceeding that which is normal or sufficient.

Ferber method: A technique invented by Dr. Richard Ferber to solve infant sleep problems. It involves baby-training children to self-soothe by allowing them to cry for a predetermined amount of time before receiving external comfort. It is a controversial method to some, primarily because the method involves a degree of crying it out.

Fetus: The name for a developing human organism from the start of the ninth week after conception until birth.

First trimester: The time period extending from conception through the 13th week of gestation.

Forebrain: Anterior part of the brain, which is the main control center for sensory and associative information processing, visceral functions, and motor functions.

Functional Behavior Assessment (FBA): Is a process that identifies specific target behavior, the purpose of the behavior, and what factors maintain the behavior that is interfering with the student's educational progress.

GI Generation: Also known as "The Greatest Generation" (1901–1924). The generation of veterans that fought and won World War II, later became the Establishment, and parents of children who later became the Baby Boomers (born 1946–1964).

Gender identity: A person's acceptance of the roles and behaviors that society associates with the biological categories of males and females.

Gender identity disorder: The psychological diagnosis that is used to describe a male or female who feels a strong identification with the opposite sex and experiences considerable distress because of his or her actual sex.

Gender schema theory: Introduced by Sandra Bem in 1981 as a cognitive theory to explain how individuals become gendered in society, and how sex-linked characteristics are maintained and transmitted to other members of a culture. According to this theory, children adjust their behavior to fit in with the gender norms and expectations of their culture.

Generativity versus stagnation: Generativity versus stagnation is the seventh stage in Erik Erikson's eight-stage theory of human development. According to Erikson, this stage occurs during middle adulthood between the ages of about 40 and 65. People in this stage are focused on nurturing or creating things that will outlast them. Feeling useful and contributing to society are important at this stage.

Goal: The result or achievement toward which effort is directed.

Goal domains: Related to the analysis of the link between life goals and life satisfaction, including self-reliance or autonomy goals, leisure time, and physical activity goals.

Goal orientation: In addition to the specific goals aspired to, goal orientation is focus on achievement, power, and the expression of personal abilities and communal life.

Goal-related action: A strong sense of self-directed goal, strengthening of life satisfaction, and sense of purpose providing renewed energy.

Grasp reflex: Primitive reflex in infants that consists of a clenching of the fingers or toes upon stimulation of the palm or sole.

Graying of America: The rapid increase of older adults, 65 years old and over (Baby Boomers), living longer, active, and healthier lifestyles.

Great Depression: It was a severe worldwide economic depression in the decade preceding World War II. The timing of the Great Depression varied across nations, but in most countries it started in 1930 and lasted until the late 1930s or middle 1940s.

Great Depression cohort: Americans born from 1925 to 1945, notably during the Great Depression (1929–1939) economic downturn in the United States and World War II (1939–1945).

Hawthorne Effect: The Hawthorne Effect refers to a psychological phenomenon in which participants alter their behavior to produce an improvement as a result of being part of an experiment or study due to increased attention from the observers.

Hindbrain: Lower part of the brainstem, consisting of the cerebellum, pons, and the medulla oblongata.

Holistic approach: Characterized by the view that a whole system of beliefs must be analyzed rather than simply individual components.

Hospice movement: A patient-centered approach for people affected by terminal illness that emphasizes the importance of giving patients as much knowledge about their conditions as possible so that they maintain some control over their care and focuses not on curing disease but on managing symptoms and pain by means of palliative care.

Human development: Includes human growth but also takes into consideration the psychological aspects of development.

Human growth: The physical aspects of development.

Human services: Programs or facilities for meeting basic health, welfare, and other needs of a society, education, or group, such as the poor, sick, or elderly.

Hypochondriasis: Also called hypochondria (sometimes referred to as health phobia or health anxiety); refers to excessive preoccupancy or worry about having a serious illness.

Hypothalamus: A center within the brain that governs hormonal activity and regulatory activities such as eating, drinking, and body temperature.

Iatrogenic: Side effects or consequences due to the activity of a physician or therapy. For example, an iatrogenic illness is an illness that is caused by a medication or physician's practice.

Identity: A consistent definition of one's self as a unique individual, in terms of roles, attitudes, beliefs, and aspiration.

Idiosyncratic: Peculiar to specific individual; a peculiarity of constitution or temperament; an individualizing characteristic or quality.

Imitative play: A child fantasizes and acts out various domestic and social roles and situations such as rocking a doll, pretending to be a doctor or nurse, or teaching school.

Intervention: The act or fact of interfering so as to modify any measure whose purpose is to improve health or alter the course of disease.

Intimacy: As in an intimate relationship is an interpersonal relationship that involves physical or emotional intimacy. Physical intimacy is characterized by romantic or passionate attachment or sexual activity.

Irrational thinking: Cognition, thinking, talking, or acting without inclusion of prudence, specifically described as an action or opinion given through inadequate reasoning, emotional distress, or cognitive deficiency.

Language development: The process where an individual acquires the ability to use the verbal symbols of his or her language for communication needs, social interaction, and the understanding and expression of complex thought.

Lanugo: Fine, soft hair that covers the body and limbs of newborns.

Lateral prefrontal lobe: It is the area of the brain located at the front of each cerebral hemisphere, and its position is anterior to (in front of) the parietal lobe and superior and anterior to the temporal lobes.

Lawrence Kohlberg's Stages of Development: Kohlberg's Stages of Development constitute an adaptation of a psychological theory originally conceived by the Swiss psychologist Piaget on this topic while a psychology post-graduate student in 1958 and expanded and developed throughout his life. Kohlberg's theory holds that moral reasoning, the basis for ethical behavior, has six identifiable developmental stages, each more adequate at responding to moral dilemmas than its predecessor.

Life expectancy: The expected number of years of life remaining at any given age.

Life satisfaction: The feeling of pleasure individuals receive when they achieve or obtain something they want.

Lifespan: The length of time that any particular organism can be expected to live.

Longevity: Length or duration of life.

Malnutrition: The condition that results from having an unbalanced diet in which certain nutrients are lacking, in excess (too high an intake), or in the wrong proportions.

Maturation: Development of personal and behavioral characteristics through growth processes.

Metacognition: "Thinking about thinking"; the ability to evaluate a cognitive task in order to determine how best to accomplish it and then to monitor and adjust one's performance on the task.

Metamemory: The ability to understand how memory works in order to use it well. Metamemory is an essential element of metacognition.

Midbrain: The middle of the three primary divisions of the developing vertebrate brain or the corresponding part of the adult brain.

Middle adulthood: The period of age beyond young adulthood but before the onset of old age. It covers the productive years from 34 to 60 and one quarter of the average lifespan of human beings.

Midlife crisis: It is experienced between the ages of 40 and 60. It was first identified by the psychologist Carl Jung and is a normal part of the maturing process. Most people will experience some form of emotional transition during this time of life.

Moral development: A human development process through which children foster proper attitudes and behaviors toward other people in society, grounded on social and cultural norms, rules, and laws.

Morality of constraint: It implies that children, until into their adolescence, will follow their parents' orders, without considering the reasoning or consequences behind them.

Moro reflex: Startle reflex; a normal reflex of young infants; a sudden loud noise causes the child to stretch out the arms and flex the legs.

Motor development: The gradual acquisition of full control of all voluntary motor movements common to the species.

National Association of School Psychologists (NASP): An organization providing a set of standards, academically and professionally, with respect to the discipline of school psychology. In addition, NASP provides a source of knowledge, professional development, and resources empowering school psychologists to ensure that all children and youth attain optimal learning and mental health.

Neglect: A condition that occurs when a parent or guardian fails to provide minimal physical and emotional care for a child or other dependent person.

Neglectful parent: An approach to child rearing in which the parents are indifferent toward their children and unaware of what is going on in their children's lives.

Neurophysiologic: The study of the workings of the nervous system, including brain function science.

Neuropsychological screening: Specifically designed tasks used to measure a psychological function known to be linked to a particular brain structure or pathway.

Neurotic crisis: Refers to mental distress that, unlike psychosis, does not prevent rational thought or daily functioning.

Nonverbal cues: Messages can be communicated through gestures and touch, body language or posture, physical distance, facial expression, and eye contact, which are all types of nonverbal communication.

Normal aging: The underlying time-dependent biological, physical, and psychological changes that are perceived as signs of deterioration or decline, independent from disease.

Objective: Not influenced by personal feelings or opinions in considering and representing facts.

Operational stage of cognitive development: This stage begins at approximately age 12 and lasts into adulthood. During this time, people develop the ability to think about abstract concepts. Skills such as logical thought, deductive reasoning, and systematic planning also emerge during this stage.

Oppositional defiant disorder: Recurring pattern of negative, hostile, disobedient, and defiant behavior in a child or adolescent, lasting for at least 6 months without serious violation of the basic rights of others.

Orbitofrontal cortex: The prefrontal cortex region in the frontal lobes in the brain that are involved in the cognitive processing of decision making.

Palliative care: Comfort care that involves services provided by caregivers from several disciplines, including a comprehensive approach to care that addresses pain management, emotional and spiritual care, and psychological support for caregivers and survivors.

Parallel play: A form of play where children play adjacent to each other but do not try to influence one another's behavior.

Parietal cortices: It is a part of the brain positioned above (superior to) the occipital lobe and behind (posterior to) the frontal lobe. The parietal lobe integrates sensory information from different modalities, particularly determining spatial sense and navigation.

Passion: It is a term applied to a very strong feeling about a person or thing. Passion is an intense emotion compelling enthusiasm or desire for anything.

Pathophysiology: A convergence of pathology and physiology. Pathology in medical terms describes conditions observed during a disease state, and physiology is biological discipline that describes processes or mechanisms operating within an organism.

Perceptual development: The process wherein the individual becomes capable of organizing various sensory stimuli into units of information.

Permissive parent: An approach to child rearing that is characterized by high nurturance and communication but little discipline, guidance, or control.

Person-environment perspective: In aging research, frequently coined "Environmental Gerontology," draws upon the idea that old age is a period of adult development influenced and shaped by the environment.

Perry's Theory of Epistemic Cognition: Proposed by William G. Perry, educational psychologist, in 1998, it is a model for understanding how college students come to understand knowledge, the ideas they hold about *knowing*, and the ways in which knowing is a part of the cognitive processes of thinking and reasoning. Perry proposed that college students pass through a predictable sequence of positions of epistemological growth.

Physical abuse: One or more episodes of aggressive behavior, usually resulting in physical injury with possible damage to one's internal organs, sense organs, central nervous system, or musculoskeletal system.

Physical development: The progressive changes in size, shape, and function during the life of an organism.

Piaget (Jean): Swiss developmental psychologist and philosopher who studied children and their hidden mind and developed a comprehensive theory about the nature and development of human intelligence

Pituitary gland: A small gland located next to the hypothalamus that regulates many endocrine functions, including the secretion of growth hormones, and hormones that, in turn, trigger hormone secretion in other glands.

Positive Behavior Support (PBS): A process for understanding and resolving the problem behavior of children that is based on values and empirical research.

Postconventional thought: Kohlberg's sixth stage, at the third level of moral reasoning. Adults base their moral standards on principles that they have evaluated and that they accept as inherently valid, regardless of society's opinion.

Postformal thought: Involves making decisions based on situational constraints and circumstances, and integrating emotion with logic to form context-dependent principles. The distinction is a useful thing to understand when dealing with emerging adults.

Postpartum depression (PPD): Moderate to severe depression after the birth of a child.

Preconventional thought: Related to the preconventional level of moral reasoning that is especially common in children, although adults can also exhibit this level of reasoning. The child or the individual at this level judges the morality of an action by its direct consequences. The preconventional level consists of the first and second stages of moral development and is solely concerned with the self in an egocentric manner. A child with preconventional morality thoughts has not yet adopted or internalized society's conventions regarding what is right or wrong, but instead focuses largely on external consequences that certain actions may bring.

Prefrontal cortex: The area of the cortex at the front of the brain that specializes in anticipation, planning, and impulse control.

Prenatal development: The process of growth and development within the womb, in which a single-celled zygote becomes an embryo, a fetus, and then a baby.

Preoperational stage: Piaget's Theory of Cognitive Development second stage. It starts when the child begins to learn to speak at age two and lasts up until the age of seven. During the preoperational stage of cognitive development, Piaget noted that children do not yet understand concrete logic and cannot mentally manipulate information. Children's increase in playing and pretending takes place in this stage.

Progressivism: Based on the idea of progress, which asserts that advances in science, technology, economic development, and social organization can improve the human condition.

Psychological abuse: A form of mistreatment in which there is intent to cause mental or emotional pain or injury.

Psychopathology: The study of mental disorder, mental distress, and abnormal maladaptive behavior. In this context, the term is most commonly used within psychiatry where pathology refers to disease processes.

Punishment: Any change in a human or animal's surroundings that occurs after a given behavior or response that reduces the likelihood of that behavior occurring again in the future.

Qualitative research: A method of inquiry employed in many different academic disciplines, traditionally in the social sciences but also in market research. Qualitative researchers aim to gather an in-depth understanding of human behavior and the reasons that govern such behavior, and it employs focus groups, in-depth interviews, content analysis, ethnography, evaluation and semiotics, open-ended survey responses, literature reviews, audio recordings, pictures and webpages. The qualitative method investigates the why and how of decision making, not just what, where, when. Hence, smaller but focused samples are more often needed than large samples to gain an understanding of underlying reasons and motivations.

Quality of life: A measurement used to evaluate the general well-being of individuals and societies.

Quantitative research: Refers to the systematic empirical investigation of social phenomena via statistical, mathematical or computational techniques. The objective of quantitative research is to develop and employ mathematical models, theories and/or hypotheses pertaining to phenomena and to quantify data and generalize results from a sample to the population of interest.

Rejectivity: An unwillingness to embrace certain individuals, groups, or ideas in one's social circle. Taking on aggressive energy drawn from the power and authority of one's status in middle adulthood.

Relativistic thinking: It is viewing all knowledge as embedded in a framework of thought. It is thinking using both reason and intuition.

Resilience: The capacity to adapt well despite significant adversity and to overcome serious stress.

Risk-taking behaviors: Risk-taking behaviors refers to the tendency to engage in behaviors that have the potential to be harmful or dangerous, yet at the same time provide the opportunity for some kind of outcome that can be perceived as positive.

Role conflict: State of tension that occurs when the demands and expectations of various roles conflict with one another.

Role overload: State of tension that occurs when there are too many role demands and expectations to handle in the time allowed.

Role spillover: State of tension that occurs when the demands or pre-occupations about one role interfere with the ability to carry out another role.

Rooting reflex: Reflex causing head-turning and sucking movements caused by gently stroking the side of the mouth or cheek.

Second trimester: The time period extending from the 14th to 27th week of gestation.

Securely attached: A relationship in which an infant obtains both comfort and confidence from the presence of his or her caregiver.

Self-concept: The individual's awareness of the self as a person; a theory about the self that explains personal experience.

Self-regulation: The ability to activate or move or regulate oneself.

Senescence: To grow old, also called biological aging or gradual deterioration of function characteristic of most complex life forms found in all biological kingdoms that on the level of the organism increases mortality after maturation.

Senility: Marked deterioration in mental organization characterized by confusion, memory loss information-processing difficulties, and disorientation.

Sensory development: Development of senses: hearing, seeing, touching, tasting, and smelling.

Sexual abuse: Assault or other crime of a sexual nature, which need not be physical. An act of a sexual nature is considered abuse if performed with minors or nonconsenting adults.

Sigmund Freud: Considered the father of psychoanalysis. He began to analyze dreams in order to understand aspects of personality as they relate to pathology.

Slow to warm: A shy, uneasy, or cautious child when put into new situations or with unfamiliar people.

Social convoys: The network of close relationships we maintain throughout life.

Social isolation: A complete or near-complete lack of contact with society for members of social species. It is usually involuntary, making it distinct from isolating tendencies or actions consciously undertaken by a person.

Social ladder: Hierarchical structure of a society; also called social scale.

Social Learning Theory: An extension of behaviorism that emphasizes the influence that other people have over a person's behavior. The theory's basic principle is that even without specific reinforcement, every individual learns many things through observation and imitation of other people.

Social referencing: Seeking information about how to react to an unfamiliar or ambiguous object or event by observing someone else's expressions and reactions.

Social role: A set of connected behaviors, rights, and obligations conceptualized by individuals in a social situation. It is an expected changing behavior and may have a given individual social status or social position.

Social self-concept: A person's understanding of who he or she is, incorporating self-esteem, physical appearance, personality, and various personal traits, such as gender and size.

Social skills: A group of skills that people need to interact and communicate with others.

Social work: A professional and academic discipline that seeks to improve the quality of life and well-being of an individual, group, or community by intervening through research, policy, community organizing, direct practice, and teaching on behalf of those afflicted with poverty or perceived social injustices and violations of human rights.

Sociodramatic play: Refers to play involving acting out scripts, scenes, and plays adopted from cartoons, books, and so on. Children take/assume roles using themselves and/or characters like dolls, figures, and puppets as they interact together on common themes. A facilitator may assist with ideas for characters, settings or props and use the children's ideas for a story. Typically occurs between 3 and 4 years of age. As a child matures, themes, sequences, plans, problem solving, characters and so forth become more detailed and they begin to organize other children (around 5 years of age) for role play with independence.

Spermarche: The beginning of development of sperm in boys' testicles at puberty; a boy's first ejaculation of seminal fluid.

Subjective: Based on or influenced by personal feelings, tastes, or opinions.

Subjectivity: A person's opinion; in philosophy it is a term used to refer to the condition of being a subject and the subject's perspective, experience, feelings, beliefs, and desires.

Symbolic thought: It is the representation of reality through the use of abstract concepts such as words, gestures, and numbers. Evidence of symbolic thought is generally present in most children by the age of eighteen months, when signs and symbols ("signifiers") are used reliably to refer to concrete objects, events, and behaviors ("significates").

Synapses: The intersection between the axon of one neuron and the dendrites of other neurons.

Temper tantrums: Unpleasant and disruptive behaviors or emotional outbursts.

Temperament: Inborn differences between one person and another in emotions, activity, and self-regulation.

Teratogens: Agents and conditions, including viruses, drugs, and chemicals, that can impair prenatal development and result in birth defects or even death.

Third trimester: The time period extending from the 28th week of gestation until delivery.

Trans-theoretical framework: The teaching of diverse therapeutic perspectives to provide opportunities for learning the best practices that exist across intervention models.

Trust versus mistrust: Erikson's first crisis of psychosocial development. Infants learn basic trust if the world is a secure place where their basic needs are met.

Undernutrition: Insufficient or imbalanced consumption of nutrients.

Ventral striatum: The emotional and motivational aspects of behavior.

Vernix: A protective deposit covering the fetus during intrauterine life, consisting of exfoliations of the outer skin layer, lanugo, and secretions of the sebaceous glands.

World Health Organization (WHO): An agency of the United Nations, established in 1948 to promote health and control communicable diseases.

Zone of proximal development: The difference between what a learner can do without help and what he or she can do with help.

Index

Bandura, Albert, 28, 286
Banerjee, R., 111
Banti, S., 64
Barbaranelli, C., 28
Barekatain, M., 64
Barger, S. D., 286
Barker, J., 229
Barnett, B., 64
Barnett, N., 199
Barton, E. A., 79
Basemore, S. D., 64
Basile, K., 57
Basin, E., 267
Bates, J. E., 203
Bauer, K. W., 145
Beach, S., 292
Beauchamp, G. K., 74
Beauvais, H. J., 203
Becker, D., 237
Beckman, A., 83
Begley, S., 216
Behavior modification therapy
    Positive Behavioral Support (PBS) preschool program
        and, 133
    for separation anxiety, 99
Behaviorist theory (Watson), 28
    Bandura's social learning theory and, 28
    natural experiments and, 40–41
    operant conditioning model (Skinner) and, 28
    B. F. Skinner and, 28
Bellis, M., 168
Belmont Report, ethical principles of, 41
Belskey, J., 170
Bem, Sandra, 102
Bennett, C., 190–191
Benson, J. W., 182
Benson, M. J., 178
Berg, S., 303
Berger, K. S., 36
Berk, L., 191, 215, 216
Berkman, L. F., 290
Berrett, K., 174
Berry, A. A., 64
Bertrand, R. M., 244
Best, K. M., 128
Beyers, W., 215
Bias of researcher, 37, 42
Biesecker, G., 80
Billings, J. A., 299
Bilszta, J. L., 64
Binge eating, 173
Biopsychosocial model, 16–17 (case illus.)
    biological system and, 15

excessive distress and, 15
of human development, 4, 14–15
integrative nature of, 15
irrational thinking and, 15
maturation and, 15
psychological system and, 15
sociocultural system and, 15
Bipolar disorder
    in late adulthood, 270
    during pregnancy, 63
Birch, H., 77
Birren, J., 286
Birth. *See* Conception and prenatal development
Biting behavior in toddlers, 107–108, 108 (case illus.),
        108 (fig.)
Bjorkqvist, K., 173, 174
Bjorvatn, B., 64
Black, M., 57
Blair, C., 80
Blake, R., 285
Blanchard, A., 64
Blehar, M. C., 77
Blewitt, P., 299
Bloom, D. E., 271
Blow, F. C., 63
Bodell, L. P., 204
Bodrova, E., 29, 31
Body image issues
    in early adulthood, 222–223
    eating disorders and, 223
    as multidimensional construct, 222
    during pregnancy, 63
    See also Eating disorders
Bondevik, G. T., 64
Bonds, D., 43
Boonstra, H., 179
Booth-LaForce, C., 151, 152
Boris, N. W., 79
Borri, C., 64
Bosch, K. R., 202
Bosworth, K., 178
Botwinick, J., 272
Bouffard, L., 267
Bowker, J. C. W., 151
Bowlby, J., 77
Bowling, A., 286
Boyce, L., 79
Boyce, P., 64
Boyce, W. T., 147
Boyd, M., 202
Boyd-Franklin, N., 183
Brandy-Smith, C., 79
Braungart-Ricker, J. M., 77

$SAGE researchmethods

The essential online tool for researchers from the world's leading methods publisher

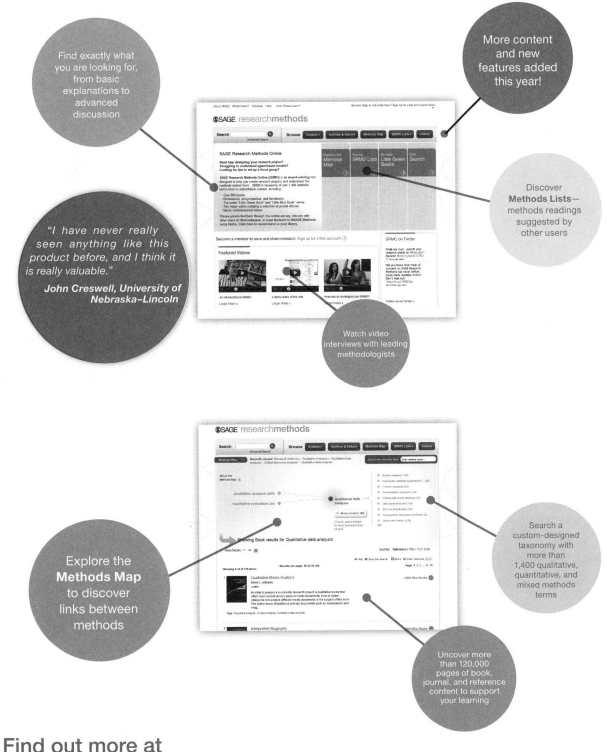

Find exactly what you are looking for, from basic explanations to advanced discussion

More content and new features added this year!

"*I have never really seen anything like this product before, and I think it is really valuable.*"

John Creswell, University of Nebraska–Lincoln

Discover **Methods Lists**—methods readings suggested by other users

Watch video interviews with leading methodologists

Explore the **Methods Map** to discover links between methods

Search a custom-designed taxonomy with more than 1,400 qualitative, quantitative, and mixed methods terms

Uncover more than 120,000 pages of book, journal, and reference content to support your learning

Find out more at
www.sageresearchmethods.com